LONERGAN

and the Philosophy of Historical Existence

ERIC VOEGELIN INSTITUTE
SERIES IN POLITICAL PHILOSOPHY

LONERGAN
and the Philosophy of Historical Existence

Thomas J. McPartland

UNIVERSITY OF MISSOURI PRESS
COLUMBIA AND LONDON

Library of Congress Cataloging-in-Publication Data

McPartland, Thomas J., 1945–
    Lonergan and the philosophy of historical existence / Thomas J. McPartland.
        p.   cm. — (Eric Voegelin Institute series in political philosophy)
    Includes bibliographical references and index.
    ISBN 0-8262-1345-6 (alk. paper)
        1. Lonergan, Bernard J. F.   2. Consciousness.   3. History—Philosophy.
    4. Voegelin, Eric, 1901–   I. Title.   II. Series.
BD995.L654   M37   2001
191— dc21   2001027424

⊗This paper meets the requirements of the
American National Standard for Permanence of Paper
for Printed Library Materials, Z39.48, 1984.

Designer: Kristie Lee
Typesetter: The Composing Room of Michigan, Inc.
Printer and Binder: The Maple-Vail Book Manufacturing Group
Typeface: Berkeley

For permissions see p. 305

*The University of Missouri Press offers its grateful acknowledgment
for a generous contribution from the Eric Voegelin Institute
in support of the publication of this volume.*

For My Parents

Contents

Preface   xi

Introduction   1

Part I. *Lonergan's Foundational Worldview*

1   Lonergan's Philosophy of Consciousness   9

    Age of Consciousness   10
    Lonergan: Philosopher of Consciousness   12
    Normative Structure of Consciousness   14
    Self and Self-Knowledge   17

2   From Classicism to Emergent Probability:
    Lonergan's Notion of Development   25

    Aristotle: Rudiments of Development   27
    Plato and Aristotle: Human Development   29
    Lonergan's Notion of Development   31
    Lonergan's Notion of Human Development   40
    Lonergan's Notion of Historical Development   45

Part II. *Historical Existence*

3   Dialectic of History   55

    Dialectic of Historical Interpretations   56
    Lonergan and Dialectic   64
    History   69

4   Historicism and Historicity:
    Two Perspectives on History   76

    Historicism   79

The Epistemological Assumptions of Historicism   82
Historicity   94
Emerging Intellectual Horizon   106

5   Reason and History   108

Classicism and Historicism   109
Reason   116
Reason and History   120

6   Cosmopolis: The Community of Open Existence   125

Cosmos and Polis   126
Cosmopolis and Historicity   129
Cosmopolis and the Challenge of History   135

7   Historicity and the Event of Philosophy   141

Lonergan and Historical Consciousness   142
Philosophy and Existence   147
    The Subjective Pole of Philosophy   147
    Philosophy and Religious Experience   150
    Noetic Consciousness and History   154
Engaging the Philosophical Past   159
    Dialectic of Philosopher and Philosophical Tradition   159
    Philosophy and Relativism   162
    Historical Consciousness and Functional Specialties   165
    Mythopoesis   168
Philosophy and Praxis   173
    Philosophical Therapy and Existential Deformation   173
    Philosophy and Intellectual Culture   177

Part III. *Authentic Existence*

8   Dread and the Horizon of Existence   183

Self-Transcendence   185
Dread   186
Suffering   187
Guilt   187
Shame   188
Ressentiment   190

9   Noetic Science: Aristotle, Voegelin, and the
     Philosophy of Consciousness   193

        Political Science and Noetic Science   194
        Voegelin and Aristotle   196
        Nous and *Theoros:* The Historical Context   198
        Episteme and *Nous*   199
            Cognitive Habits   200
            Cognitive Acts   201
            Principle of Science   202
            Nous as *Episteme*   203
            The Self-Luminosity of *Nous*   204
            Nous and *Phronesis*   205
        Limits of Aristotle's Analysis   207
        Noetic Science as Philosophy of Consciousness   209

10   Self-Appropriation in Lonergan and Voegelin   214

        Lonergan's Reflective Subjectivity   215
        Voegelin's Existential Exegesis   220
        Comparative Assessment   222

11   Equivalence of Meaning: Lonergan's Cognitional
     Theory and Voegelin's History of Symbols   226

        Response to the Crisis   229
        Lonergan's Cognitional Theory   237
        Lonergan's Expanded Cognitional Theory   245
        Historical Existence   253
        Lonergan-Voegelin Dialogue   265

     Bibliography   273
     Index   289

Preface

THIS BOOK CONSISTS OF materials that were originally articles and conference papers directed at two audiences, those already familiar with Lonergan (and, in some cases, Voegelin) and those with a more general background. Accordingly, each chapter is self-contained and can be read as an independent unit by both audiences. At the same time, as indicated in the Introduction, the order of chapters presents a cumulative case regarding Lonergan's philosophy of history, starting with his foundational and unique approach to consciousness.

I am greatly indebted to the hosts and organizers of the various conferences at which much of the material for this book was originally presented: to the late Timothy Fallon and Mark Morelli for providing me with a continuing forum for philosophical dialogue at the West Coast Methods Institute; and to Ellis Sandoz and Chip Hughes for having the Eric Voegelin Society sponsor a Lonergan-Voegelin panel in conjunction with the American Political Science Association. I am also grateful to the following editors who have encouraged my publications in their venues: the late Timothy Fallon, Philip Boo Riley, Patrick Byrne, and Mark Morelli. I likewise extend a special thanks to all those collaborators on the road of inquiry whose discussion, comments, and encouragement over the years have positively affected this project, particularly Paul Carringela, Chip Hughes, Rodney Kilcup, Fred Lawrence, Faith Smith, and Eugene Webb. I appreciate the professionalism of Beverly Jarrett, Jane Lago, and the entire staff of the University of Missouri Press and, in particular, the skillful copyediting of Annette Wenda. Last, but not least, I have been generously supported by my wife, Sue Wolfe, who, well beyond the call of duty, typed the most onerous part of the manuscript.

LONERGAN

and the Philosophy of Historical Existence

Introduction

WHEN MONTAIGNE FIRST WROTE his *essais,* perhaps establishing the genre, he intended his essays to be tests or trials of his judgment, principally about himself and secondarily about the human condition.[1] The present work is a series of essays on Lonergan's philosophy of history. Although Lonergan substitutes critical realism for Montaigne's skepticism, and whereas a cursory reading of Lonergan's magnum opus, *Insight,* would suggest that he— in total contrast to Montaigne as an incidental thinker—is the most systematic of philosophers, at least since Spinoza, the essay format is, in fact, a quite appropriate vehicle to explore Lonergan's thought. For Lonergan's task in *Insight* is to invite the reader to engage in a process of self-scrutiny, self-understanding, and self-discovery. Lonergan presents often daunting examples of precise thinking in such fields as mathematics, quantum mechanics, relativity theory, and psychoanalysis as exercises, or tests, of the reader in the project of cognitional self-appropriation. It is true that in providing these examples of cognition Lonergan shows that he is a rigorous and systematic inquirer, and indeed a commentator justifiably in awe of both the range and the depth of Lonergan's thought can offer a systematic treatment of his ideas. But this can never add up to a system. Lonergan, as he makes abundantly clear in *Insight,* is interested in the *noesis* not the *noema,* the *intentio intendens* not the *intentio intenda,* the process of inquiry not the product.[2] Lonergan would have us tread on what he would see as the related paths of Socratic self-knowledge and modern existential explication.

If with Lonergan, however, we are to enter the terrain of subjectivity, then how can we find there norms and standards? If our modern pictures of the physical universe seem to place us, ever since Pascal, disoriented and bewil-

---

1. Donald M. Frame, ed., *Montaigne: Selections from the Essays,* v.
2. Bernard J. F. Lonergan, *Insight: A Study of Human Understanding,* 4, 7, 12–16, 19–20, 23. For Lonergan's attack on rationalist and Hegelian systems, see 427–33, 446–48. Hereafter, second citings of Lonergan's texts will not include the author's name.

dered in the abyss between macroscopic infinity and microscopic nothingness, does not our contemporary proclamation of historical existence open up
another abyss, the chasm of perpetually fragmented worldviews that so fright-
ened Wilhelm Dilthey in his famous dream, where he witnessed the schools
of philosophy in Raphael's painting drifting irrevocably apart?[3] Is not the term
normative subjectivity an oxymoron?

It will be the burden of Chapter 1, "Lonergan's Philosophy of Consciousness" (and later in Chapter 11, "Equivalence of Meaning"), to establish what
Lonergan would have us discern in the realm of subjectivity as the immanent
norms of the flow of consciousness. Lonergan's answer will be deceptively
simple: the norms we seek are the norms of inquiry ingredient in the process
of inquiry itself. The process of inquiry unfolds through a structure of conscious and intentional operations; the structured process is underpinned by
a basic orientation of intentionality; the directional tendency of the process
and its attendant structure is, in turn, engulfed by an existential state of
being-in-love. The existential state, then, is the existential condition of fidelity to the basic intentionality, and fidelity to the intentionality generates the
openness of cognitional, moral, and spiritual inquiry. In a move reminiscent
of that of Polanyi in his *Personal Knowledge: Towards a Post-Critical Philosophy,*
Lonergan sees fidelity to the structured process of inquiry as the source of all
norms and standards. The self-knowledge that is at the heart of Lonergan's
philosophical enterprise is the recognition, or appropriation, of this structure
of inquiry, its orientation of consciousness, and the engulfing existential state.
Lonergan is blunt on its centrality: "Up to that decisive achievement all leads.
From it all follows."[4]

It is not the task of this book to conduct exercises that might assist in the
achievement of self-appropriation. Rather, the task is to explore "what follows" from that achievement in clarifying the status of human existence as historical existence. In pursuit of this goal two interrelated problems arise, one
methodological, the other substantive.

In the first place, Lonergan's philosophy of consciousness, it should be recalled, is deceptively simple. His terminology about the structure of con-

---

3. Blaise Pascal, *Pensées,* no. 199 (no. 72 in Brunschvicg standard edition); Karl Löwith,
Nature, History, and Existentialism and Other Essays in the Philosophy of History, chap. 6;
D. E. Linge, "Historicity and Hermeneutic: A Study of Contemporary Hermeneutical Theory," 252–53 n. 271.
4. *Insight,* 13.

sciousness can be taken as a slogan, or even mantra, and his articulation of the structure of consciousness can be misinterpreted as referring to a reified thing. In fact, the "simplicity" of the structure of consciousness will recur through all the diverse patterns of human inquiry, in all the various cultural horizons, and at all the distinct phases of development throughout human history. At times of progress and triumph it will be as conspicuous by its presence as at times of decline and breakdown it will be conspicuous by its absence. In this work Lonergan's "simple" philosophy of consciousness will serve not as a slogan but, to employ an analogy from music, as a leitmotiv working out its theme in ever changing movements.[5] Thus, the essay format of this book will play the leitmotiv in contextual variations appropriate to the set of topics listed in the Contents rather than present a system of the philosophy of history.

The second problem, the substantive one, follows by accepting Lonergan's claim that he has a normative philosophy of consciousness. Does not this claim seem similar to those of the foundational philosophers, starting with that of Descartes, so decried by the postmodernists, that would impose from some atemporal and absolute viewpoint a structure on history as an alien object? Worse yet, a foundational philosophy of consciousness might be tempted to impose something like a gnostic vision of the meaning of history, a move so denounced in classic style by Eric Voegelin.[6] By contrast, Voegelin contends that, as historical creatures, we have an in-between status: as actors in the drama of history surrounded by the aura of mystery, we are participants in a process of historical existence outside of which we cannot stand. It will be a major theme in these essays that Lonergan's philosophy of consciousness does not occupy some privileged zone outside of history. Indeed, Lonergan's philosophy is quite clear and specific on why the process of inquiry is always historically contextualized, on why the normative dimension of consciousness is a source of both historical identity and historical diversity, and on why historical existence is a challenge to assume historical responsibility. Furthermore, not only is Lonergan's philosophy of consciousness compatible

---

5. A musician and scholar of Lonergan, Paul Marcoux, once remarked to me that Lonergan's *Insight* reminded him of a work by Bach with the intricate variations on a central theme. Interestingly, Lonergan commented that listening to Beethoven helped him write *Insight*. See Bernard J. F. Lonergan, *Caring about Meaning: Patterns in the Life of Bernard Lonergan,* 194.

6. Eric Voegelin, *The New Science of Politics;* Karl Löwith, *Meaning in History.*

with Voegelin's philosophy of history but, as argued in Chapter 10, "Self-Appropriation in Lonergan and Voegelin," and Chapter 11, "Equivalence of Meaning," Lonergan's perspective of critical realism can also formulate key principles that prove identical with, or the equivalent of, Voegelin's most salient points.

As suggested above, then, the order of the chapters is not simply acciden-tal but reflects an unfolding of the major theme. The first chapter appropri-ately introduces Lonergan's philosophy of consciousness, for consciousness serves as the evidence for cognitional theory, epistemology, and metaphysics. As the second chapter spells out, the metaphysics corresponding to the phi-losophy of consciousness supports a theory of development—Lonergan's worldview of emergent probability—that regards human development under the dynamic category of historical-mindedness rather than under the static rubric of classicism.

Chapter 3 highlights what is specific about human development: the fac-tor of dialectic, where human beings take on responsibility for authenticity or inauthenticity in negotiating the tension of limitation and transcendence, the very hallmark of development. This also allows for the crucial distinction be-tween historicity and historicism. Chapter 4 clarifies the distinction by relat-ing each concept to epistemological assumptions and shows how Lonergan's cognitional theory can affirm historicity while rejecting historicism. Chapter 5 explores the role of reason in historical life by addressing a delicate ques-tion: how can one today forcefully reaffirm the thesis of progress and link it to the power of reason while, at the same time, divorcing it from rationalist or gnostic historical speculation and from conceptualist plans to dominate his-tory? This points to the possibility of a creative community of inquirers who would foster progress, a topic discussed in Chapter 6 under the heading of cosmopolis. Neither a utopian blueprint nor a dictatorship of intellectuals, cosmopolis, to emphasize the main theme of Lonergan's philosophy, is a di-mension of consciousness with a heightened sense of historicity. If cosmopo-lis and reason are linked to historical responsibility, what, then, is the role of philosophy and its relation to historicity? Chapter 7 reaches perhaps two star-tling conclusions in this regard: philosophy is a variety of religious experience that shares with other varieties of religious experience a historical context of emergence; and, accordingly, philosophy is an event that must be appropriat-ed anew in each historical situation and its therapeutic task of unrestricted in-quiry applied to concrete historical challenges.

As most chapters stress, human existence entails historical existence, and historical existence entails authentic existence. Lonergan's treatment of self-transcendence—cognitive, moral, and spiritual—ties together two seemingly disparate concerns: that for performative norms and that for a horizon of possibility. Chapter 8 shows how these two concerns are linked in the various dynamics of the existential mood of dread, which is intrinsically connected to self-transcendence. Insofar as Lonergan's philosophy of history embraces the themes of authenticity, the truth of existence, and orientation to transcendence, his ideas can be further elucidated by comparison with the remarkable parallels in Eric Voegelin's philosophy of history. With Lonergan's cognitional theory as a backdrop, Chapter 9 introduces Voegelin's philosophy of consciousness by showing how he retrieves and develops Aristotle's noetic science. Chapter 10 considers the project of self-appropriation in both thinkers, and Chapter 11 proposes a mutually enriching dialogue between the two philosophers, whose main line of inquiry, it is argued, is equivalent. The three concluding chapters end where the first chapter begins—with consciousness. The entire book, then, cumulatively explores the dynamic of consciousness: consciousness of self as an actor participating in the drama of history.

Because Lonergan sees a unity to consciousness he also sees a unity to the drama of history, notwithstanding the shock of diversity, decline, and novelty. The very mystery that surrounds the drama of history, as Lonergan understands it, is a function of this unity. In wrestling with the crisis of historicism Dilthey dreamed that Raphael's *School of Athens* fragmented into irreconcilable worldviews. Lonergan's vision of history, to the contrary, would keep the painting intact as it represents a unity of origins and a "sequence of contributions to a single but complex goal."[7]

7. *Insight*, 349–50, 412, 414, 569–72.

Part I

*Lonergan's Foundational
Worldview*

1

Lonergan's Philosophy of Consciousness

CONSCIOUSNESS IS THE ENGLISH WORD derived from the Latin *cum* (with) and *scire* (to know). The Latin original meant either knowing something in the company of others or (with *sibi*) self-knowing. In 1620 *consciousness* was used to mean awareness to oneself. In 1681 Hobbes, of all people, meant by *consciousness* "mutual knowledge." Since the seventeenth century, *consciousness* has come generally to mean perception of the mind (Locke, 1694), or the state of being mentally aware of a thing (1746–1747), or the sum total of impressions, thoughts, and feelings that make up one's conscious being (Locke, 1695).[1]

The vast usages of the term, then, provide no clear indication of its philosophical import. Indeed, it should caution us to pay careful attention to how a philosopher, such as Lonergan, might employ it. But why is it important to focus on *consciousness*? Why is it important for Lonergan? Indeed what is it for Lonergan? And what are some of the more pregnant implications of Lonergan's idea of consciousness for contemporary reflection on the self and self-knowledge?

---

1. See Charlton T. Lewis and Charles Short, *A Latin Dictionary,* s.v. "scio"; Thomas Hobbes, *Leviathan,* 31; *Oxford English Dictionary,* s.v. "conscious," "consciousness," 3–5.

Age of Consciousness

We live in an Age of Consciousness. For the past two decades we have been urged to "raise our consciousness."[2] We have seen various liberation groups—racial, ethnic, national, or gender—following precisely this injunction. Phenomenologists have insisted upon studying consciousness in its purity and givenness. Psychologists have assisted us in trying to recover our repressed consciousness. Artists have explored in symbolism and surrealism the depths of our consciousness. Marxists have sought to transform the material conditions that foster our false consciousness. Gnostic poets and politicians, gurus and revolutionaries, have promised—or threatened—to liberate our consciousness. Philosophers from Descartes to Hegel to the existentialists have taken the "turn" toward interiority and subjectivity—that is, toward consciousness. Ah, but here is the rub! Does not this turn to consciousness and interiority and subjectivity threaten to engulf us in the swamp of relativism, egoism, and indeed nihilism? Are there not as many consciousnesses as agents of consciousness? Would not to think otherwise be to reify consciousness and make it into an abstract something other than what we mean by consciousness with all its associations of interiority and subjectivity? Are consciousness and objectivity, in fact, contradictory, or, at least, contrary, notions? If so, how can we even meaningfully communicate about this obscurity?

In other words, is the contemporary concentration on consciousness itself simply one manifestation of a severe intellectual crisis? The crisis would be an *intellectual* crisis in a double sense: it would be a crisis among intellectuals, and it would be a crisis about the very integrity, nature, and value of intellectual life. It would be a *crisis* because grave doubts would have been sown by intellectuals about the real worth of serious intellectual endeavor, either about the virtue of radical attachment to the desire to know or, at any rate, about the real prospect of human reason to shed light on fundamental problems of the human condition. And with an appropriate raising of consciousness why would one need, or want, to take seriously the fully intellectual life, except perhaps as a pleasurable *divertissement*?

I believe this is more than just a caricature of our times. Whereas the claims on behalf of human reason have steadily shrunk among most intellectual leaders, the fascination with consciousness has correspondingly grown. That the

2. For a survey, see Roland N. Stromberg, *After Everything: Western Intellectual History since 1945.*

claims of reason have suffered an eclipse in the past two centuries is obvious. The followers of the empiricists and posivitists restrict reason to the gathering of facts about mere phenomena; the Kantians and neo-Kantians enclose human understanding in a cage of methodologies; conventionalists argue that even science provides only the most economical fictions; existentialists tend to consider truth as the truth we live within the bounds of practical reason or our leaps beyond reason; pragmatists look to practical reason in the most literal sense as the model for intellectual culture; such historicists as Wilhelm Dilthey proclaim the finitude of all truth and values and the emergence of an ensuing historical *consciousness* that will foster an "anarchy of convictions"; such social scientists as Max Weber deny that scientific reason can pronounce on the truth of values; and linguistic philosophers reduce human meaning essentially to the function of language games.[3]

It is true that there have been protests against consciousness. Behaviorists, for example, consider it an occult entity. Linguistic philosophers eschew consciousness as an object of investigation because they abhor the idea of private contents of consciousness that a focus on it, in their view, necessarily entails. But these perspectives give us a clue to the source of the intellectual crisis insofar as they suggest that objective method and an emphasis on consciousness are antithetical. In brief, objectivity and subjectivity are polar opposites. Both those who glorify consciousness and those who detract from consciousness apparently accept the same ground rules: subjectivity can only interfere with objectivity; objectivity can only mutilate subjectivity.

And behind these ground rules about subjectivity and objectivity lies a basic assumption about human knowing, the *confrontation theory of truth.* Objective human knowing must be analogous to an unobstructed vision of objects "out there." Subjectivity certainly obstructs this vision. Consciousness itself is often interpreted in this fashion. John Locke, for example, defined consciousness as the "perception of what passes in one's mind."[4] But, if this perception is not unconscious, then one must have a perception of it, and that perception must have a perception, and so on, as Leibniz suggested. Objective knowing of consciousness, so conceived, thus involves us in an infinite regress. We seem caught in dangerous quandaries and paradoxes.

Thus, the problem of consciousness is, in one sense, part of a larger prob-

---

3. For discussion of the cultural crisis at the turn of the twentieth century, see H. Stuart Hughes, *Consciousness and Society: The Reorientation of European Social Thought, 1890–1930.*

4. John Locke, *Essay Concerning Human Understanding*, 2.1.19.

lem of the contemporary intellectual crisis and its operative assumption about subjectivity and objectivity.

In perhaps the *reductio ad absurdum* of modern culture, deconstructionism exploits these aporias regarding subjectivity and objectivity as it simultaneously assaults both objective method and the self. Whereas deconstructionism more reveals the problem than offers a viable alternative, Lonergan would have us sweep away dominant assumptions about subjectivity and objectivity and enter into an entirely new perspective.

This perspective also allows for a new approach to the philosophy of history. For, as we shall explore at greater length in Chapters 3 and 4, the confrontation theory of truth sets the agenda for reflections on history. Historical objectivity must be, according to this view, either methodological domination of facts or passive intuition of diverse expressions of meaning. The historian either imposes methodological control on history or succumbs to historical relativism. Lonergan offers a substantive alternative to these options.

Lonergan: Philosopher of Consciousness

Interestingly enough, for Lonergan a resolution of the contemporary problem involves a return, so to speak, to consciousness.[5] Clearly, Lonergan does *not* mean by consciousness what most people, or even philosophers, mean. And by not meaning by consciousness what most philosophers mean, Lonergan will not take the search for foundations to be what most philosophers from Descartes on have claimed it to be. Lonergan instead would resuscitate the now largely discredited foundational enterprise and place it within the radically different context of his distinct interpretation of consciousness. We must first turn to why he holds consciousness to be decisive in considering foundational philosophical issues, and, second, we must examine what he means by consciousness.

Lonergan shares the deep concern of Descartes, Kant, Hegel, and Dilthey that philosophical method must address itself to the incessant wars of antagonistic philosophical *Weltanschauungen*. This calls for a critical philosophy, one that must establish a philosophy of philosophies, accurately accounting both for the genesis of correct philosophical positions and for the birth of incorrect philosophical counterpositions along the entire gamut of conflicting philosophical worldviews. Unless a genuine philosophy of philosophies can

---

5. *Insight,* 12–13, 16–17; Bernard J. F. Lonergan, *A Second Collection,* 69–86.

be constructed, the philosophical horizon of relativism may win the struggle by default; the danger lurks that the civil war of philosophies may so exhaust the mettle of the participants that the excessive practicality of common sense will triumphantly proclaim itself as sovereign over its rightful masters.[6]

Lonergan warns that the battle of philosophical horizons cannot be resolved by an appeal to the coherence of any given horizon, theory, or set of propositions within a horizon, for then every horizon would, in effect, be self-justifying. What is needed as a starting point is not metaphysics but the wisdom that generates a metaphysics. What is needed is not so much a foundational theory as a foundational reality. Or to put it another way, what is needed is not a philosophy, nor even *the* philosophy, but rather *the philosopher:* a concrete inquirer who inquires about his or her own concrete process of inquiry. Lonergan compels a higher culture worn out by centuries of irreconcilable philosophical theories and ideas to ask whether indeed the strategy of waging the foundational philosophical struggle by relying chiefly on an arsenal of theories and ideas has been the primeval fault, leading to an inevitable and exhausting dead end. Lonergan urges that contemporary philosophical culture retrace the journey in search of foundations along the path from medieval essentialism to Descartes's thinking substance, to Kant's transcendental ego, to Hegel's subject, to Kierkegaard's *this subject:* from object as object, to the subject as object, to the subject as subject. Lonergan challenges us to ask whether philosophy can reasonably embark upon any other course save that of, in his unique phrase, "self-appropriation."[7]

Lonergan does not prove that in the "subject as subject" will be found the evidence for a critique of all horizons; he claims to prove that unless we find it there we will not find it at all.[8] What does Lonergan mean by the subject as subject? He means the subject as *conscious.* He means the subject not as reflecting upon his or her operations of sensing, thinking, or willing, but the subject as simply aware while sensing, thinking, or willing. Consciousness is not an operation additional to the operations of sensing, thinking, and willing.[9] It is properly not an operation at all; it is the luminosity concomitant with operations. This is an extremely important point for Lonergan, and its radicality must be grasped and constantly kept in mind lest our understand-

---

6. Bernard J. F. Lonergan, "Horizon as a Problem of Philosophy," in *Notes on Existentialism,* 15; *Insight,* 6, 412–13, 441–45.

7. "Horizon as a Problem," in *Notes on Existentialism,* 15; *Insight,* 12–13, 432.

8. "Horizon as a Problem," in *Notes on Existentialism,* 15.

9. Bernard J. F. Lonergan, *Method in Theology,* 8.

ing of Lonergan's idea of consciousness slide into more commonplace versions fundamentally at odds with his own.

Lonergan, then, asks us to attend to our conscious activities; consciousness becomes data for our self-inquiry, self-understanding, and self-knowledge. This experiment has its uniquely personal dimensions: it is a personal philosophical reflection on our own personal activities for which we take personal responsibility. The experiment must necessarily be personal, but the results, Lonergan argues, should bear a generic resemblance. This is to say that conscious activities—at least for most persons—are not entirely amorphous, chaotic, and disoriented. There is a patterned interrelationship and a directional tendency in the flow of consciousness itself.[10]

Normative Structure of Consciousness

Let us explore what, according to Lonergan, we shall likely find as a result of a careful scrutiny of our consciousness. We can highlight seven themes.

First, consciousness is self-presence, not self-knowledge.[11] I am, for example, reading a book. While my attention is on the subject matter of the book, I am also present to myself as reading. Only if I stop and reflect upon the fact of my reading will that self-presence (that consciousness) reach my attention and become an object of my knowledge. Consciousness is an awareness immanent in appetitive, sensitive, cognitional, and volitional operations. It is self-presence in acts of desiring, seeing, hearing, touching, smelling, tasting, perceiving, imagining, inquiring, understanding, conceiving, formulating, reflecting, marshaling and weighing the evidence, judging, deliberating, evaluating, deciding, speaking, writing.[12] Consciousness, then, is an *experience* of the self, and, as such, it supplies data for self-knowledge, although it is not itself such self-knowledge. This means that a heightening of consciousness—consciousness-raising—is a necessary but not sufficient condition of self-

10. On consciousness as data and cognitional structure, see Bernard J. F. Lonergan, *Collection*, chap. 14; and *Method in Theology*, chap. 1. On the experiment of consciousness, see *Insight*, 13. On the directional tendency of consciousness, see *Insight*, 372–83; *A Second Collection*, 79–84; *Method in Theology*, 11–12; and *A Third Collection: Papers by Bernard J. F. Lonergan*, 174–75.

11. For a general discussion of consciousness, see *Insight*, 344–52; *Method in Theology*, 6–10; and *Collection*, 209–10.

12. *Insight*, 344–46, 636–38; *Method in Theology*, 7.

knowledge. Further cognitional operations are needed beyond attending to the data of consciousness if self-knowledge is to be achieved, and various biases can short-circuit the interpretation of consciousness.

Second, consciousness is not a succession of atomic units. To consider single conscious acts entails, Lonergan insists, a "violent abstraction." Sensitive acts, intellectual operations, and movements of volition are all involved in multiple correlations. As I read my book, for instance, I am seeing marks on a piece of paper, and I am moving pages; I am understanding and reflecting upon the meaning conveyed by the ordered marks; and I am deciding to carry on the above activities. Attention to sensations, perceptions, images, and memories occurs within a horizon informed by the content of cognitional operations and constituted by acts of volition. Intellectual acts, however, operate with respect to sensitive stimuli and manipulation of sensitive flow. Acts of volition, in turn, regard the contents of intellectual and sensitive operations. Hence the study of consciousness is the study of flow, direction, orientation, interest, concern. Indeed, distinct flows of consciousness constitute such distinct orientations as the aesthetic, scientific, and practical "patterns of experience." Accordingly, we can speak of the *stream of consciousness*.[13]

Third, consciousness, through various patterns of experience, flows spontaneously through successive and *expansive* levels, each qualitatively distinct but functionally related to the others.[14] These are levels of:

—*empirical consciousness* (operations of sensing, perceiving, imagining, feeling, and bodily motion);
—*intelligent consciousness* (operations of inquiring, understanding, expressing, and formulating);
—*rational consciousness* (operations of reflecting upon formulations, assessing evidence, and judging); and
—*existential consciousness* (operations of deliberating, evaluating, deciding, and acting).

These operations in their structural cooperation constitute the self-present structure of consciousness.

Fourth, according to Lonergan, spontaneously and consciously we go from the level of experiencing to inquiring about our experience; spontaneously

13. "Horizon and Dread," in *Notes on Existentialism,* 10; *Insight,* 181, 205, 324–25; *Method in Theology,* 12–13.
14. *Insight,* 346–48, 623; *A Second Collection,* 79–81; *Method in Theology,* 9–10.

and consciously we go from the level of understanding to judging what we understand; spontaneously and consciously we go from the level of judging to deliberating and deciding in light of what we know. The spontaneous flow of consciousness indicates that the stream is at once *directional* and *normative*. The spontaneity is rooted in the existential moods of wonder (as we inquire), doubt (as we reflect), and dread (as we deliberate). Lonergan would add to this the spiritual undertow of an unrestricted love and the "upwardly driven" neural base charged with image and affect.[15] The normative dimension of the flow of consciousness itself means that objectivity is the result of following these norms. Fidelity to the desire to know and to the intention of the good is the ultimate criterion of objectivity. Objectivity, as Lonergan puts it, is the *fruit* of authentic *subjectivity*.[16]

Fifth, we can speak of *the* stream of consciousness and its structure and norms because there is a unity to consciousness. And the unity is *given:* it is experienced.[17] It is the experience of self-presence, which is the luminosity of self pervading the flow and operations of consciousness.

Sixth, the normative, spontaneous flow of consciousness throughout the several levels of inquiry is *expansive* of *selfhood*.[18] The experience of self is the experience of an expanding, opening horizon of possibility. This is the true meaning of a "raising of consciousness." It is the tending of consciousness beyond. Far from falling into solipsism or narcissism, a liberation of consciousness would open up the luminous process of self-transcendence.

Seventh, though there are such conscious emotional and conative impulses as hunger and thirst, fatigue and irritability, that have no content, most conscious operations have objects. When I am self-present as reading, I nevertheless focus attention on the content of the book through combined operations of sensation, perception, imagination, memory, understanding, judging, and evaluating. This heading of awareness toward objects is what phenomenologists call *intentionality*. As there are conscious acts at distinct levels, so there are objects at distinct levels. As the flow of consciousness is not a succession of atomic units, so the contents of different conscious operations will

---

15. *Insight*, 346–48, 370, 377–80, 481–82, 623, 627; *A Second Collection*, 79–81; *Method in Theology*, 9–10, 18, 105. On dread as the existential mood of responsible consciousness, see Elizabeth Murray Morelli, "The Feeling of Freedom," 101; and *A Third Collection*, 174–75.

16. *Insight*, 404–5; *Method in Theology*, 20, 35, 37, 265, 292.

17. *Insight*, 349–50.

18. *A Second Collection*, 80; *Method in Theology*, 9–10.

merge into profiles of particular objects and different profiles of objects will be meaningfully interrelated within a *horizon.*[19]

Thus, the normative pattern of conscious and intentional operations—that is, the subject as subject—provides the basis for differentiating the normative flow of consciousness from the narrow interpretations of restrictive philosophical horizons, including the prevailing views in the contemporary climate of opinion. In so doing it also raises in the most intimate and personal manner the issue of authentic selfhood.

Self and Self-Knowledge

If this outlines the contours of Lonergan's philosophy of consciousness, what are some of its most fruitful implications about the conscious subject, or self, that circumvent the confrontation theory of truth? To cite some typical modern problems about the self: Is it an isolated monad? A pure Cartesian thinking thing? A completely transparent world-immanent project? Or so elusive and inexhaustible as to defy objectification and to preclude real self-knowledge?

We must first inquire, *what is the self?* Clearly, it is not an already preformed thing. Nor is it simply what is given in consciousness. For the spontaneity of consciousness with its directional tendency to the beyond may be blocked. Obviously, the structure Lonergan talks about is not always—or perhaps is only rarely—fully present. But that does not invalidate his claims, for the normative pattern of conscious intentionality is *self-validating:* any meaningful attempt to criticize it (that is, to inquire attentively, intelligently, reasonably, and responsibly about it) must invoke it. Consciousness, then, exhibits the self as a tension of questioner and object of the question, as choosing and as chosen. To seek authentically one's authentic self is to exhibit this tension. To fail to seek authentically one's authentic self is to exhibit loss of selfhood. The tension of authenticity and inauthenticity becomes a theme in the recovery of selfhood. The real self is engaged in a perpetual quest for authentic existence and in a perpetual withdrawal from inauthenticity.[20] But the self is not sim-

---

19. "Subject and Horizon," in *Notes on Existentialism,* 6–7; *Method in Theology,* 5–8, 30, 235–37.

20. On the self-validating nature of the structure of consciousness, see *Insight,* 359–60; *Collection,* 190, 192–93, 199–200, 204; and *Method in Theology,* 17–21. On the tension of self as questioner and self as question, see *Collection,* 229; Emil L. Fackenheim, *Metaphysics and Historicity,* 83–85; and Emil L. Fackenheim, *The God Within: Kant, Schelling,*

ply self-contained, even within these tensions of self-transcendence and re-covery. Rather, it is Lonergan's position that the self is inherently a field of ten-sion with its own unconscious depths, with other selves, and with the tran-scendent beyond. This is to ask about the relation of consciousness to the unconscious, to other selves, to the divine, to being.

We must consider, then, that, for Lonergan, consciousness is incarnate. Consciousness is an integrated consciousness, integrated with cosmic energy. According to Lonergan's holistic metaphysics, human reality consists of atom-ic, chemical, biological, psychic, and intentional levels of integration, in which higher levels are conditioned by lower ones but also sublate them.[21] The chemical level systematizes what is merely coincidental in the underlying manifold of subatomic events; the biological is a higher integration of the un-derlying manifold of chemical elements and compounds; the sensitive psyche is a higher organization of the organic; and the levels of conscious intention-ality sublate atomic, chemical, biological, and psychic manifolds. The laws of physics, chemistry, biology, and behaviorist psychology pertain to conscious intentionality such that sensations, images, and feelings are integral with the functioning of intellectual and moral projects without determining them.

At the same time, Lonergan argues that precisely because of this integration of nature and spirit the unconscious neural base is an "upwardly directed dy-namism" with "anticipations and virtualities of higher activities." Unconscious energy is a potency heading for the form of psychic energy. This arena may include what Whitehead means by "experience." There is a field of instinctu-al energy that can burst forth on the conscious level in the form of images and affects in league with the desire to know and the attraction to the good.[22] Still, this integration of consciousness is a complicated and arduous process. Depth hermeneutics has both an archaeological task of recovering repressed, Freudi-an libido and a teleological task of liberating and conscripting what Bergson calls the *élan vital*.[23] The field of energy channeled into the neurophysiologi-cal system of a given human organism is itself part of a field of cosmic ener-gy; the "personal unconscious" is related to what Robert Doran calls the "cos-

---

and Historicity, 229–30, where he cites Søren Kierkegaard, *Either/Or,* 2:179ff. On the per-petual struggle for authenticity, see *Method in Theology,* 110, 252.

21. *Insight,* 57–92, 126–61, 229–30, 284–87, 463–67, 476–94.

22. Ibid., 482, 555–57, 569–72.

23. On the "archaeological," see ibid., 214–31; and *Method in Theology,* 33–34, 67–68. On the teleological, see Bernard J. F. Lonergan, "Reality, Myth, Symbol," 33–34. In *Method in Theology,* Lonergan refers to Ricoeur's notion of the archaeology and teleology of the subject (68). See Paul Ricoeur, *Freud and Philosophy: An Essay on Interpretation.*

mic unconscious," or what Eric Voegelin, following Plato's interpretations in the *Timaios* and the *Critias,* terms the "generic unconscious" of mankind in touch with the "primordial forces of the cosmos."[24]

So Lonergan would suggest that we might add to the four levels of conscious intentionality adumbrated above a unique lower level, at the very depths of consciousness, in which a "symbolic operator" shapes the development of sensibility. This lower level, associated with psychic integration through the coordination of neural potentialities, occupies a land between unconscious and conscious operations, including materials in the "twilight of what is conscious but not objectified."[25] We must interpret Lonergan's suggestion in light of his notion of levels of integration. Accordingly, to posit a level of the symbolic operator is to retain fully the qualitative distinction of the higher operations of conscious intentionality (experiencing, understanding, judging, and deciding) and, at the same time, to recognize that the lower, sublated level of the psyche is a bridge to cognitive and volitional activities from unconscious energy. It is not really so much to "add" another level as simply to acknowledge the functional relation of the psyche to consciousness.

If consciousness has a participatory link with the unconscious depths, then, we may ask, does it not also open up a sharing of consciousness both horizontally and vertically? To put it another way, Lonergan's focus on consciousness is a focus on the subject as subject. Is there also a reality of subject-with-subject? We ordinarily interact with others, as incarnate beings, through varying degrees of interpretation, from body languages, to overt speech, to scientific analysis. However, can we also interact subject to subject with a sharing of consciousness—a participation of consciousness? Lonergan's unique definition of consciousness pinpoints self-presence as radically different from any interpretation. Can we have a noninterpretive sharing of consciousness? Interpersonally? With the divine? Is not the latter the meaning of mystical experience? It is interesting to note that Lonergan compares mystical union with the mating of lovers.[26]

Lonergan goes so far as to postulate beyond the moral operator on the level of responsible consciousness another level of consciousness, that of loving commitment, extending from interpersonal relations to embracing the whole

24. Robert Doran, "The Theologian's Psyche: Notes toward a Reconstruction of Depth Psychology," 109–10; Eric Voegelin, *Order and History,* 3:192, 198. Lonergan, in "Reality, Myth, Symbol," refers approvingly to Doran's exploration of the psyche (37).

25. Bernard J. F. Lonergan, "Philosophy and the Religious Phenomenon," 134; *Method in Theology,* 34.

26. *Method in Theology,* 77.

universe in a total engagement. This loving consciousness would seem to be a subject-to-subject sharing of consciousness, with its most radical expression in spiritual experience. Is loving consciousness, however, most properly another level of consciousness or another dimension of consciousness? If Lonergan's positing of a level of symbolic consciousness legitimately strains the metaphor of level of consciousness because the psychic level of integration is precisely the link between unconscious energy and conscious intentionality, his positing of a spiritual level strains the metaphor even more, perhaps to the point where it may be counterproductive. On the one hand, Lonergan does define levels of integration with the mathematical analogue of "operators," and the existence of a spiritual operator (unrestricted loving) would, in a move reminiscent of Kierkegaard, be a distinct operator beyond that of the moral operator. This retains the old theological idea of Aquinas that the supernatural life sublates (that is, perfects) natural existence. On the other hand, the principle of this operator, for Lonergan, is not a new set of conscious and intentional operations. The principle is, rather, "conversion," the vertical exercise of liberty that transforms a horizon and perforce transforms (sublates) the operations within the horizon—but not by a new set of operations. The issue here would seem to be whether spiritual habits are operations or existential dispositions. We may explore this issue briefly in terms of the traditional spiritual virtues of faith, hope, and charity. Lonergan does indeed speak of faith as a judgment of value born of religious love. The judgment of value, though, in this case, would seem to be an operation on the fourth level of consciousness transformed by the state of being unrestrictedly in love. Hope, Tad Dunne argues, following the pattern of Lonergan's definition of faith, is a "confident desire born of religious love"—hence an existential, affective disposition.[27] Charity is itself a state of being in love. Thus, just as in symbolic consciousness we reach the border of conscious intentionality "below," so in religious consciousness we reach the border of conscious intentionality "above." Both borders surround consciousness with transforming mystery. Genuine symbolic consciousness is an orientation from the unconscious to transcendence; the experience of transcendence reorients symbolic consciousness. Psychic vitality energizes the levels of conscious intentionality; spiritual luminosity alters the very horizon of experience, understanding, judging, and deciding.

27. "Philosophy and Religious Phenomenon," 34; on the mathematical analogy of the operator in development, see *Insight*, 490–92; on "conversion," see *Method in Theology*, 40, 237–38, 240–41; on "faith," see *Method in Theology*, 115; Dunne, *Lonergan and Spirituality: Towards a Spiritual Integration*, 123.

We might also inquire whether the "inner light" of the flow of consciousness anticipates in our own unrestricted questioning the horizon of being itself. In our consciousness do we participate in the experience of the intrinsic intelligibility of being? Is this participation the experience of the heuristic insights that ground the very process of inquiry? This suggests that we might consider consciousness, self-presence, as the primary meaning of intelligibility, a stance that seems in accord with Aristotle's and Thomas's emphasis on knowing as the identity in act of knower and known.[28] Still, our human consciousness is an anticipatory illumination of what we must always incompletely and inadequately fill out with our discursive reasoning and grasp of form. So, too, no matter how profound may be a mystical experience, it remains that transcendence, for Lonergan, takes on its elementary meaning from raising the further question—that is, from the orientation to, and not the possession of, the beyond through the desire to know and the intention of the good.[29] Similarly, no matter how intimate an intersubjective relation may be, authentic loving demands objective knowing, which, in turn, requires interpretation and judgment.[30]

The very incarnate nature of our consciousness and the discursive nature of our reasoning point to the fact that selfhood is a function of a dialectic of consciousness and horizon. The orientation of consciousness itself cannot exist apart from a "concrete synthesis of conscious living," which Lonergan identifies as a horizon, whereas the fundamental defining principle of a horizon is the orientation of consciousness. Stated succinctly, conscious operations are always performed within an already constituted horizon of meaningful, significant, relevant questions and a background of previous experiences, insights, formulations, judgments, evaluations, and decisions—just as conscious operations also constitute the very horizon itself. Lonergan's idea of consciousness as data significantly clarifies the dialectic of performance and interpretation. Conscious performance is data for interpretation, and interpretation is a basis for future performance. One is decisively tied to one's past, which is always an interpreted past; one really never acts toward the future from a present that totally constitutes itself from a blank tablet; but one can

28. On the "inner light," see *A Third Collection*, 193; for discussion of Aquinas's term *intellectual light*, see Bernard J. Lonergan, *Verbum: Word and Idea in Aquinas*, 90ff; on "heuristic notions," see *Insight*, 417; on the identity of knower and known in Aquinas, see *Verbum*, chaps. 1–2.

29. *Insight*, 658.

30. *Collection*, 220–21.

act so as to transform one's mode of living, and the new performance can, in turn, supply new data for new interpretation. The circle of past performance supplying data for present interpretation that influences future performance can be a vicious circle of inhibited performance and cumulative misinterpretation, establishing the spiral of ever narrower integrations of living amid the increasing wreckage of former psychic order. On the other hand, though, it is possible to break out of this vicious circle and bridge the existential gap between fact and possibility, between misinterpretation and genuine insight. The past can become a challenge, a *question*, crying out for creative response, for more attentiveness, greater insight, and sounder judgment to reverse the spiral and to enlarge the operational range of freedom.[31]

We must underscore, however, that although consciousness is not separate from interpretation, consciousness is nonetheless radically distinct from interpretation. To clarify this distinction of consciousness we can identify three levels of self-interpretation:

> —*theoretic* (a systematic, conceptual reflection on the self that aims at explanatory statements and definitions);
> —*commonsensical* (usually autobiographical reflections in ordinary language narratives and concrete observations); and
> —*nonthematic* (spontaneous reflections, particularly where images and affects are wedded to experience).

As Lonergan defines consciousness, *none* of these three types of self-reflection are the same as consciousness. They are performed consciously, but awareness of the *contents* of these kinds of self-interpretation is not consciousness.

To illustrate in the most extreme case, that of nonthematic interpretation, which seems to bear a likeness to consciousness: Nonthematic interpretations involve what Lonergan calls "elemental meanings," where the meaning must be experienced to be understood.[32] For elemental meanings, such experiences as those of images, feelings, gestures, and tone of voice cannot be separated from what is intended or the meaning is lost. This applies to symbolic mean-

---

31. On horizon, see "Horizon and Dread," in *Notes on Existentialism*, 10; and *Method in Theology*, 235–37. On human historicity, see *Method in Theology*, 81, 237. On psychic disorder, see *Insight*, 214–20; on "genuineness," see *Insight*, 499–503; on the "existential gap," see "Subject and Horizon," in *Notes on Existentialism*, 9. On the operational range of freedom, see *Insight*, 643–47. On Toynbee's theory of challenge and response, see *Insight*, 234; and *A Third Collection*, 103–4, 214.

32. *Method in Theology*, 57–69.

ing (for example, a flag), intersubjective meaning (frequently a spontaneous pattern of gesture, interpretation, and response), and incarnate meaning (deeds, such as Marathon, or words, such as the Gettysburg Address, that embody the meaning of a group or person). Regardless of how elusive, spontaneous, and compact our awareness of elemental meanings may be, there still remains the radical gap between consciousness of the act of meaning and awareness of the intended content. To highlight this radical gap we can consider the helpful distinction Michael Polanyi has made between two degrees of awareness: *focal awareness* and *subsidiary awareness*. To return to the example of reading a book, I have a subsidiary awareness of seeing ordered marks on a piece of paper, while I have focal awareness of the meaning of the words signified by those ordered marks.[33] This is indeed a powerful analytic distinction—but, we must note, it is within the field of intended contents of conscious acts. Subsidiary awareness, then, is *not* consciousness. To be sure, nonthematic interpretations held in subsidiary awareness may seem so unreflective, so opaque, so subjective as to be equated with consciousness. *Still they are not.* Consciousness is radically other than any intended content.

We cannot stress this distinction too much, for without it we could never have access to the *subject as subject.* Nonetheless, as Michael H. McCarthy has remarked in *The Crisis of Philosophy,* there is a perpetual temptation to define consciousness by *analogies,* whether analogies of vision (Descartes), of technological making (pragmatism), or of socially sanctioned language (Wittgenstein). All these analogies fail miserably to do justice to the reality of the subject as subject. They obscure important operations of cognition, decision, and spiritual quest, and they contribute mightily to the intellectual crisis alluded to above. And so we have apparently come full circle.

If, however, there is such a radical gap between consciousness and interpretation, can we truly know consciousness, as Lonergan conceives of it? For the moment we inquire about our conscious experience, it is gone. We must remember that consciousness is not perception of mental operations. So we must rely on memory as we inquire about consciousness. Does this reliance on memory then make knowledge of consciousness, in principle, fundamentally incomplete, suspect, impossible? Lonergan's answer would undoubtedly be that knowledge of consciousness would indeed be fundamentally incomplete, suspect, or impossible if one accepted the demand of the confrontation theory of truth that knowing involves some kind of *direct look.* As

33. See *Insight,* 577–78; Polanyi, *Personal Knowledge,* vii, 55–65.

knowledge of consciousness relies on memories of conscious operations, so scientific knowledge relies on images, memories, and percepts derived from sense experience.[34] As scientists can judge scientific theories by testing for sensible consequences, so investigators of consciousness can judge interpretations of consciousness by guiding the performance of their conscious operations to "heighten their consciousness."

Still, a critic might rejoin, to know consciousness is to know consciousness as an object, and to know consciousness as an object is necessarily to distort the reality of the subject as subject. Indeed, in the last analysis, it is Lonergan's insistence on the pursuit of relevant questions as the font of objectivity—and not on a perception of something "out there" or "in here"—that overcomes a skeptical temptation unduly to mystify consciousness.[35] That consciousness has mystery about it surely cannot be denied. The existential tensions of selfhood and the subjective relation of self to other selves, to the cosmic unconscious, and to divine being—all alluded to above—suggest that the philosopher can never attain an exhaustive understanding of subjectivity and in these areas can more point to possibility than prove. But to posit a dynamism, a structure, and a unity to consciousness, as does Lonergan, is not to distort the subject as subject. To objectify subjectivity is not to mutilate subjectivity if by object one means simply what is intended in a question and not a Cartesian extended substance or a Kantian phenomenon defined by the strictures of Newtonian science.[36]

In conclusion, if Lonergan is correct about these foundational philosophical tenets, then any contemporary exploration of consciousness that does not factor in like-minded assumptions about subjectivity and objectivity will be seriously flawed. To my knowledge, no thinker has been so precise on this score as has Lonergan. His idea of the subject as subject is, I believe, the corollary to his equally precise and unique interpretation of an object as the content intended in a question and to his equally precise and penetrating notion of objectivity as fidelity to the desire to know.

34. *Insight,* 96–97.
35. Ibid., 308–12.
36. *Method in Theology,* 262–63, 341.

2

From Classicism to Emergent Probability

Lonergan's Notion of Development

AMONG THE PROMINENT WORDS in the contemporary climate of opinion, *development* occupies a conspicuous place. Like *consciousness*—with which it is frequently linked—the term *development* carries with it a host of possible philosophical meanings. It also expresses a diversity of seemingly irreconcilable philosophical frameworks. One such viewpoint was that of Plato and Aristotle, who conceived of development, including human development, as the actualization of a nature defined by its universal properties. Modern Enlightenment thinkers, on the other hand, have seen development specifically as progress through the tutoring of culture, and hence of society, by science and through the improving of standards of living by technology. The Enlightenment idea of progress has been applied in vastly different ways to the political and economic realms by the antithetical claims, on the one hand, of the liberals, who have praised the free market and (eventually) democracy, and, on the other hand, of the Marxists, who have looked forward to the redemption of human nature by the irruption into history of socialist humanity. Both such liberals as Herbert Spencer and other evolutionary positivists and such Marxists as Friedrich Engels could later tie their respective interpretations of development, somewhat ambiguously, to a biological theory of the evolution of the universe. Romantics, however, perhaps the dialectical twins of the Enlightenment *philosophes,* have taken development to mean individual self-development, a voluntaristic expression of "self-concept," always coupled with a vital surge of affectivity and imaginative power.[1] It is indeed part of the task of a reflective and sophisticated intellectual culture to examine, analyze, and criticize the meaning of such implicitly philosophical terms. Like *consciousness, development* is in need of radical philosophical clarification.

It is instructive to consider Bernard Lonergan's notion of development, for he would build upon the foundation of ancient ideas, not simply discard them, while, at the same time, freely embracing modern concern with the heuristics of scientific method, with historical progress, and with subjectivity. Lonergan, in other words, engages in a dialogue with ancient and modern horizons. He addresses how Plato's and Aristotle's conceptions of human nature can be reconciled with modern scientific method, evolution theory, historical consciousness, and emphasis on subjectivity. How can this be achieved, a devotee of the perennial philosophy might ask, without succumbing to a materialism that would reduce intellectual, moral, and spiritual operations to mere epiphenomena—that would, in effect, replace the human soul with the human machine as true human nature—or to a relativism that would replace human nature with human history, or to a subjectivism that would replace history with the self?[2] Conversely, how can this be done, a modern might rejoin, without ignoring the claims that nature is an emergent universe, that human beings are historical beings, and that philosophy must become reflective interiority?

Our task is to survey how Lonergan's notion of development draws from both ancient and modern ideas while trying to avoid what he would judge to be the oversights of each. Conveniently, Lonergan explicitly states that in Western culture there have been roughly two major historical perspectives, two alternative horizons, two different frameworks within which philosoph-

---

1. On the methodological assumptions of the Enlightenment, see Ernst Cassirer, *The Philosophy of the Enlightenment,* chap. 1. On progress, see Robert Nisbet, *History of the Idea of Progress,* esp. chaps. 5–6; and Franklin L. Baumer, *Modern European Thought: Continuity and Change in Ideas, 1600–1950,* 237–55. For a recent critical appraisal, see Stephen Toulmin, *Cosmopolis: The Hidden Agenda of Modernity.* See Robert Bellah et al., *Habits of the Heart: Individualism and Commitment in American Life,* 27, 33–35, 333–34, for a description of "expressive individualism."

2. See Joseph Wood Krutch's searching question: "Is it really true, as I once believed, that there is no escaping the scientific demonstration that religion, morality, and the human being's power to make free choices are all merely figments of the imagination?" (*The Modern Temper: A Study and a Confession,* xii). See also E. A. Burtt, *The Metaphysical Foundations of Modern Science,* esp. 238–39; and Floyd W. Matson, *The Broken Image: Man, Science, and Society.*

ical ideas can be addressed—classicist and historically minded. The classicist outlook conceives of culture normatively and universally; it focuses on the substance of things, on unchanging essences; it relies upon a perennial philosophy, art, and ethics. Historically minded culture, on the other hand, is dynamic; it replaces the idea of fixity with a program of change; it sees culture empirically as humanly constructed, ongoing, and diverse. It should not be surprising, then, that the notion of development would take on different meanings within these two frameworks. Lonergan also emphasizes, though, that the very sequence itself of these two perspectives exhibits development, with historical-mindedness being, for the most part, a creature of the past two centuries.[3] We must see, then, what are the ancient foundations upon which Lonergan can construct his theory of development and what changes he would bring to the old perspectives.

At best, of course, these historical categories are ideal-types, useful historical models, which, however, do not claim to offer a complete description of historical reality.[4] Thus, to apply the category of classicist culture to the Greeks is neither to suggest that all Greek thinkers eschewed an evolutionary theory nor to imply that the achievement of such creative geniuses as Plato and Aristotle could be contained within any simple category. Whereas, in fact, it can be argued that Plato and Aristotle had some sensitivity about human historicity and opened up lines of inquiry that could be more readily formulated within the framework of historical-mindedness, it seems that, on the balance sheet, their metaphysics, cosmology, as well as anthropology represent more of a kind of classicism.[5] And, if Lonergan is correct about the relation of the classicist horizon to that of historical-mindedness as one of development, then we can anticipate that the ideas of development found in Plato and Aristotle will indeed exhibit basic insights but insights inviting enrichment and expansion within a higher viewpoint.

Aristotle: Rudiments of Development

Let us first consider some of the key components in Aristotle's treatment of development, for, in Lonergan's view, he articulates rudimentary principles

---

3. *Second Collection,* 92–93. See also Thomas J. McPartland, "Meaning, Mystery, and the History of Consciousness," 226–47. *Third Collection,* 169, 171.

4. See *Method in Theology,* 227–28.

5. See Ludwig Edelstein, *The Idea of Progress in Classical Antiquity,* chap. 3, who argues that Plato and Aristotle advocated cultural progress and continuous, open-minded inquiry.

that will remain valid and ought to be presupposed in a viable contemporary theory of development.

It would seem that any notion of development must, in some sense, incorporate the ideas of (1) change, (2) order, and (3) goal. Clearly, without change development is impossible. If a fetus does not change, it will not develop into an adult human. Still, change with no order, change with no intelligible pattern, change that is merely and completely random, cannot support development. Hence, the biologist studies the stages of ordered change in the development of the fetus into an adult human. However, ordered change implies direction, that is, movement toward a goal. The fetus has an ordered sequence of change precisely because it moves in the direction of becoming an adult human, the goal or end of its development.

Aristotle introduces indispensable technical terms to demonstrate the intelligible relationship of these ideas. He defines change (*kinesis*), or motion, or movement, as "the fulfillment of what exists potentially, insofar as it exists potentially." Note the key here to the definition is *potency*. Movement is potency in fulfillment. A bunch of logs lying on the ground may have a potential to become a house, but movement occurs only when the process of *building* takes place, in which case potency-for-house is fully operative—until the house is built and movement ceases.[6] Potency implies direction: it is always potency for this or that. (Even the most undifferentiated matrix, prime potency, is potency for some kind of material being.) Potency, as potency for this or that, thus sets limits on movement and hence on development. At the same time, however, it is the very principle that allows for movement, and hence for development, since a thing that is already a something also has the potency to become that which it is not yet. By including the term *potency*, then, in his definition of movement Aristotle assumes that we live in a universe not under the complete sway of chance or randomness.

In order, however, to apply this definition of motion to development Aristotle must differentiate between the movement involved in the creation of artifacts (for example, the house), where development, in the strict sense, does not occur, and the movement of natural things, the proper locus of development. So Aristotle defines nature (*physis*) as an immanent source of movement and rest.[7] There is an internal principle at work in the ordered change of nat-

6. For definition of change, see Aristotle, *Physics* 3.1.201a10–11, trans. R. P. Hardie and R. K. Gaye, in *The Basic Works of Aristotle;* for potency, 3.1.201b9–12.
    7. Ibid., 2.1.192b22–23.

ural things. The movement ceases when the goal of development has been reached. Although wood lying in a vacant lot cannot be said to develop into a house, for the source of movement of the wood into the house is external, namely, the efforts of the builders, the acorn can be said to develop naturally by its own internal principle into an oak tree.

Aristotle here adds another crucial general term: *form.* For what is the goal of development? To realize that goal is indeed the end or purpose—the final cause—of development.[8] And the goal is precisely to realize the form of the thing developing, the intelligible structure that makes it a certain kind of thing. The acorn develops into the form of an oak tree. This means that, in fact, two forms are decisive for ordinary development, the form out of which something develops and the form into which something develops.[9] Aristotle assumes that the forms in question—which, for example, define biological species—are not mere conventions artificially imposed by the human mind on data but are real intrinsic properties of kinds of things. He asserts that real emergence is taking place in nature, but he views emergence as the transformation (literally) of a less developed form to a fully developed form of the same substance within the same species.

Aristotle has also introduced a term correlative to that of *potency: act.*[10] For when the movement ends and potency is no longer operative because of success, it is then that what had potential has become actual. The form, which is the end of development, has been realized.

Aristotle, then, in explaining the principles of change, order, and goal in the process of development insists, in effect, that any viable notion of development must employ some equivalence of his terms of *potency, form,* and *act.*

Plato and Aristotle: Human Development

What, for Aristotle, is the goal of human development? The goal must be to realize the form of human being, and that form is defined as "rational animal."[11] Thus, there is a crucial, qualitative difference between the acorn becoming an oak tree and the fetus becoming an adult human in the complete sense (a *spoudaios*). Both cases, it is true, involve spontaneous organic ten-

8. Ibid., 2.8.198b34–199a33.
9. Ibid., 2.1.193b18–20.
10. Aristotle, *Metaphysics* 5.16.1021b13–1022a3; 9.6.1048a25–b34.
11. Aristotle, *Nicomachean Ethics* 1.7.1097b23–1098a5.

dencies of growth, but in the human case there are additional factors, those Aristotle associates with the human soul and its specifically rational capacities.

If the goal is to integrate "rational" and "animal," then the means are through the power of reason to choose and through the habits that support the correct exercise of that power. We must underscore the correct exercise of that power of choice. Aristotle, therefore, establishes a normative principle of human development. His standard is the prudent person, who exemplifies the norm of excellence *(areté)*. Ethical *areté,* excellence regarding the direction of human affairs, according to Aristotle's famous definition, is "a state of character concerned with choice, lying in a mean, i.e., the mean relative to us, this being determined by a rational principle, and by that principle by which the man of practical wisdom would determine it."[12]

In speaking of the "mean relative to us" Aristotle is not advocating relativism. The "mean relative to us" is always determined by the practical wisdom—the cumulative experience, insight, and judgment—of the morally mature person, the *spoudaios.* The apparent vicious circle entailed by this definition, where the morally mature person is the measure of the choices leading to maturity, might be avoided and Aristotle's sense of normativeness illuminated if we accept the process of questioning as an internal, that is, natural, principle of movement and rest:[13] the person faithful to the project of moral inquiry will grow toward true human fulfillment. Norms are therefore ingredient in the process of inquiry itself.

This is also Plato's position, probably even more so than Aristotle's, for Plato's dramatic artistry, we must admit, always highlights the dynamism of the process of inquiry. Still, Aristotle explicitly relies on Plato's normative analysis of the human soul.[14] Plato perhaps provides the closest approximation in antiquity to a phenomenological analysis of horizons in his treatment of characters and states in books 8 and 9 of the *Republic.* The basic kind of love one serves—whether the love of wisdom, the love of honor, the love of money, the love of pleasures, or the love of power—determines one's basic perspective and orientation in life. One's interests, ideas, judgments, evaluations, and decisions are functions of the framework of one's horizon. And each horizon is qualitatively distinct. The love of wisdom, however, is a self-validating

---

12. Ibid., 2.6.1106b36–1107a3, trans. W. D. Ross, in *Basic Works.*
13. See Lonergan's suggestions along these lines in *Third Collection,* 172.
14. See, for example, Aristotle, *Politics* 7.1.1323a22–b39. On Plato's focus on inquiry, see David Burrell, *Analogy and Philosophical Language,* chap. 3.

norm, and the other horizons are, consequently, distortions of human development. Plato has not so much presented a theory of actual historical sequences of personalities or constitutions—though he has some penetrating
insights here—as uncovered the basic source of development in history, the
love of wisdom, and the sources of devolution, the myriad types of bias and
distortion identified with the various counterloves.[15] Although Plato's nuanced and sensitive dramatic exploration of the many horizons acknowledges
their radical diversity, their complicated historical interplay, and the individual and communal dialectic that constitutes them, he nonetheless insists that
norms and standards pervade the process of human development. Both Plato and Aristotle ultimately agree that any viable theory of human development
must reflect norms and that those norms must appeal to the standard of human nature.

Our discussion has implied that Plato's and Aristotle's articulation of
the principles of development is foundational for any further reflection on
the topic. If this is so, then what further theoretical developments are possible when these principles are integrated within a more avowedly historical-
minded perspective? We must now turn to Lonergan.

Lonergan's Notion of Development

The key to Lonergan's notion of development is his philosophy of consciousness, adumbrated in the previous chapter. Lonergan stresses, we should
recall, that the conscious process of inquiry is a structured process of the
cognitional operations of experiencing, understanding, and judging. Thus, for
example, the scientist attends to relevant data, gains insight into the data
(formulating them as hypotheses), and tests out the hypotheses. Building
upon his phenomenology of cognition and his cognitional theory, Lonergan
adopts a critical realist epistemology. Lonergan's theory of knowledge—
in contrast to the confrontation theory of truth, whose sense of reality entails
the confrontation of a subject "in here" with objects "already out there now
real"—has, as its sense of reality, the structured directional tendency of questioning itself. Replacing the spatial and ocular model is a focus on the self-

---

15. Thus, Aristotle's criticism of Plato for empirical incompleteness in his theory of
"revolutions" is not entirely on the mark. See *Politics* 5.12.1316a1–b26.

transcending process of questioning and its correspondingly transcendent objects. If the real is not some putative realm of objects outside the horizon of questioning, then the real is simply what is to be known by fidelity to the norms of the process of questioning. And if the process of questioning has a structure of experiencing, understanding, and judging, then, accordingly, the real will have a structure correlative to the contents of experiencing, understanding, and judging. This, in a nutshell, is Lonergan's principle of isomorphism, which asserts that the human structure of knowing finds a parallel in the structure of what is to be known.[16]

Perhaps one of the most conspicuous features of Lonergan's notion of development is his extensive use of Aristotle's vocabulary of *potency, form,* and *act.* Corresponding, respectively, to the cognitional distinctions of experience, understanding, and judging are Lonergan's metaphysical distinctions of potency, form, and act.[17] When the inquirer attends to experience, the inquirer is aware of the real as potency. When the inquirer grasps insights, the inquirer is aware of the real as intelligible form. When the inquirer renders a reasonable judgment, the inquirer is aware of the real as actual. But to speak of these metaphysical distinctions of potency, form, and act is not to speak of little realities floating around independent of each other. Just as knowledge is the structured resultant of experience, understanding, and judging, so the reality of the world is the dynamic relation of potency, form, and act. This dynamic unity is the basis for Lonergan's notion of development. We need to consider in more detail potency, form, and act and how they constitute a dynamic relation.

Potency is the nonintelligible substratum that provides data for intelligent inquiry. It is the empirical residue that "consists in individuality, the continuum, particular place and time, and the non-systematic divergence from theoretically grounded anticipations." It is whatever, at any level of organization, is a merely coincidental manifold of events. Potency, then, is simultaneously the universal principle of limitation, which conditions all intelligible structure and achievement, and the objective ground of the dynamism of reality, in

---

16. For Lonergan's cognitional theory, see *Insight,* pt. 1, "Insight as Activity"; *Method in Theology,* chap. 1; *Collection,* chap. 14. For the "already out there now real," see *Insight,* 275–79. For the connection of cognitional theory and metaphysics, see *Insight,* 4–5, 22–23, 412–13. For Lonergan's meaning of "the real," see *Insight,* 22–23, 372–75, 381–83, 413, 415–21, 522–26; and *Verbum,* 20. For Lonergan's focus on inquiry as self-transcendence open to transcendence, see *Collection,* 211–14. For the principle of isomorphism, see *Insight,* 424–25, 470–71, 510–11, 522–26.

17. *Insight,* 424–25, 458.

which what is incomplete heads toward some indeterminate growth. It is a tension of opposites: for it is the aspect of reality that both restricts and makes possible intelligible unities and patterns of occurrence. Form, on the other hand, is the intelligible structure to which potency is directed and which itself becomes the possibility for determinate realization in nature. Act is the realization of possible intelligible patterns in the concrete universe.[18]

Lonergan indeed appreciates the Aristotelian distinctions while, at the same time, offering significant clarification, particularly of the relation of form to act. The differentiation of experience and understanding grounds, for Lonergan, the prototype of emergence, namely, the insight that arises with respect to appropriate images, as well as the prototype of higher integrations, namely, the insight that gives rise to higher cognitive viewpoints.[19] The distinction of form and act, which exploits Aquinas's differentiation of essence and existence, means that contingency, and not just necessity, is an appropriate category of scientific investigation.[20] Nevertheless, even these clarifications could operate within a theory committed, as apparently was that of Aristotle, to a universe that was inert, static, finished, and complete.[21] Cognitive emergence and higher viewpoints could simply point to greater human understanding of what is still a fixed universe. Development could simply be the growth of the immature to maturity within that universe of fixed species.

Lonergan, however, takes a more radical departure from Aristotle. The universe, in Lonergan's view, is a directed dynamism in which the effectively probable realization of its own possibilities means the *emergence* of new forms and new realities. Technically, this involves a transformation of universal explanatory patterns immanent in the data, or "classical laws." Such patterns are what Aristotle meant by forms. For Lonergan, classical laws regard, to employ his equivalent term, "conjugate forms," which are "defined implicitly by their empirically verified and explanatory relations."[22] In Lonergan's universe, one set of conjugate forms can give place to another. The result: the emergence of new forms. Whereas Aristotle recognized a fixed order of nature grounded ultimately on the eternal cyclic recurrence of celestial motion, Lonergan argues for a universe of emergent probability.[23]

---

18. On potency, see ibid., 463, 467–71, 475–76; on form, 457–58, 462; on act, 457–58.
19. Ibid., 506.
20. See ibid., 391–96; and *Verbum*, chaps. 1–2.
21. *Insight*, 151–52.
22. Ibid., 112–13, 460–61.
23. Ibid., 152.

Here we see perhaps one of the salient repercussions of Lonergan's precise distinction of form and act. Lonergan can formulate a theory of probability concerned with coincidental aggregates of events (acts).[24] However, unlike Aristotle, who regarded the category of the merely coincidental, such as contingent terrestrial events, as completely outside the ken of science, Lonergan can find an intelligibility by abstracting from nonsystematic processes, namely, the ideal frequency from which actual, relative frequencies do not diverge systematically.[25] Were actual relative frequencies to diverge systematically from an *ideal* frequency, the process would, of course, be subsumed under what Lonergan, as we have seen, calls classical laws and what Aristotle identifies as forms. These intelligible principles of natural processes are most often "schemes of recurrence," where, in a given series of events, "the fulfilment of the conditions of each would be the occurrence of the others." As examples of schemes of recurrence, Lonergan cites the planetary system, the nitrogen cycle, and the routines of animal life.[26] Now if we add to statistical laws the notion of a *conditioned series* of schemes of recurrence, we have the scientific apparatus to investigate a universe the immanent intelligibility of which is one of emergent probability. When the emergence of an actual order at one level (for example, the organic) is the precondition, that is, potency, for the emergence of a higher level order (for example, the psychic) and when the latter is the precondition for a still higher order (for example, the intellectual), we have a conditioned series of schemes of recurrence. And, given sufficient numbers and time, the higher orders will be likely to emerge. Emergent probability is thus "the successive realization, in accord with successive schedules of probabilities, of a conditioned series of ever more complex schemes of recurrence."[27]

The actualization of one set of potential natural forms can become the potency for the emergence of new, higher natural forms. What on one level is merely a random manifold of events can on another, higher level be an actually functioning formal pattern of events. In other words, an emergent higher integration systematizes what was merely coincidental on a lower order. Moreover, such a dynamic integration systematizes by adding and modifying until the old integration is eliminated and, by the principle of emergence, a

24. Ibid., 79.
25. Ibid., 78–89, 121–23, 152.
26. Ibid., 141.
27. Ibid., 138–50, 152, 473.

new integration is introduced. Hence, according to Lonergan, "chemical elements and compounds are higher integrations of otherwise coincidental manifolds of subatomic events; organisms are higher integrations of otherwise coincidental manifolds of chemical processes; sensitive consciousness is a higher integration of otherwise coincidental manifolds of changes in neural tissue; and accumulating insights are higher integrations of otherwise coincidental manifolds of images or of data."[28]

Lonergan claims that this worldview of emergent probability is "uniquely probable" as a metaphysical theorem. The theorem rests on two components, one a priori and the other a posteriori. Its uniqueness resides in the tight complementarity of these two elements. The a priori, or properly metaphysical, component is informed by the principle of isomorphism, rooted in Lonergan's critical realism, which proclaims, as we have seen, that there is an isomorphism between knowing and the known. We should recall the parallel between the cognitional structure of experience, understanding, and judging, on the one hand, and the metaphysical structure of potency, form, and act, on the other hand, as an instance of isomorphism, which partially grounds Lonergan's notion of development. We can also ask whether there is a parallel between the dynamism of knowing and a dynamism of the known. This parallel would seem to serve as the precise formulation of the major premise of the metaphysical component of the argument for emergent probability; it acts, in effect, as a corollary to the principle of isomorphism. The dynamism of the process of knowing then becomes a minor metaphysical premise. But can we affirm the major premise? For knowing could be dynamic and ongoing, whereas the known could be finished and static.[29]

No doubt Lonergan is more open to the metaphysical premises of the theorem of emergent probability than would be Plato or Aristotle because, unlike them, he does not view science as true, certain knowledge of causal necessity. Science, for Lonergan, arrives not at truth, in the sense of completely immanently generated knowledge, but at the best opinion of the scientific community.[30] No scientist, for example, can conduct all the experiments presupposed by his or her own investigations. Rational belief in the integrity of

28. Ibid., 464, 477–78, 487.
29. Ibid., 424–25, 475.
30. For the view of Plato and Aristotle, see, for example, ibid., 151–52; *Collection*, 238–40; *Third Collection*, 137–40, 147–48; and *Method in Theology*, 315–16. For Lonergan's contrasting view, see *Collection*, 238–39; *Insight*, 725–40; and *Method in Theology*, 41–47.

colleagues stands out even more than a healthy skepticism. Modern science likewise posits not certain judgments but probable judgments. Empirical verification, one of the keys to modern scientific method, can provide only inductive probability. To claim deductive certitude because an observable consequence of a theory, in fact, occurred as predicted would be to commit the formal fallacy of affirming the consequent.[31] Lonergan would agree with Karl Popper that, strictly speaking, a scientific theory can be only falsified and not verified in any final way.[32] Moreover, the application of any given scientific law raises further questions that head toward the systematization of the whole field; insofar as further questions are not posed or further facts raise new questions, though, the systematization is incomplete and the law open to revision. Neither are scientific judgments of fact definitive. Since measurements of facts must employ the best available instruments and observables be defined in terms of some theoretical framework, as instruments develop and theories advance so facts may be rendered obsolete. Finally, rather than seek causal connections that exist by necessity, modern science searches for verified correlations in the data that exist as a matter of fact; in addition to classical laws it also discerns statistical frequencies. Lonergan thus sees the dynamic nature of the process of scientific knowing as suggesting, though not proving, that the universe itself is a process.[33]

To articulate, as Lonergan does, the limits of science is not, in his view, to deny the objectivity of science, which he defines as fidelity to the project of questioning, where "no further relevant questions" is the norm. Nor, consequently, is it to reject the truth of science in favor of conventionalism or relativism. If, he argues, "empirical science is no more than probable, still it truly is probable. If it does not attain definitive truth, still it converges upon truth." It is the approximate truths of contemporary science that provide the a posteriori component of the theorem of emergent probability. For the empirical sciences act as "subsidiary minor premises" to support the model of

---

31. *Third Collection,* 138. The logical form of the fallacious argument would be as follows:

If scientific theory X, then observable consequences Y.
Observable consequences Y.
∴ Scientific theory X.

32. See Karl R. Popper, *The Logic of Scientific Discovery,* 40–42, 75–77, and passim. In *Third Collection,* Lonergan refers to Popper's *Conjectures and Refutations: The Growth of Scientific Knowledge,* but not in this connection (100–102, 108–9).

33. *Insight,* 327–28.

emergent world process by "vast ranges of facts." This is not, of course, to entail deductive certainty; it is to add inductive strength, making the argument more probable. Here Lonergan apparently adopts the same position he holds with respect to the field of hermeneutics. Interpretation, he urges, is like a scissors with two blades: the upper blade of philosophically generated categories and the lower blade of empirical studies. Both must interact in a mutually cooperative enterprise. When empirical facts thus combine with the metaphysical premises, the argument for emergent probability then becomes "uniquely probable."[34]

There is also another implicit argument that Lonergan seems to present. For as the three levels of the structure of scientific cognition, according to Lonergan's critical realist epistemology, are correlative to metaphysical elements—the cognitional operations of experiencing, understanding, and judging being isomorphic with the metaphysical elements of potency, form, and act—so modern scientific practice has differentiated three distinct methods of scientific inquiry, each exploiting one of the metaphysical elements. Genetic method is grounded in potency, classical method seeks form, and statistical method is concerned with acts or events. The fact that three distinct methods have been differentiated by modern science, each isomorphic with the metaphysical elements and their corresponding cognitional operations, would seem to be no accident. And, to further Lonergan's claims about the theory of emergence, it is precisely the combination of these methods that constitutes the foundations for the worldview of emergent probability.

To consider these methods in light of this assertion we can recall first what Lonergan says about classical laws. Whereas picture thinking would see classical laws as portraying imaginary bodies moving in an imaginary space and

---

34. On the criterion of scientific judgment, see ibid., 305–6, 308–12; on scientific judgments as probably true, 328; on empirical sciences as "subsidiary minor premises," 475. For the application of the scissors analogy to hermeneutics, 600–601, 603, 608–9; for its application to metaphysics and science, 337, 486, 546. The structure of Lonergan's argument about emergent probability seems to be as follows:

If knowing is a process, then the known is a process.
Knowing is a process.
∴ The known is a process.

It becomes obvious that the "subsidiary minor premises" of scientific facts, in affirming that the universe is in process, simply lend inductive support to the conclusion. Since the major premise is asserted only tentatively, as, we might say, a weak corollary of Lonergan's general isomorphism principle, the entire argument can have the status of being, at best, "uniquely probable."

in an imaginary time as they interact with each other according to the imaginary procedures of efficient causality, Lonergan, to the contrary, argues that classical laws aim at the intelligible relations among things in terms of such enriched abstractions as mathematical equations whose sensible consequences can be verified. In short, as we have seen, classical laws regard form.

When classical laws, however, attempt to explain a particular event, they run into the problem of nonsystematic process. To explain a certain event Z, a certain antecedent circumstance Y must be present, but for the antecedent circumstance Y to be present a certain set of positive conditions (P, Q, R . . .) must obtain and a certain set of negative conditions (U, V, W . . .) must be absent. Further analysis of each of these conditions in the two sets reveals that each of them has a set of positive conditions that must be met and a set of negative conditions that must be in abeyance, and so forth. We are faced here, Lonergan contends, with a concrete series of diverging conditions. But we are not confronted with chaos. For insight is possible into ideal frequencies of the occurrence of events from which actual events do not diverge systematically. Thus, we can, in principle, make judgments about probability states, and indeed a principle of uncertainty is axiomatic for natural processes investigated by statistical method, whether evidenced in the unmeasured uncertainty of Boltzmann's classical statistics or the measured uncertainty of Heisenberg's equation.[35] Unless one is committed, however, to the determinist universe of picture thinking, statistical method is not simply a cloak for ignorance. God does roll dice! Whether one claims that God knows the results of the roll depends upon whether one holds, as does Lonergan in the Augustinian and Boethian tradition, that, for God, there are no future contingents or whether one holds that, for God, there is an open future.[36]

Genetic, or developmental, method concerns the possibility of emergence of new schemes of classical laws and statistical laws. The emergence of new intelligible relations, we should recall, is grounded in the metaphysical element of potency, which is simultaneously the basis of limitation (by providing the antecedent conditions) and of transcendence (by offering a range of possibilities). What is nonsystematic at one level, say the subatomic level, can become systematic at another, higher level of integration, say that of chemical compounds. The ideas of development and genuine novelty contradict a

35. *Insight,* 70–89, 117–24.
36. Ibid., 685–86; Bernard J. F. Lonergan, *Grace and Freedom: Operative Grace in the Thought of St. Thomas Aquinas,* chap. 5.

consistent reductionism, based on picture thinking, that would find the dynamism of potency not captured by the imagination. Indeed, to grasp the principle of potency requires, according to Lonergan, neither representative imagination nor direct intelligence but, rather, what Lonergan calls an inverse insight.[37] Thus, it is the dynamism of potency combined with forms of classical laws and the events of statistical laws that gives rise to the immanent intelligibility of world process that Lonergan names emergent probability.

We are now in a position to summarize Lonergan's notion of development. Stated succinctly, it is a "linked sequence of dynamic higher integrations." More precisely, he defines development as a "flexible, linked sequence of dynamic and increasingly differentiated higher integrations that meet the tensions of successively transformed underlying manifolds through successive applications of the principles of correspondence and emergence."[38] Lonergan's notion of development, then, simultaneously rejects both static essentialism (focusing on fixed forms, perhaps within the permanent hierarchy of the great chain of being) and reductionism (focusing exclusively on the material substratum).

Lonergan does indeed recognize, as does Aristotle, forms in nature, and he would grant, as does Aquinas, that form is a kind of potency, or second potency, for act. What exists in nature is conditioned by intelligible patterns in nature. But act is also potency for new forms. And development, in fact, witnesses the emergence of true new forms in nature. Furthermore, higher integrations meet precisely the tensions of transformed lower manifolds. Higher integrations are solutions to problems. Higher integrations neither have a temporal priority over less complex forms in nature nor exist by some metaphysical necessity.

By the same token, Lonergan is opposed to reductionism: no explanation of a lower manifold is adequate to explain the intelligible structure of a higher integration that is itself a solution of tensions in the underlying manifold and is, consequently, more differentiated. What is merely potential in the lower manifold is an actualized form in the higher integration. Thus, life cannot be completely explained in terms of chemistry, nor intelligence in terms of biology. New forms, however, are not arbitrary eruptions in an essentially chaotic nature. According to the principle of correspondence, they must conform to the potentialities inherent in the underlying manifold. Lower manifolds

37. *Insight,* 43–50.
38. Ibid., 478–79.

condition but do not determine the exact properties of new forms. Chaos theory is correct in discerning enormous diversity and complexity in nature and in refuting reductionism. However, from the framework of Lonergan's notion of development, its label of "chaos" stems from its conception of mechanistic determinism as the only viable alternative. Lonergan instead would emphasize the importance of probability schedules as the way out of the disjunction of either mechanistic determinism or chaos. For development is of linked sequences of higher integrations, where the linkage of potency, form, and act is a function as probability schedules. Given sufficient time, increasingly differentiated forms in nature are likely. This is not because of some mechanistic necessity, nor because of some external push or pull from beyond nature. Development, for Lonergan, is simply the immanent intelligibility of natural process.[39]

Lonergan's Notion of Human Development

What does this suggest about human development? Are there implications here that would carry us beyond a classicist framework for interpreting human nature? What would higher integrations be on the level of human development? New species? Supermen? Indeed, how much light does emergent probability shed on specifically human development if such development is one of emergence, as Lonergan defines it? Is there an ideal frequency that can be abstracted from the nonsystematic process of human history? Although Lonergan's notion of development in general takes him beyond the perspectives of Plato and Aristotle, will his notion, as applied to human development, take him beyond the normative views of these thinkers? What can it add qualitatively to enrich and go beyond their normative explication of the human situation?

Whereas Plato objectifies cognition as process in his artistic dialogues, Lonergan objectifies cognition as structure. Whereas Aristotle duly emphasizes the cognitive roles of experience and insight, he tends to relegate judgment to a mere synthesis of concepts, thereby neglecting its full import in the process of knowing. By contrast, Lonergan claims that he can establish the full range of cognitive activities and their nexus in adult consciousness, the developmental stages needed to achieve fully differentiated mature consciousness,

---

39. On principle of correspondence, see ibid., 477; on development, 476.

and the kinds of bias that both block the growth of cognitional structure itself and prevent adequate performance of cognitional operations. Lonergan can exploit Aristotle's definition of nature and argue that the immanent principle of movement and rest on the level of human consciousness is the raising and answering of questions.[40] For it is the process of questioning that is the origin of genuine human cognitive and moral activity, and it is the process of questioning that contains the standards by which human striving can genuinely come to rest. Lonergan can also locate precisely the kinds of questions appropriate to the different levels of consciousness (namely: What is it? Is it so? What ought I to do?).

Is this, however, basically an enrichment within the Platonic and Aristotelian frameworks? Is it essentially the same theoretical higher integration simply systematizing different, or more differentiated, manifolds? Lonergan, I suggest, has transgressed crucial limits of the earlier horizons, and he does so by introducing three major transformations into the theory of human development.

In the first place, Lonergan does not explain human development in terms of the growth of that substance, or thing, defined as "rational animal." Rather, he explains human development in terms of the internal growth of the "subject," a self with distinct levels of conscious operations. Hence, such interpreters of Lonergan as Walter Conn and Daniel Helminiak can graft onto Lonergan's general structure various contemporary theories of cognitive, affective, and moral development. Lonergan insists on the inadequacy of investigating human reality exclusively in metaphysical terms (for example, the Aristotelian seriation of objects, acts, habits, potencies, and essences).[41] By the same logic, the general categories of development framed by Lonergan as part of his metaphysical method would be in themselves insufficient to explain specifically human development. They must be supplemented by terms and rela-

---

40. Lonergan contrasted his objectification of cognition with that of Plato in a private conversation with me at Boston College, June 1978. On Aristotle, see *Verbum*, 62; and *Insight*, 390–91. Although Aquinas, according to Lonergan, grasped the components of cognition in their full integrity, he did not thematize his introspection but cast his cognitional theory explicitly in metaphysical terms. *Verbum*, 5–6; *Insight*, 431–32. On questioning as "nature," see *Third Collection*, 172.

41. On the expansive nature of the subject, see *Second Collection*, 73; Walter Conn, *Conscience: Development and Self-Transcendence*, dealing with the developmental theories of Piaget, Erikson, and Kohlberg; David A. Helminiak, *Spiritual Development: An Interdisciplinary Study*, pt. 1. On Aristotelian metaphysical analysis, see *Verbum*, 4–6; and *Second Collection*, 73.

tions appropriate to the level of human development, and those terms and relations are precisely those concerned with the subject.

By his cognitional analysis of the subject Lonergan can fully explore the dynamism of questioning, where understanding becomes the potency for affirming truth, the attainment of knowledge at any given point becomes the
potency for further knowledge, insight gives rise to higher viewpoints, intellectual breakthroughs transpose the entire set of original assumptions, and inquiring becomes a self-correcting process of learning.[42] The mind, for Lonergan, is no more fixed than its content:

> The mind is not just a factory with a set of fixed processes. Rather it is a uni-
> versal machine tool that erects all kinds of factories, keeps adjusting and im-
> proving them, and eventually scraps them in favor of radically new designs.
> In other words, there is not some fixed set of a priori syntheses. Every in-
> sight is a priori; insight follows on insight to complement and correct its pre-
> decessor; earlier accumulations form viewpoints to give place to higher view-
> points.[43]

Lonergan emphasizes, then, the emergence of new ideas, values, viewpoints,
horizons. He also stresses that the dynamic process of questioning occurs in
such diverse patterns of experience as the intellectual, the practical, and the
artistic currents of consciousness, each opening up to a distinct world of
meaning. No field of inquiry, therefore, is the total paradigm for the emergence of meaning in the process of human development. We can, says Lonergan, set aside the classical definition of the human being as a rational
animal and instead employ the definition of symbolic animal.[44] Still, the symbolic animal, no less than the rational animal is, most fundamentally, the questioning animal.

We must note here that a change in objects is a change in the subject; a change
in ideas, viewpoints, perspectives is a change in the human self. This highlights a second cardinal transformation Lonergan brings to the notion of human development. Lonergan introduces not only the human subject but also
the human *existential subject*. For there is a higher integration of cognitional
activities by the operations of deliberating, evaluating, and deciding.[45] In

42. *Insight*, 37–43, 197–98.
43. Ibid., 430–31.
44. On patterns of experience, see ibid., 196–205, 207–10. On "symbolic animal," see
Collection, 241–42.
45. *Second Collection*, 79–84; *Method in Theology*, 34–41.

those operations the issue is not "What am I?" but "Who ought I to be?" In those operations I am not only deciding to do X, Y, and Z but also, more basically, deciding who I am by doing, or not doing, X, Y, and Z. At stake in this self-constitution is not simply my universal human characteristics—not even my nature as a questioning animal—but my being, my historicity, that is, the set of meanings, values, and choices from my past that inform my perspective in the present as I face the possibility of my future. In short, relevant to human development is individual development, the unique development of *unique selves.* The general categories of development must again be supplemented—in this case to account for the historicity of the self.

Perhaps the first major philosopher to address this issue was Leibniz. Leibniz viewed individual development in terms of his theory of monads: each monad, absolutely unique and causally unconnected ("windowless") to the world, had a "complete individual notion," the sum total of the details of its "career" known by only God but obscurely anticipated through its perception. Its internal programming was such that it was in constant activity, striving for self-realization of its individual notion. This process of maturation and individuation was a continuous one in which past states of mind foreshadowed future states, bringing to realization contents that had existed in only obscure and latent form.[46] We need not accept the framework of Leibniz's peculiar, if ingenious, combination of metaphysical atomism and epistemological conceptualism in order to profit by his focus on individual growth and historicity.

For Lonergan, the historicity of the self is not grounded in a philosophical speculation on divine foreknowledge and the moral necessity of a best of all possible worlds.[47] It is grounded in the directional tendency of our questioning who we are to be. The self to be chosen always challenges and calls the presently choosing self. Our being is constituted by inquiry about being. So Lonergan remarks that "being oneself is being, and by being is . . . meant . . . the concrete goal intended in all inquiry and reflection."[48] The object of inquiry includes the true self, the self who authentically follows the norms of cognitive, moral, and spiritual inquiry in the concrete circumstances, situa-

---

46. Baron Gottfried Wilhelm von Leibniz, *Discourse on Metaphysics,* in *Basic Writings,* 8, 9, 13; Leibniz, *Monadology,* in ibid., 7, 10, 11, 12, 14, 15, 22; Nicholas Rescher, *The Philosophy of Leibniz,* chap. 5.

47. For a critique of what Lonergan calls the method of "concrete deductivism," see *Insight,* 429–31.

48. *Collection,* 229.

tions, and possibilities of concrete life. The inauthentic self, of course, may be a fact, but, as such, it does not, however, participate in being; it is a privation of authentic possibility. We might say that the inauthentic self is the chasm between openness as a demand and openness as an achievement. This chasm is usually connected to another gap, that between authentic possibility and distorted interpretation of possibility. The struggle for the emergence of authentic existence, which always stands outside present attainment, is a struggle within the dialectic of performance and interpretation, where interpretation mediates performance in concrete living and performance becomes data for further interpretation. The tension of this dialectic is heightened because some interpretations decisive for individual development are nonthematic, spontaneous affect-laden images.[49]

We turn here to a third change Lonergan introduces to the notion of human development. The subject—including the existential subject—is, Lonergan argues, not simply an integration of organism and consciousness but, rather, a "triply compounded movement of successive higher systems." Aristotle, by contrast, did not grasp the fact that human development required the integration of organic, psychic, and intellectual components.[50] The psyche with its imaginative power and affective energy cannot ignore or run ahead of organic demands; neither can conscious operations function at odds with the psychic base. The integration of the psyche, then, as mediating between organism and conscious operations is complicated, difficult, and crucial. The mind cannot simply control the psyche but must, so to speak, negotiate with it. The psyche is not an isolated faculty, or thing; it is a potency for intellectual development. As potency, it is a source of limitation—and hence the lurking danger of neurotic compulsions or, in the extreme, of psychotic turbulence in a badly integrated psyche. However, it is also a source of transcendence, as when the conscripted psychic energies of eros and wonder inspire, support, and sustain the process of inquiry. Here Lonergan, who was influenced by Bergson's *Creative Evolution,* would see the directional tendency of human consciousness as the *élan vital* emerging from more primordial tendencies of development in nature.[51]

49. On the gap in openness, see ibid., 186–87. On performance and interpretation, see ibid., 192–93, 199–200, 203–4. For intersubjective, symbolic, and incarnate meanings, see *Method in Theology,* 59–61, 64–69, 73.

50. *Insight,* 494–504, 507.

51. On psychic disturbance, see ibid., 214–31; on psychic source of transcendence, 482, 555–56; on the *élan vital,* see "Reality, Myth, Symbol," 33–34, 37.

Indeed, the tension of limitation and transcendence is a hallmark of all human development.[52] Development, in general, we should recall, is a solution to problems. Human development is always from the context of particular circumstances, whether organic, psychic, or intellectual, at particular times and places, and, simultaneously, oriented to what is beyond those circumstances. Both the pole of limitation and the pole of transcendence must be respected. But this means that human development is always a matter of the existential subject negotiating between these poles. The goal is self-transcendence; the means is authenticity. Hence, authenticity is both the criterion of human development and irreducibly unique. As criterion, it refutes the relativist tendencies of romanticism; as irreducibly unique, it supports the valid insights of romanticism into the self. There are, to be sure, universal standards of human nature, but in constituting the "second nature," the personal edition we call the self, the application of those standards of human nature is always to the concrete situations in a concrete process of negotiating the tension of limitation and transcendence. It is not a mistake to appeal to universal standards, or to learn from the example of others, or to profit from one's past. It is a mistake, however, ultimately to compare oneself with anything or anyone other than one's own authentic self. The true norms of human development are not so much directly tied to discernible achievement or attainment, but, rather, defined in terms of maximum operative capacity, that is, the fulfillment of potency as potency in the constant movement of self-transcendence.

Lonergan's Notion of Historical Development

To speak of individual development, of course, is not necessarily to imply that individual development is a monadic process. For Lonergan, there is a dialectical relation between the horizon of the subject and the horizon of society. Individual development is conditioned by historical development, as historical development is conditioned by individual development. On the one hand, technological inventions, economic differentiations, political decisions, and cultural innovations present the situations wherein individual development occurs through socialization, education, and acculturation. On the other hand, the cumulative product of the insights of the concrete, individual person is the source of technological, economic, political, and cultural break-

---

52. *Insight*, 497–504, 650.

throughs. Development of an individual, for example, in a tribal society will differ from development of an individual in an urban society precisely because the former lives in a tribal society and the latter lives in an urban society. The development from tribal society to urban society, however, may also be, in part, the fruit of a creative minority of outstanding individuals. To be sure, the principles of the dialectic are not new, for we can extrapolate them as far back as Plato's *Republic,* books 8 and 9. The constitution of characters and the constitution of states mutually influence each other. The gradual transformation of lovers of honor, for instance, into lovers of wealth effects the transformation of timocracy into oligarchy. At the same time, the education of young people in the oligarchy will be an education into the values of the love of wealth.[53] What, then, does Lonergan add to such reflections?

Above all else, Lonergan insists that historical-mindedness is the awareness that human beings bear *collective responsibility* for the creation of the human world. In the field of human history, human beings take on responsibility for the direction of emergent probability. Increasingly, the effective realization of what is potential results not merely from physical, chemical, biological, psychic, geographical, or demographic processes but also from human insights, judgments, and decisions. The growth of technologies evokes economic developments; economic developments spur political institutions to communicate and bring about decisions regarding the more complicated technological higher viewpoints and economic organizations; the growth of tools and material facilities, of the procedures for producing goods and services, and of political specializations offers the challenges to which culture can respond by analysis and critique. The agricultural revolution, then, was the potency for high civilizations; the high civilizations were the potency for theoretical culture, which reflects on spontaneous culture; and theoretical culture was the potency for historically minded culture, which, in its turn to interiority, reflects on theoretical culture. These cultural transformations were accompanied by differentiations of consciousness.[54]

As in the case of individual development, so in historical development what is most significant is not the outer, objective developments—the advance of

53. For the dialectic of subject and society, see ibid., 237; Chapter 7 below. For acculturation, socialization, education, see *Method in Theology,* 79; and *Third Collection,* 180–81. For Lonergan's appropriation of Toynbee's term *creative minority,* see *Third Collection,* 10, 103, 214. Plato, *Republic* 550c–551b, 553a–e.

54. *Insight,* 232–36, 252, 261–63; *Method in Theology,* 305–18; McPartland, "Meaning, Mystery, and History."

technology, the specialization of economic life, the evolution of the polity, the differentiation of culture—but the emergence of new, shared experience, understanding, judgments, and decisions. For common experience, understanding, judgments, and decisions are constitutive of community itself.[55] Thus, human beings can transform their collective horizons. Here we witness the historicity of communities.

Does this suggest that although Lonergan would not simply equate the advance of technology and science with progress, he would nevertheless embrace the progressivist vision of history as the inevitable march of cultural enlightenment? Or would he accept the Marxist interpretation of history as the final reconciliation of social structure and authentic human consciousness?

Lonergan would challenge any one-sided emphasis on progress. In the self-constitution of human reality there are false starts, breakdowns, aberrations, and corruptions as well as stability, emergence, sanity, and honesty. Emergent probability "makes no pretense to provide an aseptic universe of chrome and plastic. Its trials will far outnumber its successes, but the trials are no less a part of the programme than the successes." More and more, the success of developing the technology, economy, polity, and culture, for which human beings bear collective responsibility, depends upon human beings adhering to the norms of the process of inquiry in the recurrent pattern of challenge and response. The coalescing of insights is the key to the cumulative process of progress, whereas the proliferation of oversights in the flight from understanding is the source of the cumulative process of decline.[56]

Indeed, as Lonergan says, we can chart a pure line of progress, an ideal frequency, prescinding from all the pitfalls and all the freaks of historical development. But we must not misinterpret the results. To formulate such a pure line of progress we must consider not only technological inventions, economic expansion, political improvement, and cultural discoveries but also the complex relations among these complicated factors. We must restrict our detailed formulation to developments within the limits of a given set of initial conditions. We must recognize that, at best, our formulation is an account of generic tendencies that necessarily ignores the concrete facts of historicity. We must admit that such a formulation can never fully anticipate all the challenges that arise from greater complexity itself. The positing of a pure line of

---

55. *Method in Theology,* 79; *Third Collection,* 170.

56. *Insight,* 8, 475. On Toynbee's ideal-type of challenge and response, see ibid., 234; and *Third Collection,* 103, 104, 214.

progress thus is more retrospective than prospective. Most important, we must not forget that it is only an ideal. The reality of development includes trials, dead ends, and oversights. Emergent probability, warns Lonergan, "does not undertake to run the world along the lines of a kindergarten."[57]

Nevertheless, Lonergan does urge higher intellectual culture to grasp the historical origins of any given contemporary situation and to criticize it in light of the dialectic of progress and decline. Moreover, he proposes the functional cooperation of science, scholarship, and philosophy to effect precisely such a critical culture as a catalyst to historical development.[58] Will this eliminate decline? To ask a related question, where will the ideal line of progress head? Toward a substantive transformation of human nature, such as Marxists and other revolutionaries have envisioned?

There have been those who have taken historical development very seriously. Anticipating the emergence of a radically new historical epoch in which decline would become obsolete, they have presented a vivid portrait of the goal of historical development. Jewish rebels against Rome believed that the New Jerusalem described by the prophets was about to dawn. Yellow Turbans awaited the restoration of the golden age of the *Tai Ping* with the overthrow of the Han dynasty. Almost a thousand years later the Red Turbans awaited the reincarnation of a Buddhist bodhisattva who would usher in the perfect society after liberating China from the Mongol yoke. In medieval and early modern Europe, chiliastic flagellants, Apostolic Brethren, Taborites, Adamites, left-wing Anabaptists, and Fifth Monarchists all proclaimed the coming of the millennium. Progressivists in the modern period opted for a gradualistic vision of human perfection, while Jacobins, Marxists, and National Socialists actively sought to lay the ax to evil through radical revolution.

These groups raised the decisive question for any advocate of historical development: will historical development lead to the emergence of a new human nature? If not, what can historical development really mean? In response, we might turn the question around: if historical development leads inexorably to the emergence of a new human nature, how can we take *historicity* seriously? For, as in the case of the historicity of the individual, so the historicity of the collectivity—whether the destiny of local communities, of civilizations, or of the human race—is rooted in the tension of limitation and transcendence. The source of human "going beyond" is the process of questioning,

57. *Insight,* 474, 588–89.
58. Ibid., 264–66. See Lonergan's notion of functional specialties in *Method in Theology.*

which is always that of a concrete, incarnate consciousness, a compound of intellectual, psychic, and organic components. The immanent source of transcendence is also the limit of possibility, and this limit is, to use Aristotle's language, the specifically human principle of movement and rest, namely, human nature. Lonergan would caution us against the foolish hope that any historical transformation will put a new human nature in the saddle.[59] What historical developments bring are vast changes and higher integrations of that "second nature," both intelligible and intelligent, which the process of human inquiry, insight, reflection, and decision (in other words, human nature) creates. More complexity in the humanly constituted world, which means the transcendence of present limitations, becomes the potency for more development and the setting of new limitations in a spiral of differentiations and integrations. No development, though, not even that of a critical culture, can guarantee immunity from that primal limitation called the *mysterium iniqui- tatis*. Lured by the attractive power of bias, human beings are free to forsake the project of questioning. Critical culture itself may become inauthentic. Even an authentic critical culture may find its voice drowned out by the clamor of biases and, accordingly, made ineffective on the stage of history.

We must recall that the goal of individual development was not some achieved state but, rather, the fulfillment of operative capacity. So, too, for historical development. If we are to judge historical periods and historical groups, then we must judge them in terms of fidelity or infidelity to the norms of inquiry under the concrete, particular, and unique circumstances and challenges to which persons in that period or in that group had to respond. No formulation of a pure line of progress can capture the irreducible and unique quality of collective historical being. Thus, Ranke was, in a sense, correct to insist that every historical age is equal under God.

There is a further, and final, complication to the tension of limitation and transcendence. If authentic historical existence means radical, unrestricted openness to what is beyond, then history is at the intersection of time and eternity. And if history is at the intersection of time and eternity, then both poles of the tension are constitutive of historicity and must be respected: the temporal pole is the source of historical diversity and uniqueness and limitation; the transcendent pole is the source of change and unity. The plot of history is comprehended by the mystery of the known unknown. There may indeed be a genuine history of religion, a story of development and emergence,

---

59. *Insight,* 264–65.

but that drama, too, is at the intersection of time and the timeless, reflective of the tension of limitation and transcendence. Modern Enlightenment thinkers would bar mystery from the cultural vocabulary; Marxists would replace questions about ultimate being with questions about worldly matters. However, the very openness of questioning itself embraces concern for transcendent being—for a reality correlative to the unrestrictive thrust of inquiry—and, in Lonergan's view, makes real deflection of that concern an act of obscurantism supporting a process of devolution.[60]

If Lonergan's worldview of emergent probability rejects intellectual obscurantism, it equally opposes, as we have seen, reductionist materialism. The possibility for humans of higher integrations is the possibility of self-transcendence, and the possibility of self-transcendence is the possibility of a higher integration of human nature with transcendent spiritual reality. Such an experience of participation—attested by all the major religious traditions—far from violating the principles of human nature and the intelligibility of emergent world process would serve as a call to genuine inquiry and to maximizing the operative capacity of human nature. This open horizon of the religious infrastructure might be contrasted with any authoritarian and dogmatic tendencies of the institutional superstructure. Lonergan would argue, then—against both rightist and leftist currents of modern culture—that a vigorous reaffirmation of the possibility of progress ought to properly be tied to a sense of the sacred.[61]

But where does this leave historical development? Is human reality emerging into some higher state of being, perhaps into deity itself? Lonergan's own affirmation of transcendent being would preclude, for him, the latter possibility. He would also seem to warn against predictions about emergent world

---

60. Ibid., 657–62. For debate on the relation of Lonergan's notion of transcendence and that of process philosophy, see Michael Vertin, "Is God Process?" in *Religion and Culture: Essays in Honor of Bernard Lonergan,* ed. Timothy P. Fallon and Philip Boo Riley, chap. 4; and Thomas Hosinski, "Lonergan and a Process Understanding of God," in ibid., chap. 5.

61. This is also the conclusion of Nisbet in his sweeping analysis, *History of Progress,* epilogue. On the experience of participation, Lonergan cites Friedrich Heiler, "The History of Religion as a Preparation for the Cooperation of Religions," in *Second Collection,* 146, 149. Lonergan's worldview of emergent probability allows for the possibility of this spiritual integration. His theodicy argues that the divine solution to the problem of evil is precisely such divine presence operating in history according to the probability schedules of world process. See *Insight,* 718–25. For Lonergan's distinction of the religious infrastructure and the religious superstructure, see *Third Collection,* 57–58.

process beyond some general heuristic anticipations. According to his reasoning, it is likely that there will be further development along lines of greater complexity of consciousness, at least with respect to human "second nature." Beyond that it would be dangerous to speculate.[62] We should recall that positing some pure line of progress is legitimate only retrospectively, and then only under severely limiting conditions. Furthermore, Lonergan's worldview of emergent probability does not postulate a goal, or final cause, of the entire process. Indeed, as we have argued above, we can employ Aristotle's notion of final cause fruitfully as we examine the development of any given species. Still, as Lonergan surveys the entire directional tendency of emergent probability, he makes it clear that his theory is dealing with formal cause, not final cause, with the immanent intelligibility of emergent world process, not with its ultimate goal.[63]

This brings us full circle to the beginning of this study and to contemporary confusions. A focus on development cannot be a substitute for a soteriology cult. The classicist worldview, to be sure, avoided this problem, but at the price of conceiving of development within a world of fixity, or, at least, of cosmic cycles. It underplayed emergence and historical perspective, while being entranced by permanence. The more contemporary worldview, on the other hand, has its peculiar dangers and fascinations. Leibniz spoke of divine prescience of the career of each monad and of the careers of the sum total of all monads in history. Many contemporary efforts—ranging from the most crude popularizations to the most sophisticated intellectual speculations—have aimed at appropriating such a God's-eye view of development. To the contrary, all reflections on development must acknowledge: we have no such God's-eye view, neither by the philosopher, nor by the historian, nor by the scientist, nor by the psychologist, nor, least of all, by the ideologist.

Thus, what Lonergan claims to offer in his worldview of emergent probability is a philosophical alternative to a nonevolutionary theory of the universe, which, at the same time, avoids reductionist and gnostic tendencies and, as a set of heuristic notions rooted in what he calls generalized empirical method, is consonant with any future scientific developments.

---

62. See *Insight*, 473–74.
63. Ibid., 476. Lonergan would relate final causality to the ultimate ground of value of the universe (679–80).

Part II

Historical Existence

3

Dialectic of History

OUR CONTEMPORARY SCIENTIFIC worldview, as Bernard Lonergan argues, is properly defined as one of "emergent probability." We must acknowledge that the universe is truly a world in process. Indeed, to grasp the intelligibility of emergent world process we need to employ—in addition to the method of classical, Newtonian physics—the methods of statistical analysis and of development. Human history, too, according to Lonergan, is under the sway of emergent probability. However, it has this difference: it is intelligent as well as intelligible. Moreover, in human history we have not only an intelligent intelligibility but also a nonintelligent unintelligibility. As in all processes of the universe, human history has trials and errors, triumphs and failures, breakthroughs and breakdowns, but in human history these are largely conscious. Historians must use methods appropriate to ascertain the interior dimensions of history: they must interpret the ideas, meanings, values, and purposes affecting events from the "inside." In short, they need a hermeneutical method. Lonergan would furthermore pinpoint a key component in the investigation of human affairs as dialectical analysis.[1] Thus, to study human

1. On emergent probability, see Chapter 2; *Insight*, chap. 2, esp. 144–51, chap. 4, 437–507, esp. 505–6. On emergent probability and human affairs, 5–6, chap. 7, esp. 235–36, 255–61, 324–25. On the interiority of human affairs, see *Method in Theology*, 81, 175–80. On dialectic, see *Insight*, 242–43, 260–61, 265, 509; and *Method in Theology*, 245–46.

history we require a distinct method, and this distinct method must be a dialectical hermeneutic. Our purpose in this essay is to explore why dialectical method is, in fact, such a key component.

To speak of both dialectic and history, then, implies that neither history nor historical accounts are simply chaotic, that there is an identifiable dynamism to historical life, and that the historical dynamism includes opposed principles. A dialectic of history must embrace both subject and object, knower and known, written history and the history that is written about. We must, accordingly ask: What is dialectic? What is history? And how does dialectic apply to history?

Dialectic of Historical Interpretations

Aristotle practiced a kind of dialectical analysis by considering the views of his predecessors.[2] We might gain a preliminary understanding of dialectic by examining prevalent frameworks for interpreting history, which incorporate, in varying degrees, some kind of dialectical element. Our analysis, following Aristotle's procedure, might itself be a preliminary exercise of dialectical method.

First, let us recall the most widely used framework for history: the three-stage division of history into ancient, medieval, and modern periods. We should note that this convention applies most appropriately to Western history, which perforce becomes the standard for world history. Furthermore, there is a set of evaluative criteria at work with respect to the conventional division of Western history itself. In the Renaissance, Vasari articulated these standards as he divided the history of painting into an ancient period, which saw the birth and flourishing of the arts; a medieval time, which witnessed the barbarization and decline of the arts; and, finally, his contemporary era, which was giving rebirth to the arts. Later Voltaire and D'Alembert would adopt the convention of a birth, extinction, and progress of the human spirit as the great leitmotiv of history. This grand-scale Enlightenment construction of history was a replacement for the older, biblical theory of history, with its notion of a sacred history extending from Creation to the Fall, to Redemption,

---

2. See, for example, Aristotle, *Metaphysics* 1.3–10.983ff; *Nicomachean Ethics* 1.5–6.1095b13–1097a14; and *Insight*, 242.

to eschatological future. The modern view has "immanentized" the eschaton; it is decidedly a progressivist interpretation.[3] In the nineteenth century it became secular dogma, setting up as standards of modern progress both the advance of science and technology as well as liberal and humanitarian political ideals. Its residue, of course, still remains to a degree in our textbooks and contemporary outlooks. Our vision of a utopian future as an aseptic, efficient, demythologized world is but one example of the sway of this interpretation.

This conventional view surely has a dialectical component: there is an epochal battle between enlightenment and the inertial forces of superstition and ignorance. We here need point out only the most questionable premise underlying the dialectic, namely, a rigid scientistic conception of reason that consigns all human understanding outside its narrow frame to some form of superstition and ignorance. Without necessarily adopting this premise we can, however, extrapolate real insights. There *is* a phenomenon in history we can call progress: for there are technological innovations, such as writing, steam power, and electricity; economic improvements, such as market economies; political advances, such as constitutional governments, mixed regimes, and the abolition of slavery; and cultural achievements, such as cumulative discoveries in mathematics, physics, and scholarship. If we are willing to label such developments as progressive, we must also admit that they are the fruit of human reason.

Perhaps the inherent weakness in this conventional historical interpretation is reflected in the fact that most professional historians are loath to refer to it, at least explicitly. In fact, there is an increasing tendency in college curricula in the United States to replace Western civilization courses with world civilization courses—and, we should add, an increasing tendency to accord non-Western civilizations their "fair share" in world civilization textbooks.

We turn, then, to a second model, one emphasizing parallel developments of civilizations (with some cross-fertilization apparently allowed). Here all standards and norms are those of the particular civilizations themselves. No external principles are allowed. The antecedent of this model is clearly the romanticist emphasis on the irreducible uniqueness of each culture, as found in

3. Giorgio Vasari, *Lives of the Artists,* 1: pref. Jean le Rond D'Alembert, "Preliminary Discourse," 1–43; Eric Voegelin, *From Enlightenment to Revolution,* chap. 1. On immanentizing, see Voegelin, *New Science of Politics,* 29, 120–21; Voegelin, *Modernity without Restraint: "The Political Religions," "The New Science of Politics," and "Science, Politics, and Gnosticism,"* 110, 185–86; and Löwith, *Meaning in History.*

the program of such historicists as Herder. The historian, following the romanticist hermeneutic, must absorb his or her horizon totally into the meanings and values of the horizon under investigation.

But what room is there for dialectic? With each hermetically sealed cultural horizon basking in its individuality, this multicultural outlook would seem
to have no patience with dialectical analysis. Herder, for instance, could place
all seeming tension and opposition, all seeming historical discord, within the
greater harmony of the grand symphony heard by only the God of history.[4]
Perhaps if any dialectic were allowed within this perspective, it would entail
the struggle of cultural autonomy against the forces of imperialism, including
what might be regarded as Western intellectual universalism. A loophole in
this model, by which social Darwinists would actually glorify the battle of
competing cultures, no longer seems fashionable.

The strength of this model is its insight into the existence of relative horizons, those perspectives at particular times and places whose questions, concerns, and assumptions are informed by traditions, historical experiences, and
linguistic frameworks. Yet, herein lies a danger: relative horizons imply the
philosophy of relativism. For the romanticist hermeneutic would, in principle, destroy all standards save those of the relative horizon under observation
as those standards apply to itself. It would deny the possibility of what Gadamer terms a fusion of horizons between interpreter and subject matter of investigation.[5] It would automatically rule out of court any appeal to universal
standards. Would not, though, this romanticist horizon itself simply be one
relative horizon among many more, whose own claims would have no validity beyond the horizon of romanticist interpreters, unless the romanticist
hermeneutic were to aspire to universality in flagrant violation of its inner
principles?

Third, there remains the possibility of recognizing historical diversity by
seeing amid the diversity a scientific pattern in cycles of historical development. Polybius, for example, drawing on the ideas of Plato and Aristotle, proposed that the forms of government—monarchy, tyranny, aristocracy, oligarchy, democracy, and mob rule—tended to revolve in a historical circuit.
Vico held that societies pass through specific developmental stages of growth,
maturation, and decay; his *corsi e ricorsi* ran from the Age of the Gods, to the
Age of Heroes, to the Age of Man. Spengler saw each civilization go through

4. See Isaiah Berlin, *Vico and Herder: Two Studies in the History of Ideas,* 145–216.
5. Hans Georg Gadamer, *Truth and Method,* 273ff, 337.

a cycle analogous to the seasons. Sorokin argued that cultures gradually shift from a Sensate phase (dominated by sense experience), to an Ideational phase (dominated by religious intuition), to an Idealist phase (dominated by a balance of faith and reason).[6]

Whatever we may conclude about the empirical merits of any of these cyclical typologies, they all suffer from a major defect. Dialectic, at best, is an inborn and necessary series of contradictions that impels the movement from one cyclical phase to another. But can the historian claim to operate and judge outside the cycle any more than can the advocate of a romanticist hermeneutic consistently claim some kind of neutrality of horizon? And can the historian completely avoid evaluation when describing, for example, one phase as barbaric, another as senile? To be sure, this cannot obscure the merit of grasping the insight that there are schemes of recurrence in human affairs, whether in demographic trends, economic cycles, or patterns of political institutions. Nevertheless, is it not possible for individuals and whole peoples to respond to historical challenges through intelligence and freedom, to transcend inherited schemes of recurrence, and to effect the emergence of new schemes? Polybius, in fact, wrote glowingly of how the Romans created a scheme of recurrence, their constitution, that avoided precisely the Polybian cycle of revolving forms of government with its attendant violence and upheaval. His historical account, in turn, helped to inspire the framers of the United States Constitution to adopt the schemes of recurrence of checks and balances in a mixed constitution, where the specific intent was to escape none other than the Polybian cycle itself.[7]

Fourth, if cyclical theories putatively offer a diachronic solution to the problem of diverse worldviews, Dilthey is foremost among those who would offer a synchronic solution. Rather than being scandalized by the contradictions among the seemingly irreconcilable worldviews of positivism, the idealism of freedom, and objective idealism, Dilthey would have us embrace them as eternal tensions. They arise perpetually from the unbounded vitality of human life. Ultimately, Dilthey offers us an aesthetic appreciation of the wealth and variety of human opinion. This mind-set has indeed inspired many a program

6. Polybius, *Histories*, 6:3–9, in *The Portable Greek Historians*, ed. M. I. Finley, 475–81; Giambattista Vico, *The New Science of Giambattista Vico*, bk. 4; Oswald Spengler, *The Decline of the West*; Piritim Sorokin, *Social and Cultural Dynamics*.

7. Polybius, *Histories*, 6:11–18, in *The Portable Greek Historians*, ed. Finley, 483–89. For a discussion of the attempt to avert the decline of a republic, see Forrest McDonald, *Novus Ordo Seclorum: The Intellectual Origins of the Constitution*, 70–71, 81, 84–87.

of humanistic studies or intellectual history. It preaches toleration and the liberation from the finitude of every historical phenomenon, every human or social condition, and every kind of faith.[8]

Its dialectic, if it has a dialectic, is a war against dogmatism. But this is a frozen dialectic, and it really provides no solution. For it has its own dogmas: it is a form of skepticism. And it negates its most powerful insights. Dilthey correctly perceives that there are recurrent tendencies throughout intellectual history toward certain worldviews, stances based upon philosophical assumptions. However, is not his worldview just one among many, or does it somewhat miraculously have a privileged position? The philosopher must ask: Why are there the "eternal" options of the human mind? Is there a philosophical explanation for the recurrent multiplicity? Dilthey proclaims that philosophy is barred from any such explanation because to ground adequately such an explanation philosophy would have to penetrate beneath the multiform expressions of meaning, value, and purpose to the conscious acts that engender them, and to go beneath the expressions of consciousness, says Dilthey, philosophy cannot do. Here certain dogmatic assumptions about consciousness, subjectivity, and objectivity preclude pursuing the question. But the questions persist: Is Leibniz correct when he insists that philosophers are generally correct in what they affirm and erroneous in what they restrict? Is it possible to explore consciousness, the forbidden zone, to discover some universal viewpoint of hermeneutics? Whether in the romanticist case, with its appeal to the equality of all worldviews, or in the diachronic case, with its fascination with the intelligibility of the cycle, or in the synchronic case, with its attraction to the eternal options, the adoption of a relativist position begs the question of norms.

Fifth, when we turn to Hegel, we do indeed find a philosopher who analyzes consciousness and argues for a universal viewpoint. And, for Hegel, dialectic is an integral part of the very movement and meaning of history. Various ideas, worldviews, philosophies—as they develop, oppose each other, and fuse in higher viewpoints—partake of a necessary, intelligible direction. History is a logical moment in the eternal self-making of the Absolute.[9] The Absolute Idea, with its own inherent dialectical movement, externalizes itself

---

8. Wilhelm Dilthey, *Pattern and Meaning in History,* 167.
9. Fackenheim, *Metaphysics and Historicity,* 28–34; Fackenheim, *The God Within,* 128–30.

as nature and returns to itself through reflective consciousness in history, thereby attaining self-awareness as Spirit.

Hegel has profound insight into dialectic as an intrinsic component of historical process. He abundantly demonstrates the role of ideas through developing, clashing, and shifting historical circumstances. He, furthermore, has some comprehension of history as a movement both in time and beyond time. History, startlingly enough, is a process "located" in time and eternity. He speaks of a tension in historical existence: "I raise myself in thought to the Absolute . . . thus being infinite consciousness; yet at the same time I am finite consciousness. . . . I am the struggle between them." His method and the wealth of his historical reflections have had an enduring influence on the disciplines of the history of philosophy and intellectual history. Obviously, though, if we reject the standpoint of Absolute Idealism, we reject Hegel's notion of dialect. If we reject the idealism, we reject the necessitarian and conceptualist aspects of his dialectic. If we reject the absolutism, we reject the gnostic tendencies in his system, as, for example, when he places history essentially within the life of the Trinity and speculates on the divine before the creation of the world.[10]

Sixth, Marx offers what he believes is the antidote to Hegel's abstract conceptualism while preserving Hegel's brilliant discoveries. Marx makes Hegel concrete by, so to speak, standing him on his head. Marx has rich insights into the contradictions within the field of practical intelligence. He understands the significance of material conditions and highlights the contradictions between those conditions and economic organization. Perhaps his greatest achievement is to address the pervasive effect of group bias on historical decline. But Hegel stood on his head is still Hegel. Marx's dialectical materialism is a monocausal system with absolutist claims on the goal of history. He holds that science can demonstrate the inevitable rush of history through an apocalyptic revolution toward the liberation of humanity from the primary source

10. On the tension of existence, see Georg Wilhelm Freidrich Hegel, *Lectures on the Philosophy of Religion,* 1:65, quoted in Fackenheim, *Metaphysics and Historicity,* 68; and Fackenheim, *The God Within,* 140. On Hegel's influence, see Karl Löwith, *From Hegel to Nietzsche,* 50–52. For Hegel's God's-eye view of creation, see Hegel, *The Phenomenology of Mind,* 750–85; Hegel, *Reason in History: A General Introduction to the Philosophy of History,* 52; Voegelin, *Order and History,* 4:260–66; Voegelin, *Science, Politics, and Gnosticism,* 40–44; Voegelin, *Modernity without Restraint,* 271–74; Voegelin, *Published Essays, 1966–1985,* chap. 8, esp. 222–31.

of evil in society. The overthrow of the capitalist order will usher in this age of freedom with the epiphany of Marx's version of Rousseau's general will. Here we encounter, in Marx's dubious notion of humanity as the concrete universal, "species-being," fundamental metaphysical problems involving the old philosophical controversy about universals and particulars. We also see remote analogies with Zoroastrian dualism, gnostic themes of alienation and esoteric knowledge, and prophetic temptations to predict the metamorphosis of the human condition.[11] Marx, though he would perhaps deny the charge, implicitly claims, as does Hegel, to stand at an Archimedean point beyond history. How can we articulate a universal viewpoint of dialectical hermeneutics from within historical existence?

Seventh, the temptation might be to give up on the entire venture. If the interpretive frameworks adumbrated above seem, despite their promise, to lead nowhere, then, most academic historians have seemed to argue, they should be abandoned. Historiography should eschew prejudices and idle speculation, eliminate dialectic, and stick to the facts. Max Weber is a striking example of a thinker who bears witness to this trend. Although Weber is most often celebrated as a founder of contemporary sociology, his reflections, in principle, apply not only to the configurational analyses of sociologists but also to the developmental and situational analyses of historians. Although recognizing that scholars themselves are committed to the values of intellectual culture and of scientific objectivity, Weber insists that the very commitment to objectivity demands that scholars divest themselves of all values when they assess the past.[12] Precluded therefore is any possibility of objective value judgments about the historical past, about its values, its persons, its events.

No doubt the strength of this position lies in its avowal that, regardless of partisan stance, historians must strive to determine objectively what happened. But, we must inquire, does this insight necessarily discredit a dialec-

---

11. For the toppling over of the abstract synthesis of Hegel into the concrete materialism of Marx, see Löwith, *From Hegel to Nietzsche,* 144–46. For Marx's version of the general will, 233–37, 242–44. For the input of Rousseau on Hegel and, through him, on Marx, see George Armstrong Kelly, *Idealism, Politics, and History: Sources of Hegelian Thought.* For the problem of universals and particulars in political thought, see Charles N. R. McCoy, *The Structure of Political Thought: A Study in the History of Ideas,* chaps. 9–10. On gnostic themes and prophetic analogies, see Voegelin, *Order and History,* 1:452; Voegelin, *Science, Politics, and Gnosticism,* 22–28; Voegelin, *Modernity without Restraint,* 262–65; Voegelin, *From Enlightenment to Revolution,* chaps. 10–11; and Friedrich Heer, *The Intellectual History of Europe,* 460–61.

12. See Gunther Roth, "History and Sociology in the Work of Max Weber," 308–18; and Max Weber, "Science as a Vocation."

tical method of evaluating? Is not moral life an integral part of historical process, past and present? If a historian, for instance, describes an act of genocide as one of "murder" rather than as one of "killing," might not the former description be a more accurate assessment of the historical deed? Does murder ever happen in history, or is that appellation *always* the merely subjective judgment of a culture or of an interpreter? Are values of historical interest solely as indicators of tendencies to act in the past? We face here a broader philosophical issue: Are values simply emotive and irrational, incapable of rational treatment save as historical relics, as petrified remains of a distant, subjective concern for the good? Can we, in fact, preserve both objective determination of what happened in the past and the critical role of intellectual culture in wrestling with values and offering direction to civilization?

A further problem, however, remains with this essentially positivist method, which assumes that science is preeminently a matter of looking at the facts. Suppose that the "facts" are not the starting point of investigations but the terminal point. Suppose that Kant is correct and data in themselves are chaotic until understanding intervenes. Suppose, moreover, that facts do not precede interpretation (with interpreters perceiving facts) but that interpretation precedes facts (with interpreters establishing facts). And are not interpreters always operating with respect to certain questions of selection, to principles of organization, and to frameworks?

Eighth, then, we face a final alternative. Admit that "subjective" perspectives invariably inform historical interpretations.[13] The real chaos is not a chaos of facts but a chaos of interpretations. As legal pragmatism holds that the Constitution of the United States is what the Supreme Court says it is, so this position would allege that history is simply what the historian says it is. There can be no consistent meaning of dialectic other than the dialectic of viewpoints among historians. Here, however, gnawing questions interpose: Can we methodologically allow for this diversity without capitulating to subjectivism? Can we, in short, envision the possibility of critical philosophy critically engaging dialectical positions?

We can see the fruit of our Aristotelian dialectical procedure in the following series of questions: Can we speak meaningfully of standards of progress without taking those standards from a particular civilization at a particular phase? Can we reconcile a universal viewpoint of interpretation with recognition of the integrity of relative horizons? Can we acknowledge both recurrent patterns in history and divergent worldviews—and, at the same time, tie

13. See Raymond Aron, "Relativism," 153–61.

each to transcultural standards? Can we embrace historical change equally on the level of ideas and on the substratum of material processes? Can we preserve historical objectivity while pursuing historical evaluation? Can we follow a critical method that would handle dialectically divergent historical accounts? No satisfactory dialectical method can avoid coming to term with such problems.

Lonergan and Dialectic

Lonergan's foundational enterprise promises a dialectical method that would embrace these concerns. We must now turn to Lonergan's alternative by first examining what he means by dialectic.

A cursory reading of Lonergan's work would suggest that by dialectic Lonergan means a method at once critical and evaluative. It is a method that uncovers a dialectical process in which the flourishing of insights is countered by the blocking of insights, in which progress is opposed by decline, and in which historical interpretations compatible with fundamental philosophical critique are contradicted by historical interpretations not so compatible.[14] Although the cursory reading is correct insofar as Lonergan does incorporate precisely these elements into his dialectical procedure, a more comprehensive reading would spot a more comprehensive notion of dialectic. Lonergan, in fact, defines dialectic as follows:

(1) there is an aggregate of events of a determinate character;
(2) the events may be traced to either or both of the principles;
(3) the principles are opposed but bound together; and
(4) they are modified by the changes that successively result from them.

Lest there be any doubt that dialectic, as Lonergan conceives it, has a generic application, he goes on to say: "It is adjustable to any course of events, from an ideal line of pure progress resulting from the harmonious working of opposed principles, to any degree of conflict, aberration, breakdown, and disintegration."[15] To be sure, when Lonergan speaks of either "harmonious working" or "aberration" or "breakdown," he is invoking norms. These norms are ingredient in the self-transcending process of consciousness with its directional tendency and levels of operations. The norms of consciousness always

14. *Insight,* 21, 242, 269, 293, 446–47; *Method in Theology,* 224, 245–49, 251–53.
15. *Insight,* 242, 269.

take us beyond: beyond experiencing to understanding our experience, beyond understanding to judging the adequacy of our understanding, and beyond knowing to deliberating, deciding, and acting. These norms are self-transcending; they require no extrinsic validation or critical grounding; they themselves are the source of validation and grounding. For to deny these norms and the cognitional and volitional operations they underpin is to invoke them if the denial claims to be attentive to experience, intelligent, reasonable, and responsible.

The norms of the self-transcending process of authentic conscious living embrace, to use Robert Doran's terms, both a dialectic of contraries and a dialectic of contradictories.[16] It is self-transcendence that must negotiate the myriad tensions of human existence—to ensure the "harmonious working of opposed principles"—in the dialectic of contraries. And it is self-transcendence itself that must battle against the forces arrayed against it, where no negotiations are acceptable, in the dialectic of contradictories. Let us briefly consider each of these dialectics.

Although Lonergan does not explicitly name a dialectic of contraries, he does elucidate in some detail various tensions in human existence that need to be balanced. On one level, the human sensitive psyche intersects unconscious biological energy and the intelligent world of cognitional and moral operations. At this intersection of organic vitality and intentional operations the psyche is a sensitive flow associated with nonintentional states and trends; with cognitional and volitional operations on distinct strata; with varying degrees of reflective awareness, ranging from the twilight of nonthematic elemental interpretation, to commonsense understanding, to theoretical meaning; and with a dispositional, directional tendency, a teleology toward the beyond. The neural demands of the organic base must be respected, as must the conscious and intentional demands of intellectual, moral, and spiritual life be respected—that is, the demands must be negotiated in order to promote self-transcendence.[17]

---

16. Doran uses the language of Aristotle, for whom the existence of contraries is compossible and the existence of contradictories is impossible (*Theology and the Dialectic of History,* chap. 3; and "Duality and Dialectic"). Whereas Lonergan defines dialectic in a generic fashion, the ordinary context of his usage tends to be that of the "distorted dialectic," whether of blockage of insights (*Insight,* 242–43), of distortion of consciousness by counterpositions (509), of conflicts (*Method in Theology,* 128–30), or of mutually and fundamentally opposed horizons (247). "Conflicts," however, can be incomplete viewpoints whose mutual encounter leads to development. On the latter, see Bernard Lonergan, *The Way to Nicea: The Dialectical Development of Trinitarian Theology.*

17. *Insight,* 214–31, 499–503; *Method in Theology,* 34–35.

If the individual must work through the tension of a dialectic within, the individual is also implicated in a dialectical relation to the community. Neither can the individual exist without the community nor can the community exist without the individual, yet neither is reducible to the other. The individual need not be simply the plaything of larger technological, social, or cultural forces. By the process of inquiry individuals can transcend their communal situations, and a creative minority can carry the tradition of a community beyond itself. Conversely, a community is not necessarily the sum of its parts, for its material products, institutions, and cultural sedimentations can transcend their points of origin along with their individual carriers, and there is a communal drama (its destiny) of a society, a civilization, the human race, which can not be reduced to an aggregate of individual wills.[18]

In addition to the creative tension between the microhorizon of the individual and the macrohorizon of the community, there is a tension within community itself between the spontaneous intersubjectivity of groups and the colder imperatives of practical intelligence.[19] Symbols, feelings, and passions cannot be ignored any more than can economic necessities and political responsibilities. Furthermore, the creatures of human intelligence—technology, economy, polity, and culture—which can take on an objective reality and perdure through time, themselves constitute a series of dialectical relations and mutual conditioning with each other, although Lonergan argues that more of the conditioning comes from the direction of the technology to the economy, of the economy to the polity, and of the polity to culture.[20]

Self-transcendence, however, must negotiate not only a complicated series of tensions within the human situation but also the human situation itself, with human inquiry as a response to an abiding sacred presence of nothingness and mystery. To repress the experience of divine mystery would be to risk an atrophy of the orientation to transcendence, but to abnegate the human condition would be to destroy the human base for an ascent to the divine.[21]

---

18. On subject and society, see *Insight,* 8, 235–36; *Method in Theology,* 47–52; *Third Collection,* 106, 180–81; and "Horizon and History," in *Notes on Existentialism,* 13. On the creative minority, see *Method in Theology,* 255–56; *Verbum,* 37; and *Third Collection,* 10, 103, 214. On destiny, see *Insight,* 234–35, 725–40; *Method in Theology,* 41–47; "Horizon and History," in *Notes on Existentialism,* 13; and Bernard J. F. Lonergan, *Topics in Education: The Cincinnati Lectures of 1959 on the Philosophy of Education,* 231–32.

19. *Insight,* 237–44.

20. Ibid., 233–34, 261–62.

21. Ibid., 749–50. For parallel analysis by Voegelin, see Glenn Hughes, "Balanced and Imbalanced Consciousness," chap. 7.

Throughout these variegated tensions of human living, which we have by no means exhausted, there runs a constant theme, implied in Lonergan's cognitional theory:[22] the dialectic of performance and interpretation. Performance becomes data for interpretation, and interpretation informs future performance. The opposed principles are therefore linked. This is the inherently hermeneutical dimension of human existence. It can be a regressive circuit, in which distorted interpretation conspires with constricted performance. Or it can be an open circuit, in which insightful interpretation before the audience of self, community, and being can support self-transcending performance.

Three comments are in order here about the dialectic of contraries. First, they are continuations, on the human level, of the basic principles of emergent probability. Lonergan's generic notion of development focuses on higher integrations as solutions to the problems of living, meeting the tensions of transformed lower manifolds. Both the immanent dynamism of emergent world process and universal limitation are grounded in potency, which hence is a "tension of opposites." In terms of human development, this tension of opposites is the "tension of limitation and transcendence."[23] Self-transcendence is always a limited move beyond, a process always requiring an ongoing negotiation to balance limitation and transcendence.

Second, then, human development is a dialectic of transcultural norms and particular situations, of transcendental standards and concrete exigencies— of basic horizon and relative horizons. The basic horizon defined by the desire to know and the intention of the good never exists by itself in some pure "transcendental realm" but always is a participant in concrete syntheses of conscious living at particular times and places. The a priori of the horizon of openness is met by the bodily a priori, the communal a priori, and the temporal a priori. It is precisely the tension of these a prioris of the human condition that accounts for both identity and difference in human history. It is precisely this tension that accounts for the dialectics of divine and human, intelligence and affectivity, community and individual, performance and interpretation. Neither absolutism nor relativism triumphs in this in-between status of human being.[24]

---

22. *Insight,* 210–12; *Method in Theology,* 325; *Collection,* 192–93; *Third Collection,* 170–71; "Horizon and History," in *Notes on Existentialism,* 13–14; Bernard J. F. Lonergan, "Philosophy of History," 73–74.

23. *Insight,* 476, 479, 497ff.

24. See Chapter 11, pp. 258–59, below.

Third, although the dialectic of contraries is a continuation, on the human level, of the fundamental principles of emergent probability, it is also a trans-formation of the problems of prehuman development. Indeed, the tension of opposites on the prehuman level is properly a dialectic, in Lonergan's sense, only in potency. For the dialectic of contraries is a dialectic because the tensions of human existence must be negotiated and this "must" ordinarily entails an "ought," namely, the imperative of self-transcendence. The imperative, in turn, implies the possibility of the kind of success or failure for which human beings are responsible. Dialectic, for Lonergan, works on this human stage of responsibility.[25]

The failure of self-transcendence means the failure to negotiate the dialectics of contraries. Although the very desperateness of the resulting situation can act as an invitation to restore the balance, and hence can trigger a kind of correcting mechanism, that restoration cannot take place over the long run without the restoration of self-transcendence.[26] The failure of self-transcendence itself, however, is part of a qualitatively distinct dialectic, that of contradictories, the perpetual struggle of the openness of existence against biases. The negotiation of the dialectic of contraries requires commitment to the desire to know and the freedom to implement that commitment. These are the sources of individual growth, communal development, and historical progress. They operate both on the level of ideas and throughout the entire panoply of technological, economic, and political structures associated with those ideas. Arrayed against open existence are the forces of decline: such biases as psychoneurosis, egoism, group narrowness, and practical shortsightedness—all endemic to the nourishing soil of such existential conditions as flight from anxiety, the sickness unto death, and *ressentiment*.[27]

Finally, we must note a curious dialectic, which partakes, in a sense, both of the antithetical nature of contradictories and of the enriching possibilities of contraries. Lonergan indeed sees fundamental incompatibilities between

---

25. Lonergan's dialectic, as normative, is differentiated from the developmental method appropriate to prehuman processes. See ibid., 447. For articulation of this theme, see Glenn Hughes, "A Critique of 'Lonergan's Notion of Dialectic' by Ronald McKinney, S.J.," and "A Reply to Ronald McKinney, S.J."

26. "Horizon and History," in *Notes on Existentialism*, 14.

27. On bias, see *Insight*, 214–31, 244–69; and *Method in Theology*, 53, 80, 110. On the desire to know and freedom, see *Insight*, 8, 259, 494–504, 643–47. On the sweep of the dialectic, see *Insight*, 232–34, 261–63, 619–21; *Method in Theology*, xi, 47–52, 78; and "Horizon and History," in *Notes on Existentialism*, 12–13. On the existential roots of bias, see Chapter 7, pp. 173–77, below.

those philosophical and intellectual pronouncements consonant with actual cognitive, moral, and spiritual practice ("positions") and those distorted interpretations intrinsically at odds with such performance ("counterpositions"). However, insofar as counterpositions are formulations of thinkers genuinely pursuing the desire to know, and are not simply ideological rationalizations of inauthenticity, then the counterpositions, along with the efforts to articulate them and the insights that inspired them, play a positive role in cultural development. These counterpositions are the work of self-transcendence. All positions invite development; all counterpositions invite reversal. In the latter case, the "existential gap" between counterpositional interpretations and authentic human performance, cognitive and volitional, will eventually be revealed if inquirers after truth persist in inquiry. The reversal can not only "separate the thinker's discovery from its author's bias" but also illuminate the problems under consideration. Hence, for example, Lonergan can regard the historical series of philosophies as a sequence of contradictory "contributions to a single but complex goal."[28]

We have gathered together sufficient material on Lonergan's notion of dialectic to apply them to history. We shall argue that dialectic, so conceived, sheds fundamental light on history and on its study. We have already laid the foundations to answer the questions posed in the previous section.

History

We can conceive of reflection on history in three veins. First, when we examine history as a constitutive element of human being, what continental philosophers call "historicity," we have an *ontological philosophy of history*. Second, when we consider the nature and scope of historical method, we have an *epistemological philosophy of history*. And, third, when we ponder general patterns or grand-scale ideal-types covering the broad sweep of historical events, we have a *speculative philosophy of history*. We must now explore each of these varieties.

History is a project. It is the search, individually and collectively, for meaning, with the goal hurled in front of the quest as its objective. It is a neverfinished project. The questions about human being, the concrete challenges

---

28. *Insight,* 413–14, 509; *Method in Theology,* 251–54. For "ideology" as self-interpretation of inauthenticity, see *Method in Theology,* 357. On the "existential gap," see "Subject and Horizon," in *Notes on Existentialism,* 9; and *Collection,* 192–93, 204.

of history, and the perplexities of the mystery of the human condition do not dry up. The quest—and all the acts and meaning and valuing and deciding that go with it—carries norms of self-transcendence. But the quest can falter. Biases can obscure insights. As ideas and discoveries are embodied not only in cultural forms and institutions but also in technological innovations, economic breakthroughs, and political enlightenment, so distorted meanings and prejudiced views can not only infect culture but also present ever narrower and twisted options for the technology, the economy, and the polity. The quest, however, can continue through the exigency of genuineness, through the demand to uncover bias, and through the desperate imperative to bridge the existential gap between authentic human possibility and atrophied human fact.[29] The project of history is a drama, where we are actors and critics, performers and interpreters, midway between material process and the transcendent beyond that is anticipated in the full sweep of our questions.

History, for Lonergan, is complex: It is as complex as are the various dialectics that must be negotiated or engaged. It can be reduced to neither individuals ("great men") nor the larger collective forces; to neither psychic influence nor intellectual operations; to neither ideas nor material circumstances; to neither aspirations of groups nor cold practical necessities; to neither a purely world-immanent nor a purely otherworldly perspective. History has a multiplicity of horizons, each reflecting particular traditions, experiences, and challenges. Self-transcendence itself demands this multiplicity. Nonetheless, the norms ingredient in the self-transcendence of the quest form a transcultural unity. History witnesses progress when those norms are followed, decline when they are violated.[30]

Thus, history has a directional tendency, a goal, a transcendental ideal of historical action amid the multiplicity of scenes and acts in the unfolding drama. And as the drama unfolds, *that* becomes data for further interpretations, further action, further questions. History is a hermeneutical project revolving around the dialectic of performance and interpretation within the transcendental ideal of historical action. Human existence, then, entails historicity,

---

29. See *Insight* on uncovering bias, 214–31 (dramatic bias), 246–47 (individual bias), 249–50 (group bias), and 259–67 (general bias); on genuineness, 494–504; on reversal of counterpositions, 413; on reversal of ethical counterpositions, 626, 630; and on critique of mistaken beliefs, 735–39. See also *Method in Theology*, 231–32; and "Horizon and History," in *Notes on Existentialism*, 14.

30. *Insight*, 8, 259–60; *Method in Theology*, 55, 231–32; "Horizon and History," in *Notes on Existentialism*, 12–14.

hermeneutics, and dialectic, with each mutually defining the other. This is why dialectic is such a cardinal feature of Lonergan's philosophy of history.

If history is the drama of the gaining, the losing, and the regaining of the direction of existence, then surely it is not a pure line of progress. Still, it need not be a recurrent circle of growth and decline. Any rigid organic analogy misses the kind of higher integration that human living can be and ignores the possibility of assuming historical responsibility for the direction of history.

It is here that we see one of the most revolutionary contributions of Lonergan. For he ties together the emphasis of historicity (present interpretation of past performance oriented toward the future) with academic history. Every person has an individual history, composed of memories of significant and meaningful events, which through anticipations, expectations, hopes, and fears guides the person in the future. The wise person can reflect critically on his or her past and learn from it, challenge its distortions, overcome its blind spots, and expand his or her horizon for the future. So, too, every society has an existential history, a collectively significant core of memories that defines that society's past meaning, present values, and future purposes. When a society has differentiated a reflectively critical intellectual culture, that society can scrutinize its past in light of dialectic, reassess its identity, and take on more collective responsibility for directing its own history.[31]

If the history that is written about is, as Lonergan maintains, a dialectic process, then historiography must be able to depict its dramatic tensions and dialectical contradictions. This is a tall order for historiography.[32] How can it preserve objectivity yet conduct evaluation? A narrow positivism would exclude evaluation in the name of the pure, objective description of facts. A narrow relativism would exclude objectivity in the name of the inevitability of intrusions by subjective, evaluative interpreters. Lonergan's cognitional theory handles the problem in a twofold manner by a twofold differentiation.

First, Lonergan claims that there are two types of objectivity, associated, respectively, with two distinct levels of consciousness and animated by two distinct kind of questions. There is an objectivity issuing judgments of fact, rooted in insights into the data, and responding to the question: what happened? There is another objectivity issuing judgments of values about the facts, responding to the questions: Was it worthwhile? Was it a true theory?[33] His-

31. *Insight,* 259–67, 587–91; *Method in Theology,* 168; *Collection,* chap. 16; *Second Collection,* 21, 91–92, 103–4; *Third Collection,* chap. 11.

32. *Insight,* 260–61; *Method in Theology,* chap. 10.

33. On judgment of facts, see *Insight,* chap. 10, esp. 302–12; and *Method in Theology,* chap. 8, 201–3. On judgment of values, see *Method in Theology,* 36–41, 232–33.

torical evaluation, we must observe, cannot take place without prior judgments of historical facts. On the other hand, determination of historical facts can occur without explicit evaluation. Indeed, the judgment of historical facts can include three distinct historical styles: basic description, explanation of causes, and dramatic narrative, with the latter based on the former.[34] In all of these cases, judgments of historical fact need not be encumbered by considerations of evaluation. How, though, can we speak at all about objectivity of evaluation? And does not evaluation creep in the back door to cloud even judgments of fact? To the first question, Lonergan would point out that the transcultural norms that guide the drama of history also guide the historian. The norms of the open horizon of questioning define a universal viewpoint of hermeneutics, from which a historian can examine challenge and response, cultural flourishing or cultural fragmentation, political responsibility or political bias, economic growth or economic breakdown.[35] Historians can render evaluations in two genres, one emphasizing a narrative component, the other focusing on analysis. In either style, however, the historian can, for example, encounter moral character of persons, identify progress and decline in social and political history, recognize insights or blind spots in cultural history, or grasp the salutary effect of the tension of positions and counterpositions in intellectual history.

Second, in answer to the question about evaluations clouding judgments of fact, Lonergan would make a further differentiation: one between dialectical history, either narrative or analytic, and dialectical studies of the historians themselves. Although Lonergan would agree that values affect historical investigations, he would argue that they need not cripple honest efforts at judging what happened. For there is a methodological safeguard, a dialectic, covering the many layers of historiography. In addition to descriptive history, explanatory history, factual narrative, evaluative narrative, and evaluative analysis, there is the distinct specialty of dialectical analysis of the works of

---

34. Two of the historical styles are explicit in *Method in Theology:* 128 (basic history), and 128, 209–10, 230 (specialized, explanatory history). The style of dramatic narrative is rooted in the drama of human living, the "primordial drama that the theatre only imitates" (*Insight*, 211). This dramatic narrative is reflected in "existential history," or "the history that is written about," which, as the group's unreflective self-interpretation, has, accordingly, a strong aesthetic component (*Method in Theology*, 182, 210–11; *Topics in Education*, 229–31). To communicate adequately the drama of living the historian must do so artistically (*Topics in Education*, 253). Indeed, "this is the fundamental problem in general history" (254).

35. *Insight*, 587–91; *Method in Theology*, 245–47, 249–53.

historiography. This dialectic examines the writings of historians to uncover significantly divergent assumptions. This opens up historical interpretations (interpretations of the interpretations of existential history) to an encounter with critical philosophy. Far from eliminating dialectical contradictions, this approach would illuminate such differences and by so doing, in the context of effective academic freedom, would make it more likely that all could contribute in the long run to a single goal through the process of developing positions and reversing counterpositions.[36]

A fuller clarification and exposé of Lonergan's epistemological philosophy of history would entail a more extensive foray into his cognitional theory. Here we have been content to outline the broad lines of his sophisticated approach.

Lonergan, at first glance, might seem to have no speculative philosophy of history. He acknowledges, for instance, that history is not a pure line of progress, for progress intermingles with decline. Nor does it, according to him, follow an ironclad cyclical scheme of recurrence. To be sure, such factors in history as the cumulative nature of progress, the spiraling fragmentation of long-term decline, and the oscillation of dominant and repressed groups in the shorter cycle of decline, as nurtured by group bias, all provide historians and social scientists the data through which they can construct patterns of development and devolution. The mystery of human freedom, however, makes no such patterns inevitable, and, as we have just recounted, self-transcendence can erect new schemes of recurrence to deal with the challenge of old schemes of recurrence.[37] Nor does Lonergan offer the hope of a revolutionary transformation of the human condition, either by gnostic intellectual advances or by apocalyptic political transformation. He chides those who believe the dominance of society by a new, immaculate group will put a new human nature in the saddle.[38] Therefore Lonergan would not endorse the theories of either Vico, or Condorcet, or Hegel, or Marx.

Nevertheless, Lonergan proffers a modified speculative philosophy of his-

---

36. On the distinction between dialectical history and dialectical studies, see *Method in Theology*, 249–50, 253. On historical studies as an interpretation of interpretations, see ibid., 210–11, 250; and "Philosophy of History," 71–74. On dialectical development and reversal in scholarship, see *Method in Theology*, 250, 253–54. Note that, for Lonergan, liberty is the principle of progress (*Insight*, 259).

37. On the mating of progress and decline, see *Insight*, 8; and *Method in Theology*, 251. On patterns of progress and decline, see *Insight*, 234–36; and *Method in Theology*, 180, 211–12. On self-transcending responses to challenges, see *Insight*, 252–53; and *Topics in Education*, 257.

38. *Insight*, 264–65.

tory in the form of the *ephocal* differentiations of consciousness. Lonergan would not have the investigation of the history of consciousness be dogmatically a priori. Indeed, a philosophy of consciousness can supply explanatory tools in this endeavor, but these tools are grand-scale ideal-types (not constructs of a universal history), and they can be employed, enriched, tested, and revised in an ongoing fashion by the various specialized historical disciplines.[39] In antiquity, for example, as Lonergan postulates it, theoretical culture differentiated itself from one almost entirely dominated by a fusion of myth and common sense. The resulting horizon shift erected a cultural superstructure to examine, criticize, and evaluate the more spontaneous apprehension and communication of meaning.[40] More recently, theoretical activities have been differentiated into empirical science, historical method, and a philosophy of interiority. Lonergan is definitely not presenting an updated rendition of the positivist three-stage model of history (from myth to metaphysics to science). It is here that dialectic intervenes.

Lonergan is well aware that the tension of limitation and transcendence is operative in these horizon shifts. Differentiation may necessarily precede integration, but integration must follow. The cultural past is not simply discarded. Differentiation raises new problems, to which integration is the response. Myth is not superseded by theory, but once theory is differentiated the tension between intellectual culture and symbolic culture must be negotiated.[41] The differentiation of scientific method, historical consciousness, and interiority does not abrogate myth, common sense, or metaphysics but sets up challenges for adequate integration. Self-transcendence in the contemporary world cannot embrace the easy solutions of scientism, historicism, or relativism any more than it can conduct an easy retreat into the seductive rhythms of myth, the practicality of common sense, or the formal splendor of dogmatic metaphysics. The history of consciousness is one theme in the drama of history, but it does not eliminate the dialectical character of a drama unfolding always midway between knowledge and ignorance.

---

39. On differentiations of consciousness, see ibid., 587–95, 600–601, 608–16; *Method in Theology*, 302–18; and McPartland, "Meaning, Mystery, and History." On the use of grand-scale ideal-types, see *Insight*, 600–601; and *Method in Theology*, 228–29, 251, 284–88.

40. *Second Collection*, 21, 91–92, 103–4.

41. *Insight*, 569–72; *Method in Theology*, 64–69; *Collection*, 241–43; "Reality, Myth, Symbol," 32–34.

To summarize Lonergan's position on the dialectic of history, we can recall our earlier dialectical inquiry into theories of history and sharpen Lonergan's views by way of contrast. Although Lonergan would wish to reinvigorate the idea of progress, he would deny the hubris of the Enlightenment as it made progress the axis of history in a desacralized world devoid of mystery. Rather than retreating to a romanticist hermeneutic of hermetically sealed horizons, he would insist on the dialectic of relative horizons and basic horizon. He would applaud the construction of ideal-types by Toynbee and others, but he would deny that they are comprehensive descriptions of the self-transcending project of history. Whereas Lonergan would agree with Dilthey about the efficacy of a critique of historical reason, he would contend that underpinning the divergent structures of meaning and patterns of experience are universal norms both present in consciousness and accessible to philosophical exploration. He would appreciate the discoveries of both Marx and Hegel but would, perhaps ironically, sublate both materialism and idealism in a higher viewpoint of critical realism.[42] Lonergan would join with the positivists in their demand for historical objectivity, but not at the expense of evaluation. He would join the relativists in their claim about the operative influence of values in the frameworks of historians, but not at the price of denouncing the prospect of historical objectivity in general, let alone of objective historical evaluations precisely in light of the dialectic. Finally, Lonergan would urge as a specialty in historical studies a dialectical procedure to handle different interpretive frameworks themselves.

Lonergan's notion of a dialectical hermeneutics is the vision of a methodologically insightful cooperation among all concrete, specialized disciplines as they examine all concrete historical details. The strength of his position ultimately rests on the strength of his analysis of consciousness, and the strength of that analysis rests on his ability to discern the nuances of consciousness: its norms, levels, patterns, and differentiations. Lonergan's ultimate challenge, however, is not simply to adopt his theory but to attend to our own consciousness as actors in history—with all of its dialectical complexity.

---

42. On the hubris of the Enlightenment, *Insight,* 572, 711. On the limits of ideal-types, see *Method in Theology,* 228–29. On critical realism, see *Insight,* 22, 266, 446–48.

4

Historicism and Historicity

Two Perspectives on History

TO DESCRIBE OUR AGE as one marked by a high degree of "historical consciousness" is to utter more than a shibboleth. Books and articles touching upon every facet of human history pour forth continuously. There is no lack of historical monographs and no dearth of research topics. Nonetheless, there still remains a pressing need for a comprehensive understanding and evaluation of what often seems a mass of uninterpreted information. Indeed, modern society seems overburdened with a plethora of undigested facts, facts that frequently point to only the "relativity" of truth and values. Modern society thus finds itself caught in the web of a cultural crisis, which Franklin Baumer has discussed under the title of the "triumph of becoming." To a significant degree, this crisis centers upon what Ernst Troeltsch called the "crisis of historicism." According to Troeltsch, "We see here everything in the flux of becoming. State, law, morality, religion, art are dissolved in this flux, and intelligible to us only as ingredients of historical developments. . . . Historicism shook all eternal truths."[1] Recognition, however, of the radically temporal dimension of human existence and the historical conditionedness of truth and values—that is, recognition of *historicity*—does not in itself lead to *historicism*.

---

1. Baumer, *Modern European Thought,* pt. 5; Troeltsch, "Die Krise des Historismus," quoted in ibid., 501.

76

The perception that all human thinking is historically conditioned does not require the radical conclusion that what is true is true *only* from the context of a certain point in time and of the intellectual and social setting in which the context is embedded.[2] The equation of historicity and historicism, in fact, becomes compelling only from within the perspective of certain epistemological and metaphysical assumptions, assumptions that have long held sway in Western intellectual life. If those assumptions are challenged in a comprehensive and reflective manner, as they were by thinkers in the twentieth century, then there is opened up a new and possibly fruitful approach to interpreting the meaning and significance of historicity. This chapter explores the relation between historicity and historicism by examining it in terms of the pervasive assumptions underlying much of modern intellectual history and of the rejection of precisely those assumptions by some contemporary intellectuals. This contemporary trend, which includes thinkers such as Heidegger, Gadamer, Habermas, and Lonergan, has yet to receive adequate attention by intellectual historians. This study aims to identify the trend and indicate some of its most significant features.

The "crisis of historicism" is a progeny (though not necessarily a legitimate one) of the rise of historical consciousness in the modern world. The long path of this epochal transformation of human thought can be traced in such diverse milestones as the expansion of the European horizon through contact with the peoples and cultures of the Americas, Africa, and Asia; the scientific revolution, which opened the way for a clearer distinction between nature and history; the feeling of participating in an epoch of history as a result of the experiences of the transformations wrought by the Reformation, scientific revolution, Industrial Revolution, and French Revolution; the Enlightenment's critique of tradition; the romantics' glorification of the Gothic ages; Hegel's philosophy of history; Marx's demand for a practical history; the refinement and maturation of historical scholarship in the nineteenth century, associated especially with the names of Barthold Niebuhr and Leopold von Ranke; Dilthey's effort at a critique of historical reason; and Heidegger's contention that time is an essential dimension of human being.

The rise of historical consciousness has emphasized the vast divergence of ideas, beliefs, customs, and mores that can be found at different times and places in human history, and it has stressed that human actions are not sole-

---

2. *Historicity* is a translation of the German term *Geschichtlichkeit*, used by Heidegger and others. *Historicism* is a translation of *Historismus*. On the history of *Historismus* and bibliography, see Maurice Mandelbaum, "Historicism."

ly the results of natural processes but rather are largely the expressions of human consciousness and understanding. As Nietzsche observed, animals have no history.[3] Technological, economic, social, political, and cultural phenomena are, to a great extent, although to varying degrees, the products of human thought.

In part, the rise of historical consciousness has created a cultural problem of significant magnitude because rarely, if ever, in Western culture has there been such an acute awareness of the historical dimension of human existence. Hence, both the validity of traditional ideas and their relevance to modern concerns have become problematic. In brief, the traditional *answers* have become suspect or opaque if they are not seen to be answers to *questions* flowing from the spring of modern historical consciousness. We may find, in response to this situation, either a complacent skepticism with respect to the Western intellectual tradition or an effort to rethink the problem, drawing on the insights of earlier thinkers.

The rise of historical consciousness, moreover, has become a pressing social as well as cultural concern. An unprecedented mastery over nature coupled with a greatly expanded awareness of human historicity has given modern men and women an unparalleled opportunity to meet the challenge of assuming larger responsibility for intelligently directing history. At the same time, the urgency of meeting that challenge has never been greater. For modern civilization is also confronted with an unparalleled problem. Through modern technology, human beings have made striking advances in the ability to create their own world by control over nature and over human beings themselves. There has been no similar advance in the ability to utilize this newfound power for reasonably and responsibly determined human ends. The technological forces we have unleashed threaten to dominate us. That the flowering of modern historical scholarship has led to an enormous extension of our knowledge of the past is beyond doubt; that this increased knowledge has resulted in an enhanced capacity for us to direct our future responsibly is at least open to question. Although the study of history has in many instances inspired a liberation of the human spirit from the dogmas and prejudices of the past, it has frequently done so at the price of inviting a new kind of dogmatism in the form of relativism and skepticism. Modern scholarship, according to Bernard Lonergan,

---

3. See R. G. Collingwood, *The Idea of History,* 216–17; Friedrich Nietzsche, *The Use and Abuse of History,* 5.

takes the whole of human history for its kingdom to compare and relate lan-guages and literatures, artforms and religions, family arrangements and cus-tomary morals, political, legal, educational, economic systems, sciences, philosophies, theologies, and histories. New books pour forth annually by the thousands; our libraries need ever more space. But the vast modern ef-fort to understand meaning in all its manifestations has not been matched by a comparable effort in judging meaning. The effort to understand is the common task of unnumbered scientists and scholars. But judging and de-ciding are left to the individual, and he finds his plight desperate.[4]

The *fact* of the historical dimension of human existence must be distin-guished from the *interpretation* of the meaning, significance, and implications of that fact. There are two broad perspectives for interpreting and dealing with the phenomenon of human historicity. One perspective—which includes both historical relativists and many of their more vehement opponents, those, for example, who urge a dogmatic appeal to a metaphysical system, religious authority, or the conventions of society—is that defined by crucial presup-positions that have long prevailed in European intellectual life. The other per-spective marks a decided break with the assumptions of modern intellectual culture, and its interpretations, consequently, do not follow the usual rules of the game. In this study we shall focus on the distinction between these two perspectives.

Historicism

We have spoken of a "crisis of historicism," yet "historicism" has been giv-en a variety of definitions in the literature on the subject, and the controver-sy over its nature still rages. In order to arrive at a satisfactory working defi-nition of the term *historicism,* let us briefly consider some of the more pertinent treatments of the issue.

Carlo Antoni, in his comprehensive description of historicism in *L'His-torisme,* has helped us locate, if not define, this phenomenon by placing it in historical perspective. Antoni claimed that in the eighteenth century there emerged a peculiarly modern attitude toward history, absent in classical, me-dieval, and Renaissance cultures, and going against the grain of Enlighten-ment thought—against a mechanistic worldview and against the idea that

---

4. *Collection,* 244.

history was a collection of abuses and superstitions. Instead, eighteenth-century thinkers such as Burke, Vico, and Herder proclaimed that history itself was the key to the understanding of humans as social and political beings. Antoni went on to say that historicism opposed not only Enlightenment ideas but also the universalism of the French Revolution and its attempt to reconstruct society along bureaucratic centralist lines. Thus, historicism supported the traditionalism of Burke and other Englishmen, as well as the reactionary glorification of the Middle Ages found in French and German writers. By mid-nineteenth century, the stream of historicism had become a torrent, discernible in German, French, and English historiography and such theorists as Comte and Marx. Among the foremost later historicist thinkers were Dilthey, Spengler, and Croce.

Friedrich Meinecke's monumental work, *Historism,* which in many respects paralleled that of Antoni, pinpointed a cluster of ideas that, for Meinecke, defined the essence of historicism.[5] According to Meinecke, there was a general tendency among historicist thinkers to interpret historical reality as the realm of becoming and flux, where the reigning categories were those of the "individual," the "concrete," and the "unique." The historical world was incapable of being subsumed legitimately under rational or scientific categories that sought universal laws and patterns. Perhaps the weakness in Meinecke's theory was that it applied more characteristically to German historicism than to the phenomenon as a whole.[6]

In Karl Popper's *Poverty of Historicism,* we find another, very different, definition of historicism. Popper identified "historicism" with the propensity of Comte, Hegel, and Marx to argue that there are laws of communities qua communities (that is, laws of societies as a whole) and that once these laws can, by definition, be ascertained the future can be predicted. Such a definition, of course, was the very antithesis of Meinecke's.

The historicism spectrum, therefore, is wide, and contradictory, and ranges from an emphasis on what is concrete, unique, and irrational to a concern for arriving at general laws of historical development. Perhaps the term *historicism* can be given an adequate working definition for our purposes if we concentrate more on the *method* underlying historicism than on any particular set of ideas or theories of particular historicist thinkers. If we focus on histori-

---

5. Meinecke, *Historism,* lv–lx, 3–4.
6. "[H]istorism is nothing else but the application to the historical world of the new life-governing principles achieved by the great German movement extending from Leibniz to the death of Goethe" (ibid., lv).

cism as a methodological principle with its own distinct metaphysical perspective, its central features become clearer. It involves what Maurice Mandelbaum has suggested is a *genetic method* of explanation, namely, each event in history is to be understood and evaluated by viewing it exclusively in terms of a larger process of which it was a phase; only by understanding the nature of the process can one fully understand or evaluate concrete events.[7] All understanding of history, then, is based on the nature of the historical process itself.

This method, furthermore, should not be viewed as merely restricted to the method of historiography or social science. It is more fundamental than that, for it is a way of apprehending truth and human reality. It posits a new concept of truth: *all philosophical questions become historical questions.* And, according to this line of thinking, there is a new concept of human nature: *human nature is that which is made by humans in history.* Consequently, there is no universal human nature. It varies from historical age to historical age, much as philosophical truth varies from one *Weltanschauung,* or worldview, to another. Historical relativism is the logical outcome of the methodological assumptions of historicism, although, in practice, historicist thinkers have been hard-pressed to avoid appeal to some extrahistorical or historical absolute.[8]

This philosophical stance has penetrated the fields of historiography, social theory, psychology, and education to demand a rigorous separation of facts and values. As a result of relativism, scholarship has been in danger of becoming pedantry or aestheticism. Its confidence in itself as a source of wisdom has been undermined. Historicism has also filtered down to the level of popular culture to combine with currents of extreme subjectivism, hedonism, and irrationalism to become the conventional wisdom of the day—the conviction found in newspapers, stylish journals, and conversations that claims, with respect to truth, that all we have are opinions and all opinions are equal and, with respect to ethics, that each person ought to "do his or her own thing."

7. Mandelbaum, *History, Man, and Reason: A Study in Nineteenth-Century Thought,* 42.

8. Burke, for example, saw history as the march of God's Providence; Hegel claimed to know the Absolute Idea; Marx looked forward to the advent of "socialist man"; Nietzsche spoke of the "myth of the eternal return"; and Dilthey appealed to Life. Of course, the extent to which these thinkers should be considered "historicists" may be subject to debate. On the historicist transformation of the concept of human nature, see Fackenheim, *Metaphysics and Historicity* and *The God Within,* chap. 8.

The Epistemological Assumptions of Historicism

Some of the key assumptions underlying the historicist viewpoint, indeed the crucial ones, are also assumptions that have been dominant in modern European thought for centuries. The debate, for example, between advocates of historical relativism and those arguing for eternal truths has usually been circumscribed by premises to which both sides adhere. To a remarkable degree, the pervasive dichotomies, antinomies, and alternatives of modern thought —dogmatism versus skepticism, Enlightenment versus romanticism, rationalism versus irrationalism, objectivism versus subjectivism, eternal truths versus historical relativism—have been defined and established within the same basic framework of intellectual presuppositions. In other words, the debate has been conducted with the same set of ground rules.[9] These ground rules are fundamental assumptions regarding subjectivity, objectivity, truth, and reality. These assumptions maintain the premise that there is a necessary and irreparable bifurcation of subjectivity and objectivity.

Hence, the problem of historical relativism is a striking manifestation of a wider problem in modern intellectual culture as a whole over the past few centuries, and in order adequately to comprehend and perhaps to wrestle critically with the problem of historical relativism, we must consider the larger problem. We can best proceed by briefly considering the examples of Wilhelm Dilthey and Max Weber, both brilliant pioneers in the development of historical scholarship and social science, who saw that modern historical and scientific culture was a two-edged sword.

No one was more aware than Dilthey of the fact that the data for historical research are not simply given like the objects in the external world studied by the natural sciences, or of the fact that history is mediated by acts of meaning and valuing. He insisted that such data are the expression and objectification of human living and that the expression and objectification of human living are living's own interpretation of itself. Dilthey poured tremendous energy and erudition into the tasks of differentiating between the cultural and natural sciences, identifying the various kinds of meaning expressed in historical process, and delineating the dynamic systems of interaction (*Wirkungszusammenhangen*) in which meanings, values, purposes, and activities are interconnected and interdependent.[10]

9. For a discussion of modern intellectual debate, see Wayne C. Booth, *Modern Dogma and the Rhetoric of Assent,* 17–19.

10. Dilthey, *Pattern and Meaning,* chaps. 5–6; R. E. Palmer, *Hermeneutics: Interpretation Theory in Schliermacher, Dilthey, Heidegger, and Gadamer,* 100–114; H. A. Hodges, *The Phi-*

Still, no one illustrates more the "crisis of historicism" than Dilthey. For, although he made enormous advances in understanding the patterns of meaning in history, Dilthey, as H. Stuart Hughes has argued, struggled—without success—for an "escape from the skeptical and relativist implications of his own thought."[11] He could not establish a critique of meaning, since his study of history led him to assert the relativity of values. Dilthey, it is true, proclaimed that "the historical consciousness of the finitude of every historical phenomenon, of every human or social condition and of the relativity of every kind of faith, is the last step towards the liberation of man." Consciousness of historical relativity, however, though it served as a potent antidote against dogmatism, did not satisfy Dilthey's legitimate yearning for an undogmatic foundation for values and action—a prerequisite for intelligent and deliberate making of history. Consequently, he asked where the means were to be found for overcoming the "anarchy of convictions" threatening to break in after the "liberation" of the human spirit by historical consciousness. He expressed his own personal dilemma in the face of conflicting philosophical horizons through his moving description of a dream in which he was present at the scene depicted in Raphael's *School of Athens*. In the dream, Dilthey saw the three groups of philosophers gathered there gradually drift apart into physically different areas and cease communication. He dramatically related how "the unity of my own being seemed sundered as I was drawn passionately first to this group and then to another, and I strove to master them."[12] In the end, Dilthey's historical consciousness left him with an aesthetic resignation, a romantic contemplation of the variety and diversity of human achievement and creativity, with no basis for evaluating the past and for guiding the future. It has been suggested that Dilthey sought to escape from the consequences of relativism by his typology of worldviews.[13] Whether this interpretation is cor-

---

losophy of Wilhelm Dilthey; Rudolf A. Makkreel, *Dilthey: Philosopher of the Human Studies;* Linge, "Historicity and Hermeneutic," pt. 1; Gadamer, *Truth and Method.*

11. Hughes, *Consciousness and Society,* 199.

12. On liberation by historical consciousness, see Dilthey, *Pattern and Meaning,* 167. On the "anarchy of convictions," see Linge, "Historicity and Hermeneutic," 252. On the dream, see ibid., 252–53 n. 271; Wilhelm Dilthey, *Gessamelte Schriften,* 8:233, trans. in ibid., 253 n. 271; Introduction, pp. 2, 5, above.

13. According to George Iggers in *The German Conception of History,* Dilthey was convinced that the *Geisteswissenschaften* transcend history by discovering the recurrent types of philosophical world images (142). Iggers claims that Dilthey had a view of history as a process that was still within the German idealist tradition (143). Carlo Antoni has argued that Dilthey's concept of types reduced historiography to sociology (*From History to Sociology: The Transition in German Historical Thinking,* 33). Jürgen Habermas has maintained that the objectivity of Dilthey's classification of worldviews is fallaciously grounded in a

rect is immaterial, since no typology, however sophisticated and "empirical," can in itself resolve the problem of relativism. The agony of Max Weber bears witness to this fact.[14]

One of the founders of modern sociology, Weber realized, as did Dilthey, that a scientific study of human beings must start from the factor of meaning in human living. Weber developed Dilthey's typology into a methodology and applied it to a vast range of empirical data. Employing his celebrated notion of ideal-types, Weber sought to correlate certain tendencies of action with corresponding initial assumptions and values. However, there was a tension in Weber's outlook between his conception of a social science (a conception in many important respects applicable to historiography) and his deep anxiety over the increasing "rationalization" of modern civilization associated with the advance and influence of science. He was foremost in proclaiming value-free social science and, at the same time, was haunted by the specter of bureaucratic domination and depersonalization in the modern world.[15] Weber affirmed scientific activity as a value, yet he saw science contributing to increasing bureaucratic organization. Science, for Weber, determined means—it established cause and effect relationships and probable modes of human behavior in society. It could not pronounce on the validity of ends, since values could not be determined rationally. Certainly, he sought to sidestep relativism and nihilism in that he believed that one must articulate one's values with intellectual integrity.[16] Nevertheless, Weber denied that a conflict among value systems could be rationally resolved: *we* must choose our values, and this choice can have no rational basis. The implication seemed to be that it is the

---

philosophy of vitalism (*Knowledge and Human Interests,* 183–84). Linge, however, in "Historicity and Hermeneutic," warns against interpreting Dilthey's typology too rigidly (243). He insists that Dilthey's primary interest was never in cataloging types, but in understanding how worldviews emerge from the basic dynamic of life that is man's historicity. Linge also mentions elements of Dilthey's thought that emphasize creative shaping of the future (see 260–66). And, indeed, Makkreel argues in *Dilthey* that these elements, found especially in Dilthey's writings on aesthetics, constitute a "critical hermeneutics." Linge concludes, though, that this aspect of Dilthey's philosophy is "submerged . . . in the aesthetic and contemplative whole" (263).

14. For a well-balanced, brief discussion of Max Weber, consult H. S. Hughes, *Consciousness and Society,* 287–335. Hughes describes Weber as pushing all the contradictions of his time to their point of maximum lucidity "with a kind of perverse vocation for self-torment" (290, 330).

15. Weber, "Politics as a Vocation" and "Science as a Vocation."

16. This is a point that tends to be overlooked in interpretations of Weber. See Reinhard Bendix, *Max Weber: An Intellectual Portrait,* 263 n. 8.

will to power that decides the set of values that is dominant in a society, a sobering thought. For Weber, then, neither historiography nor social science could offer an effective critique and evaluation of history. At best they could give a certain type of explanation of events. Critique of the past, or explicit attempts at recovery of lost or obscured meanings and values, was, in principle, precluded. Weber inherited from Dilthey the "crisis of historical understanding," and he left it where he found it.[17]

Thus, we see that Dilthey praised the human liberation ushered in by modern historical consciousness from the dogmas of the past but simultaneously shuddered at the "anarchy of convictions" that threatened to flow out of that very liberation by historical consciousness. Weber realized that precisely the kind of rationalism central to social science, when rigorously applied to investigate the beliefs, ideas, and sentiments of traditional philosophy, morals, and religion, was creating a distinctively modern aura of "disenchantment," one he feared would make the future "a polar night of icy darkness and hardness."[18]

In no small measure, the "crisis of historicism" associated with this problem of value-free history can be attributed to the prevalence in modern culture of certain fundamental assumptions regarding truth and objectivity. It was precisely from within this framework that Dilthey and Weber grappled with the problem of relativism and were saddled with the alternative of either dogmatism or skepticism. Dilthey and Weber both adhered to what can be called a "confrontation theory of truth." According to this view, there is a gap between knower and known, subject and object. The way in which the gap is overcome is through an act that is similar to seeing. Objectivity is conceived as unimpaired *perception* of objects. It is as though we "look at" the "world" through a pair of glasses and "subjective" influences tend to fog up the lens, distorting our vision, and making it objectively unreliable.

In terms of historical understanding, this "confrontation theory of truth" holds that the historian with his or her horizon—namely, his or her perspective of beliefs, attitudes, sentiments, values, and ideas—confronts a horizon within which people in the past thought and acted; objectivity is interpreted as unimpaired, undistorted perception of how people in the past thought and acted in their horizon, perception unmarred by intrusions and impositions from the horizon of the historian. Evaluative historiography is thereby pre-

17. Gerhard Masur, *Prophets of Yesterday: Studies in European Culture, 1890–1914*, 201; Voegelin, *New Science of Politics*, 13–23; Voegelin, *Modernity without Restraint*, 98–105.
18. Weber, "Science as a Vocation," 155; Weber, "Politics as a Vocation," 128.

cluded. Or, if evaluation is considered desirable, then historical analysis is construed as making the past "relevant" for present concerns, interests, and problems; in short, the past is merely a mirror reflecting the present, there being no way for the historian to escape the distortions created by his or her own subjectivity.

Historians tend to be caught on the horns of a dilemma that proceeds from two affirmations: historians correctly affirm both the existence of horizons in the past within which people thought and acted and the existence of horizons in the present within which historians themselves operate. Then comes the dilemma. If historians bracket out their own horizons in order to understand how people in the past thought and acted in their horizons, they can attain "objectivity," but forsake critique; they can achieve a value-free interpretation. If, on the other hand, historians attempt critique or do not bracket out their horizons, they are necessarily prey to the "biases" of their horizons and cannot attain "objectivity."

In fact, historians cannot conduct their investigations with minds that are blank tablets: their knowing is inescapably tied to past experiences, insights, judgments, and decisions. Indeed, operative in the interpretations of historians are implicit and usually inchoate philosophical assumptions regarding truth, objectivity, and values. If a pure value-free history is therefore impossible, are we, then, stuck with relativism? Must historians inevitably fail in their attempt to gain an "objective" view of the past, because they cannot succeed in bracketing out their own horizons? And must critique of the past ultimately fail also, because the critic cannot escape the "prejudices" that flow from the relativity of his or her own horizon?[19] These questions mask a particular view of what understanding and valuing are, and they are questions that make effective sense only if their assumptions are accepted.

Dilthey strove to avoid obstruction of the historian's understanding of other periods by positing an affinity or sympathy with the experience of the people under investigation: the historian would creatively *reproduce* or copy the pattern of those experiences in himself or herself. Dilthey's theory of knowledge had as its model the ideal of "objective" contemplation and pure description. Insofar as we see Dilthey seeking a kind of creative "empathy" with the experience of the past, we notice romantic strains in his thought (strains

---

19. We see here the relativism of the historicist thinker rebounding to undermine the objectivity of the historical method itself. See Iggers, *German Conception of History,* 186; and Baumer, *Modern European Thought,* 499–500. Both Iggers and Baumer refer to Troeltsch, "Die Krise des Historismus."

revealed in a much more extreme form in Ranke's dictum that the historian must "efface the self"), and insofar as we see Dilthey espousing the ideal of contemplation and pure description, we observe positivist strains in this thought. The positivist strain is the legacy of the Enlightenment, which identified objectivity with scientific detachment and description. The confrontation theory of truth, operative in the method and ideas of Dilthey and Weber, was also the basic epistemological model for the Enlightenment. This model was likewise a decisive factor in the romantic movement. We must now examine the horizon of modern European thought in light of the predominance of the confrontation theory of truth.

Romanticism was not merely a reaction against the Enlightenment, the antithesis to Enlightenment rationalism, but also, in one important and decisive respect, its dialectical twin, sharing with the Enlightenment many of the same basic assumptions. These assumptions revolved around the premise that the sole valid form of human knowing was scientific knowing, that reason was essentially, and indeed exclusively, scientific reason. Romanticism, then, for all of its complexity, variety, and ambiguity, tended to accept the basic ground rules laid out by the Enlightenment, accepted the Enlightenment's interpretation of rational and irrational, but rejected the Enlightenment's appeal to rationality, so understood, and became captivated instead by the "irrational," the "mysterious," the "mythic" as conveying deeper levels of truth.

Behind the Enlightenment's and romanticism's specific idea of scientific reason stood René Descartes's more generic interpretation of reason and objectivity. It was Descartes who—under the impact of the scientific revolution and the gnawing skepticism that grew out of the Reformation controversy over authority—formulated the modern presupposition that conceives of objectivity as a dispassionate otherworldly mind *confronting* an alien world.[20] The Cartesian juxtaposition of mental substance (*cogito*) and matter (extension) was a radical articulation of the fundamental, rigid bifurcation and confrontation of subject and object, and it presented a central problem for subsequent thinkers: how to bridge the gap between subject and object. The Cartesian split of subject and object, mind and matter, had repercussions beyond what may seem to be the "ivory tower" concerns of epistemology, for it entered into the self-interpretation of human beings in the modern world.

On the one hand, the affective, spontaneous, and subjective side of human existence tended to be repressed, since it was categorized as belonging to the

---

20. See Burtt, *Metaphysical Foundations*, chap. 4; and Richard Popkin, *The History of Scepticism from Erasmus to Descartes*, chaps. 9–10.

nonobjective realm. This intellectual and psychological stance clearly reinforced, and was reinforced by, the growing phenomenon of bourgeois man—soulless, efficient, alienated. The dualism of mind and matter was "resolved" by those who reduced the mental to the material sphere, starting with Hobbes. The project of the Enlightenment—to employ the scientific method that was so successful in understanding nature to the study of human beings—made the subject matter, human beings, into an object (in the Cartesian sense) through the dictates of the method of research.[21] E. A. Burtt has eloquently summarized this trend that declared the irrationality of "secondary qualities":

> The world that people had thought themselves living in—a world rich with colour and sound, redolent with fragrance, filled with gladness, love and beauty, speaking everywhere of purposive harmony and creative ideals—was crowded now into minute corners in the brains of scattered organic beings. The really important world outside was a world hard, cold, colourless, silent, and dead; a world of quantity, a world of mathematically computable motions in mechanical regularity. The world of qualities as immediately perceived by man became just a curious and quite minor effect in that infinite machine beyond.[22]

On the other hand, the stress on "objectivity" provoked the periodic irruption of movements that glorified the irrational, the romantic, and the abnormal and led to an exaltation of subjectivity in the form of an otherworldly mind (for example, the transcendental unity of apperception of Kant, the absolute subject of German idealism, or the transcendental ego of the earlier Husserl). As Whitehead has pointed out, one particularly compelling reason for the attraction to subjectivism was the "discrepancy between the materialist mechanism of science and the moral intuitions which are presupposed in the concrete affairs of life."[23]

Included in this reaction against modern objectivism was historicism. The Enlightenment's endorsement of scientific method as the paradigm of human knowing carried with it an appeal to nature "out there" as the norm and standard in the realm of values and meaning. Enlightenment thinkers hoped to

21. Matson, *Broken Image.*

22. Burtt, *Metaphysical Foundations,* 238–39. For the impact of "objectivism" on poetry, see Basil Willey, *The Seventeenth-Century Background: Studies in the Thought of the Age in Relation to Poetry and Religion.*

23. Hannah Arendt, *The Human Condition,* pt. 6; Thomas Prufer, "A Protreptic: What Is Philosophy?"; Mario Praz, *The Romantic Agony;* H. S. Hughes, *Consciousness and Society,* chap. 9; Masur, *Prophets of Yesterday,* chap. 3; Alfred North Whitehead, *Science and the Modern World,* 116.

derive values from the facts that modern empirical science ascertained, to derive *prescriptive* statements from the *descriptive* statements of science. In this task, they employed the analytical, reductionist, and genetic method, developed by Descartes, Galileo, and Newton, which they proclaimed as the essence of scientific investigation. The great model of scientific inquiry into the realm of human nature was John Locke, who, not without some confusion, applied Newton's "historical, plain method" to analyze human knowledge and human society by breaking down (reducing) these phenomena into their components and tracing their origins. The genetic element of this method, it should be noted, was more *logical* than historical, as is seen, for example, in Locke's discussion of a state of nature, basically ahistorical, prior to the formation of a social compact that occurred at no verifiable point in history. The whole project of perceiving values "out there" in nature, however, began to meet with serious resistance in the eighteenth century. We are reminded, for instance, of Hume's criticism of the fallacious jump between statements of *is* and statements of *ought* (later labeled by G. E. Moore as the "naturalistic fallacy") and Kant's distinction between *origin* and *validity*.[24]

It was therefore to history that intellectuals turned in an attempt to discover the meaning that the Enlightenment had not found as long as its gaze was fixed on the laws of nature. Certain strands of thought in the Enlightenment itself were fundamental to the nineteenth-century effort to establish philosophical, moral, and spiritual truth by an appeal to history. Hume and Montesquieu, for example, tried to find transcultural, rational historical laws, and D'Alembert and Voltaire sought a pattern of meaning in the extinction and resurrection of reason in history. History increasingly replaced nature as the norm and standard, for it was in the historical world that one could study the genesis of ideas and values, that is, confront not merely a world that is but also, and more important, a world permeated, indeed constituted, by ought. By the late eighteenth century, the genetic method was becoming a real historical method in the work of thinkers such as Herder.[25] Nevertheless, sim-

24. On the question of method, see Burtt, *Metaphysical Foundations;* and Cassirer, *Philosophy of the Enlightenment,* chaps. 1, 3. Locke, *Essay Concerning Human Understanding,* 1:27. On the "naturalistic fallacy," see David Hume, *Treatise of Human Nature,* 3.1.1; G. E. Moore, *Principia Ethica,* chaps. 1–4; and Immanuel Kant, *Critique of Pure Reason,* A84, B116.

25. On Burke's historicism, for example, see Rodney Kilcup, "Burke's Historicism." On the eighteenth-century background, see also Meinecke, *Historicism,* pt. 1; Antoni, *L'Historisme,* chaps. 2–6; Cassirer, *Philosophy of the Enlightenment,* chap. 5; and Peter Gay, *The Enlightenment: An Interpretation,* vol. 2, *The Science of Freedom,* 368–96. Rodney Kilcup, introduction to *The History of England,* by David Hume; Robert Shackleton, *Montesquieu:*

ply recording the historical origins of ideas and values cannot in itself validate or invalidate those ideas and values, and, in entertaining such an aspiration, "historicism" committed the "genetic fallacy." It left in its train the specters of relativism and nihilism.

The resulting relativism and skepticism, we should recall, were in large part a legacy of Descartes, whose formulation of the confrontation theory of truth established the ground rules for much of intellectual debate.[26] Still, the problems posed by the epistemological and metaphysical assumptions of Descartes had their historical background in an older tradition, the Scotist, Ockhamist, and Thomist schools of medieval philosophy. The epistemological horizon of modern culture has its roots in the medieval period, at least as far back as the conceptualism and essentialism propounded by John Duns Scotus in the High Middle Ages and its influence on later medieval philosophy and Renaissance Scholasticism, which, in turn, set the background from which modern philosophy emerged.[27]

European history, consequently, for all its immense variations, shifts, and transformations over the past six hundred years, reveals a startling unity if we examine it in light of the persistence of the decisive epistemological assumption that we have called the "confrontation theory of truth." Much of European intellectual culture in the past few centuries has been devoted to exploring the

---

A Critical Biography; Thomas L. Pangle, *Montesquieu's Philosophy of Liberalism;* J. H. Brumfitt, *Voltaire, Historian;* Löwith, *Meaning in History,* chap. 5; Voegelin, *From Enlightenment to Revolution,* chap. 1. See Berlin, *Vico and Herder,* 145–216.

26. This is not to say that Descartes caused the ideas of subsequent thinkers, or that later thinkers were Cartesians at heart, but is to say that Descartes formulated many of the compelling assumptions that, to a great degree, conditioned, limited, and restricted the range of relevant answers for later thinkers.

27. Scotus made the act of understanding *seeing* a nexus between *concepts;* he posited concepts first, then the apprehension of the nexus between concepts (see *Verbum,* 38–39; Scotus, *Philosophical Writings,* 103–39; Allan Wolter, *The Transcendentals and Their Function in the Metaphysics of Duns Scotus;* and John K. Ryan and Bernardine M. Bonansea, eds., *John Duns Scotus, 1265–1965*). According to Etienne Gilson, the "essentialist" philosophy of the Renaissance Scholastic F. Suarez tended to reduce being to essence even more than that of Scotus (*Being and Some Philosophers,* 102–3). For the theory of knowledge of Suarez, see Francisco L. Peccorini, "Knowledge of the Singular: Aquinas, Suarez, and Recent Interpreters." Suarez influenced Wolff whose School of Pure Reason Kant critiqued (see Frederick Copleston, *A History of Philosophy,* 3.1:128–29, 6.1:128–29). Lonergan maintains that Kant's *Critique of Pure Reason* is, in effect, a critique of the human mind as conceived by Scotus (*Verbum,* 38–38 n. 126). A wide-ranging survey of "essentialism" is given in Gilson, *Being and Some Philosophers,* 84–153; and Löwith, *Nature, History, and Existentialism,* 30–50.

possibilities, ramifications, and implications of this assumption that knowing is essentially taking a look at something "out there." In this process, there has been a recurrent and increasing tendency toward skepticism.

In the Late Middle Ages, for instance, we witness, with respect to the power of speculative reason, the skepticism of the nominalist movement arising to attack the speculative metaphysics of Scotus, who posited an unconscious look at the relations among concepts as the source of understanding.[28] Later we observe British empiricism, reaching its logical culmination in Hume's skepticism, opposing the continental rationalism of Descartes, Spinoza, Malebranche, and Leibniz, whose approach to metaphysics was similar to that of Scotus. Both empiricism and rationalism, it should be emphasized, shared the wider horizon delineated by the confrontation theory of truth. Continental rationalism, which asserted an intellectual intuition of objects, was further assaulted by Kant's devastating critique. According to Kant, the only intuition, the only immediate perception of objects, was sensible intuition, and, because human knowledge of objects required understanding and judgment as well as sensible intuition, human knowledge was thereby mediate and limited to appearances, limited, that is, to the ways in which the human mind organized the data of experience.[29] There was no immediate intellectual apprehension of "things in themselves."

The growing realization that there was no intellectual perception that could guarantee the validity and objectivity of knowledge did not, as one might suspect, lead to the demise of the confrontation theory of truth as a fundamental factor in the horizon of recent Western culture. In the nineteenth century, it still largely determined the meaning of the terms *reality, truth,* and *objectivity.* Positivism, for example, took as reality what could actually be perceived, that is, contents of sensations. Positivism, however, did not genuinely have what can be considered a philosophically articulated theory of knowledge. Instead, for philosophy it substituted a profession of "faith," which amounted

28. William of Ockham, *Philosophical Writings,* 3–48; Ernest A. Moody, *The Logic of William of Ockham;* Philotheus Boehner, *Collected Articles on Ockham;* Julius R. Weinberg, *A Short History of Medieval Philosophy,* chaps. 11–12; Gordon Leff, *The Dissolution of the Medieval Outlook: An Essay on the Intellectual and Spiritual Change in the Fourteenth Century,* chap. 2; John Herman Randall Jr., *The Career of Philosophy,* 1:31–43; Copleston, *A History of Philosophy,* 3.1:1–34, 164.

29. "Objects are *given* to us by means of sensibility, and it alone yields us intuitions; they are through the understanding, and from understanding arises *concepts*" (compare with Scotus, n. 27 above) (Kant, *Critique of Pure Reason,* A19, B33); judgment is mediate knowledge of objects (A69, B93); human knowledge is of phenomena (B310).

to a dogmatic belief in scientific knowing (rather narrowly defined) as the sole kind of knowing.[30] Not surprisingly, it could substantiate this posture neither scientifically nor philosophically.

It is significant to note that positivism attempted to supply science with meaning in terms of a philosophy of history (Comte's "three stages" of history, culminating in the "age of science"). The positivist "philosophy" of history was hardly scientific, in any rigorous sense, or grounded in what could legitimately pass as philosophy. Indeed, it has been suggested that it is a variety of gnostic theorizing on the essence of history. Akin to the positivist construction of history was the much more sophisticated brand of speculative gnosis in German idealism. Whatever the genuine merits and insights of German idealism in the sphere of philosophy, in claiming to *possess* a kind of knowledge of which philosophy, the love of wisdom, is always *in search,* it went beyond the limits of philosophy. To counteract the gap between subject and object, German idealism proclaimed a philosophy of identity: behind the veil of appearance the object was, in fact, the subject. Alienation and estrangement of subject and object were interpreted as necessary moments in the eternal self-making of the Absolute, an alienation overcome in absolute knowledge, when self-consciousness becomes aware of itself.[31]

In spite of the challenge to the confrontation theory of truth, this theory remained, and still remains, a potent factor in Western culture, because the notion that human knowing had to be like seeing objects continued to hold sway. In light of the disjunction that either there is such picturelike knowing or there is no objective knowing at all, the manifold of alternatives taken in nineteenth- and twentieth-century intellectual history becomes more intelligible. If there is no picturelike knowing, then there is opened up the Pandora's box of nihilism, irrational philosophies of life, varieties of romanticism, skepticism, and the reduction of science to mere instrumentality, to a chopping up of experience to serve pragmatic ends; or the attempt is made to salvage objectiv-

---

30. Habermas, *Knowledge and Human Interests*, 67.

31. On positivist appeals to the philosophy of history, see ibid., 71. On attempts to define the "essence" of history, see Voegelin, *New Science of Politics*, 111–13, passim; and Voegelin, *Modernity without Restraint*, 185–87. See also the frequent references to "neognostic" sentiments and ideas in modern European intellectual history in Heer, *Intellectual History of Europe*. For a survey of ancient gnosticism, see Hans Jonas, *The Gnostic Religion*. On speculative gnosis in German idealism, see Voegelin, *New Science of Politics*; Voegelin, *Science, Politics, and Gnosticism*, 40–44, 67–80, 105–6; Voegelin, *Modernity without Restraint*, 271–74, 286–92, 308; Jürgen Habermas, *Theory and Practice*, 214–16; and Habermas, *Knowledge and Human Interests*, 7–24. Hegel, *The Phenomenology of Mind*, 789ff.

ity by a dogmatic faith in positive science that is restricted to *perceptual observable* "facts"—a faith appealing to an esoteric philosophy of history to guarantee the meaning of science; or a *superhuman* knowledge is sought through gnostic revelation, as in German idealism.

In an effort to escape from the bog of epistemological uncertainty and confusion (and to step into the vacuum brought about by a vigorous assault on Christianity and classicist culture), positivism, romanticism, the dazzling systems of German idealism, and, on a practical level, neognostic revolutionary movements of the Right and Left all sought meaning in the process of history. Yet, history as the court of appeal, so it seems, has not provided the meaning and order so earnestly sought, but, rather, as Dilthey feared, has decreed and legitimated an "anarchy of convictions." In the twentieth century, severe doubt was cast on the possibility of attaining superhuman gnosis, the shadow of historical relativism hovered over culture and mores, and the fact of totalitarianism apparently put some damper on revolutionary ardor and discredited apocalyptic expectations among intellectuals in the Western world. Skepticism once again became a powerful torrent in Western culture, threatening to sweep away the possibility of rational insight and conviction.[32]

By the twentieth century, intellectuals tended to deny strenuously that there is such an "intellectual look" and struggled mightily to come to grips with the seemingly inescapable conclusion that there is no objectivity at all, either cognitional, moral, or spiritual.[33] The attempt to salvage rationality by placing it within the restricted field of "scientific" determination of "facts" does not, as we have seen in the case of Weber, reestablish moral objectivity. It is within this intellectual crisis brought about by epistemological assumptions that we must place the specific problems created by awareness of human historicity. Hence, we witness the crisis of historicism in the twentieth and twenty-first centuries.

We can conclude that the cultural crisis of the twentieth and twenty-first centuries, of which the crisis of historicism is a part, is not a rare flower blossoming forth strangely and inexplicably out of the garden of seventeenth-, eighteenth-, and nineteenth-centuries lofty hopes in human reason, but is a flower nourished in that very soil of European thought. It is an end point, a logical culmination, perhaps even a *reductio ad absurdum,* of the pervasive as-

---

32. For a general discussion, see Baumer, *Modern European Thought;* Masur, *Prophets of Yesterday;* H. S. Hughes, *Consciousness and Society;* and W. Warren Wagar, *World Views: A Study in Comparative History.*

33. See, for example, the searching analysis of Krutch, *Modern Temper.*

sumptions dominating and defining the modern intellectual horizon, and indeed the late medieval horizon.[34]

Historicity

Still, to affirm the fact of the radically historical nature of human existence need not in itself lead to a position of historical relativism, if the framework for *interpreting* that fact is significantly different from that which we have been considering. Beginning in the early decades of the twentieth century and gaining momentum after World War II, there has been a challenge to the basic intellectual assumptions of modern culture far-reaching enough to constitute a major and radical horizon shift in twentieth-century intellectual history. This intellectual movement, building on the foundation of such isolated nineteenth-century thinkers as Kierkegaard and Nietzsche, marks a decided break with the paradigm or horizon of the confrontation theory of truth.

This new intellectual horizon is defined by a sense of questioning and spirit of exploration held by thinkers in a wide range of fields, including philosophy of science, phenomenology, history of religions, existentialist philosophy, hermeneutics, critical social theory, classics, and theology. It involves thinkers such as Werner Heisenberg, Michael Polanyi, Edmund Husserl, Mircea Eliade, Martin Heidegger, Hans Georg Gadamer, Jürgen Habermas, Eric Voegelin, and Bernard Lonergan. Although these intellectuals work in different fields and may be interpreted as belonging to different "schools" of philosophy, their most significant characteristic, and what has not received adequate notice, is what they have in common, namely, their concern with those dimensions of subjectivity that they take to be the core of objectivity itself. Their diverse approaches and perspectives complement one another and highlight various aspects of the relation between subjectivity and objectivity. I intend to discuss briefly these figures and the implications of their approach for the interpretation of human historicity.

In the twentieth century, there was a revolution within the seemingly impregnable citadel of Cartesian objectivity, natural science. Werner Heisenberg, one of the pioneers of quantum mechanics, has argued that what the scientist observes is not nature in itself but nature exposed to our questioning, that the

34. This argument deals exclusively on the level of ideas. It is not intended to deny the significant impact of economic, social, and political factors on the cultural crisis of the twentieth century.

questioning activity of the scientist must be brought into our picture of the world, and that the world of physics therefore cannot be conceived as a world separate from ourselves. Michael Polanyi has carried this assault on the old Cartesian notion of a detached observer further by stressing the personal elements of responsibility, commitment, and passion that go to the very heart of scientific objectivity. Scientific knowledge is rooted in a process of inquiry and discovery, and, according to Polanyi, "from the first intimation of a hidden problem and throughout its pursuit to the point of its solution, the process of discovery is guided by personal vision and sustained by a personal conviction."[35]

If we follow Heisenberg in concentrating on the questioning activity of the scientist and Polanyi in emphasizing the personal process of scientific inquiry, we also focus on the dynamism behind the transformation of scientific ideas: we focus on the scientist revising concepts, postulates, axioms, and methods when existing theories, procedures, and modes of analysis cannot handle scientific data and results of experimentation satisfactorily. Here we likewise encounter an especially important element of the *historicity* of scientific thought. In its fullest scope, the historicity of scientific thought means that scientific formulations have historical conditions, that these formulations are framed within the context of partially unacknowledged intellectual assumptions, and that the formulations are not final and definitive. Whether the historicity of scientific knowledge necessarily entails the relativity of scientific truth clearly emerges, then, as a fundamental and crucial issue. The approach of Polanyi is unmistakable in denying validity to the claims of historical relativism. Personal knowledge, Polanyi insists, is a process of self-transcendence, requiring personal submission to universal intellectual standards, standards that make sense only by a commitment to them, by acknowledging their jurisdiction. The scientist, in his or her passionate, personal commitment to truth, strives to attain an understanding that transcends his or her own whim and fancy, and the criterion of success in this venture is precisely faithfulness in the pursuit of truth itself, with its personal ingredients of devotion, attentiveness, and creative insight. Thus, personal knowledge must be totally separated from subjectivism in the pejorative sense with its relativist implications.[36]

35. Heisenberg, *Physics and Philosophy: The Revolution in Modern Science;* Polanyi, *Personal Knowledge,* 301.

36. Polanyi, *Personal Knowledge,* 300–303. When objectivity is not interpreted as rooted in the personal dimensions of scientific knowing, in the questioning activity of the scientist, but is interpreted principally in terms of logical rigor, concepts, or observable facts,

In large measure the separation of historicity and historicism in contemporary intellectual life can be attributed to the influence of Edmund Husserl. Nevertheless, Husserl did not always perceive the import of his ideas, particularly in the domain of history, and he frequently disagreed vehemently with the direction taken by such followers as Heidegger. Husserl, the founder of phenomenology, placed beside the modern scientific method of investigating the data of sense a rigorous method for studying the data of consciousness without explaining consciousness away or reducing it to drives, motives, or unconscious forces, a method that has found widespread application in social science, history of religion, psychology, and philosophy.[37]

One of the decisive breakthroughs by Husserl in his treatment of subjectivity was his notion of "horizon." A horizon comprises two "poles," one consisting of acts of consciousness with their orientation and direction, and the other composed of what is intended by those conscious acts. Furthermore, acts of consciousness have a certain priority insofar as the questions, concerns, interests, and orientations of the "subjective" pole of a horizon specify and delimit the objects, actual and possible, in the "objective" pole. Hence, a horizon is defined more by the range of relevant and meaningful questions than by answers; answers to questions that are meaningless, insignificant, or not worthwhile from within the perspective of a given horizon are, in fact, excluded from the horizon, and thereby from the world of that horizon. The upshot, for Husserl, is that the "world" is not *simply given* in advance. It is not an object "out there" confronting a subject "in here," but is rather a world for a subject. What we interpret to be the "world"—the objective pole of our horizon—is constituted, though not created out of nothing, by the subjective pole of our horizon. Husserl viewed his own work as clearing a radical path for further inquiry. He claimed he could see "the infinite open country of the true

---

then, indeed, a book such as Thomas S. Kuhn's *Structure of Scientific Revolutions* may seem to point to conventionalism and relativism. Kuhn argues for the occurrence of revolutions in scientific thought—the replacement of one conceptual and instrumental framework, or paradigm, by another framework. For the debate surrounding the book, see Imre Lakatos and Alan Musgrave, eds., *Criticism and the Growth of Knowledge*.

37. In social science, see Alfred Schütz, *Collected Papers* and *The Phenomenology of the Social World;* and Peter Berger and Thomas Luckmann, *The Social Construction of Reality: A Treatise in the Sociology of Knowledge.* In religion, see Gerhardus van der Leeuw, *Religion in Essence and Manifestation: A Study in Phenomenology;* and Mircea Eliade, *Patterns in Comparative Religion, The Sacred and the Profane,* and *Cosmos and History.* In psychology, see Ludwig Binswanger, *Being-in-the-World: Selected Papers of Ludwig Binswanger;* and Rollo May, *Love and Will.* In philosophy, see the works of Martin Heidegger, Jean-Paul Sartre, Maurice Merleau-Ponty, and Paul Ricoeur.

philosophy, the 'promised land,'" but he himself would never set foot on that land.[38]

One area where the method of phenomenology has been fruitfully employed is in the terrain of religious symbols, and among its advocates, though not without some ambiguity, is the historian of religion, Mircea Eliade. Eliade maintains, contrary to much of Enlightenment opinion, that more affective and symbolic modes of thinking—for example, the myths of archaic societies—can be valid and compelling forms of human understanding in their own right. He thus breaks with conventional presuppositions that either debunk myth as fable and primitive science or applaud it as a supreme manifestation of the irrational. Instead, Eliade regards myth as a symbolic form of expression and understanding, legitimate within its own sphere, and uniquely suited to explore and come to grips with the boundary conditions of existence (such as origins and death) that strain the capacity of more conceptual thinking in the face of mystery. According to Eliade, if we enter the horizon of *homo religiosus,* that is, if we get caught up in the *problems* and *questions* that define the religious horizon, then we must encounter the boundary situations of human existence and the recurrent, symbolic responses to these ultimate and mysterious situations, namely, the archetypal images and symbols. The study of the history of religions, consequently, discloses both diversity and change in religious life as well as the continuity of questions and archetypes. In other words, with reference to religious life, it seems to argue for historicity but not historical relativism.[39]

"Husserl," claims Quentin Lauer, "saw, however vaguely, that transcendental phenomenology would ultimately be viable only in a historical framework." It was Martin Heidegger, at one time a student of Husserl, who, in an ambitious, original, and penetrating manner, broadened the perspective of Husserl's "transcendental" phenomenology to include explicitly the dimen-

---

38. Husserl, *Ideas: General Introduction to Pure Phenomenology,* 11, 21.

39. On continuity and change, see Mircea Eliade, *Images and Symbols,* 33–37. Eliade, as an interpreter has pointed out, complements his phenomenological approach with a structuralist method, probably motivated by an ontology rooted in Indian philosophy. See Guilford Dudley, *Religion on Trial: Mircea Eliade and His Critics.* The methods of phenomenology and structuralism parallel respectively time and the timeless, becoming and being. The emphasis of Eliade, however, is on the timeless and being. For this reason, Eliade and Husserl are the two figures in this discussion who are least sympathetic to the notion of historicity. Yet, as Husserl's method opened paths of inquiry into historicity, so, in the judgment of this author, Eliade's pioneering phenomenological-structural method, in spite of its ambiguities and weaknesses, suggests the distinct possibility of a study of religion that gives due weight to its historicity without succumbing to historical relativism.

sion of history. Heidegger, in his "hermeneutical" phenomenology, took the preliminary steps toward a possible rejuvenation of higher intellectual culture through uncovering its existential foundations. He sought to explicate the existential roots of philosophy and ethics, of human understanding and human living, by divorcing himself completely from the Cartesian assumption of an alienation of subject and world. We are not, for Heidegger, self-contained transcendental subjects observing an alien world; we *ex-ist,* stand outside ourselves, immersed in the body and in the world. We do not exist without a world, and to speak of a world-in-itself "out there" is profoundly misleading. Our being is being-in-the-world—not as water "being" in a glass, as one "thing" being "in" another "thing" (as might be suggested by the spatial metaphor), but as a conscious *dwelling* in the world, even as we contemplate it and differentiate ourselves from it.[40]

Nevertheless, our dwelling in the world can be authentic or inauthentic. We are inauthentic when we constrict our existence to that of a thing among other things in a "world" composed of things. We are authentic when our stream of consciousness, existential stance, or basic orientation—that which defines our horizon—is one of "care" *(Sorge),* and "care" means attending to, taking up, heeding the call of the most basic and most concrete of *questions:* what does it mean to be?—the question of Being. This is the essence of humanity, fidelity to the very question of what it means to be, openness to Being. A basic norm therefore inheres in the project of human existence itself and shatters the foundations of any thoroughgoing relativist viewpoint. Nonetheless, humans are radically temporal creatures since their personal existence is not simply given like that of a substance or thing, nor is it created in an absolute, infinite freedom. It is rather constituted by finite and limited decisions as a constant projecting into the future from the standpoint of the present conditioned by the past. Heidegger thus affirmed historicity as the very core and basis of human existence, while, at the same time, acknowledging the presence of a norm and a standard at that core itself.[41]

40. Lauer, introduction to *Phenomenology and the Crisis of Philosophy,* by Husserl, 56. Martin Heidegger, *Being and Time,* 79–80; see also William Luijpen, *Existential Phenomenology,* 54–83; and Calvin O. Shrag, *Experience and Being: Prolegomena to a Future Ontology,* 257–69.

41. On inauthenticity, see Heidegger, *Being and Time,* 67ff, 167, 219ff. On the being question, see ibid., 29. On the being question as the essence of humanity, see Heidegger, "Letter on Humanism," 209. For an explicit attack on historicism, see Heidegger, *Being and Time,* 448. For a brief discussion of the ambivalence toward historicism in some of the works of the "later Heidegger," see Fackenheim, *Metaphysics and Historicity,* 77–79 n.

Hans Georg Gadamer, a cardinal figure in the "hermeneutical school," has applied Heidegger's idea of historicity to the temporal structure of communal existence, exploiting the notion of Heidegger that human being is being-in-the-world. For the world in which one dwells is a communal world, not a private world. Thus, in the project of human living, one anticipates the future not solely from the context of one's own past experience but also, and in a decisive way, from the perspective of the past of one's community. Gadamer forcefully rejects the Cartesian and Enlightenment model of tradition as an object to be confronted and thoroughly critiqued.[42] Tradition, for him, is a society's living, ongoing interpretation of its past, a process of identity and difference, continuity and innovation. It is a process, furthermore, operating, for the most part, on the level of sentiments, attitudes, images, and commonsense insights communicated through the myriad insinuations of daily living. The richness of tradition, then, can never be fully conceptualized, and human thought can never attain a basis of completely acknowledged presuppositions. Human knowledge is fundamentally horizon-bound. We cannot climb to a standpoint outside of history to judge history, we cannot critique tradition *as such,* and we cannot achieve a totally alien distance from a "past-in-itself."

This, of course, is not to say that we must remain passive subjects upon which the force of tradition impinges through acculturation, socialization, and education. Indeed, Gadamer argues, one appropriates tradition in terms of an active dialogue with it. And it is precisely dialogue that also becomes the model of genuine historical understanding. The historian does not, any more than the member of society appropriating tradition, *confront* a past-in-itself. He or she *encounters* the past as a text to be understood: in order to understand the past, the historian must enter into its horizon, and to enter its horizon he or she must understand *the questions* that constituted it. Yet, according to Gadamer, entry and understanding hinge not on the extinguishing of the horizon of the interpreter, as Dilthey, for example, alleged, but, rather, depend upon the wealth, depth, and expansiveness of the horizon of the interpreter—that is, on his or her capacity to ask questions. In Gadamer's words, "to understand a question means to ask it." Consequently, the condition of the possibility of historical understanding is getting caught up in the question, and by getting caught up in the question one eliminates neither the horizon of the

---

44; Fackenheim, *The God Within,* 227–28; and Karl Löwith, *Martin Heidegger and European Nihilism.* On historicity, see Heidegger, *Being and Time,* 370ff, 428.

42. Gadamer, *Truth and Method,* 241–45; see also Gadamer, *Philosophical Hermeneutics;* Palmer, *Hermeneutics,* 62–217; and Linge, "Historicity and Hermeneutic," pt. 2.

past nor the horizon of the present. One engages in a *fusion* of horizons, a fusion that places in questioning both the horizon of the past and that of the present.[43] In short, the standard is neither the past nor the present but the stance defined by the activity and logic of questioning. The questioning of the interpreter implies *distance* from the past and *continuity*, and in this we see the fundamental hallmark of tradition. Gadamer, therefore, perceives in the very fact that we are historically bound creatures the fact that we also are bound to the norms, standards, logic, and openness of questioning.

Jürgen Habermas, formerly of the Frankfurt Institute for Social Research and influenced by Gadamer's hermeneutical philosophy, has likewise departed from the Enlightenment ideal of a detached social observer confronting the social world as an alien object, but he allows for the project of social critique by replacing the paradigm of a confrontational relation between social critic and society, subject and object, with that of a dialectical relationship. The dialectical relationship is this: human beings collectively acting in history create, through both pragmatic control of material conditions and cultural interaction, the objective historical situation (language, institutions, artworks), and, at the same time, the objective situation is the framework for the historical action of human beings.[44] The social scientist cannot rise above the dialectical relationship as a detached observer. He or she is deeply implicated in the social matrix, for the social scientist either affirms it implicitly by treating the objective historical situation as given human reality or negates it by critique.

Habermas takes to task positivist social science and its "value-neutral" idea of objectivity for making its basis a *descriptive* analysis of what is simply "given"—the phenomena of a given society, a given objective historical situation. Such a descriptive social science, however, cannot, in Habermas's judgment, attain a truly theoretical, and therefore critical, stance: it cannot determine whether and to what extent the social facts are products of bias, distorted understanding, and irrationality; it cannot unmask false consciousness (ideology, in the Marxian sense); it cannot escape legitimating by its merely descriptive approach the given (and possibly irrational) social order. Still, according

43. On dialogue as the model of hermeneutic, see Gadamer, *Truth and Method*, 245–74; on questioning as decisive, 338; on "fusion of horizons," 273ff, 337.

44. For a history of the Frankfurt Institute, see Martin Jay, *The Dialectical Imagination: A History of the Frankfurt School and the Institute of Social Research, 1923–1950*; on the interpenetration of Gadamer's hermeneutics and the Frankfurt School's critical theory, see Gerard Radnitzky, *Schools of Metascience*, 193–351. On historical dialectic, see Habermas, *Knowledge and Human Interests*, 191–97 and passim.

to Habermas, another interpretation of objectivity is possible, one that views objectivity as rooted in the norms of the "emancipatory interest," the orientation that negates, critiques, and *questions* any given horizon, social order, or historical circumstance to uncover bias, narrow prejudice, and ideological rationalization. The emancipatory interest aims at restoring a balance to the dialectical pattern of history when the emphasis is on human beings as the *products* of history, and it thereby seeks to promote more responsible direction of human history by human beings as *producers*. The emancipatory interest is the normative drive conditioned, but not determined, by historical situations.[45]

Eric Voegelin, a philosopher and historian of symbols, has discerned an emphasis in Greek intellectual culture, which crystallized in the philosophy of Plato and Aristotle, that was similar, if not identical, to Polanyi's "personal knowledge," Heidegger's "care," Gadamer's "open horizon of the question," and Habermas's "critique." These Greeks were preoccupied with the *act of questioning,* with an orientation of consciousness and existence defined by the state of questioning unrest, a spontaneous wonder and passionate search for the true and the good. This, for Voegelin, was the life of reason in the classical sense, with quite pronounced moral, affective, and religious dimensions.

The font of cognitive, moral, and spiritual objectivity, the norm and measure, was the *performance* of such a person as Socrates, who by embodying the love of wisdom was a genuine *philosopher,* faithful in the quest of the true and the good. The unrestricted openness of the lover of wisdom gained entrance to the common world of intelligibility and reality and left behind, however precariously, the private world of bias and "idiocy" (the *idios kosmos* of "subjective opinion"). The philosopher, moreover, was in a state midway between knowledge and ignorance, since to ask a question presupposes both insight—the sense of the question—and ignorance. For this reason, Voegelin sees the philosopher as representative of humanity in the drama of history, humanity essentially ignorant of both the full scope of the drama and its role

---

45. For critique of positivism, see Habermas, *Knowledge and Human Interests,* chaps. 4, 8, and 11; Habermas, *Toward a Rational Society: Student Protests, Science, and Politics;* see also Albrecht Wellmer, *Critical Theory of Society;* Thomas McCarthy, *The Critical Theory of Jürgen Habermas.* On the "emancipatory interest," see Habermas, *Knowledge and Human Interests,* 184–86, 197–98, 211, 212, 209, 284–85. For the Gadamer-Habermas debate over the limits of critique of tradition, see Gadamer, "On the Scope and Function of Hermeneutical Reflection," chap. 2 in *Philosophical Hermeneutics;* Habermas, "Summation and Response"; and Theodore Kisiel, "Ideology Critique and Phenomenology: The Current Debate in German Philosophy."

in that drama, hence historically finite, yet cognizant that there are a drama and a role about which to inquire, hence transcending a relativist viewpoint, which would deny that there are a drama and a role defining what it means to be human.[46]

To consider a final example illustrating this trend: Bernard Lonergan— philosopher, methodologist, and theologian—has located the transcultural basis of culture in an "intelligent subjectivity." This "intelligent subjectivity" encompasses the full range of human understanding from science to myth and contains its own immanent norms, demands, and imperatives, fidelity to which, Lonergan maintains, is the source and real meaning of objectivity. Arguing that there is an identity in all historical horizons, Lonergan suggests that we probe beneath the ideas, attitudes, sentiments, judgments, and actions of a period and focus on the personal acts of meaning and decision that constitute its horizon. If we shift attention from the "objective" to the "subjective" pole of historical horizons, we can penetrate to a basic concern, orientation, interest, or existential stance. Lonergan identifies this basic concern with the "desire to know" (the drive to understand reality) that underlies the structure of knowing and the "intention to bring about the good" (the demand of the moral ought) that underlies the structure of moral action in human living. The desire to know and the intention of the good are two elements of a single basic orientation of "intelligent subjectivity," since knowing is a value chosen and moral action is informed by understanding.[47]

It is Lonergan's contention that cognitional objectivity properly understood is nothing less than fidelity to the desire to know. In his view, objectivity does not mean a correct look at something "out there," whether concepts, essences, or individual things. For Lonergan, as for Polanyi, it means faithful exercise

---

46. On the classical view of reason, see Eric Voegelin, *Anamnesis,* chap. 6; Voegelin, *Published Essays, 1966–1985,* chap. 10. In *Order and History,* 3:300, and *New Science of Politics,* 64–65 (in *Modernity without Restraint,* 138–39), Voegelin refers to Aristotle's discussion of the "mature man" (*spoudaios*) as the norm and measure. See Aristotle, *Nicomachean Ethics* 3.4.1113a29–35. On the "private world," see Voegelin, *Order and History,* 2:229–39. Voegelin refers to the fragment of Heraclitus: "Those who are awake have a world one and common, but those who are asleep each turn aside into their private worlds" (B89). On the drama of history, see Voegelin, *Order and History,* 1:1–3, 4:183–92, 218–38. Voegelin mentions Plato's symbol of the metaxy, the "in-between" tension of human existence, in the *Symposium,* 202A–203A. A standard English edition of Plato is *The Collected Dialogues of Plato Including the Letters.*

47. *Insight,* 372–73, 584, 622ff, 636ff, 645–46, 681; *Method in Theology,* 34ff, 38, 94, 122, 340; *Second Collection,* 82–84.

of one's own intelligence and reasonableness. In this sense, then, objectivity is the fruit of *authentic* subjectivity.[48] The quality of one's objectivity is contingent upon the quality of one's attention, insight, and discrimination in judgment. Similarly, moral objectivity is fidelity to the intention of the good. Moral objectivity is not a matter of accurate perception of a system of values "out there," but is faithfulness to one's sense of responsibility.[49] Statements about values are the formulations of moral insights. Hence, moral understanding derives not from a look at a system of values but, rather, from insights achieved through the concern, questioning, and involvement of moral agents.

The orientation that Lonergan talks about is an existential stance, a way of living, that constitutes what can be called a "basic horizon" of operations. These operations include acts of questioning, grasping insights, judging, apprehending values, deliberating, and deciding—the operations of the structures of knowing and moral living. Normativeness arises from the fundamental orientation, concern, and direction of basic horizon; that is to say, norms are immanent in the desire to know and the intention of the good. Adherence to the norms of basic horizon generates the structure of knowing and of moral action, whereas violation of the norms makes the structures inoperative or only partially operative. The basic horizon of operations is, therefore, the identity in all different historical horizons, for unless there were a modicum of intelligence and responsibility at work, no human society could be created or perpetuated. To be inattentive, unintelligent, unreasonable, and irresponsible is to invite decay, corruption, breakdown, disaster, and collapse. Thus, Lonergan argues that following the norms of basic horizon is the source of progress in history and that violating those norms is the cause of decline in history.[50]

From the perspective of Lonergan's philosophy of history and human understanding, the historian does not confront a totally alien horizon in his investigation. Rather, as Gadamer has suggested, the historian is engaged in a

48. On critique of the confrontation theory of truth and objectivity, see *Method in Theology,* 262–63; and *Insight,* 11–15, 22, 111–12, 260–61, 276–78, 344–45, 396–97, 410–12, 431, 437–41, 448–50, 519–20, 603–8, 657–58, 669. On intelligent and rational objectivity, see *Insight,* 404, 408; and *Method in Theology,* 35, 263. On objectivity as genuine subjectivity, see *Method in Theology,* 265.

49. *Method in Theology,* 35; *Second Collection,* 83.

50. On the operations of basic horizon, see *Method in Theology,* 7. On the intentionality of basic horizon, see ibid., 18; and *Insight,* 404–5. On progress and decline, see *Insight,* 6–8, 259–60.

fusion of horizons.[51] When the historian is performing intelligently and reasonably, he or she is operating within basic horizon. Historiography, then, although it is always undertaken from the standpoint of one relative horizon, necessarily is an activity within basic horizon. Because it is such an activity, it places in question every determinate historical horizon, including the historian's. Basic horizon, consequently, is not any particular concrete historical horizon. As an existential stance committed to questioning, understanding intelligently, judging reasonably, evaluating, deliberating, deciding, and acting responsibly, it is the identity in historical horizons. Still, it is, at the same time, a fundamental and inexhaustible source of difference in historical horizons. Basic horizon is essentially defined, bounded, limited by the range of the pure unrestricted question; it extends as far as does human questioning, questioning that regards both what is and what ought to be. Therefore, no determinate horizon can be equated with basic horizon: no determinate horizon can answer all the questions, no determinate horizon can ask all the questions, and no determinate society can perfectly realize the good. Thus, we notice here, as with the other thinkers discussed in this section, the conclusion that historicity does not entail historicism.

In all these thinkers we can perceive a concern with common problems, problems that revolve around a central assumption as their nucleus. The assumption, to be sure, is articulated and held with varying degrees of intensity, emphasis, and exactness.[52] Indeed, it has been implied in this study that Lonergan has formulated the core epistemological assumption most clearly.[53]

---

51. *Method in Theology,* 274.

52. Convergence on common problems, of course, does not preclude disagreement, as we have seen with the Gadamer-Habermas debate, n. 45 above. Neither Lonergan nor Polanyi, with their stress on personal commitment to the desire to know, would agree with Habermas's restriction of the "scientific interest" to pragmatic control. For criticism of Habermas on this score, see Radnitzky, *Contemporary Schools of Metascience,* 206. To cite a third example, Voegelin, *New Science of Politics,* 64 (in *Modernity without Restraint,* 138–39), and Habermas, *Knowledge and Human Interests,* app., offer two differing interpretations of Greek *theoria.* Furthermore, the extent to which many of these thinkers have broken completely from Cartesian assumptions can be questioned. Husserl's refusal to consider the metaphysical status of the world, for instance, may harbor residues of a Cartesian notion of a self-contained *cogito* (see Luijpen, *Existential Phenomenology,* 112–17). And Heidegger's understanding of scientific objectivity as well as Gadamer's interpretation of method may possibly be challenged as too Cartesian by Polanyi's and Lonergan's interpretations of science and method (Heidegger, in *Being and Time,* 413–14, secs. 14–24; Gadamer, *Truth and Method,* 417; Lonergan, *Method in Theology,* 1–6, 262–65; *Insight,* 67–68).

53. See, in particular, Chapter 1; Chapter 7, pp. 142–47, 159–68, 177–79; Chapter 10, pp. 223–24; and Chapter 11, pp. 238–47, 266–70.

This core assumption denies a fundamental opposition between subjectivity, rightly understood, and objectivity: it holds that subjectivity can no longer be placed exclusively in the realm of the irrational and the vital, and it insists that one can attain a full, comprehensive, and insightful view of cognitional, moral, and spiritual objectivity only by a discriminating analysis of their roots in structures of interiority. It urges, in short, contemporary culture in its search for norms and standards to shift attention from the *products* of thought to the *process* of thinking.

From this assumption follows a particular interpretation of historicity. If the project of questioning is taken as being the foundation and meaning of objectivity, and not a set of answers or even a set of formulated questions, then the differences among historical horizons do not in themselves imply relativism. Extreme relativism (emphasis on only the difference in human world-views) denies human historicity. Human history is not simply a process but also a project. At the very least, this project revolves around seeking to understand what it means to be human and striving to implement that understanding. The project, then, is oriented toward a goal, an "ideal." The very wealth and diversity of human ideas, inasmuch as they are not the result of bias, distortion, stupidity, and irresponsibility, can be attributed to the fact that the goal is more definite than any concrete historical achievement. If this notion of objectivity is accepted, then the myriad instances of *authentic* human understanding and acting acquire a unity, since they are all within the basic horizon of the project of history: they are all intellectually or morally objective. In these cases, differences would arise among historical horizons because different questions would be posed, or the same questions would be posed in different contexts, or the same questions would be answered in compatible though not equally penetrating manners.

By the same token, positing a set of eternal truths "out there" likewise denies human historicity. It is the position of most of the advocates of "intelligent and authentic subjectivity" that the human being is a known unknown; the goal of the project of history is like an x in an algebraic equation. What it means to be human is known in the sense that it is the "ideal" of historical action; it is the object of the question. What it means to be human is unknown in the sense that it is revealed only in the performance of searching for the goal, a performance that never ceases; it is a question, and no answers are definitive. Thus, human history consists of the basic orientation of questioning and the answers formulated at particular times and places. The basic orientation does not exist apart from the historically situated answers. Identity does not exist without difference. Such is the tension of human existence, the condition of human beings as radically historical creatures.

According to this position, then, articulated most forcefully by Lonergan, a proper understanding of the basic orientation of intelligent subjectivity allows, and requires, us to affirm fundamental ethical values and intellectual standards while, at the same time, acknowledging that human conduct and thinking are radically conditioned by historical circumstance. It also demands that contemporary science and scholarship attain a more critical and normative stance. For the norms of intelligence and valuing can be followed authentically, or they can be violated through such forms of inauthenticity as ideological bias, national and social prejudices, and egoism. By focusing on the concrete interplay of authenticity and inauthenticity in historical existence, science and scholarship would possess, in principle, an objective criterion for differentiating in cultural and social life between progress and decline, order and disintegration, insight and oversight. Such an empirical and normative *Geisteswissenschaften*, its advocates claim, would contribute toward more reflective, deliberate, and responsible choice in the direction of human affairs.[54]

Emerging Intellectual Horizon

We can summarize the two perspectives we have been discussing by suggesting that the first—the one dominated by the confrontation theory of truth and tending to advocate either relativism or dogmatism—holds to the *ultimacy of answers* as an ideal, as the norm, even if it cannot be attained, and that the second holds to the *ultimacy of the question,* interpreting the act of questioning not in a subjectivist fashion but as the very core of objectivity itself. The first perspective sees historicity as *necessarily* entailing historical relativism; the second perspective sees historicity as the human condition, in Plato's words, midway between knowledge and ignorance, and in the language of a later tradition, at the intersection of time and eternity, a condition involving both continuity and difference, insight into the order of being and ongoing reformulation of insights.

In this study, we have considered the distinction between historicity and

54. This is a point emphasized in particular by Lonergan and Habermas. For discussion or examples of critical history and social theory, see *Insight,* chap. 7; *Method in Theology,* 365–66; *Verbum;* Habermas, *Knowledge and Human Interests;* Gadamer, *Truth and Method,* historical secs.; Voegelin, *Order and History,* vols. 1–4; Voegelin, *From Enlightenment to Revolution;* and Gibson Winter, *Elements for a Social Ethic: Scientific Perspectives on Social Process.*

historicism and have explored the possibility that the distinction becomes intelligible if related to two broad interpretations of human history rooted in crucial epistemological and metaphysical assumptions. The discussion has been presented in the spirit of a *Problemstellung,* aiming not at exhaustive description or typology but at opening up lines of inquiry. Investigating these matters from a wide historical perspective may, it is hoped, lead to fuller appreciation of the significance of certain directions in modern intellectual history and perhaps clarify to some degree the nature of contemporary discussion of historicity.

The twentieth century has been rightly characterized as an age when intellectuals were acutely, and often painfully, aware of the diversity and impermanence of beliefs, sentiments, ideas, and values. This situation must be tied to two profound intellectual transformations, the scientific revolution and the historical revolution, which have molded specifically modern intellectual culture. The scientific revolution has seemed to prove as illusory the Greek idea of *kosmos,* the idea of a harmonious, beautiful, and meaningful order transcending the realm of human affairs. The historical revolution has destroyed the plausibility of a "perennial philosophy" and the ideal of a culture valid for all time. Yet, neither science nor history has succeeded in filling the shoes of discredited philosophy. It would not be too bold, then, to suggest that the central issue of twentieth-century intellectual culture was precisely the significance, integrity, and validity of intellectual culture itself, which is to say, of philosophy in its broadest (and most traditional) sense. The issue, to state it another way, was whether, amid the flux of becoming, one could discover, or rediscover, being—rediscover the possibility of meaning. At the end of his book on modern European intellectual history, Baumer has concluded that "intellectual creativity of the highest sort depends on a healthy mixture, or tension, between being and becoming, between the permanent (permanent ideals, even if one does not yet know what they are in any final or complete sense) and the impermanent."[55]

The contemporary intellectual trend described in this chapter can be summarized best by saying that it addresses itself to this problem of establishing a balance between being and becoming. It breaks with the epistemological assumptions of modern thought in an effort to recapture the sense of being, which the ancient Greeks had, but from a perspective that recognizes the decisiveness of modern science and modern historical consciousness.

---

55. Baumer, *Modern European Thought,* 517.

5

Reason and History

BERNARD LONERGAN'S PHILOSOPHY of history posits an intimate connection between reason and history. Reason, according to Lonergan, is indeed operative as a constitutive element in historical life. Reason is capable of grasping historical truth. And reason is capable of grasping long-term configurations of historical process, including, and especially, the history of thought. However, for Lonergan, reason does not necessarily rule over historical existence. Reason cannot encompass the totality of historical truth. Nor can reason comprehend the meaning of history.

Lonergan's philosophy of history differs from ancient and medieval perspectives on history that would relegate history to the domain of mere contingency beyond the proper ken of reason and would view patterns in history as essentially cyclical. Lonergan also differs from modern thinkers who, in recognizing the historicity of human existence, attach that recognition either, as does Foucault, to various deconstructions of human nature, or, as does Dilthey, to historical relativism, or, as do Hegel and Marx, to a priori constructions on the meaning of history.

Although Lonergan has conducted studies in the history of ideas and has written numerous lectures, articles, and chapters on the philosophy of history, his chief contribution to the philosophy of history lies in his uncompromising focus on philosophical foundations and the strategic implications of that foundational analysis for the philosophy of history.[1] Accordingly, we must

---

1. For Lonergan's historical work, see *Way to Nicea; Verbum;* and *Grace and Freedom.* For Lonergan's chief reflections on the philosophy of history, see *Insight,* pref., chaps. 7,

ask: What differentiates Lonergan's idea of history both from ancient and medieval ahistorical tendencies and from characteristically modern historical consciousness? What is Lonergan's distinct interpretation of reason that so distinguishes his idea of history? And what relation, then, does Lonergan see between reason, so conceived, and history?

Classicism and Historicism

Lonergan would have us negotiate between the frozen shores of classicism and the turbulent chaos of historicism. This advice may indeed seem banal, except that the alternative route between the extremes would seem as rarely traversed with success as that between Scylla and Charybdis. If classicism places reason above history, not in the sense of reason comprehending history in its totality but in the sense of form being above chaos, then historicism places history above reason insofar as historical development defines, or determines, or subsumes the life of reason itself. The following historical sketch of classicism and historicism can shed some light on Lonergan's views by contrast, although, to be sure, it makes no pretense of being historically exhaustive.

The classicist worldview, which Lonergan associates with Greco-Roman, medieval, and Renaissance cultures, is, we can argue, a refined formulation of ideas found in hunter-gatherer societies, agricultural villages, and the pre-classical civilizations.[2] Commonsense reason, of course, in these societies lacking a fully differentiated, critical intellectual culture had made impressive achievements—as any observer of the pyramids of Giza can attest—but commonsense reason was not concerned with the details of historical life save to find ways to escape from the "terror of history." More essential to the grasp of the core of meaning than the exercise of commonsense reasoning was the recollection of the primordial models established "in the beginning" and recounted in myth. In ancient Mesopotamia, for example, civilization, and along with it the norms of human nature, was founded "when kingship was

---

17, 20; *Method in Theology,* 52–55, 85–99, 175–234, 245–47, 249–50, 302–26; *Collection,* chap. 16; *Second Collection,* chap. 1; *Third Collection,* chaps. 7, 11; and "Analytic Concept of History." For Lonergan's foundational analysis, see *Insight; Method in Theology,* chap. 1; and *Collection,* chap.14.

2. For Lonergan's discussion of "classicist culture," see *Second Collection,* 91–93, 101, 141, 160–61, 182.

lowered from Heaven." Tradition was important not as an ongoing hermeneutic of the society's historical existence but as a precarious link to the meaningful, archaic time so far removed from the here and now as to be beyond
the ordinary time of historical life. The only history worth knowing about was
this sacred history, and it was known through the medium of myth. To be sure,
there were occasional hints of lines of meaning in time (for instance, in the
Sumerian king list), although they were usually associated with the institu-
tion of sacred kingship, which paralleled the lastingness of cosmic-divine order, or with the temporal framework of permanent astronomical cycles. More
typically, history was identified with decline as such. Any hope of betterment
was conceived not as action within history but as restoration of transhistori-
cal order. Thus, in Paleolithic societies, the shaman reversed decline and re-
instituted order by contact with the spirit world. In agricultural communities,
the decline, or dying, of the year was overcome at New Year's—in the spring-
time—when the earth and humankind were renewed. Here was progress of
a sort. In traditional China, when calamity visited the *Tian Xia* ("Everything
under the Heavens"), the *Tian Ming* (the "Mandate of Heaven") was withdrawn
from the ruler and a new mandate bestowed. In these examples of archaic societies and civilizations, progress and decline were symbolized in a compact,
undifferentiated, and inchoate fashion—usually tied to a sense of time as cosmic.[3] Decline was the downward stage in the eternal return; progress was the
upward surge of the cycle. In the extreme, the desire to escape decline could
be so overwhelming that it became the desire to escape the cycle altogether,
as in Indian culture and its search for *moksha*.

Whereas the preclassical societies viewed a shaman, priest, or king as mediator between meaningful social order and cosmic-divine reality, the intellectual leaders of classical civilization in Hellas tended to replace the earlier
figures with the philosopher as representative of true order. This epochal
breakthrough heralded a deeper sensitivity to historical existence. Herodotus
told the great tale of the Hellenic resistance to the encroachment by the universal empire of Persia, while Thucydides analyzed the momentous *kinesis*
that tore apart the Hellenic world and threatened the very cosmion of order
that had been preserved in the earlier struggles against Persia. Plato, living in

---

3. On the "terror of history," see Eliade, *Cosmos and History.* For the Mesopotamian idea
of kingship, see "The Sumerian King List," in *Ancient Near Eastern Texts, Relating to the Old
Testament,* ed. James B. Pritchard, 265; and Voegelin, *Order and History,* 4:59–67, 82–100.
Mircea Eliade, *Shamanism: Archaic Techniques of Ecstasy.*

the age of the god Nous, detailed the noetic source of order in society and of progress in his masterful, dramatic presentation of the nature of the psyche. Moreover, he gave a probing critique of disordered psyches and portrayed the cumulative process of decline from the timocratic regime, ruled by honor; to the oligarchic, ruled by love of money; to the democratic, ruled by love of all pleasure; to the tyrannical, enslaved by love of unnecessary pleasure.[4]

Still, even the creative Hellenic thinkers muted their awareness of historical existence. Herodotus, for example, seemed to situate his investigations (*historia*) within the framework of the Anaximandrian law of compensation, where greatness (the Persian Empire) would pay its penalty (defeat) according to the ordinance of time. Plato's foundational analysis of progress and decline was apparently tied to the notion of cosmic cycles, expressing the mystery of existence and of evil. Furthermore, Plato conceived the object of true science (*episteme*) as the eternal forms beyond space and time. The good polis was, at best, a temporary spatial refuge against the ravages of time, and perhaps the ideal polis was simply a paradigm in the heavens that could resonate in the soul of the lover of wisdom. Aristotle sought wisdom in the knowledge of the unmoved mover, clearly beyond history, and in the contemplation of the immanent forms that constituted the permanent fixture of nature. In contrast to eternal verities and certain causal necessity was the sheer contingency of the world of history. This did not preclude accurate knowledge of the past. What it precluded was historical knowledge attaining the status of real science. Such Platonists as Plutarch might, at the most, employ history as a pedagogical tool for moral instruction. Aristotle would see even poetry as more successful in painting the universal features of human nature. According to Aristotle's language, the essential properties of human nature were, in a sense, defined by the past—not the past, however, of the flow of history, but the infinite past of the form of a thing whose actualization was the immanent principle of movement and rest called its "nature." For Aristotle, the essence of a thing was its "what-it-was-to-be" (*to ti en einai*). If history approximated a science at all, it was when it revealed cyclical patterns over human time. Plato, Aristotle, and Polybius all saw the scope of human effort and historical responsibility as very circumscribed: the most that humans could hope for, in

4. On Greek historical sensitivity, see Voegelin, *Anamnesis,* 122–13; *Order and History,* 2: chap. 12. For Plato on the psyche, see his *Laws* 713E–714A; *Republic* bks. 4, 7–9; and Voegelin, *Order and History,* 4:218–27. For Plato on decline, see *Republic* bks. 8–9.

applying the lessons of history, would be to erect, probably for a brief time only, political edifices—mixed constitutions—that would contain, though not eliminate, evil.[5]

"Classicist culture," needless to say, is an ideal-type that cannot reflect the ideas of all the creative minds of antiquity let alone capture the nuances of the great thinkers mentioned above. Its central themes, however, are prevalent enough over broad periods of history from antiquity to the modern period to bear summarizing. Although classicist culture, then, emphasized that reason could play a decisive, if not necessarily successful, role in creating true order in society, it did not stress reason creating order *in history.* Historical knowledge was indeed possible, though of no great import other than for moral edification. What history seemed to attest to was the rise and fall of societies, states, and empires. The truth in this classicist view would seem to be that human affairs do mirror the rhythms of nature, the mystery of creation and destruction, the cycles of life and death. But is there something missing? The romantic poet Shelley in his *World's Great Age* detected a world-weariness that could ensue:

> Heaven smiles and fates and empires gleam,
> Like wrecks of a dissolving dream.
> . . . .
> The world is weary of the past.
> Oh, might it die or rest at last.

Shelley breathed in a culture long accustomed to accord deeper significance to historical time. In a large part this was the legacy of the Israelite sense of divine presence in the flux of history—a divinity present there even more so than in the recurrent cycles of cosmic order. The Chosen People could look forward to a new, redeemed future. In the same religious perspective, Christians and Muslims would equate sacred history with the scale of human time.

---

5. Anaximander, fragment B1; Voegelin, *Order and History,* 2:336–37. On cosmic cycles, see Plato, *Statesman* 269–74; and Voegelin, *Order and History,* 3:151–69. For the escape from time, see Plato, *Republic* 592B; and John G. Gunnell, *Political Philosophy and Time,* chaps. 5–6. For Aristotle's denial of any science of the accidental, see *Metaphysics* E6.2.1027a19. For poetry and history, see Aristotle, *Poetics* 2.1448a1–18. On Aristotle's definition of essence in terms of the past, see B. A. Van Groningen, *In the Grip of the Past: Essay on an Aspect of Greek Thought,* 22; Aristotle, *Physics* 2.1.195b21–22. On mixed constitutions, see Plato, *Statesman* 300B–303B; Aristotle, *Politics* 3.7.129a22–b10, 4.8–9.1293b22–1294b41, 4.11–12.1295a25–1297a13; Polybius, *Histories,* 6:3–9.

Christian writers would also speak of Pilgrims' Progress, of the dignity of the individual soul in the journey of mundane existence. There was likewise the temptation to claim to have a God's-eye view with respect to collective history: to predict the direction of history, the coming of the millennium, or to declare oneself to be among the saved, "godded men" of the new dispensation.[6]

Nevertheless, the mainstream Judeo-Christian emphasis on history was attached for centuries to the classicist intellectual culture. Christian sacred history, for instance, which was linear, operated, according to the dominant premodern view, in a preordained and fixed hierarchal cosmos, which included in it a secular history that was largely the sad, monotonous tale of rise and fall of empires. The prevalent Augustinian theology of history downplayed the eschatological hope of a transformed future by making its primary relevance for believers a symbolism of the fate of the individual soul in the beyond.[7] For all practical purposes, the *eschaton* was postponed to a far distant future.

Surely, the tension of such a postponement was reaching a crisis point by the modern period. One solution, which undoubtedly contributed to the rise of modern historical consciousness, was to transfer the *eschaton* to secular history. Indeed, a sense of historical epoch accompanied the experiences of global exploration, trade, and conquest; the collapse of feudalism; the Renaissance assault on medieval culture; and the Reformation attack on the leading institutions of Christendom. Equally decisive was the scientific revolution. When God (according to Pope) said, "Let Newton be," and there was light—it seemed that the laws, if not the secrets, of nature were revealed for the first time. Gone was the hierarchal cosmos. In its place was a more democratic, or at least Whiggish, universe, where the laws of motion applied throughout. The human world would gradually become more democratic, too, and modern intellectuals would begin to hold that collective humanity could have a say in its history. Indeed, the primary symbol of legitimacy would become that of "the people" (witness the appeal from below by regimes embracing such diverse ideologies as puritanism, liberal democracy, communism, fascism, and national socialism), replacing the old symbol of legitimacy from above, that of sacred kingship. It is not surprising that the intellectual movement of the

6. On the Israelite view of history, see Eliade, *Cosmos and History,* 102–12; and Voegelin, *Order and History,* 1: chap. 4. On millennialism, see Voegelin, *Order and History,* 1:452–58; Norman Cohn, *The Pursuit of the Millennium.*

7. Saint Augustine, *City of God,* 20:7–9; Cohn, *Pursuit of the Millennium,* 29; Voegelin, *New Science of Politics,* 109; Voegelin, *Modernity without Restraint,* 176–77; Löwith, *Meaning in History,* chap. 9.

Enlightenment, the first systematic attempt to formulate a specific modern worldview, emphasized collective historical responsibility. Paradoxically, the Enlightenment focus on historical development implicitly placed the Enlightenment thinker at an Archimedean point above history as its observer, a position perhaps explicated to its fullest by Hegel with his God's-eye view of historical process. Ironically, the Enlightenment standpoint, carried through by positivist historiography, neo-Kantian methodology, and Weberian social science, not only eventually immersed the objects of observation totally within the stream of history but ultimately engulfed the observer as well.[8]

The progressivist, Hegelian, and Marxist a priori constructions of history concentrated on the universal principles of historical development, whereas the romanticist hermeneutic stressed the irreducible historical uniqueness of each tradition, culture, or civilization. In either case, however, the historical project was to understand and evaluate each event in history exclusively in terms of the larger process of which it was a phase or part.[9] Since the Enlightenment enterprise of creating a new human science to replace classicist theories of human nature appealed normatively to the laws of nature, thereby succumbing to the naturalistic fallacy, increasingly intellectuals sought the proper method of dealing with meaning, purpose, and value by an appeal to the one area where human beings created meaning, purpose, and value, namely, the process of history.[10]

Human nature, then, is what is made by humans in history through human thinking, deciding, and acting. Does not human nature vary from historical age to historical age, much as truth varies from one *Weltanschauung* to another? This includes historical truth, for the historian cannot escape the relativi-

8. On the secularization of the millennium, see Voegelin, *New Science of Politics*, 28–29; Voegelin, *Modernity without Restraint*, 110–11; and Ernest Lee Tuveson, *Millennium and Utopia: A Study in the Background of the Idea of Progress*. On the symbol of the people, see Voegelin, *New Science of Politics*, 41–45; Voegelin, *Modernity without Restraint*, 120–23; Heer, *Intellectual History of Europe*, 1; Edmund S. Morgan, *Inventing the People: The Rise of Popular Sovereignty in England and America*; Karl Dietrich Bracher, *The Age of Ideologies: A History of Political Thought in the Twentieth Century*; and Cassirer, *Philosophy of the Enlightenment*, chap. 5. On Hegel, see Karl Barth, *Protestant Thought: From Rousseau to Ritschl*, 278–80. To suggest that Hegel's system may contain elements of speculative gnosis is not necessarily to deny his tremendous wealth of insight into historical context and historical development, particularly the dialectic of subject and object. On the crisis of positivist historiography, see H. S. Hughes, *Consciousness and Society*, esp. chap. 6.

9. Mandelbaum, *History, Man, and Reason*, 42.

10. See, for example, Peter Hans Reill, *The German Enlightenment and the Rise of Historicism*.

ty of horizons. Does not the historian with his or her ideas, sentiments, and values confront a horizon within which people in the past thought, willed, and acted? And would not objectivity demand that the historian be divested of all "subjective" intrusions from his or her horizon as he or she looks at the horizons of the past? If the historian, however, cannot conduct an investigation with a mind that is a blank tablet, if the historian's interpretation is inescapably tied to past experiences, insights, judgments, and evaluations, then not only would the object of historical investigation be completely relative but also the position of the observer would be irredeemably subjective. When grandiose a priori constructions of history would no longer be fashionable or conceivable, then what general pattern of history could the historian still discern? The historian may indeed be left to formulate mere ideal-types in a much more subjective fashion than Weber ever envisioned or to empathize, as Dilthey recommended, with the diversity of worldviews, basking in an aesthetic appreciation of otherness and of the vitality of the elusive, inexhaustible human spirit. Perhaps the *reductio ad absurdum* of historicism is, as Foucault has urged, the deconstruction of history itself.[11] With historicism carried to its logical extreme, human nature disappears. So, too, does history.

Thus, historicism, whatever its original pretensions and goals, placed reason within the flux of historical process, and hence under it; it relativized historical truth; and, in the limit, it somewhat ironically witnessed, amid a chaos of clashing *Weltanschauungen,* history fading away. All this is premised on the confrontation theory of truth. The methodological assumptions of historicism—whether articulated in positivist, neo-Hegelian, Marxist, romanticist, neo-Kantian, or pragmatist versions—presuppose a confrontation of historian subject with historical object. All of its tensions, dilemmas, and contradictions flow from here.

The classicist mentally tended to put a premium on concepts, universal standards, and fixed ideas, while neglecting the questions and insights that generated the concepts and the judgments that tested them. The historicist mentality, on the other hand, at least when purified of idealist metaphysics and naturalistic principles, focused on the particular, the concrete, and the

11. On the historicist idea of human nature, see Fackenheim, *Metaphysics and Historicity,* 24–28; Fackenheim, *The God Within,* 127–28. On Dilthey and Weber, see H. S. Hughes, *Consciousness and Society,* 192–200, chap. 8; Dilthey, *Pattern and Meaning,* 167. Emphasizing the "space of dispersion" and "discontinuity" in history would seem to head in the direction of its deconstruction (see Michel Foucault, *The Archeology of Knowledge,* 10–11).

unique contents of historical horizons; it acknowledged the process that generated these contents but as a process mysterious and incapable of objectification. In Lonergan's view, both classicism and historicism suffer from a fatal flaw because they highlight only fragments of the process of cognition and, correspondingly, do justice only to fragments of human reality.

Reason

For Lonergan, the challenge of contemporary culture is to negotiate a fusion of horizons: to embrace both natural right and historical-mindedness, to emphasize both human nature and historical being, to replace a classicist hierarchy from above and a modern cosmic chaos with an emergent series of higher viewpoints from below—in a word, to accept transcultural norms without classicism, historicity without historicism. To accomplish this task Lonergan urges us to embark on the prior task of a foundational analysis of reason.[12]

Lonergan's own writings clearly reflect his own experience as a person in the twentieth century, a time in which belief in progress was shattered by bloody world wars, ghastly concentration camps, and the frightening specter of nuclear holocaust. In one sense, all of *Insight,* Lonergan's magnum opus, was a response to this challenging situation. Hence his emphasis on the theme of progress and decline in the preface. Hence the dramatic transformation of style and energy in the chapters on common sense. What specific contribution, then, does Lonergan make to the topic of the philosophy of history? The line of the answer is obvious. In the measure that Lonergan is correct when he claims that his foray into the territory of insight is a foray into something at once overlooked and central to philosophy, culture, and civilization—in that measure his philosophy of history ought to reflect his penetrating insight into insight. In short, if Lonergan has articulated a uniquely foundational philosophy and if he is consistent in applying his principles to the philosophy of history, then we can anticipate a uniquely foundational analysis of history. Not surprisingly, Lonergan loudly proclaims the relation of insight to concerns in the philosophy of history: Insight into insight, he says, "is the very key to practicality." Insight is the motor of progress, oversight the brake of decline. "The

---

12. On fusion of norms and historicity, see *Third Collection,* chap. 11; on emerging higher viewpoints, see *Insight,* 144–52, 157–62; on the foundational task, see ibid., 4–6, 83.

challenge of history," Lonergan insists, "is for man progressively to restrict the realm of chance or fate or destiny and progressively to enlarge the realm of conscious grasp and deliberate choice."[13] These statements may seem commonplace enough. But Lonergan's nuanced treatment of the structure of cognition, the conditions of insight, the unfolding of insight, and the thwarting of insight through the biases of neurosis, individual egoism, group egoism, and commonsense shortsightedness—Lonergan's three hundred pages of cognitional analysis—provides the basis for a nuanced treatment of historical existence, historical knowledge, and theories of history.

To cite among the more prominent themes: Lonergan argues that through human reason human beings are not inevitably constrained by cosmic cycles. Human lives are indeed functions of "schemes of recurrence" on various strata of human being, whether subatomic, chemical, biological, psychic, demographic, sociological, or economic. Insight itself, though, by its grasp of possible schemes of recurrence, can make them not only possible but also likely and probable and actual. Human intelligence and freedom can intervene to make humans the executors of emergent probability in the field of human history.[14] Since Lonergan conceives of nature in terms of an immanent directedness of world process toward more complexity in accord with probability schedules, human reason, for him, is not the contemplation of fixed cosmic cycles and hierarchies; rather, human reason is a natural agent bringing about greater complexity and development in the emergent world order.

Reason, however, in driving this process is not the empirical reason of Enlightenment *philosophes* and positivists, nor the conceptualist reason of modern rationalists, nor the voluntarist reason of many romanticists, existentialists, and pragmatists. For these schools of thought, as stated above, tend to focus on fragments of the process of inquiry, the net effect of which is to lend support to the mutation of historical reason and the deconstruction of history. For Lonergan, on the contrary, reason is a creative process of inquiry structured by distinct and related activities, embracing the operations of experiencing, of understanding (whose formations may be concepts), of judging, and of deliberating and deciding. The point of cognitional analysis is to grasp comprehensively the parts (the distinct operations), to see how they form a unified structure of knowing, and to appreciate that this structure attains its

---

13. *Insight*, 8, 253, 259–60.
14. Ibid., 141–48, 232–37, 252, 258. Lonergan's worldview of emergent probability adds statistical and developmental laws to classical laws while rejecting radical indeterminism (see Chapter 2 above, pp. 31–40).

unity by the unfolding of the desire to know in the process of questioning. And it is here in fidelity to the desire to know—not in facts per se, or in logical coherence, or in practical success—that objectivity lies. Moreover, the process of inquiry includes all avenues of questioning and not simply those in the natural sciences.[15] The process of inquiry is at once nuanced, structured, and normative.

Still, the mere activity of reason does not guarantee progress. Reason can be abused, manipulated, distorted by various biases and accompanying existential moods. The principle of progress itself, according to Lonergan, is not reason but liberty, and liberty implies *possibility:* the possibility of failure as well as success, the possibility of freely choosing to restrict the operational range of effective, responsible freedom, that is, the possibility of enslaving reason. Lonergan, of course, would not look for a gnostic vision of the movement of history toward a world-immanent perfection, as in progressivism or Marxism. The irresponsible abuse of freedom to destroy freedom creates an unintelligible humanly formed world, what Lonergan calls the "social surd," that is nonetheless a fact.[16] So there is the possibility of progress, the possibility of decline, the possibility of progress being mated with decline, and, finally, the possibility of an authentic exercise of freedom reversing decline.

Because Lonergan highlights the intentionality of reason (the desire to know and the intention of the good), his concept of reason cannot be divorced from those experiences that would inspire reason, support the activity of inquiry, and heal the biases—experiences both psychic and spiritual, whether the affectively charged images of wonder and awe or the silent undertow of the mystics. Unlike Enlightenment thinkers, Lonergan does not dissociate progress from a sense of the sacred. What is experienced as "openness as a gift" (not to be identified with the constricting attitude of dogmatism), in fact, would enhance the operational range of freedom.[17] The spiritual dimension

15. The notion of "patterns of experience" is crucial here. See *Insight,* 204–12. On cognitive structure, see *Collection,* chap. 14; *Method in Theology,* chap. 1; and *Insight,* pt. 1. *Reason* in this chapter is employed as the equivalent of the entire structure and intentionality of cognitional operations. Lonergan's technical use of the term tends to restrict it to the operational level of judging. On the central intentionality of the desire to know, see *Insight,* chap. 13, esp. 404–5; and *Method in Theology,* 37, 238, 263, 265, 338.

16. On the possibility of restricting reason, see *Insight,* 259–60, 631–47. Lonergan would reject "the nonsense that the rising star of another class or nation is going to put a different human nature in the saddle" (264–65). On the "social surd," 255.

17. On the psyche and intentionality, see *Insight,* 210–14, 229–30, 482, 555–58, 569–72; *Method in Theology,* 64–69. On spiritual consciousness and the reversal of decline, see *Insight,* 710–25, 740–50; *Method in Theology,* chap. 4, 240–43, 288–91; *Col-*

of human existence, rightly interpreted, neither destroys reason and eliminates freedom nor provides hope for a millenarian transformation of the tensions of history. Thus, for Lonergan, the area where humans take on responsibility for progress or decline is situated between cosmic cycles and absolute transcendence.

The intentionality of the process of reason also means that, in a sense, questions have priority over answers. For questions define the range of meaningful, relevant, and significant answers—and, consequently, the directional tendency of the whole cognitional process. In brief, questions define the horizon of inquiry. But questions, on the other hand, are influenced by answers, including the contents of partial steps on the way to answers. Indeed, prior experiences, ideas and concepts, judgments, and decisions all constitute the background of the horizon and can, accordingly, weaken or strengthen the efficacy of questions, transform questions, or spawn new questions. The process of reason is horizon-bound in the historical interplay of questions and answers.[18]

One crucial feature of a person's horizon is the self-interpretation of the subject of the horizon. Self-interpretation, running the continuum from nonthematic, elemental meanings (such as intersubjective or symbolic),[19] to common sense, to concepts, involves a reduplication of the process of inquiry. The primal datum is who the person is, and who the person is, to a large degree, is the person as faithful or unfaithful to the imperatives of attending to experience, understanding intelligently, judging reasonably, and acting responsibly. The interpretation is nothing else than attending to this datum, understanding it, and judging the accuracy of the understanding. Performance, then, provides data for interpretation, and interpretation informs performance. This ongoing hermeneutics of performance and interpretation is at the core of a person's historicity.

Since, for Lonergan, the process of reason is not the achievement of isolated human monads, the hermeneutical dimensions of human existence are also found on the level of collective history. There is an ongoing circuit in which individuals share common experiences, understanding, judgments, and decisions to constitute communities, and in which communal meanings

---

lection, chap. 12; *Second Collection,* 271–72; "Analytic Concept of History," 15; and *Third Collection,* 106–8, 115–28, 173–75. On "openness as a gift," see *Collection,* chap. 12.

18. *Method in Theology,* 235–37, 312–14.

19. Ibid., 57–69, esp. 63, 67.

and achievements—sedimented in culture, institutionalized in the polity and economy, and embodied in the technology—develop individuals "from above" through acculturation, socialization, and education. A creative minority, particularly geniuses, add to the common fund of ideas, but not even geniuses operate in a vacuum outside a cultural horizon. Reason not only is the source of immanently generated knowledge but also embraces reasonable belief as part of the ongoing dialogue we call tradition.[20]

Reason and History

Having seen how Lonergan's cognitional theory allows precision in dealing with progress and decline, horizon, the hermeneutics of human existence, and historicity, we are now able to assess more specifically Lonergan's position on the relation of reason to history.

When we focus on "existential history," the history that is lived and written about, we discern a somewhat paradoxical connection between time and history, which provides us with a clue to the dynamics of reason and history. If by "time" in its elementary sense we mean the lastingness of the physical universe, either explained by the geometrical frameworks of physics or measured by the commonsense reference frames of personal and public life (for example, clocks), and if by "eternity" we mean the lastingness intimated in the experience of openness to the transcendent beyond our unrestricted questioning, then history, and the activity of reason, is neither purely in time nor purely in eternity. By contrast, there is a psychological dimension of time, explored by Bergson and mentioned by Lonergan.[21] The basis of this "psychological time," I would suggest, is the experience of historicity, namely, present interpretation of past performance informed by past interpretation, all comprehended by the generic openness of the pure desire to know oriented to transcendence.

20. On community, see ibid., 356–57; on technology, economy, polity, and culture, see *Insight*, 232–37, 261–63; on development from "above," see *Third Collection*, 106, 196–97. On Toynbee's idea of a "creative minority," see *Third Collection*, 10, 103–4, 214. On the role of genius, see *Verbum*, 37–38; and *Insight*, 443–44. On belief, see *Insight*, 725–39; and *Method in Theology*, 41–47.

21. On "existential history," see *Insight*, 725–39; and *Method in Theology*, 41–47. On time, see *Insight*, 166–68; and *Method in Theology*, 29, 83–84, 102–7. On psychological time, see *Method in Theology*, 175–78; and Henri Bergson, *Time and Free Will: An Essay on the Immediate Data of Consciousness*.

To approach the same topic from a slightly different angle, the agents of history operate simultaneously in relative horizons (limited by the locus of consciousness in a particular body, circumscribed by the concrete communal and social preconditions of human living, and subject to the cumulative effects of progress and decline) and in a basic horizon (defined by the openness of the pure desire to know and the intention of the good). Neither does basic horizon exist apart from the particular perspectives of relative horizons in some disembodied, self-enclosed, timeless realm, nor could relative horizons exist for long without some fusion with basic horizon (for that divorce would mean total inauthenticity, and total inauthenticity—total inattentiveness, total stupidity, total unreasonableness, and total irresponsibility—would mean total annihilation). Basic horizon with its transcultural norms of fidelity to questioning is the identity amid historical differences, either by way of participation in it (progress) or by way of privation (decline). It is also the source of genuine diversity, for it challenges every fixed idea, every established system, every horizon, with the further question. History is a project, a search for meaning and a quest for value, with the object of questioning hurled in front of the questioner as that which gives a direction to life. It is a hermeneutical project revolving around the dialectic of performance and interpretation within the basic, or transcendental, horizon of the objective of meaningful historical action.[22]

Thus, reason—as a normative process nourished by spiritual experience, structured by horizon, and implicated in the hermeneutic of performance and interpretation—is neither above history nor below history. Reason and history exist in the in-between at the intersection of time and eternity. The field of historical existence is precisely a tension, what Lonergan calls the "tension of limitation and transcendence."[23] It is when this tension breaks apart that we witness the extremes of either historicism or classicism.

Historical reason (academic history) bears a relation to existential history. The exigency of reason to reverse decline can, under certain temporal conditions of development, reside in a critical, reflective superstructure of intellectual culture. There, the imperative arises both to know objectively past performance in history through the cognitional structure of experience, un-

22. On being oneself as the object of the question, see *Collection*, 229. The project of history, I would suggest, constitutes the dramatic character of historical existence, part of the "primordial drama that the theatre only imitates" (*Insight*, 213). This, in turn, establishes the significance of narrative historiography (see Paul Ricoeur, *Time and Narrative*).

23. *Insight*, 497–503.

derstanding, and judging and to evaluate that performance in light of the dialectic of progress and decline. By positing a basic horizon of inquiry amid the diversity of historical perspectives, Lonergan preserves the prospect of historical objectivity along with that of historical evaluation, or, more exactly, of both objective determination of facts and objective evaluation. Rather than depict objectivity on the model of the confrontation theory of truth as a subject perceiving an object "out there," Lonergan defines objectivity as fidelity to the process of inquiry, whether cognitional or moral. Historical knowledge and historical evaluation are possible and compatible because authentic inquiry opens to a universal viewpoint of hermeneutics that grounds a heuristic anticipation of all possible horizons. According to Lonergan's cognitional theory, all possible horizons will be grounded, along a continuum of authenticity, in the unfolding of the desire to know and the intention of the good, through distinct conscious and intentional operations, within diverse patterns of experience, at different stages of cognitional development.[24]

Nevertheless, the universal viewpoint of hermeneutics is not knowledge of universal history. For Lonergan acknowledges the historicity of historical reason. Lonergan sees critical historiography as part of an academic praxis that embraces functional specialties proportionate to the differentiated structure of cognition as it meets the past, encounters historical tradition, and responds to the challenge of the future.[25] Thus, a nuanced critical culture would have tasks devoted, for example, to research of data, to interpretation of texts, and to assessment of historical events and trends. Out of the encounter with historical tradition it would evaluate historical movements and explore basic philosophical assumptions underlying present culture. In accepting historical responsibility for the future it would have other tasks devoted to affirming authentic goals of the tradition, to developing ideas and plans consonant with those goals, and to communicating ideas as a contribution to the responsible direction of the future. The ongoing character of this circuit of functional specialties should be clear enough. If existential history is self-interpretation, then critical history is critical interpretation of self-interpretation, which can, in turn, inform performance and then become data for further interpretation.[26] There is no genuine room for closure here.

24. On the intellectual superstructure, see *Collection,* 235–38; *Second Collection,* 102–3; and *Method in Theology,* 304–5. On objectivity of judgments of fact and of value, see *Method in Theology,* chap. 9, 245, 250. On objectivity as fidelity to inquiry, see ibid., 265, 292. On the "universal viewpoint," see *Insight,* 585–616.
25. On the historicity of the intellectual superstructure rather than universal history, see *Insight,* 564; and *Method in Theology,* chap. 5.
26. *Method in Theology,* 209–11.

Furthermore, we must underscore that actual interpretation can inform historical performance. There is no guarantee, however, that the carriers of intellectual culture will be successful in influencing society, nor even that they will be completely faithful to the imperatives of reason. Reason indeed has the task of helping direct history, but reason cannot control history and eliminate the social surd. The hope perhaps is that the love of wisdom—the true spirit of intellectual community—may have some salvific effect in the long run.

Lonergan's sophisticated analysis of reason would surely preclude any simplistic monocausal interpretation of history that might create the illusion of finality. He would urge instead the ongoing methodological cooperation of all historical disciplines, including the various fields dealing with the history of thought. Technological, economic, political, and cultural factors in history mutually condition each other. Reason, in all of its complicated modes, is embedded in, but not determined by, technical and social circumstances. And where Lonergan would paint the contours of a discipline that would see broad patterns of historical development as the result of differentiations of consciousness (for example, the main horizon shifts accompanying theoretical consciousness and historical consciousness), he would envision what we may call the "history of consciousness" as a fruitful combination of philosophically grounded ideal-types and empirical research.[27] Cognitional theory can supply the categories that regard differentiations of consciousness; historical investigations can refine these categories. The story of the progress of reason does not lead to a gnostic intuition of the meaning of history. Most emphatically, Lonergan would oppose any theoretical construction that would absolve the tension of historical being, ignore the horizon-boundedness of human inquiry, and eliminate the ultimate mystery of human existence.

To say that Lonergan has hit upon fundamental cognitional facts is not to say that he has explicitly formulated and systematically treated all the salient issues in a philosophy of history, nor that he has exploited in full the implications of his own positions. Nor is it to say that he is the only thinker who has wrestled creatively with the issues of cognition and historical process.

It is to say, however, at least to those who would be convinced of the truth of his foundational perspective, that Lonergan's cognitional theory offers a propaedeutic to any coherent and thoughtful philosophy of history that would eschew both classicism and historicism.

Lonergan's philosophy of history challenges contemporary thinkers to

---

27. Ibid., 85–99, 293, 302–12, 314–18; McPartland, "Meaning, Mystery, and History," 203–67.

avoid a disjunction that seems almost inevitable, given the modern intellectual horizon: the disjunction of either affirming, on the one hand, the norms
of reason (conceived as abstract, universal, and atemporal truths divorced
from the accidents of mere historical being) or affirming, on the other hand,
historical existence (conceived as sheer contingency cut off from any notion
of transcendence). Both extremes make philosophy irrelevant to address contemporary issues at the point of maximum consequences for human welfare,
the former by abstracting from the concrete conditions of historical responsibility, the latter by denying, through subjectivism, the critical base necessary
for an intelligent exercise of historical responsibility. Deconstructionism, to be
sure, is a contemporary philosophy that is not satisfied with the disjunction.
It assaults the claims of abstract reason and, at the same time, as in the case
of Foucault, deconstructs history and the subject. But what is left? An antiseptic with no criteria for differentiating between progress and decline, a
movement of criticism with no adequate foundation for social and cultural
critique. Whereas deconstructionism is a genuine plea to go beyond the assumptions of the modern intellectual horizon, Lonergan's philosophy of history would offer, as an alternative to that horizon, a creative framework that
embraces both reason and history.

6

Cosmopolis
The Community of Open Existence

ALTHOUGH LONERGAN'S most detailed and clearly stated discussion of his notion of cosmopolis is in *Insight,* his first articulation of the idea reveals its essential structure. There he describes cosmopolis, in bold strokes, "not as an unrealized political ideal but as a long-standing, non-political, cultural fact." It is a fact that resides in the field of communication; it is the "bar of enlightened public opinion"; it is nothing less than the "tribunal of history." If we wish to understand the core of Lonergan's notion of cosmopolis, then we must comprehend the central role of historical consciousness. Indeed, in an earlier writing Lonergan refers to a linguistic equivalent of cosmopolis, the "great republic of culture," as persons holding "esteem of great men of the past, on whose shoulders they stand," and having "devotion to men of the future, for whom they set the stage of history."[1] Applying this principle to Lonergan's own work we might inquire: What are the historical antecedents to Lonergan's idea of cosmopolis? What is the intrinsic relation of cosmopolis to historicity? How might cosmopolis meet the challenges of the future in Lonergan's day, and ours?

1. *Collection,* 39, 109.

Cosmos and Polis

Cosmopolis is a term coined by Diogenes, the Cynic, who declared, "I am a citizen of the cosmos."[2] He differentiated the foolish attachment to the artificial world of family and city from the wise participation in the simple world of nature. Cosmopolis later attained currency as the Stoic ideal of world citizenship indifferent to class, nation, or race. The term, of course, is derived from the Greek words *cosmos* and *polis*. It can assume various shades of meaning in various contexts, depending, to a large extent, on what is the interpretation of "cosmos" and of "polis." As we explore Lonergan's idea of cosmopolis, we must first contrast his view with other major interpretations of "cosmos" and "polis."

First, when cosmos is the mysterious cosmic-divine order, whose pulse is the movement of celestial bodies and the rhythm of vegetation cycles, as in the earliest civilizations, then society is civilized, meaningful, and legitimate, solely because of its integration into the larger, permanent cosmic order, usually by the mediation of kingship. Cosmopolis is an ideal even before the technical language was developed to express it. It is the harmonious society "in the beginning," at the golden age when the cosmos was formed and "kingship was lowered from heaven." Nevertheless, each year—as the decay of time diffuses original cosmic energy—decline sets in. Reality has to be restored by cult and ritual each New Year's, society to be resuscitated, the link between cosmic-divine substance to be reestablished. Although these archaic civilizations clearly appreciate the mystery of existence and the unity of being, they place little premium on human responsibility. Meaningful historical causality is vertical, coming from above.[3]

Second, when cosmos instead is an intelligible, beautiful, harmonious or-

2. Diogenes, fragment 7.

3. For general treatment of cosmological civilizations, see Henri Frankfort et al., *The Intellectual Adventure of Ancient Man: An Essay in Speculative Thought in the Ancient Near East;* Frankfort, *Kingship and the Gods: A Study of Ancient Near Eastern Religion as the Integration of Society and Nature;* Voegelin, *Order and History,* 1: intro. On sacred kingship, see Eliade, *Cosmos and History;* "The Sumerian King List," in *Ancient Near Eastern Texts,* ed. Pritchard, 265. On the cultic restoration of reality, see, for example, "The Babylonian Creation Myth," in *Ancient Near Eastern Texts,* ed. Pritchard, 265–67. On the sense of the mysterious unity of being, see Thorkild Jacobsen, *The Treasures of Darkness: A History of Mesopotamian Religion,* chap. 1; R. T. Rundle Clark, *Myth and Symbol in Ancient Egypt;* and Voegelin, *Order and History,* 1:3. On vertical causality, see, for example, Jacobsen, *Treasures of Darkness,* 86–91.

der, and when the physical universe is considered a cosmos because the world itself is an intelligible, beautiful, harmonious order—as it was for most Hellenic philosophers—then the true polis is an intelligible cosmion, an island of justice amid a sea of chaos, a spatial refuge against the ravages of time.[4] The model of human order is not a mysterious cosmic-divine substance whose story is recounted by myth but a rational network of necessary causal connections whose permanent intelligible structure is contemplated by the human mind; nature is not a Thou subject to the play of divine will but an internal principle of development subject to final causes; the mediator of the true polis is not a king but a philosopher. The teleological order of the universe is mirrored in the soul of the philosopher, the standard of actualized human nature.[5] Cosmopolis can therefore be explicitly articulated as a polis in which the spirit of the love of wisdom, and the presence of philosophical culture, is the spirit of the laws. The essence of cosmopolis, then, is a cultural community of radical openness—openness to true order in society, to the order of the cosmos, and, indeed, to ultimate order beyond. If other loves predominate in culture—the love of honor, or the love of wealth, or the love of all pleasures, or the love of power—then in that measure the empirical polis will be a deflection from the true order of the best regime.[6] It is here that human responsibility obtains. For the philosopher through self-knowledge can control the meaning that informs human living.[7] The philosopher can carry out the Socratic enterprise of exposing the illusions of the cave. To be sure, the prospects of founding, let alone perpetuating, such a cosmopolis outside the

4. Plato, *Gorgias* 508A, follows the Pythagoreans in calling the universe a *kosmos*. See Heraclitus, fragment 30. For a standard English edition, see Kathleen Freeman, *Ancilla to the Pre-Socratic Philosophers*. On the polis as cosmion, see Voegelin, *Order and History*, vol. 2; and Gunnell, *Political Philosophy and Time*, chaps. 5–6.

5. Thus, Aristotle defines science as the true grasp of necessary causal connections (*Posterior Analytics* chaps. 2, 4–8). For nuanced interpretation, see Patrick H. Byrne, *Analysis and Science in Aristotle*, 204–7. For Aristotle's definition of nature, see *Physics* 2.1.192b21–22. See Plato, *Republic* 473C–D, on the mediating role of the philosopher. On the "state within" measured by eternal standards, see Werner Jaeger, *Paideia: The Ideals of Greek Culture*, 2:354–57. Aristotle's *spoudaios* achieved the *areté*, or excellence, of actualized human nature (*Nicomachean Ethics* 2.4.1105b5–8).

6. The love of wisdom animates the political culture of the "aristocratic" type of polis Plato envisions in his *Republic*. Heraclitus praises the lover of wisdom whose logos is operative in the "common world" in contrast to the "sleepwalker" who dwells in a private world (fragments B1, B2, B35, B45, B72, B73, B89, B113, B115). Plato portrays the shadow loves in *Republic* bks. 8–9.

7. *Collection*, 235–36.

soul of the philosopher may seem dim. Perhaps the cyclical tendency in nature rules also in human affairs.[8]

Third, when the cosmos, as conceived by Hellenic philosophers, is, on faith,
believed to be the creation of a god incarnate in history, then the polis becomes
the city of God. In the medieval Christian worldview, secular history might
continue to witness the rise and fall of states and the precarious harmony of
human society with the standards of the fixed, hierarchical cosmos. However, in addition to profane, secular history there is a sacred history in human
time whose carrier is the city of God. In the city of God grace can sustain both
reason and virtue and can inspire a vision of participating in universal, catholic
order. Whereas the heart of cosmopolis—and the source of order in human
society—would be those souls touched by God's grace, the mediating function of institutional authorities, laws, and cult is also highlighted by the prevalent Augustinian theology, resonating with Plato's *Laws*.[9] This at least seems to
parallel the natural hierarchy of the cosmos. It likewise seems to capture the
archaic civilizations' mystique of ritual attunement to order.

On the other hand, if the cosmos is neither the cosmic-divine order of archaic civilizations nor the teleological universe of Hellenic thought, then what
is the nature of the polis? What is cosmopolis?

Fourth, when the cosmos is a machine composed of matter in motion, operating according to mathematically determined mechanical laws, then the
polis is, as Descartes perhaps ironically imagined in his *Discourse on Method
in Theology,* a machine to be constructed, refined, and reformed by Enlightenment social engineering. As Stephen Toulmin has argued in his recent work
Cosmopolis, the hidden agenda of modernity is a model of human society that
is as rationally ordered as is the Newtonian universe. Scientific progress would
propel moral progress. Cosmopolis would be a community of enlightened intellectuals supporting such projects as the *Encyclopedia* and gradually educat-
ing the masses, or perhaps cosmopolis could be created instantaneously by
establishing, as Robespierre hoped, the Republic of Virtue, or, as Marx predicted, socialist humanity. If conceptualist blueprints, however, modeled on

8. Plato, *Republic* 546A–547A; *Statesman* 269–74.
9. On Augustine, see Löwith, *Meaning in History,* chap. 9; Cohn, *Pursuit of the Millennium,* 12; Voegelin, *New Science of Politics,* 107–10; Voegelin, *Modernity without Restraint,*
175–78; and Voegelin, *History of Political Ideas,* vol. 1, *Hellenism, Rome, and Early Christianity,* ed. Athanasios Mouklakis, vol. 19 of *The Collected Works of Eric Voegelin,* 206–23.
On Aquinas, see *Grace and Freedom.* On the Platonic connection, see Voegelin, *History of
Political Ideas,* vol. 2, *The Middle Ages to Aquinas,* ed. Peter von Sivers, vol. 20 of *Collected
Works of Voegelin,* chap. 3; and Jaeger, *Paideia,* 3:252.

geometric precision, do not seem to do justice to the evil propensities of unredeemed humanity, then a gritty realism that recognizes the principle of force in nature could in the place of cosmopolis substitute Hobbes's Leviathan or, in the limit, as Lonergan calls it, "totalitarian practicality."[10]

Can the old notion of cosmopolis be resurrected—but simultaneously divorced from an antiquated science that holds a classicist disregard of historicity and purged from modern rationalist conceit?

Fifth, when the cosmos, as it is for Lonergan, is an emergent order of higher viewpoints operating according to probability schedules (rather than either a preestablished hierarchical order or a machine functioning according to rigid determinist principles), then the polis is human cooperation in process, conditioned by the emergence of the higher viewpoint of human reason, and locked in perpetual struggle against the counterpulls of decline.[11] The polis is no longer a static haven against the cycle of decline, nor a rationalist utopia. It is informed by an awareness of historical consciousness and an assumption of historical responsibility, with no illusions about ideal republics.[12] Cosmopolis offers a control of meaning equal to the challenges of history.

We must, then, tie Lonergan's notion of cosmopolis to his idea of human historicity.

Cosmopolis and Historicity

History, for Lonergan, is not simply a natural process but a hermeneutical project. Lonergan, of course, would have no quarrel with those who would claim that we can make valid assertions about human nature, about essential properties that define human beings as the kind of things, or substances, we call human. But the key to understanding human nature, if we follow the Aristotelian procedure of identifying "nature" as an immanent principle of move-

---

10. René Descartes, *Discourse on Method*, pt. 2. D'Alembert, "Preliminary Discourse"; Leo Gershoy, *The Era of the French Revolution, 1789–1799: Ten Years That Shook the World*, reading no. 10; J. M. Thompson, *Robespierre and the French Revolution*; Karl Marx, *Early Writings*, esp. 155. Hobbes, *Leviathan*, chap. 11; *Insight*, 257.

11. On emergent probability, see *Insight*, 138–51, 456–88; and Chapter 2 above, pp. 31–40. On emergent probability and human affairs, see *Insight*, 234–36, 252–53, 492–504; and Chapter 2 above, pp. 40–51. On human cooperation, see *Insight*, 233–34; and *Method in Theology*, 47–52. On the struggle against decline, see *Insight*, 8–9.

12. *Insight*, 252–53, 264–65.

ment and rest, is to grasp the specifically human principle of movement and rest. The answer, according to Lonergan, is clear: questioning.[13] The drive of questioning moves us through conscious and intentional operations of experiencing, understanding, judging, and deciding to rest with answers and deeds.

The drive of questioning, underpinned by the desire to know and the intention of the good, is not the activity of a mere substance; it is the activity of a conscious subject whose objective is being. In whatever knowledge the subject seeks and in whatever action the subject deliberates about, the subject is also constituting himself or herself. In whatever question the subject raises, the subject also, at least implicitly and unthematically, raises the question about himself or herself. Comprehended in the objective of being is being oneself.[14] Thus, human existence is a pro-ject, with the question of being hurled ahead of oneself. For the self is precisely the tension of the self as having been chosen, the self as choosing, and the self to be chosen, namely, the object of the question. No theory of human nature that treats human being as a substance can do justice to the intricacies of the project of selfhood. The project of selfhood, though, is not the project of isolated monads. Each person develops "from above" through acculturation, socialization, and education, through interpersonal encounter, through dialogue with inherited tradition. And persons come together with common experiences, understandings, judgments, and decisions to share in the destiny and responsibility of a historical community.[15] The project of selfhood is also—as writ large—the project of historical existence.

It should already be evident that this project is hermeneutical. The self as choosing is informed by the interpretation of the reality of the self as having been chosen, and as the self to be chosen performs, then that performance becomes data for further interpretation to inform further deliberation about who the self is to be. By analogy, the same hermeneutical project obtains on the macroscale of historical existence, where tradition, which is ongoing interpretation of the meaning of the past, informs collective decisions, which, in

---

13. On human nature, see ibid., 538; on nature as principle of questioning, see *Third Collection*, 172–75.

14. *Collection*, 229. On the subject and being, see *Second Collection*, chap. 6. On self-constitution, see *Method in Theology*, 38–39; *Collection*, 222–24; and *Second Collection*, 83.

15. On humans as not monadic, see *Insight*, 237; on development "from above," see *Third Collection*, 181; on "community," see *Method in Theology*, 79, 256–57; on "historical destiny," see *Topics in Education*, 231.

turn, becomes data for further interpretation. The meanings and values of a historical community become materialized in technological innovations, habitualized in the cooperative patterns of institutions, and sedimented in cultural products. These objectifications of historical life condition future performances and become data for further reflection.[16]

Because of the hermeneutical dimension of historical existence, control of meaning is possible. As we have seen, meanings and values constitute the emergent human world. Self-constitution involves self-interpretation. However, because the hermeneutical project of human self-constitution is normative, control of meaning can be the task precisely of cosmopolis. Self-interpretation can be critically and responsibly reflective. The possibility and nature of cosmopolis rest on two facts: 1) there are norms inherent in human existence; 2) the norms can be violated. Let us explore these two facts.

Human nature carries with it norms, for the immanent principle of questioning is the ultimate standard, a standard that can be captured in the simple formula, "fidelity to the project of questioning." As Lonergan argues, objectivity is the fruit of authentic subjectivity, that is, fidelity to the desire to know and the intention of the good, through the entire structure of cognitional and volitional operations. A reflective appropriation of the normative pattern of authentic human existence grounds a cognitive "turning around," or intellectual conversion; habitual commitment to the norms inherent in the intention of the good grounds moral conversion; the acceptance of an unrestricted love of being, experienced as openness as a gift, grounds religious conversion.[17] To state the point another way, ingredient in cognitional and volitional operations is an openness to transcendence. Hence, we can speak of a basic horizon of inquiry shared by all authentic persons and authentic historical communities. This, and nothing less than this, is the true meaning of cosmopolis as a normative community that transcends any local bounds. To deny the possibility of cosmopolis in the name of authentic inquiry would be to be implicated performatively in a transcendental contradiction.

Nevertheless, cosmopolis has no utopian commission. There is no basic horizon apart from concrete, particular relative horizons. Human subjectivity is an incarnate subjectivity, rooted in the physical here and now, in the mysterious union of body and consciousness; human existence is social existence, situated in the technical, economic, political, and cultural world that tran-

---

16. "Horizon and History," in *Notes on Existentialism,* 12–14.

17. On the norms of questioning, see *Insight,* 404–5; and *Method in Theology,* 37–38, 55, 104, 231, 265, 288, 292. On "conversion," see *Method in Theology,* 238–43.

scends its creators and perdures with its carriers; and individual and social existence is historical existence, conditioned by past achievements, schemes of recurrence, and probabilities. Thus, the bodily, social, and temporal a prioris limit human existence, making it horizon-bound. There is a necessary and creative dialectical tension between basic horizon and relative horizons. Without basic horizon relative horizons would neither exist nor be sustained; without relative horizons basic horizon would be a mere transcendental ideal. This tension is another word for historicity. It is what Lonergan calls the tension of limitation and transcendence. It is what Voegelin, echoing Plato, calls the tension of the in-between. It is the foundation neither of a classicism nor of a relativism but of a "perspectivism" that recognizes in the openness of the question, at once, the identity of historical horizons (hence the universal viewpoint of cosmopolis) and the source of diversity among historical horizons (hence the unrestricted thrust of cosmopolis to challenge every fixed position, every system, every formulation, as it does homage to the desire to know).[18]

Cosmopolis therefore cannot succumb to the rationalist pretensions of modernity. It cannot be lured by the gnostic dream of instantaneously transforming heuristic anticipations into determinate content. It cannot, on the other hand, capitulate to the postmodern fascinations of relativism, skepticism, obscurantism, or deconstructionism. What, then, is its positive task? It seeks to promote through persuasion and example the free conversion to the norms of basic horizon, to appeal to the latent openness of individuals and groups, to support the struggle for authenticity, to tap the psychic energy of awe and wonder—in a word, to promote self-transcendence. Nonetheless, the tactic of cosmopolis must always recognize limitation; always address the meaningful concreteness of the historical situation, the particular configuration of particular social reality, the affectivity of incarnate consciousness; always speak to the heart as well as to the mind. Thus, cosmopolis in its positive task is not restricted to theoretical culture—that is, philosophy, narrowly

---

18. On the bodily a priori, see *Insight*, 538–44, 577, 592–95, 615; and *Method in Theology*, 70, 216, 255–57. On the social a priori, see *Insight*, 232–37, 725–39; *Method in Theology*, 41–52, 269, 302; *Second Collection*, 233; and *Third Collection*, 176–77. On the historical a priori, see *Method in Theology*, xi, 85–99, 124, 235, 301–2, 315, 326; *Second Collection*, 92–93, 100, 264; and *Third Collection*, 170–71, 177–79. On the tension of limitation and transcendence, see *Insight*, 497–99. On the "in-between," see Voegelin, *Order and History*, vol. 4; *Third Collection*, 188–92, 196, 218–21; and Plato, *Symposium* 203B–204B. On perspectivism, see *Method in Theology*, 216–18. On universal viewpoint, see *Insight*, 587–91.

conceived, and science—but embraces necessarily art, the media, and historiography.[19]

Cosmopolis, however, has a second task, what Voegelin has termed its "therapeutic" function. Every society has its existential, or lived, history, its interpretation of the meaning of its past that informs its current values and its purposes. Existential history is always tied to existential philosophy, implicit assumptions about reality, truth, and the good. Cosmopolis, as self-reflective, adds to existential history critical history, to existential philosophy explicit, thematic philosophy. Were human history solely the story of authenticity, of fidelity to the openness of questioning, then critical history and explicit philosophy would be entirely positive in scope. Although neither progress nor decline is necessarily the case in history, it remains that de facto progress has been mated with decline; intelligible schemes of recurrence have been punctured by the unintelligibility of the social surd.[20] Since cosmopolis addresses the historical challenges of the concrete situation, it must have in its arsenal a therapeutic option.

Lonergan provides a quite specific analogue, on the individual level, for the therapeutic enterprise of cosmopolis that is reminiscent of Habermas's analogue of depth hermeneutics as the model for emancipatory culture.[21] In his treatments of scotosis (the state of neurotic blindness) and of genuineness, Lonergan outlines the following factors in the breakdown and recovery of dramatic living:[22]

a) a bias of understanding spawns an existential gap between performance and interpretation;
b) the interplay of inhibited performance and distorted interpretation leads to a cumulative process of breakdown;

19. On gnostic delusion, see *Insight*, 565. On promoting self-transcendence, 263–67; and "Horizon and Dread," in *Notes on Existentialism*, 10–12. On cosmopolis addressing the heart, see *Insight*, 261–62; "Horizon and Dread," in *Notes on Existentialism*, 12; and *Second Collection*, 3–6. On cosmopolis and nontheoretic culture, see *Insight*, 266, 647–49; and *Method in Theology*, chap. 3, pt. 2.

20. Voegelin, *Order and History*, 1:xiv. On critical history and thematic philosophy, see *Insight*, 265–66, 585–617, 735–39; *Method in Theology*, chaps. 8, 9, 10; and *Third Collection*, 179–81. On progress, decline, and the social surd, see *Insight*, 8, 259–60, 265–66.

21. See Habermas, *Knowledge and Human Interests*, chap. 10.

22. *Insight*, 210–31; *Method in Theology*, 33–34.

c) the result of the breakdown is the surd of unintelligible performance in dramatic living;

d) genuineness demands that less than fully conscious components of change be brought to light;

e) therapy strives to overcome bias by inverse insights;

f) a vertical exercise of liberty can effectively reconstitute the disordered dramatic horizon;

g) therapy involves the therapist's knowledge of psychogenic aberration and of specific case history; and

h) the therapist must be free from scotosis.

Lonergan would perhaps be more careful than Habermas to stress the merely analogical character of the pattern of psychic malady and therapy as it serves to illustrate vividly a similar, but not identical, pattern in the crisis of the social world. Granted, then, that individual neurotic bias is but one of many biases to flood the plain of history; that other biases may be tied more intimately to deliberate human irresponsibility, alienation, and inauthenticity and more directly to an assault on intelligence and will; and that an entire society is unlikely to seek therapy from cosmopolis—cosmopolis can nevertheless expect to find the following parallel to the healing of psychogenic disease in its own therapeutic endeavor:[23]

a) an existential gap between performance and interpretation created by bias;

b) a cumulative process of decline;

c) a social surd;

d) an explanatory and evaluative historiography to uncover the sources of inauthenticity;

e) the possibility of critique to offset decline through inverse insights;

f) the necessity of a vertical exercise of freedom to reverse decline, effectively if not definitively;

g) a theory of the dialectic of history and the history of consciousness to complement specialized historiography; and

h) the imperative for cosmopolis to purge itself from bias.

The normative project of human existence therefore demands that, under appropriate historical conditions, cosmopolis meet the challenge of history to

23. On disanalogy between individual psychic malady and social decline, see *Insight*, 8–9, 253–57, 262, 650–55, 710–15. On analogy between individual psychic malady and social decline, 8, 235–36, 252–53, 260–61, 265–66, 735–39; *Method in Theology*, 40, 245, 302, 318; McPartland, "Meaning, Mystery, and, History"; and "Horizon and History," in *Notes on Existentialism*, 12–13.

increase the scope of responsible human action and respond to the desperateness of a civilization in the throes of decline. Still, the task is perpetual. The struggle of authenticity against inauthenticity, the narrowing of the gap between basic horizon and aberrant relative horizons, is never finished. No revolution can usher in the great new age wherein the opposition between authenticity and inauthenticity will cease. No police force can carry out the mission of cosmopolis, for even a benevolent despotism would attack liberty, the very principle of progress, whereas cosmopolis manifests authenticity as a dimension of culture and of consciousness. Authenticity, for Lonergan, remains an ever precarious withdrawal from inauthenticity.[24]

Cosmopolis and the Challenge of History

What guidelines does Lonergan's philosophy suggest to cosmopolis as it meets the challenge of history in the concreteness of the early twenty-first century? We might focus on five areas.

First, Lonergan offers a nuanced analysis of tradition that clearly allows for critical culture but eschews the Enlightenment's exaggerated claim to dominate history. Paul Ricoeur has claimed that an aporia exists between, on the one hand, Gadamer's rehabilitation of tradition and assault on the "prejudice against prejudice" and, on the other hand, Habermas's espousal of a culture informed by emancipatory interests. Lonergan, I would argue, overcomes the aporia by canceling out the contradiction between tradition and critique. If tradition, as Alasdair MacIntyre confirms, is the ongoing interpretation of the meaning of the past, then critique is not inherently outside the bounds of tradition, unless the tradition were essentially inauthentic.[25] Tradition is not an object "out there" to be confronted, known transparently, and dominated by Enlightenment intellectuals. It is impossible to extricate oneself fully from the assumptions of one's own tradition. Not even if universal doubt were feasible would it be desirable. The hermeneutics of historical being points to tradition as a condition of thinking, including critical thinking. Even at best, our own knowledge is only partly immanently generated; most of it rests upon belief.

---

24. On response to decline; see "Horizon and History," in *Notes on Existentialism*, 14; on cosmopolis as a dimension of consciousness, see *Insight*, 263–64; on authenticity as withdrawal from inauthenticity, see *Method in Theology*, 110, 252.

25. Ricoeur, "Ethics and Culture: Habermas and Gadamer in Dialogue"; MacIntyre, *After Virtue: A Study in Moral Theory*, chap. 15.

How, then, is critique possible? As we need not, according to Lonergan, grasp all the facts of the universe and their interconnections to be able to make a virtually unconditioned judgment about any particular fact, so we need not comprehend in its totality tradition in order to make a judgment about any particular error. And when we expose one error, through the self-correcting process of learning, we can spot related errors and eventually a whole network of errors.[26]

Second, cosmopolis must battle against the "supremacy of facts." Perhaps the chief bias it must combat is that of common sense, with its shortsighted, narrow practicality. If the facts are the facts of the social surd, then just being practical about the facts is the realism of a prisoner in the cave. Cosmopolis must give witness to the norms of self-transcendence and the possibility of authentic existence in the face of ever more fragmented, incoherent, and impoverished interpretations that only nourish the performance that seems to verify them.[27] Since cosmopolis addresses both the mind and the heart, its witness of self-transcendence must be both in the area of critical human science and evaluative history and in the area of art.

Lonergan's explication of the historicity of the cultural superstructure in terms of the interlocking of distinct but related functional specialties is decisive here. Evaluative history, for example, is not the enemy of factual history. Rather, evaluative history rests upon the achievements of more descriptive and explanatory history, as descriptive and explanatory history rests upon the achievements of philology, as philology rests upon the achievements of research disciplines. At the same time, the dynamics of cognitional structure points beyond factual history to evaluative history. The same applies to the relation of descriptive social science and critical social science. To refuse to identify decline as decline and progress as progress is to refuse to deal with essential facts of historical existence and to rule out of court the dynamics and dramatic character of historical life. No doubt, to support and to sustain historical scholarship, cosmopolis must wrestle with such foundational issues of philosophy as truth, objectivity, and the good. These foundational concerns, however, are not a relic of Greek classicism, or medieval dogmatism, or mod-

---

26. On undesirability of universal doubt, see *Insight,* 737. On belief, 725–28; *Method in Theology,* 41–44; and *Third Collection,* 180–81. On concrete judgment of error, see *Insight,* 366–71, 736. On critique of error, 197–98, 311–12, 314–16, 736.

27. On the bias of common sense, see *Insight,* 250–67; on the facts of the social surd, 255–57, 259, 262; on witness to self-transcendence, 264–65.

ern rationalism gone awry. The endeavor of establishing philosophical foundations is more relevant than ever if evaluative historiography and normative human science are to be pursued with intellectual integrity.[28]

Art has a leading role to play in the enterprise of cosmopolis. By collapsing insights, judgments, and evaluations onto the flow of experience, art in the bare presentment of experience explores the possibility of human living. By its very nature, then, true art challenges every limited view of human being as it portrays the many moods of human straining for being. Art is a release from the drag of biological purposiveness and the confines of practicality. Art, though, does not merely stimulate aesthetic pleasure, for aesthetic pleasure is a response to aesthetic meaning, which, through insinuation and indirection, at its best is ultimately ethical, metaphysical, and spiritual. Through humor and satire, art represents the social surd as absurd, as contradicting the expectation of intelligibility, and thus is a key element of the therapeutic endeavor of cosmopolis.[29]

Third, the universal viewpoint of cosmopolis is not opposed to specializations as such. It is indeed opposed to specializations conceived according to nominalist or skeptical canons. It is not opposed, however, to specializations allied with a vision of human reality sufficiently nuanced to ground their meaningful and distinct cooperation. In fact, cosmopolis would defy its mission and encourage obscurantism were it to reject the contribution of specialists. Rather, cosmopolis promotes the integration of specialized tasks by inviting methodical cooperation. Collaboration on the level of methods ensures that cosmopolis will retain its open-ended, dynamic character. Thus, its unity is not found on a theory, metaphysical or otherwise.[30] Instances of fruitful collaboration abound. To illustrate, we can cite three regions: functional specialization, field specialization, and artistic specialization.

28. On functional specialties, see *Method in Theology*, chaps. 5–10. For an example of contemporary historians discovering the decisiveness of epistemological issues in historiography and the need of a "practical realism" to mediate between positivism and relativism, see Joyce Appleby, Lynn Hunt, and Margaret Jacob, *Telling the Truth about History*.

29. On the horizon of art, see *Method in Theology*, 61–62; and *Topics in Education*, 211–22. Lonergan refers to Suzanne K. Langer, *Feeling and Form: A Theory of Art;* see also Joseph Fitzpatrick, "Lonergan and Poetry," 441–50, 517–26. On art as liberation of human straining for being, see *Insight*, 208–9. On the substantive nature of aesthetic meaning, see Hugo Meynell, *The Nature of Aesthetic Value,* chaps. 1–2. On the functions of humor and satire, see *Insight*, 647–49.

30. *Insight*, 7, 415–21; *Method in Theology*, xi, 6, 81–83, 93–96.

Lonergan's idea of functional specialties links scholarship, philosophy, and social policy in an ongoing circuit that adds heightened, critical awareness to the dialectic of performance and interpretation. Here theory is not opposed to practice. Theoretical culture is needed to grasp the long-term developments, which persons of a practical bent would tend to overlook. Practical intelligence is needed to transform the insights of intellectual culture to meet concrete challenges and to communicate philosophical, historical, and scientific insights to persons in the commonsense world.[31]

An example of the cooperation of field specializations could be found in the history of thought, where psychohistory, the history of culture, the history of ideas, intellectual history, and the history of philosophy examine, respectively, the expression of meaning in increasingly explicit philosophical form. A sophisticated cognitional theory can assist in this methodological cooperation, although the basis of this collaboration is the native operation of the human mind through the structure of cognition, in diverse patterns of experience, over differentiations of consciousness.

The different styles of art explore complementary facets of human possibility. Sculpture is a visual realization of the interior feeling space of the person. Architecture, on the other hand, expresses objective axes of reference for the group. The physical horizon of the Middle Ages was dotted by castles and cathedrals, whereas the contemporary Western city displays its fundamental values through the domineering skyline of stock exchanges, banks, and office buildings. As sculpture is to architecture, so epic poetry and drama are to lyric poetry, the former representing a narrative of a group's past or an image of a people's destiny, the latter expressing the moods, orientations, and existential dispositions of the self. Painting more than any other spatial art form is a release of potentiality, an upsurge of energy exploring the possibilities of human living. Painting takes us beyond the space of the ordinary world. Omitting all kinesthetic and auditory elements, its pattern of colors, forms, and textures, bounded by its frame, reveals, in Suzanne Langer's words, a "virtual world." Music, however, represents an image of experienced time. The time of music, a nonspatial shape corresponding to the manner in which feelings multiply and change, is the time of Bergson's *durée pure*.[32]

Fourth, cosmopolis must promote education that reflects the above con-

---

31. On theoretical analysis, see *Insight*, 252–53, 255, 258–61, 265–66; on practical communication, 266, 585–87; and *Method in Theology*, 78–79.

32. On sculpture, see *Topics in Education*, 225–26; on architecture, 226–27; on poetry, 228–32; on painting, 223–25; on music, 227–28.

siderations. Thus, education must embrace the creative tension of tradition and critique. It must, on the one hand, foster a pedagogy that encourages appropriation of the normative pattern of inquiry in all of its complexity; it must support the psychic and social conditions for such an appropriation. On the other hand, particularly in higher education, it must carry on dialogue with tradition through its great books, classics of impenetrable depth.[33] It must nourish appreciation of the long-term view, of theoretical culture, and of learning for its own sake. It must insist on a liberal education to prevent the putatively educated from being, in fact, "educated barbarians."[34] It must not, however, conceive of liberal education as opposed to any technical, professional, or specialized training. Indeed, the leaders of technical, professional, and specialized fields need liberal education so that they might be participants, at least unthematically and indirectly, in the larger community of the lovers of wisdom.

Fifth, cosmopolis must be open to transcendence. The very openness of the desire to know compels the authentic inquirer beyond. The very openness is an unrestricted openness, experienced as being drawn to inquiry and as participating in unrestricted love. Thus, openness is simultaneously oriented to transcendence and pulled by a sacred presence that heals, renews, and sustains the orientation of self-transcendence. Lonergan would join Robert Nisbett in reversing Enlightenment procedure and tying the idea of progress to a sense of the sacred. He agrees with Voegelin's refusal to detach reason from a range of spiritual experiences.[35] Cosmopolis can identify itself neither simply with the outward panoply of religion, its institutions, practices, and creeds, nor with the *ressentiment* and scotosis of a purely secular culture.

Where, then, does cosmopolis reside? In tradition as such? But it may be inauthentic. In the authorities who are the custodians of tradition? But they may be inauthentic, even if the tradition is not. In the receivers of tradition, those subject to authorities, who are called to believe or not to believe? But they may be inauthentic and hence unreasonable believers or unreasonable unbelievers.[36] In the independent thinkers who challenge a tradition or forge

---

33. *Method in Theology,* 161–62.
34. Lonergan's term in discussion session, Lonergan Workshop, Boston College, 1970s.
35. *Third Collection,* 188–92, 219–21. On spiritual openness and progress, see *Collection,* 185–87; and *Method in Theology,* 240–43. See Robert Nisbett, *History of Progress,* 355.
36. *Third Collection,* 5–12.

a new one? But they may be inauthentic and biased. Clearly, cosmopolis resides in fidelity to the norms of inquiry, whether in the creative minority who mold tradition, the authorities who carry it, or the rank and file who believe it. More precisely, cosmopolis resides in a community of those faithful to the norms of inquiry, where there would be a healthy tension between the questioning subject and the heritage of tradition. Ideally, to match the universality of cosmopolis, the community would be global. More realistically, it would be on a much more restricted scale. In the extreme, it would have to reside in oneself alone, where one's openness would be the nucleus of a true community. But, in any case, cosmopolis cannot reside apart from individual persons converted to the horizon of openness. And one's own starting point must be oneself. To paraphrase Socrates at the end of book 9 of the *Republic:* build cosmopolis in yourself.

7

Historicity and the Event of Philosophy

THE TRIUMPH OF HISTORICAL consciousness in the past two centuries has hurled an acute, even seemingly insuperable, challenge to the ideal of objective philosophical truth—and perforce has rendered problematic the relationship of philosophy to culture and to religion. Even Kant's modest claims for critical philosophy have been overthrown by the dominant currents of logical positivism, linguistic analysis, and Sartrean existentialism, each in its own right, among other imperatives, attempting to salvage some residue of philosophy from the ravages of historical consciousness. One of the burning questions that most agitated Descartes and Kant, namely, how to surmount the plurality of antagonistic philosophical schools, has apparently now begun to consume philosophy itself in the flames of relativism. Hegel's dazzling Gnostic speculation on the meaning of history notwithstanding, more characteristic of the spirit of the age has been the tortured ambivalence of Dilthey's critique of historical reason, simultaneously displaying a kind of pantheistic enthusiasm and then a deeply felt frustration and foreboding over the restriction of philosophy to an aesthetic contemplation of the diversity of irreconcilable philosophical worldviews. The contemporary assault on philosophy, however, has had as a fomenter not so much historical consciousness per se as the strident pronouncements of historicism, an inchoate philosophy that would consign truth solely to the cultural context, if not the vagaries, of a certain point in time and of the social and technological setting in which the context is embedded: thus, human nature, according to historicism, varies from historical age to historical age much as philosophical—and presumably religious—truth varies from one *Weltanschauung* to another. Historicism, not surprisingly, is one of the more conspicuous perpetrators of the cultural crisis of the twentieth century, a crisis in which the decisive issue is ultimately the nature, value, and integrity of higher intellectual culture itself, which is to say, of philosophy in its most generic sense. Hence, the dubious relation of philosophy to culture and to religion in the climate of opinion of the twentieth century simply reflects the dubious status of philosophy—along with the dubious status of culture itself and of religion.[1]

Historical consciousness has unquestionably dislodged from its previous position of ascendancy the kind of culture that viewed itself as a set of universal and permanent standards. In the bosom of this "classicist culture," to use Bernard Lonergan's term, philosophy, no matter how debatable might be its other attributes, would inevitably aspire to be a perennial philosophy; moreover, by supplying rudimentary metaphysical principles this perennial philosophy would prepare the ground for theological reflection on the timeless truths of religion.[2]

But when classicist culture has been jettisoned, can it be supplanted? Can philosophy arise again like the phoenix from the ashes of the cultural crisis? Can philosophy once again speak to religion of the concerns of epistemology and metaphysics?

Lonergan and Historical Consciousness

No one has been more resolute in responding to this challenge than Bernard Lonergan. Nevertheless, he has not been alone in this endeavor; there was indeed at work in the twentieth century a creative minority of philosophers, theologians, social theorists, and historians—such thinkers as Martin Heidegger, Michael Polanyi, Hans Georg Gadamer, Jürgen Habermas, and Eric Voegelin, earlier preceded by such nineteenth-century precursors as Kierkegaard and Newman—all of whom, with varying degrees of intensity and exactness, have been breaking away from the intellectual horizon reigning ever since the late

1. For general discussion of the crisis of historical consciousness, see Baumer, *Modern European Thought*, pt. 5. Dilthey, *Pattern and Meaning*, chaps. 5–6; Linge, "Historicity and Hermeneutic," pt. 1, esp. 252–53 n. 271. On historicism, see Chapter 4 above, secs. 1–2; Mandelbaum, "Historicism" and *History, Man, and Reason*, pt. 2; Fackenheim, *Metaphysics and Historicity* and *The God Within*, chap. 8.
2. *Second Collection*, 101, 182.

Middle Ages, the hallmark of which has been the confrontation theory of truth.[3] With an arc of influence, immediate or indirect, extending from conceptualist metaphysics to nominalism, from rationalism to empiricism, from Kantianism to positivism, from idealism to historicism, the confrontation theory of truth has asserted, as its fundamental premise, that knowing must involve, at least in some analogous sense, an unimpaired vision of reality, whether the emphasis be given to looking at sense data, concepts, or ideas. The historicist position, for example, depicts historical objectivity as an empathic entry by a historian divested of any personal evaluation into the horizon under investigation; although some of the more sophisticated historicists, such as Dilthey, have advocated reexperiencing the creative moments beneath the tangible expressions of the horizon, still such a creative process is subjective, and it offers no objective criteria by which to discriminate among the myriad expressions of meaning and value.

Lonergan provides what is arguably the most comprehensive alternative to the confrontation theory of truth. He suggests that we probe beneath the oftentimes bewildering heterogeneity of ideas, concepts, and values found in historical horizons as finished products to the conscious activities that constitute them. He would have us ask whether waging the struggle for philosophical foundations principally in the arena of theories and concepts has been, in fact, a strategy of capitulation to the confrontation theory of truth, leading inexorably to the battle fatigue and exhaustion of the present cultural crisis. Lonergan urges contemporary philosophical culture to retrace the journey in search of foundations along the path from medieval essentialism to Descartes's thinking substance, to Kant's transcendental ego, to Hegel's subject, to Kierkegaard's *this* subject: from object as object, to subject as object, to subject as subject. The venture of cultural reconstruction must take the road of, in his unique phrase, "self-appropriation." By this Lonergan means that epistemology, metaphysics, and all other branches of systematic philosophy, including the philosophy of religion, must rest on an existential underpinning; they must be grounded on an explication of the conscious activities of the self as knower. Through a studied application of the old Socratic injunction "know thyself," issuing in what Lonergan styles "cognitional theory," we can, he claims, fashion a basic philosophical semantics. Truth, objectivity,

---

3. Among the key works: Heidegger, *Being and Time;* Polanyi, *Personal Knowledge;* Gadamer, *Truth and Method;* Habermas, *Knowledge and Human Interests;* Voegelin, *Order and History;* Søren Kierkegaard, *Concluding Unscientific Postscript;* John Henry Newman, *An Essay in Aid of a Grammar of Assent.* See also Chapter 4 above, sec. 3.

and reality now assume meaning in terms of the norms ingredient in the very process of inquiry with its directional tendency. The knower, then, rather than being a self-contained *cogito* "in here" confronting a world "out there," is a self-transcending subject dwelling in the luminous openness of the horizon of being, and knowing is precisely fidelity to the project of questioning through its recurrent cognitive structure of experiencing, understanding, and judging. Fundamental differences in metaphysics, ethics, and epistemology can usually be reduced, explicitly or implicitly, to differences in cognitional theory, and those differences can be resolved, and only be resolved, by an appeal to the data of consciousness.[4] Such is Lonergan's tack. His focus on self-appropriation and the systematic expansion of the positions of cognitional theory into all domains of philosophy stands as his most original achievement and perhaps as an enduring legacy to the history of philosophy. For he allows philosophy, with its refurbished critical apparatus, once again to address itself to the normative concerns of culture and to the vital issues of religious truth. Furthermore, by keeping in full perspective in his philosophy both the subjective pole of self-appropriation and the objective pole of cognitional theory, Lonergan strives to avoid the twin dangers of either subjectivism, irrationalism, and romanticism, on the one hand, or objectivism, essentialism, and conceptualism, on the other hand. And by discovery of a normative and transcultural pattern in subjective operations he empowers philosophy to outflank historicism in the very territory of historical consciousness itself.

Increasingly throughout his work, Lonergan has sought to exploit the riches of historical consciousness in order to erect what he calls a basic science of human living.[5] Cognitive life, integral as it is to human living, is not the totality of the human existential situation. Indeed, Lonergan remarks, "a life of pure intellect or pure reason without the control of deliberation, evaluation, responsible choice is something less than the life of a psychopath."[6] Thus, he emphasizes how the intention of the good is the fuller flowering of the desire to know, the animating principle of cognitive operations; how cognitive self-

---

4. On the movement toward interiority, see *Method in Theology,* 316; "Horizon as a Problem of Philosophy," in *Notes on Existentialism,* 14–15. On self-appropriation, see Chapter 9 below; and *Insight,* 11–17, 352–57, 359–60. On the self as knower, see ibid., 11–14, 343–62, 421–26, 626–28, 659–62. On basic philosophical semantics, see ibid., pt. 1; *Method in Theology,* chap. 1; and *Collection,* chap. 14. On truth, reality, and objectivity, see *Insight,* 22–23, 372–75, 381–83, chap. 13, 413, 415–21, 572–85. On consciousness as foundational, see Chapter 1 above; and *Insight,* 4–6, 413, 626–28, 646–53, 699–708.

5. Bernard J. F. Lonergan, "Questionnaire on Philosophy."

6. See *Method in Theology,* 122.

appropriation, or intellectual conversion, has, as existential conditions, a conversion to values and a conversion to the sacred; how, conversely, moral conversion and religious conversion preserve, enrich, and carry forward the essential features and properties of intellectual conversion; how the life of inquiry—cognitive, moral, and spiritual—is that of an incarnate subject whose knowing and deciding are driven by the power of feeling, image, and symbol, releasing the energy of the *élan vital* with its teleological momentum; how the incarnate inquirer undergoes "a development that is social and historical, that stamps the stages of scientific and philosophic progress with dates"; how at the core of historical process is the ongoing project of self-interpretation; and how human self-interpretation—and with it the entire panoply of institutions and cultural forms—can become distorted, in desperate need of critique.[7]

All these elements point in one direction—to human historicity. Although Lonergan has more outlined than systematically explored the region thus opened up, the implications of his approach are clear. We might say that, for Lonergan, human existence is an odyssey: a search for meaning and a quest for value. It is constituted by a process of inquiry one can flee but not escape. The search and the quest are tasks never finished. The meaning and value sought are elusive, never fully grasped. The interpretation of what it means to be human is always ongoing, where past performance becomes data for present interpretation and present interpretation informs future performance. This holds for individual biography as well as for communal destiny, in which the participants interact and live with each other, are nurtured by a common past named tradition, and are called to collective responsibility. The search and the quest are a search and a quest for "something," a "something" that gives a sense and direction to inquiry, and simultaneously a "something" that remains the mysterious object of the question. What it means for humans to be is known in the sense that it is the "ideal" of historical action; it is the object of the question. What it means for humans to be is unknown in the sense that it is revealed only in the performance of seeking the goal, a performance that never (authentically) ceases; it is a question, and no answers are so com-

7. On the intention of the good as enrichment of the desire to know, see *Second Collection*, 82. On the existential conditions of intellectual conversion, see Lonergan, "Bernard Lonergan Responds," 233–34. On moral and religious conversions as expansions of intellectual conversion, see *Method in Theology*, 241–42. On subject as incarnate, see *Collection*, 204; *Method in Theology*, 30–31, 66; and "Reality, Myth, Symbol," 33, 37. On subject as historical, see *Collection*, 204, 242–43. On subject as self-interpreting, see *Method in Theology*, 212; and "The Philosophy of History," 72–74. On distorted self-interpretation, see *Collection*, 204.

plete as to end the seeking. The tension of knowing and ignorance, of knowing ignorance and the mystery of the known unknown, pervades the field of
history. Neither knowledge nor ignorance is total, absolute. Understanding
can be both gained and lost, self-understanding both advanced and distorted. The gaining and the losing, the questioning direction, and the striving and
fleeing all suggest a normative dimension to historical life. (Does not the normative dimension of history, surrounded by the aura of tension and mystery,
capture the old root meaning of *culture,* stemming from the Latin *cultus,* namely, "to cultivate and to educate"?)[8] Excellence, taste, style are the emblems of
true culture, true *paideia,* but not as frozen in the immobile standards of classicist culture; rather, they properly adorn the heuristic ideals of the process of
inquiry; the norms of culture are immanent in the search for meaning and the
quest for value and in the story that necessarily emerges from that perilous
journey. Thus, the odyssey of history bears with it existential overtones of a
drama. Like any drama, this "primordial drama that the theatre only imitates"
is essentially a matter of movement and countermovement, a primal battle of
striving and fleeing, gaining and losing.[9] And if inquiry is an infinite striving,
an unrestricted openness to what is experienced as a sacred pull, then the
movement and countermovement of the drama of history are fundamentally
that of sacred presence and human response. The unity and the diversity of
history stem from the same dynamic source: the search and the quest, as forging the continuity of questioning, and as impelling diversity through the challenge of every particular formulation, every limited viewpoint, every given
horizon.

   The tenor of Lonergan's reflections, then, attests to the intimate relation of
culture and religion to historicity. This immediately serves as a springboard to
our major theme. For central to our purpose in this chapter is the question:
where does philosophy fit into the portrait sketched above? If the odyssey of
historical existence is indeed the odyssey of everyman, how is the journey of
the philosopher different? If Lonergan, as we have earlier remarked, sees cognitive self-appropriation, or intellectual conversion, as presupposing moral
conversion and religious conversion, does this observation pertain to philosophy as its core? If he views moral conversion and religious conversion as sub-
lating cognitive self-appropriation, does this likewise apply to the essence of

   8. See Lewis and Short, *A Latin Dictionary,* s.v. "cultus"; for the ancient Greek interpretation of culture, see Jaeger, *Paideia.*
   9. *Insight,* 211.

philosophy? If he associates feeling, image, and symbol with heuristic insights and the momentum of inquiry, does this association embrace in a substantive way the activity of philosophy?

Lonergan, as we have maintained, more than any other contemporary philosopher, emphasizes both the existential and the systematic character of philosophy; to ignore either would be to distort philosophy, heading for either subjectivism or objectivism. His philosophical perspective includes more than the systematic positions derived from cognitional theory. Yet, Lonergan, for all the wealth of his existential analysis, tends to accord the systematic dimension of philosophy more treatment. And when he makes his most penetrating statements about existential issues, he addresses them more to the topic of human living in general, and of religious and cultural communities in particular, than to the topic of philosophy per se.

Our main goal here must be to place in some higher unity Lonergan's ideas about the subjective pole of philosophy. That higher unity is captured in the notion of historicity. This is by no means to downgrade the significance of systematic philosophy or the perpetual relevance of metaphysics. For the existential nature of philosophy itself demands metaphysics. It is by no means to divorce philosophy from the exigency of cognitive self-appropriation. It is rather to supplement, not replace, cognitive self-appropriation with the category of historicity.

Philosophy and Existence

If we are to develop adequately the train of Lonergan's thought on the existential nature of philosophy, we must eventually arrive at a startling conclusion, which goes to the very heart of philosophy, its origin, destiny, and historicity: philosophy is a variety of religious experience. It is precisely the religious essence of philosophy that defines its unique cultural mission and, as we must presently explore, links together the two poles of philosophy. We must first examine carefully these two poles.

The Subjective Pole of Philosophy

Philosophy, to repeat a leitmotiv of this essay, has been an existential aspect and a systematic aspect; both are intrinsically related to each other as subjective and objective poles of the horizon of philosophy. The existential pole is the experience of the philosopher as a lover of wisdom, an incarnation of the desire to know with its cognitive structure of experiencing, understanding, and judging. But because philosophy is a search for complete intelligibility, the systematic imperative emerges. Thus, systems, expositions, and treatises arise ever anew to do homage to the desire to know. The subjective pole therefore specifies the objective pole. The philosopher does not look at an objective pole of essences, of systems, of being; the philosopher is immediately related to being in the philosopher's questioning unrest.

We must not, however, confuse the existential pole—the philosopher as subject, the concrete philosopher as consciously engaged in the pursuit of wisdom—with objectifications of that activity in the objective pole. Indeed, if we follow Lonergan's revolutionary stress on cognitional theory, we must distinguish within the objective pole itself a subjective dimension and an objective dimension. In the latter case (object as object) we have metaphysics and allied fields, fundamental positions about the structure of reality, the ultimate ground of being, and the relationship among the various sectors of being investigated by the several intellectual disciplines. In the former case (subject as object) we have cognitional theory, an explanatory account of the process and structure of knowing present in consciousness. Now, for Lonergan, metaphysics must be critically grounded in cognitional theory; metaphysical positions on reality must be consonant with basic positions on knowing, truth, and objectivity derived from cognitional theory; erroneous metaphysical statements are those, explicitly or implicitly, tied to a faulty cognitional theory, usually some variation of the confrontation theory of truth; correct metaphysical statements are those, explicitly or implicitly, joined to a cognitional theory in which the process and structure of questioning is given full play. The sense and meaning of reality, the metaphysical status of what is known, is determined by the orientation, pattern, and norms of inquiry.[10] Hence, within the objective pole metaphysics is conditioned by cognitional theory.

However, the objective pole itself is conditioned by the subjective pole. Another way of putting this is to say that metaphysics is conditioned by methodology and methodology by method. Lonergan has proclaimed that one of the most profound transformations in modern philosophy is the transition from logic to method. We may judge that Lonergan is speaking in two senses here. In the first place, metaphysics rather than simply founding itself upon the logical ordering of propositions must assume the exigency of method, namely,

10. *Collection,* 211–14; *Second Collection,* 40–41; Bernard J. F. Lonergan, *Understanding and Being: The Halifax Lectures on Insight,* 149–70; *Verbum,* 20; *Insight,* 22.

one in which its conclusions would be verified by an appeal to cognitional theory and the conclusions of cognitional theory, in turn, would be verified by an appeal to cognitional fact. In the second place, cognitional theory is nothing but methodology, where methodology is a systematic reflection upon method, an objectification of method. Cognitional theory, then, is a reflection on the basic method of questioning, not on any given science or academic discipline or field of inquiry as such, but on the basic, or transcendental, structure of cognitional operations. This structure with its immanent norms embraces not only purely intellectual endeavors but also practical reason, the self-correcting process of moral learning, the subtle path of spiritual inquiry, and the creative project of the aesthetic imagination. Lonergan defines method as "a normative pattern of recurrent and related operations yielding cumulative and progressive results."[11] Although perhaps Lonergan has principally in view the procedures of the sciences, the spirit, and probably the letter, of his definition, I believe, can legitimately be extended to include the orientations and structures mentioned above.

Now if method is restricted in meaning to the mere following of rules or to the interpretation accorded it by positivists and neo-Kantians, then, of course, Lonergan would join those, such as Gadamer, who attack the modern preoccupation with "method" as technique.[12] If, however, "method" is taken in its etymological sense as "way" (*methodos*) and is seen as referring to the numerous ways of apprehending and communicating meaning, then the proper existential contours of method can be illuminated. Basic method is a way of apprehending and communicating meaning that is structured by sets of operations, and structured only because it is oriented to a *goal*—which is to say that it is underpinned by an intentional and existential orientation: the desire to know, the intention of the good, and unrestricted loving. The orientation of the pure question specifies a basic horizon that bears a normative relation to all concrete, historically relative horizons. The method of basic horizon is a road toward fuller and deeper understanding, a creative journey toward its goal. At the same time, method is both a way of knowing and a way of being. A horizon, according to Lonergan in his celebrated lectures on existentialism, is a "concrete synthesis of conscious living."[13] Basic horizon has its intellectual openness to a reality correlative to the pure desire to know, its unlimited moral concern, its affective power and drive toward being and the good, and

---

11. *Method in Theology,* 4; on the shift from logic to method, 94, 305.
12. See ibid., 5–6, 157–58, 169, 223–24.
13. "Horizon and Dread," in *Notes on Existentialism,* 10; *Collection,* 148.

its undertow of religious consciousness. It is the concrete integration of cognitive, moral, affective, and religious facets of existence. It is, moreover, the concrete integration of the concrete living of a concrete person. Herein we encounter a distinctly hermeneutical factor. For when an individual faithfully pursues the goal of inquiry—thereby actualizing the basic method of inquiry—this performance becomes data for self-interpretation, for self-knowledge of who the person is and can be. It likewise evokes some notion of reality, typically a commonsense interpretation, and, as such, one often inchoate and liable to confusion by the potent, omnipresent extroversion of biological consciousness, which generates the confrontation theory of truth. The quality of performance within basic horizon, its sophistication and authenticity, together with the ongoing dialectic of performance and interpretation, each decisively influencing the substance of the other, reveal the unmistakable traits of historicity. We must conclude that if we are not to reify method, we must always connect it with horizon, hermeneutics, and historicity.

Philosophy therefore is clearly an interpretation of basic horizon. It is equally self-interpretation. It has this irreducibly personal dimension because the experiential foundation of philosophy is the performance of the person, and the creative and responsible effort of the person is the sine qua non of philosophizing. In this vein, Lonergan can contrast the self-appropriating philosopher with the "plaster cast" philosopher, the one whose philosophy Kant described as relying exclusively on outside authority.[14] As thematic self-interpretation, philosophy is the objectification of interiority, and this interiority is a luminous performance in the drama of living, a performance structured by a basic method, a basic orientation, a basic horizon. Given the dialectical interplay of performance and interpretation at the core of personal existence, philosophy must be intimately tied to the horizon it objectifies; philosophy is not a matter of a look at a distant interiority; indeed, because a horizon is a concrete synthesis of conscious living, philosophy is a way of life, a kind of conscious living. It is conscious living ordered by inquiry, by the search for meaning and the quest for the good.

Philosophy and Religious Experience

What, then, to return to a question posed earlier, distinguishes the philosopher from "everyman," for "everyman's" existence, too, is bound up with the imperatives of inquiry, which he or she follows or flees? Insofar as the philoso-

---

14. *Understanding and Being,* 34–35; Kant, *Critique of Pure Reason,* A385–86, B863–64.

pher is an inquirer (or at least called to inquiry), he or she is the *same* as "every-man." But insofar as the philosopher raises inquiry to a thematic focus, identifies and names the authentic performance of "everyman" as inquiry, inquires about inquiry itself (and inquires about the metaphysical objective of inquiry), then the philosopher is *different*. Nevertheless, as implied above, this difference does not mean that the philosopher is just like "everyman" except that he or she takes a closer look at "everyman's" conscious performance. The personal horizon of the philosopher differs in two crucial respects.

In the first place, the philosopher is unlike "everyman" in that his or her performance must be a *sufficient* incarnation of the spirit of inquiry to be adequate datum for interpretation of basic horizon. Furthermore, if fidelity to the norms of inquiry carries with it attunement or correspondence or participation between the being of the inquirer and the being intended in the search and the quest, because there is an immediate relation between inquiry and its objective, then the philosopher as an incarnation of inquiry is also an incarnation of being. Although sufficient incarnation is not the same as perfect incarnation, we might reasonably expect that the representative philosopher (a Socrates) would likewise be a representative to mankind of genuine human possibility. But, we must ask, what is it about the horizon of the philosopher that leads him to inquire about inquiry itself?

In the second place, then, the existential disposition of the philosopher has a certain distinct quality and definition, his or her orientation of consciousness a certain focus and clarity, and his or her experience a certain range of intensity—all of which nourish and sustain the particular devotion of the philosopher to the pursuit of the true and the good. The specifically philosophical differentiation of consciousness, as it was articulated by the ancient Greeks, was experienced as a response to a call, a pull, a transcendent sacred presence. Plato, for example, depicted his prisoner as leaving the cave because he had been drawn out. Voegelin perceptively describes the Greek philosopher's search for meaning as an inner trial of the soul whose victory is the saving of his life in response to the divine pull; the symbols of the philosopher, according to Voegelin, originate in the engendering experience of a mutual participation of human and divine. Moreover, to sustain the activity of philosophical inquiry requires a continuing openness to reality that so far transcends human moral impotence as to be termed, in Lonergan's language, "openness as a gift," again the experience of a sacred presence.[15] Finally, the

---

15. See Plato, *Republic* 515E. Voegelin, *Published Essays, 1966–1985*, chaps. 7, 12, pp. 267–73; Voegelin, *Anamnesis*, 91–97. For Lonergan's favorable comments, see *Third Collection*, 189–91, 194–96, 219–21. On openness as a gift, see *Collection*, 186–87.

philosopher, literally the "lover of wisdom," experiences and embodies an un-restricted love of the true and the good, a generic wonder, an unqualified openness to reality. Now these elements of call, gift, and unrestricted love, at the heart of the existential dimension of philosophy, constitute an experien-tial unity that displays unmistakable traits of religious experience.

What is the core of this experience? What distinguishes it from other vari-eties of, or even what we might ordinarily mean by, religious experience? Of the three elements of the religious experience of the philosopher—the call, the gift, and the unrestricted love—the unrestricted love seems to be the key to understanding the philosophical nature and unity of the experience, since the call is precisely the unrestricted attraction to inquiry, and the gift of open-ness sustains the unrestricted desire to know. The experience of unrestricted love, of course, would not be externally observable sense experience; it would be the self-presence of one with a certain orientation of consciousness and mode of life, a *bios*, as the Greeks styled it. The experience of the love of wis-dom would likewise carry with it an interpretation, what Lonergan calls an "elemental meaning," a meaning whose understanding is intimately and nec-essarily bound up with a set of acts of experiencing. Philosophical inquiry would be grounded in a heuristic insight, a knowing ignorance, a knowledge rooted in religious love. The experience of the love of wisdom would be an understanding born of unrestricted love and the discernment of value; the philosopher's unrestricted love would thus give rise to a "faith," in the sense of the term employed by Lonergan to refer to the "knowledge born of religious love." But faith in what? The generic wonder, the unqualified attraction, and the pure openness of the gift would be unrestricted because they would be correlative to an unrestricted goal, and the unrestricted goal would be pre-cisely the goal of the philosopher because it would be a goal of unrestricted or complete or intrinsic intelligibility.[16] So the distinguishing stamp of phi-losophy as a variety of religious experience would seem to be the experience of, and the faith in, the intrinsic intelligibility of being and the intrinsic intel-ligibility of the good. Is this not also to say that philosophy is an experience of participation in unrestricted love—with this specific difference, which

16. Lonergan regards being in love in an unrestricted fashion as the essence of religious experience (*Method in Theology*, 105–7). On classical philosophy as a way of living with spiritual exercises, see Pierre Hadot, *Philosophy as a Way of Life*. On "elemental meaning," see *Method in Theology*, 67, 75; and *Insight*, 592–93. On "faith," see *Method in Theology*, 115ff. On the intrinsic intelligibility of being, see *Insight*, 522–26, 576, 619, 628–30, 675, 695.

marks it off from other varieties of religious experience—that the experience is of the divine as intrinsically intelligible? The love of wisdom is a participation in the same divine reality sought as the objective of questioning. Aquinas, accordingly, views the human intellect as the created participation in the uncreated light of divine understanding. Lonergan, following Aquinas, describes divine reality as "the unrestricted act of understanding, the eternal rapture glimpsed in every Archimedean cry of Eureka."[17] The experience of the participation of human reason in, as the Greeks speak of it, the divine Nous or the divine Logos grounds an unrestricted *love* of truth, a *faith* in the intelligibility of reality, a *hope* in gaining insight and knowledge about reality (without ending the mystery of the divine beyond). The Greek philosopher Heraclitus, who perhaps first called philosophy by name, attested to an existential disposition of faith, hope, and love as the infrastructure of the search and the quest of the philosopher. Perhaps it is no coincidence that such philosophers in antiquity as Xenophanes, Parmenides, Heraclitus, Plato, Aristotle, and Plotinus were mystic philosophers or that such medieval philosophers as Augustine, Anselm, Albert, Bonaventura, and Aquinas were recognized as saints by their tradition.[18] Is the shift to interiority in modern philosophy, for the most part, only an incipient attempt to recollect the true experiential heart of philosophy?

To summarize the relation between philosophy in its existential sense and philosophy in its systematic sense—or, we might say, the relation between the philosopher and philosophy—we must avoid any trace of a radical subject-object dichotomy, where the philosopher is a subject confronting philosophy as an object, a system "out there." On the one hand, the philosopher is the foundation of philosophy. Philosophy is an interpretation of basic horizon, and this interpretation is self-interpretation. On the other hand, the philosopher intends philosophy; that is, the unrestricted desire to know opposes all obscurantism, for the search for intelligibility and truth demands the continuing development of conceptual formulations, theoretical tools, and systematic accounts ever adequate to the exigencies of the search. Similarly, we must not postulate any false dichotomy between faith and reason. The philosopher, while participating in the drama of history as a fellow inquirer with "everyman," is different not only by his or her more thematic interpretation but also by his or her more intense—religious—experience of the intrinsic intelligi-

---

17. *Insight,* 706; on Aquinas, see *Verbum,* 90–94, 98, 100.
18. See n. 15 above. Heraclitus B18, B35, B86; for translations of these and other presocratic fragments cited in n. 21 below, see Freeman, *Ancilla.*

bility of being, which gives philosophy its mass and momentum and direction. Indeed, it is the religious experience of the philosopher that impels him or her on the path toward explicit intellectual conversion. The "noble piety" of the philosopher, according to Kierkegaard, or, as he phrased it, of the "simple wise man," must be to acknowledge that all persons are equal under God but that he is different.[19]

Noetic Consciousness and History

The religious dimension of philosophy is historical. It happened first in Hellas among mystic philosophers. We must, of course, consider the possibility that something parallel was happening in China and India. In these two civilizations, however, the outburst of philosophy seems incomplete, with different religious overtones. Chinese civilization has boasted its countless schools of philosophy, but, if we are to accept Voegelin's careful assessment, its mode of differentiation was subdued and muted; neither the Confucian nor the Taoist sage was able to break away completely from the older, more compact cosmological order since both sought, in their different ways, attunement with (relatively) undifferentiated cosmic order.[20] "Philosophy" in Indian civilization, in spite of its obviously penetrating insights in logic, psychology, metaphysics, and other fields, is possibly a misnomer, because the animating force of Indian higher culture is the desire for *moksha,* spiritual liberation, rather than the Hellenic love of wisdom.

Philosophy attained full stature and identity in Hellas. The Ionians saw the divine in *physis,* the ground of cosmic order; the social philosopher Solon wrote in his lyric poetry of the divine "unseen measure" of human conduct; the Pythagoreans and Empedocles were deeply influenced by the Orphic tale of the purification of the soul; Xenophanes proclaimed his *areté* (excellence) as noble wisdom, which enabled him to critique unseemly, anthropomorphic images of the divine; Parmenides, perhaps influenced by the Greek notion of "like to like," posited some kind of identity between thinking and being, between human *nous* and ultimate divine being; Heraclitus, unlike the sleepwalkers, who live in their private worlds, was open through his discourse *(logos)* to the common world *(koine cosmos)* of the divine Logos, the "Alone Wise"; Anaxagoras pictured the divine Nous as the ordering principle of the

---

19. Kierkegaard, *Concluding Unscientific Postscript,* 205.
20. Voegelin, *Order and History,* 1:62; 4: chap. 6; Voegelin refers to Peter Weber-Schaefer, *Oikumeme und Imperium: Studien zur Ziviltheologie des chinesischen Kaiserreichts.*

cosmos; Socrates faithfully obeyed the divine command emanating from his *daimon* to seek wisdom; Plato, who coined the term *theology*, spoke of the philosopher as the "son of Zeus," an incarnation of the divine Nous; Aristotle categorized human reason *(nous)* as being either "divine or only the most divine element in us."[21]

More revelatory of the sacred character of Greek philosophy were the origins of two dominant terms in the Greek philosophical vocabulary, *nous* and *theoros*. As Douglass Frame has demonstrated, the root of *nous* was tied to myths of the sacred cycle of the sun god, who sojourned and struggled in the dark underworld each night; it originally conveyed the idea of a return home from death and darkness to light and consciousness. The dramatic imagery of *nous* pervaded the story of Odysseus, "the wanderer," who "saw the townlands and learned the minds of many distant men." Odysseus in his return home to Ithaca had to contend with the forces of darkness; the cave of the infamous Cyclops (from which his *nous* extricated him); the cave of the seductive Calypso; the cavernous bay of the Laistrygones, where "the course of night and day lie close together"; and the region of the fogbound Kimmerians, over whom a glum night is spread. He had to encounter fabulous creatures whose very names echoed the myth of the cycle of the sun; the Cyclops, Circe, and Calypso. These themes were conspicuously present at the opening of Parmenides' great poem: he was carried on the renowned road of the goddess "who leads the man who knows through every town"; there, leaving the "abode of the night" and far "from the beaten track of men," he was granted the vision of being through the exercise of his *nous*. We should also recall the most famous allusion to the original meaning of *nous* in Plato's allegory of the cave.[22]

21. On the Ionians, see Werner Jaeger, *The Theology of the Early Greek Philosophers*, chap. 2. On Solon, see Voegelin, *Order and History*, 2:194–99. On the Orphic tradition, see F. M. Cornford, *From Religion to Philosophy: A Study in the Origins of Western Speculation*, 194–214, 224–42. Xenophanes, B2, B11–12, B14–16, B23–26; Voegelin, *Order and History*, 2:171–80. Parmenides, B3; Voegelin, *Order and History*, 2: chap. 8; Jaeger, *Early Greek Philosophers*, chap. 6. Heraclitus, B1–2, B32, B89, B114; Voegelin, *Order and History*, 2: chap. 9. Anaxagoras, B12–14. Plato, *Apology* 28e, 30a, 31d, 33c; Plato, *Phaedrus* 252–56. Aristotle, *Nicomachean Ethics* 10.7.1177b30ff.

22. Frame, *The Myth of Return in Early Greek Epic*. Odysseus the "wanderer," *The Odyssey of Homer*, trans. Robert Fitzgerald, 1.3.7; the Laistrygones, *The Odyssey of Homer*, trans. Richmond Lattimore, 10.86; the Kimmerians, Homer, *The Odyssey*, 11.14; Parmenides, B1, translation in G. S. Kirk and J. E. Raven, trans., *The Presocratic Philosophers*, 266; Plato, *Republic* 514–517D.

We likewise find the theme of a sacred journey—the search for meaning and the quest for value—in the word *theoros*. The original Greek meaning of *theorist* referred to a person sent on a sacred mission to oracles or to religious festivals, such as the Olympic Games. The theorist was to question and to transmit faithfully a divine message; he had to venture forth, searching along the road, in order to hear the voice of God. The *theorion*, according to the poet Pindar, was the place where theorists competed in the games as official participating delegates; they were simultaneously spectators and participants on their journey, not disengaged Cartesian observers. Thus, the theorists traversed beyond the pale of the everyday to the "festive and awesome realm of the divine," guarding, along the way, against uncritical acceptance of the dominant values of their native surroundings, but eventually to return, transformed, to the home country, where the journey began. For Plato in his *Laws*, the *theoroi* were to embark upon a course of inquiry to inspect the doings of the outside world, most especially to visit divinely inspired men, only to come back to the native polis to share the spectacle. Out of this religious background emerged the Greek idea of reason; gradually, *theoria* came to be associated with travel inspired by the desire to know, as in the visits of Solon, and eventually it referred to the experience and knowledge acquired while traveling.[23]

We can postulate that behind the statements of the major Greek philosophers and behind the use of the terms *nous* and *theoria* was an eruption of divine reality. This was not an event extrinsically imposed upon history, conceived as a closed world-immanent process, for, as we have argued above, the divine-human encounter is at the center of historical existence itself, whose locus is the tension of "time" and "eternity." The enduring of the physical universe may be called "time" in its elementary sense; to order totalities of such durations we employ frames of reference, whether the explanatory theories of physical science, the personal descriptive language of such terms as *soon, re-*

23. On the original meaning of *theorist,* see Gadamer, *Truth and Method,* 111; Bernd Jager, "Theorizing, Journeying, Dwelling," 235–60; John Navone, *The Jesus Story: Our Life as Story in Christ,* 103–9; and H. Koller, "Theoros und Theoria." On *theorion,* see Gadamer, *Truth and Method,* 111; and Koller, "Theoros und Theoria," cited by Jager, "Theorizing, Journeying, Dwelling," 236. Jager, ibid., 235, following Koller, "Theoros und Theoria," 284, suggests that the origin of *theoros* may "echo" a combination of *theo* and *eros.* One of the roots of *theorion* and *theoros* is *theaomai,* meaning "to look on, gaze at, view, behold"; a second root, more specific to the motif of religious ambassador, is a combination of *theos* and *ora* (care); see Henry George Liddel and Robert Scott, *A Greek-English Lexicon,* s.v. "theaomai" and "theoros." On the journey of the theorist, see Jager, "Theorizing, Journeying, Dwelling," 239–40; and Navone, *Jesus Story,* On Plato, see Jager, "Theorizing, Journeying, Dwelling," 237–38. On *theoria,* see ibid., 237; and Navone, *Jesus Story,* 104.

cently, long ago, or such public measurements as clocks and calendars. And if by *eternity* is meant the lastingness intimated in the experience of openness to the transcendent beyond (and hence not the enduring proper to a thing in the world), then human beings, as historical creatures, are at the intersection of "time" and "eternity." In addition to the time of the physical universe and the lasting of transcendence is the existential experience of time, the *dureé* described by Bergson, in which the "now" is not a mathematical point but a psychological present, a time span of overlapping moments.[24] This psychological dimension of time, I would suggest, is grounded in the conscious intentionality of the human subject: the subject, an identity of conscious acts, by his or her intentionality reaches into a past through memories and into a future through anticipations; this experience of time is an experience of historicity, first, since the field of memory is present interpretation of past performance informed by past interpretations and, second, since the field of anticipations, with which it is fused, is comprehended by the generic openness of the pure question oriented to the beyond. To cut off the experience of transcendence is to cut off the openness of questioning. A purely world-immanent history is the equivalent of the closed horizon of Heraclitus's sleepwalking idiots.

Philosophy, then, is a constitutive event of history, a discovery of human participation in the divine Nous on the road to inquiry. We can detect this sense of historical epoch in Plato's myth of the age of the great god Nous replacing the previous ages of Cronos and Zeus. We can speculate with Voegelin about the actual impact of philosophy on Greek historiography: he suggests that historiography arose in Hellas in a fashion similar to its birth in Israel and in China, when a carrier of spiritual meaning came into conflict with, or was threatened to be absorbed by, an empire with universal aspirations; in the case of Hellenic civilization it was the carrier of the spiritual outburst of philosophy, the cutting edge of the culture of the polis, and the clash with the Persian Empire made the struggle worthy of historical memory. We can further note that Herodotus, the "father of history," was probably influenced by the ideas of Anaximander and the Greek faith in the intelligibility of cosmic order; the Herodotean law of compensation, the inevitable fall of great empires and of great men, seems to be an expression of Anaximander's dictum that all

---

24. On time, see *Insight*, 167–68. For the experience of the intersection of time and the eternal, see Voegelin's formulation of the "flux of presence in the Metaxy" (*Order and History*, 4:331, 333–35). Bergson, *Time and Free Will*; *Method in Theology*, 177.

things come out of and return to the *apeiron* (the "boundless"), paying their penalty according to the assessment of time.[25]

Now if the event of philosophy was born in particular and irreducible circumstances, is it forever limited to the spiritual and political context of its origins? Is it inextricably bound to what Voegelin has characterized as the "burden of the polis," the wedding of philosophy to the abiding sense of political community present in the classical polis? Is the essence of philosophy, as a variety of religious experience, restricted completely to the compactness of, to use Voegelin's words, the "Dionysiac soul"?[26] Granted that the contemplative vision of the philosopher is neither the Christian beatific vision, nor the Hindu *moksha*, nor the Buddhist *nirvana*, still must it remain entirely circumscribed by the Greek experience of the cosmos?[27] Needless to say, even to begin to broach these issues would require the most intricate of historical investigations and of theological reflections; this chapter has the more modest endeavor of posing the questions in their most striking terms. Nonetheless, this much we can hazard to state: Surely, the very nature of philosophy as an unrestricted love of wisdom points to something universally human, transcending, though not leaving behind, the peculiar religious tradition of Hellas. The spirit of philosophy is open to communion with other varieties of religious experience, especially when the misleading duality of "faith" and "reason" is dissolved. Nevertheless, genuine interaction can happen only as a dialogue with the tradition of Hellenic philosophy in which the cardinal goal is authentic appropriation of the love of wisdom, albeit under different historical and religious conditions that obtained in Hellas. To argue thus for the integrity—the sui generis character—of philosophy as a variety of religious experience is not to argue that it is the only variety of religious experience or that its universality renders it the supreme form of religious experience.

Historical diffusion has, in fact, spread philosophy to the religious traditions of Judaism, Christianity, and Islam. Although the usual treatment of

25. Plato, *Laws* 713c–714b; see Voegelin, *Order and History,* 4:226–27. Israel, with its spiritual outburst in the person of the prophets, went on a collision course with the major empires of Babylon, Persia, and the Seleucids, thus occasioning the writing of the history of the conflict; in the case of China, sages witnessed the absorption of classical Chinese society by imperial dynasties. Voegelin, *Anamnesis,* 122–23; see also *Order and History,* 1:6. Anaximander, B1; see Kirk and Raven, *The Presocratic Philosophers,* 105–7.

26. On the "burden of the polis," see Voegelin, *Order and History,* 2:169–70; on the "Dionysiac soul," 3:62, 70, 92, 115–16.

27. At the same time, can we simply bypass the Greek idea of the divine depths of the cosmos and of the philosophical relevance of myth, as formulated, for example, in Plato's *Timaios*? Must not these insights be reappropriated?

"Jewish philosophy," "Christian philosophy," and "Islamic philosophy" tends to place a premium almost solely on the level of doctrine, the more profound and substantive approach would be to stress the existential pole. What specific religious experience will be that of a philosopher who is a Christian? Will such a philosopher, for example, express his radical philosophical experience in terms of the central Christian experience of the Trinity, equating the love of truth with the spirit of truth, hearkening to Plato's language of the son of god in describing the fidelity of the philosopher, and identifying the objective of the desire to know with the father? What will be the unique fusion of religious horizons of a Jewish philosophy? Of a Muslim philosophy? Of a Confucian or a Hindu or a Buddhist lover of wisdom?

We can conclude that once the spiritual breakthrough of the love of wisdom has burst forth on the stage of history, a twofold imperative emerges to continue it: first, to engage and appropriate the meaning of the original tradition and, second, to cultivate the inner life of the unrestricted love of wisdom, which initially spawned the tradition. These two imperatives are allied and necessarily reinforce each other.

Engaging the Philosophical Past

The continuation of philosophy is an ongoing historical achievement embracing the dialectic of community and person in their historicity.

Dialectic of Philosopher and Philosophical Tradition

Historical existence in general witnesses a dynamic, complex, and dialectical relation between individual and community. The communal reality is more than the sum total of its individual ideals and deeds; it is precisely the horizon, the organization, and the pattern of what is common to many individuals; it has its own historical life that persists over time (though not apart from individuals); and its historical destiny is a linking of successive situations by a set of decisions that is greater than the sum of the individual wills of its participants. Nevertheless, it is not a collective will that questions, gains insights, and judges. It is not a collective will that deliberates, decides, and acts freely. There is no group entity or substance existing in itself above and beyond individuals, as idealists and essentialists allege. The person cannot be reduced to a mere function of the technical, social, or cultural milieu. Individuals cooperating together constitute the nucleus of the community, and the perduring communal life, in turn, becomes the objective historical situation in which individuals are born, are reared through socialization and acculturation, and are nourished by education. There is, then, a historical circuit in which subjects create community and community creates subjects.[28]

The historical existence of philosophy, too, shares this dialectic. On the one hand, the outer word of philosophical tradition carries the expression of philosophical meaning and mediates personal philosophical self-appropriation. The existential truth of philosophy is conveyed in the memory of such representative philosophers as Socrates; the life of Socrates, as portrayed in Plato's magnificent dialogues, is a vivid instance of incarnate meaning, where the entire personality of Socrates evokes the spirit of the love of wisdom. Without the recollection (*anamnesis*) of the exemplary philosophers, the spark of philosophy may not be lit or may only flicker.[29] The most precious literary treasures of philosophy, both existential and systematic, are the great classics, works of impenetrable depth and amazing richness, which are perpetual challenges, inexhaustible fonts of questions that invite the interpreter into ever fuller exploration of the subject matter. Without the philosophical classics, the ship of philosophy would flounder adrift in a wild sea, having lost its venerable charts. The horizon of the interpreter is always at risk in meeting the classics; the enterprise opens the interpreter up to the possibility of self-transcendence, to more profound self-knowledge; he or she may have to lift his or her horizon up to the level of that of the author of the text, for an existential condition for understanding the ideas of a thinker of the caliber of a Plato or an Aquinas is that the interpreter must initially reach up to the mind of Plato or Aquinas. This is a never-ending task. "A classic," wrote Schlegel, "is a writing that is never fully understood. But those that are educated and educate themselves must always want to learn more from it." The classics, Lonergan argues, "ground a tradition, creating a milieu in which they are studied and producing in the reader through the cultural tradition the mentality, the *Vorvenstandis,* from which they will be real, studied, interpreted."[30]

---

28. On historical destiny, see *Topics in Education,* 231–32, 257. On the individual origin of meaning, see *Method in Theology,* 255–56; *Verbum,* 37. On cooperation and communal meaning, see *Method in Theology,* 70. On the communal basis of meaning, see ibid., 41–47, 79, 90–92, 257–58, 269; *Insight,* 558–59, 725–35; *Collection,* 226–27, 233–34; and *Third Collection,* 170–71, 196–97.

29. On *anamnesis,* see Plato, *Meno;* on the encounter of a "Zeus-like soul," see *Phraedrus* 252C–253A; for a brief allusion to the passing on of tradition, see *Timaios* 20D–21A.

30. For the challenge of the text to the interpreter, see *Insight,* 769–70; and *Method in Theology,* 161. Schlegel quoted in ibid.; for discussion of a "classic," see ibid., 161–62.

On the other hand, the outer word of the philosophical tradition in and of itself is merely the carrier of the expression of meaning; the insights behind the expressions can be grasped only by the creative art of interpretation; the mind of the individual philosopher must come into play. To be sure, the interpretation will have its necessary complement of communal collaboration, but it will also have its irreducibly personal dimension: the self-appropriation of the individual philosopher. In addition, the tradition itself is forged and constantly replenished by the influence of those philosophical geniuses of the ilk of Plato, Aristotle, Aquinas, Descartes, and Kant who mark decisive turning points in the history of philosophy, either by inaugurating bold new lines of inquiry (Plato, Descartes, and Kant) or by synthesizing previous developments through masterful overarching insights (Aristotle and Aquinas). The original genius fashions new linguistic usage, molding philosophical culture.[31]

The particular circumstances behind the flowering of genius provide a most striking illustration of the dialectic of person and community. The genius does not operate in a vacuum; he or she profits from the human cooperation that supports vital cultural institutions; he or she ordinarily relies on the largely unnoticed work of countless lesser figures. "For the genius," Lonergan observes, "is simply the man at the level of his time, when the time is ripe for a new orientation or a sweeping reorganization."[32] The path of philosophical genius must have been cleared by the intellectual efforts of predecessors. Furthermore, the genius is implicated in the general movement of the zeitgeist. The cross-fertilization of ideas, the raising of questions, and the repercussions of discoveries can generate certain intellectual currents that define the general assumptions of an age; these assumptions, born by philosophical communities, schools, and sects, are probably unknown, or not very well known, by most contemporaries, even geniuses, since, for the most part, they are taken for granted and function behind the scenes; moreover, precisely because they direct, foster, or impede inquiry, these pervasive assumptions deeply affect most contemporaries, even geniuses. The genius, of course, may challenge the zeitgeist with reflective awareness or may use the categories of the zeitgeist as a springboard to leap to intellectual heights heretofore beyond the reach of the dominant horizon, but, in either case, he or she will be responding to the general assumptions of the age and, consequently, will be decisively influ-

31. *Verbum*, 37.
32. *Insight*, 444.

enced by them. Still, however propitious the time may be for a wholesale redirection of thought, it nevertheless requires the mental force, the creative edge, the singular dedication of genius to exploit the situation.

Philosophy and Relativism

Having outlined the dialectic of philosophical community and philosophers, we must now examine in more detail the historicity of each element, keeping in mind the dynamic interrelationship of each to the other. The achievements of philosophical community—and thereby of individual philosophers—are severely conditioned by the general historical situation, with its technological, economic, political, and cultural components. Thus, the development of philosophical culture in Hellas was promoted by the technological invention of writing and was contingent upon sufficient economic differentiation to allow for leisure time. The philosophy of Plato was as much colored by the crisis of the polis as the philosophy of such contemporary existentialists as Marcel, Jaspers, and Heidegger is affected by the crisis of modern technological civilization and political bureaucracy.[33] Greek and medieval philosophy typically labored under the assumption of a hierarchical, and oftentimes cyclical, cosmos, whereas twentieth-century philosophy had to take account of an emergent universe and historical consciousness.

The most telling historical conditions, however, reside within philosophy itself. There is a historical movement internal to philosophy. If philosophy is like a four-story structure, with metaphysics at the top built upon epistemology, and epistemology resting upon cognitional theory, and cognitional theory grounded upon the performance of the authentic lover of wisdom at the foundation below—if, in other words, philosophy is based on performance, not premises—then it follows that as cognitive performance develops so will philosophy, in its systematic form, be able to advance. Lonergan for example, sees progress in modern mathematics, empirical science, depth psychology, and historical method as supplying new, precise evidence for philosophy. New data on the operations of the human mind stimulate new insights and break-

---

33. Lonergan suggests that cognitive self-appropriation is conditioned by what Hegel called "objective spirit," the historical objectification, manifestation, and embodiment of subjective processes (*Understanding and Being*, 219–20). On the effect of writing on philosophy, see Eric Havelock, *Preface to Plato*. On the crisis of the polis, see Jaeger, *Paideia*, 2: chap. 1. Gabriel Marcel, *Man against Mass Society*; Karl Jaspers, *Man in the Modern Age*; Martin Heidegger, *The Question Concerning Technology and Other Essays*.

throughs in philosophical understanding. Accordingly, any theory of the human mind "is bound to be incomplete and to admit further clarification and extension."[34] Philosophical interpretation can never totally capture the richness and elusive movement of philosophical performance. This is historicity but not historical relativism. Philosophical formulations are framed within horizons, networks of interlocking questions and answers, usually relying upon partially unacknowledged presuppositions. Neither the formulations nor the horizons are final and definitive. The living act of philosophical insight is not necessarily exhausted by linguistic expressions.[35] The intention of philosophical truth does not rest content within any historically given philosophical horizon. Philosophical understanding can advance within established contexts and then move beyond those contexts to effect a genetic sequence of philosophical horizons perhaps available only to the retrospective glance of the historian. Indeed, the historian can frequently apprehend philosophical interconnections and similar paths of questioning better than the original contributors. By submitting to the norms of the pure question—the identity amid historical difference—genuine philosophers extend the import of their work beyond their own particular horizons and enter into the philosophical dialogue of the basic horizon of inquiry. Although truth does not exist apart from minds and the context of their operations, the basic horizon of inquiry establishes both the link among those contexts and the criteria by which to judge them.[36] Philosophical positions that, on the surface, seem incompatible may, in fact, be revealed as complementary, consonant, or sequences in a line of progress. Upon closer scrutiny, differences in philosophical positions may come about because different questions were raised, or the same questions were raised in different contexts, or the same questions were answered in compatible, though not equally penetrating, manners. The march

34. On intellectual progress and philosophical development, see *Insight*, 15–16, 412–13. On incompleteness of any theory of the mind, see *Method in Theology*, 19. Philosophical positions invite development (*Insight*, 413).

35. On the framework of horizons, see *Method in Theology*, 163–64; and *Collection*, 198–99. On the finitude of horizons, see *Method in Theology*, 325; *Second Collection*, 15, 25, 199, 207–8, 233, 259; and *Third Collection*, 186–88, 193–94. On the limits of linguistic expression, see the Lonergan-influenced article of Norris Clark, "On Facing the Truth about Human Truth."

36. On the retrospective insights of historians of philosophy, see *Method in Theology*, 178–79, 192, 250; and *Insight*, 412, 609. On philosophical works entering basic horizon, see *Insight*, 412. On the norms of the universal viewpoint, see *Method in Theology*, 325–26; and *Second Collection*, 207–8.

of philosophy, of course, is not along a smooth road. Philosophers have been many, disparate—and contradictory. The fragmentation of philosophical world-views, not to mention rancorous squabbling of antagonistic philosophical sects, all too conspicuously occupies the pages of the history of philosophy. No doubt, psychoneurosis, egoism, group bias, commonsense obscurantism, and neognostic exploitation of metaphysical profundities can poison the love of wisdom. But the products of such corruption belong to the history of ideology, in its pejorative sense, not to the history of philosophy, as conceived in this chapter. The history of philosophy must contend, rather, with the disturbing fact that dialectical opposition among philosophical horizons occurs in spite of fidelity to the intention of truth. Does relativism triumph after all? Not if the norms of inquiry are rigorously and thoroughly applied to expose any contradictions between a given philosophical interpretation and the actual performance of philosophizing. In other words, the failure to attend to the complexity of cognitional operations and, in particular, the failure to differentiate the confrontational element of biological consciousness from the more sophisticated activities of the mind generate philosophical errors, what Lonergan calls the "counterpositions."[37] Still, counterpositions can be profoundly helpful as they ruthlessly hammer out the inevitable implications of dubious assumptions; they can also be intimately tied to fruitful insights. Can the battle of philosophies play an ultimately positive role in the drama of philosophical understanding? Continued fidelity to the desire to know entails reversing the counterpositions, separating insights from oversights and extrapolating genuine discoveries from the constricting framework in which they were embedded. The very struggle with rudimentary philosophical misconceptions leads to a further enrichment and strengthening of authentic philosophical positions that could not have been so clarified otherwise. Beneath the myriad conflicts of doctrine, then, the history of philosophy displays a startling unity of program, goal, and intention.[38] Yet, the aim can be sought only by participating in the historical drama of philosophy.

37. On the contradictions among philosophies, see *Insight*, 386. Lonergan defines ideology as rationalization of alienated existence (*Method in Theology*, 55). On the dialectic of performance and interpretation, see *Collection*, 198–200. On counterpositions, see *Insight*, 413; on the problem of "biological extroversion," 15–17, 205–7, 275–79, 410, 413–14, 431, 437–41, 448–50, 603–5; and *Method in Theology*, 28–29, 238–40, 263–65.

38. On the fruitfulness of counterpositions, see *Insight*, 413–14. On the unity of philosophy, 412–14. "The Historical series of philosophies would be regarded as a sequence of contributions to a single but complex goal" (414).

Historical Consciousness and Functional Specialties

Coming to grips with the historical tradition of philosophy, therefore, is not merely an antiquarian interest of the historian; it is an integral moment of the project of philosophy, which demands that the insights of the philosophical tradition be appropriated and developed—cognitively and existentially. In order to appropriate the tradition, philosophers must first know it; conversely, in order to know it well, they must also appropriate it; and in order to add to its capital, they must have first appropriated its substance. We must explore this hermeneutical circle of a philosophical community.

Lonergan has implicitly demonstrated how this encounter with the philosophical tradition is precisely a community endeavor, requiring the specialized efforts of its members. To encounter the past philosophers must know it, and philosophers know the past the same as they know anything: through the cognitional pattern of experience, understanding, and judging.[39] Suppose, to pursue Lonergan's ideas of functional specialties, that specialists would focus in particular on one cognitional stage in this process. Some specialists would assemble the relevant philosophical data by preparing manuscript collections, critical editions, indices, tables, repertories, bibliographies, handbooks, dictionaries, and encyclopedias; other specialists would interpret the meaning of philosophical texts, producing commentaries or monographs on an author's treatment of discrete topics, on the single opus of an author, or on an author's entire corpus; and still others would judge the historical links among authors, schools, and eras by tracing genetic and dialectic sequences, by detailing the major horizon shifts, and by identifying the unique turning points, the transcending breakthroughs, that irrevocably alter the pattern of philosophical thinking. Each kind of specialist, to be sure, would employ the full range of cognitional operations of experiencing, understanding, and judging. However, by paying primary attention either to the experiential basis of the sources, or to understanding the texts, or to assessing historical trends, each kind of specialist would functionally cooperate with experts in other domains: histo-

---

39. The structure of the appropriation of tradition by a religious community—thematized by Lonergan in one of his more profound and original ideas—can, he suggests, be applicable to other cultural communities (*Method in Theology*, 364). Compare with James Collins, *Interpreting Modern Philosophy*, 24–34, 406–17. Collins, in his "working hypothesis," sees the components of historical investigation as the sources, historical questions, the interpreting present, and the teleology of historical understanding. On the cognitional structure, see *Method in Theology*, 133.

ry would be mediated by interpretation and interpretation by research, whereas interpretation (extending the hermeneutical circle to the zeitgeist) would be influenced by the conclusions of history and research by the conclusions of interpretation and history.[40] Only the dedicated cooperation of these functional specialists, each combining philosophical sensitivity with professional skill, would be able to promote a sophisticated, open-ended knowledge of the philosophical past. Even as the overriding goal of these researchers, interpreters, and historians would be that of objective knowledge of the philosophical past, already their philosophical perspectives would necessarily enter into the picture: for researchers must rely upon principles of selection and organization; the horizon of the interpreter, as Gadamer has so brilliantly demonstrated, is an integral part of the hermeneutical circle; and historians have as their proper commission not mere doxiographical description of reified ideas and sectarian dogmas, but an explanatory account of the historical unfolding of the desire to know.[41]

Once, however, an explanatory account has been rendered, the subjectivity of the philosopher becomes more intensely engaged. The history of philosophy is the drama of the multitude of philosophical horizons, some apparently irreconcilable. And the multitude of philosophical horizons in the history of philosophy seems matched only by the multitude of philosophical horizons operative in the historians, interpreters, and researchers themselves. The philosophical past hurls its challenge at the philosophical present. The conflicts among philosophies and among historians of philosophy have the salutary effect of further clarifying basic philosophical issues. It is incumbent upon philosophers to analyze the nature of the dialectical oppositions, to discern ultimate philosophical assumptions, to classify the crucial differences, to pronounce upon which assumptions are compatible with self-appropriation and which are not, to draw out implications of true "positions," and to correct false "counterpositions."[42] The functional specialty of what Lonergan calls "dialectic" seeks to safeguard dialogue with the philosophical tradition from the indiscriminate onslaught of blatantly a priori assumptions.

The challenge of the past impels the philosophical community to penetrate anew the foundations of philosophy in the meaningful concreteness of the

40. On research specialties, see *Method in Theology,* 127, chap. 6, passim; on interpretation specialties, 127, chap. 7; on historical analysis specialties, 128, chaps. 8–9; on interpenetration of specialties, 141.

41. *Method in Theology,* 161, 220–24, 246–47; *Insight,* 609.

42. On conflicts of philosophical horizons among scholars, see *Method in Theology,* 246–47; on clarifying philosophical issues, 253; on critical dialectical analysis, 249–50.

present, posing a series of pointed philosophical questions about objectivity, truth, reality, and the good that calls for the response of self-appropriation. As philosophical tradition is an ontological dimension in the life of philosophy, so the scholarly and dialectical mediation of the history of philosophy is an intrinsic component of philosophy. Reflectively articulate philosophical thinking originates through such an encounter with the past.[43] Although the past must be open to criticism, it can never be erased or eliminated by a program of universal doubt; it can never be dominated as a Cartesian object. The act of philosophizing is indeed a communication situation, in the words of Paul Ricoeur, "someone saying something about something to someone."[44] This is a situation in dialogue, where the partner in philosophical discourse, the "someone" in the horizon specified by the logic of questioning, is equally the self, the Wholly Other (the divine Nous), the other "sons of Zeus," and the patrimony of tradition. The outer expression of philosophical meaning, however, can be integrated satisfactorily only by philosophers involved in self-appropriation. The communal prerequisites of philosophy notwithstanding, this is, in the final analysis, a personal task, where performance of the philosopher as an incarnation of the desire to know becomes data for self-interpretation. The horizon of philosophy is the horizon of the philosopher. Fidelity to questioning the question entails a threefold philosophical conversion: a religious conversion, the experience of unrestricted love of being, inspiring a faith in its intrinsic intelligibility and a hope in the efficacy of inquiry; a moral conversion, the passionate commitment to the love of wisdom as a worthy mode of life; and an intellectual conversion, the identification of truth, objectivity, and reality with the directional tendency of inquiry. Such a profound transformation of horizon requires a "vertical exercise of freedom," the selection of a new concrete synthesis of conscious living.[45] Intellectual conversion, with its "startling strangeness," no less than the existential transfigurations, leads the philosopher on a journey, the journey of the *theoros* away from the homeland, only to return someday. The journey of philosophical self-appropriation, as a radical expansion of horizon, means that the philosopher

43. Extrapolated from ibid., 130, 246–47, 250, 365.

44. On the role of tradition, see *Insight*, 725–40; and *Method in Theology*, 41–47, 182, 223, 244. On the fallacy of the Cartesian program, see *Insight*, 433–36, 737. Paul Ricoeur, *The Conflict of Interpretations: Essays in Hermeneutics*, 83–88; for a Lonergan-influenced commentary, see Emil J. Piscitelli, "Paul Ricoeur's Philosophy of Religious Symbol: A Critique and Dialectical Transposition," 288.

45. On religious, moral, and intellectual conversions, see *Method in Theology*, 237–44; on "vertical exercise of freedom," 40, 237–38, 269.

must face the dread of his new possibility in the universe of being: dread, that is, in the Kierkegaardian sense of a "sympathetic antipathy." The prisoner leaving Plato's cave is blinded by the bright rays of the *agathon* and can acclimate himself or herself to its luminosity only by stages.[46] The budding philosopher is simultaneously attracted to the radiance of the *agathon* and disoriented by the loss of his or her cave mentality in the shadow world. Hence, the personal intellectual history of the philosopher is decisive.

The uniquely subjective effort of self-appropriation, issuing in what Lonergan describes as a "decisive personal act," is the foundation of philosophy. This self-knowledge can then be formulated in theoretical terms, and with these theoretical tools philosophers can address the future through functional specialties that reverse the cognitional pattern of experiencing, understanding, and judging. The philosophical community can critically affirm the essential truths of the philosophical tradition. Beyond that, philosophers can seek to develop its salient themes through systematic understanding. Finally, philosophers can communicate to diverse audiences what they have systematically understood and developed, affirmed, and selected from out of their encounter with the past tradition.[47] The performance of developing the authentic patrimony of the philosophical tradition becomes part of the tradition itself; it becomes data for future interpretation of the past. Thus, the philosophical community recovers, renews, and carries forward the event of philosophy, thereby displaying its historicity.

Mythopoesis

The communication of the meaning of a philosophical tradition legitimately utilizes all the dynamic resources of art, symbol, myth, drama, and narrative—and there is something inherent in philosophy that even demands such expression.[48] This pronounced affective character of philosophy, represented in its most mature form in the dramatic artistry and mythopoesis of Plato, however, has rarely been given due recognition since the time of that Hellenic genius.[49] If philosophy is, above all else, the love of wisdom, then

46. On the disorientation of intellectual conversion, see *Insight*, 22; Søren Kierkegaard, *The Concept of Dread*, 38; and Plato, *Republic* 515C–516B.

47. On self-appropriation, see *Insight*, 13. On the functional specialty of "doctrines," see *Method in Theology*, 132, chap. 12; on functional specialty of "systematics," 132, chap. 13; on functional specialty of "communications," 132–33, chap. 14.

48. *Method in Theology*, 356.

49. See Voegelin, *Order and History*, 3:10–14, 151–57, 183–94; John Sallis, *Being and*

philosophical communication must have as its task, above all else, the issuance of an invitation to philosophize, a call with all the subtlety, richness, and power of image and affect.

Philosophy itself is a drama of the psyche of the lover of wisdom against the counterpulls of inauthenticity and disorder, and the journey of the *theoroi* over the ages, constituting the grand tradition of philosophy, is part of an ongoing, still open, still unfinished story. The art of reappropriating the meaning of a philosophical tradition must necessarily recast the story of its origins and development, its trials and struggles. From the perspective of the present the drama of the past assumes new proportions—unbeknownst to the earlier actors. To borrow a metaphor Lonergan is so fond of using when he speaks of historical movement in general, there is to the history of philosophy a transpersonal dimension analogous to the course and outcome of a battle, which is not determined by the conduct of individual soldiers simply as individuals, or necessarily known by them, or inevitably in accord with the plans of the generals, the philosophical geniuses. To encounter the philosophical past is to gain a retrospective glimpse of the destiny of the philosophical tradition. For destiny, in Lonergan's estimation, is the linking of successive situations by a set of decisions by the participants in the drama that is not the decision of anyone in particular.[50] Destiny is not only a fact but also a mystery, because abiding in the drama of the philosophers on their voyage of inquiry there is the presence of the divine partner, experienced in the attraction to truth, the gift of the generic openness of questioning, and the participation in the divine thrust of unrestricted love. /

The drama of philosophy is an orientation to the mystery of the known unknown and must, therefore, have its complement of seemly myths and symbols. Why? Because the desire to know has its psychic infrastructure, its disposition of images and symbols impelled by the teleological drive of recurrent archetypes arising from the unconscious cosmic depths and by the spiritual energy released in anagogic symbols at the border of transcendence. Approximating Bergson's *élan vital*, these images and symbols, and the meanings they bear, are suffused by the experiences of call, openness, and unrestricted love.[51] This is to say that philosophical symbols, along with their narrative ac-

---

Logos: The Way of Platonic Dialogue, intro.; and Hans Georg Gadamer, *Dialogue and Dialectic: Eight Hermeneutical Studies on Plato*, chaps. 1, 3.

50. On the military metaphor, see *Method in Theology*, 179, 199; on destiny, see *Topics in Education*, 231–32, 257.

51. "Reality, Myth, Symbol," 33–34, 37. See Robert Doran, *Subject and Psyche: Ricoeur,*

companiment of myths and stories, carry heuristic insights, pointing philosophy, with a majestic power, in the direction of intrinsic intelligibility. The love of wisdom generates the understanding of faith and the affect-laden wings of hope. The philosophical triad of eros, faith, and hope has as its primordial expression those carriers of meaning whose very form keeps intact the heuristic nature of the philosophical enterprise.

To be sure, the functional specialty of communication will play its distinct role of bringing the message of the new tale of philosophy. It has the crucial mission of telling the story. But does it create the story? Is telling the tale simply a matter of translating into myth what is, after all, clearly definable and intelligible in conceptual language? Would this not be to reduce myth to either allegory or mere pedagogy? The appropriation of a philosophical tradition, we can suggest, spawns a philosophical artistry and a philosophical mythopoesis. Most significantly, for the purpose of this chapter, we can discern three elements in the process, each corresponding to a mode of historicity: the past, the present, and the future.

First, the encounter with philosophical tradition supplies the evidence for a narrative of the story of philosophy. Indeed, since the history of philosophy is the history of the drama of the psyche, historiography must convey that sense of drama. The historian of philosophy must have the requisite combination of philosophical sensitivity to the "serious play" of philosophy and artistic talent to portray it. Striking examples are Werner Jaeger's *Paideia*, an explanatory account of the development of Greek cultural ideals, particularly those of Plato, often painted in a powerful epic stroke, and Voegelin's *Order and History*, an existentially engaged presentation of the epochal struggle of the Hellenic lovers of wisdom against the disorder of their age.[52] Philosophical biography likewise has a similar dramatic and artistic obligation, namely, to capture the incarnate meaning of a philosopher revealed in his or her personal fidelity and passionate devotion, his or her patient frustration and rapturous delight, on the road of inquiry. The incarnate meaning of a philosopher can also inspire art forms that transcend biographical narration per se, Plato's dialogues about the life and death of Socrates being the supreme illustration. Perhaps bearing some likeness to Plato's dialogues—because it exhibits the mode of what Kierkegaard called "indirect communication"—would be an evaluative intellectual history of the kind that would render judg-

Jung, and the Search for Foundations, 210–52; Doran, "The Theologian's Psyche," 107–11, 120–21; Doran, "Subject, Psyche, and Theology's Foundations."
52. Jaeger, *Paideia*, vols. 1–3; Voegelin, *Order and History*, vols. 1–3.

ment in that peculiar style in which form becomes, or enters into, content: its judgments would come in the dramatic arrangement of themes, the juxtaposition of prominent thinkers, and the focus on the historical consequences unfolding from rudimentary philosophical assumptions; highlighting the challenge of possibility, it would be a powerful invitation for personal philosophical reflection on foundational issues.[53]

Second, the activity of self-appropriation in the present plunges myth into the creative vortex of the psyche purged of bias and blind spots, opening up the directed dynamism of the *élan vital*. This energy must be co-opted by philosophy in a critical philosophical hermeneutic with real poetic, mythic, symbolic depth. For philosophy is not the wisdom of divine omniscience but the love of wisdom, a process of inquiry that has no immediate access to the idea of being, no direct insight correlative to the intrinsic intelligibility of being, no total understanding of all there is to be known. Nor will it ever have. The contours of the known unknown may be constricted but the mystery never eliminated. The wither and whence of the drama of existence, the boundary situations, existentially at the center of our concern, cognitionally at the border of our horizon, will remain ever shrouded in mystery. To be sure, philosophy can pronounce on the great truths of the self, world, and God. These affirmations of philosophy, however, do not exhaust our questioning. Philosophy maps out the boundaries of reality but still leaves open vast territory to be explored. Myth is a genuine, if unique, form of understanding, which, as an expression of the generic openness of inquiry, precisely explores that territory. It thereby becomes a constitutive element of philosophy.[54] Accordingly, philosophy must negotiate along the strange paths at the border of the dynamic unconscious, bringing its own critical acumen, its own differentiated awareness, into the depths to determine the adequacy of myths to express philosophical truth. Far from being an exercise in romanticism the enterprise must be one of philosophical appropriation. The treasure of symbols must be carried back to fund the project of philosophy. Myth would be not only a prior historical condition of the emergence of philosophy, not only a prior occasion for philosophical inquiry, not only a pedagogical device for artistic commu-

53. Kierkegaard, *Concluding Unscientific Postscript,* 68, 74, 246–47, 319–21.

54. Lonergan seems to applaud Plato's recourse to myth and Aristotle's attraction to it in his later years ("Reality, Myth, Symbol," 33). On the lack of an idea of being, see *Insight,* 372–76, 383–86. On mystery, see ibid., 569–72; and *Method in Theology,* 110, 113–14, 321–23, 341–45. For Lonergan's metaphysical affirmations, see *Insight:* on self, 352–57, 362–66, 533–43; on world, 484–507; on God, 692–708.

nication, but also a genuine moment within philosophy, a reservoir of heuristic insights at the very foundations of inquiry.

Philosophical appropriation must therefore reflect the inherent historicity of myth itself. The teleological outpouring of the energy of the *élan vital* anchored by the demands of the nervous system is an a priori component of mythopoesis counterbalanced by two a posteriori components relevant to our concern here: first, the store of traditional themes and motifs, circumscribing the range and substance of myth, and, second, the personal life drama of the individual philosopher. This last point suggests implications of an earlier remark. If the intellectual biography of the philosopher is crucial, then the philosopher must appropriate that intellectual history. What intellectual interests shaped the entry into the philosophical life? What were the cardinal intellectual shifts along the journey of inquiry? What experiences were a springboard to philosophical conversion? What wisdom figures inspired the enterprise? What symbols, dreams, and life scenarios played, and continue to play, a formative influence on philosophizing? Thus, philosophical self-appropriating entails a venture of *anamnesis,* a recollection of the concrete symbols and narrative episodes that underpin the desire to know in the philosopher's personal drama of life. It is within this context that William Matthews has applied the seminal work of Ira Progoff's journaling of one's life story. Philosophical training, insists Matthews, should include an introduction to the skills required to write the story of one's philosophical search. The whole project of cognitional appropriation is rooted in the story of one's intellectual development, a personal wisdom story. To reinforce philosophy as a way of life—to take up existentially the truth of philosophy—one must articulate one's conversion story. Along similar lines, Voegelin has maintained that systematic reflection is never "a radical beginning of philosophy or can lead to such a beginning." Rather, the beginning lies in the "biography of consciousness," "the experiences that impel toward reflection and do so because they have excited consciousness to the 'awe' of existence." Voegelin then conducts "anamnetic experiments" to recount such experiences, some conspicuous for a long time in his memory, some readily recalled but without clear meaning, some remembered only after having been long forgotten.[55]

55. William Matthews, "Journalling Self-Appropriation" and "Personal Histories and Theories of Knowledge"; Ira Progoff, *At a Journal Workshop: The Basic Text and Guide for Using the Intensive Journal Process, The Practice of Process Mediation,* and *The Symbolic and the Real: A New Psychological Approach to the Fuller Experience of Human Existence.* On journaling and philosophical training, see Matthews, "Journalling Self-Appropriation," 105,

Third, there is the dimension of the future. Mediated by critical scholarship, rooted in the psychic foundations of the love of wisdom, myth can be linked to the affirmation of the basic truths of the philosophical tradition. Moreover, isomorphic with systematic development of that tradition can be further exploration of foundational symbols, myths, and poetic themes. Might we even anticipate that the rich exploration by such metaphysical poets as Rainer Maria Rilke and T. S. Eliot would herald subsequent more systematic treatment of philosophical problems?

The *theoroi* must navigate the wide ocean of basic horizon from their barks of homebound relative horizons. They must attain a distance from tradition only to renew it. And must not this renewal contain a story—and a myth—of the theorists themselves on their awesome, risky voyage of inquiry?

Philosophy and Praxis

Philosophy indirectly, but decisively, is concerned with the future conduct (*praxis*) of human affairs. Indirectly: it offers neither conceptualist generalities nor blueprints. But decisively: through the existential example of the philosopher and through systematically developed insights on the long-term perspective and on the eclipse of reality it addresses the issues of greatest import for the human good. It urges assumptions of historical responsibility. In so doing it devotes itself to pressing concerns of religion and of culture.

Philosophical Therapy and Existential Deformation

Philosophy, as a variety of religious experience, offsets the enervating effects of historical decline at the roots. As Lonergan has so lucidly demonstrated, the principle of historical decline is the poison of bias, which can take on the shapes of neurosis, individual egoism, group egoism, and commonsense shortsightedness.[56] We can suggest, however, that bias has existential sources, that if we penetrate beneath the biases adumbrated above we can uncover radical precipitants of existential deformation, and that such radical factors, al-

---

129; on personal wisdom story, see ibid., 106, and Matthews, "Personal Histories"; on the story of philosophical conversion, see Matthews, "Journalling Self-Appropriation," 106. Voegelin, *Anamnesis*, 36–37.

56. *Insight*, 214–27, 242–67.

ways subsisting in an explanatory relationship with each other, are dread, concupiscence, and *ressentiment*. Let us examine this existential complex, which
ravages both individuals and societies and of which it is the mettle of philosophy to combat.

The authentic self is engaged in a continuous process of self-transcendence
oriented to absolute transcendence. The pure desire to know is unrestricted
in its search for intelligibility; the intention of the good is unreserved in its attraction to what is worthwhile; the love of God is both the otherwordly pull
of the Wholly Other and the experience of participation in infinite divine reality. Thus, self-transcendence, even as it is always limited by its concrete human, historical, and personal situations, likewise always displays what Lonergan calls "vertical finality." The pure question by raising the existential issue
of future possibility challenges the self as presently constituted, occasioning
the experience of dread.[57] Accepting the challenge gracefully, one may expand
one's horizon in accord with vertical finality. Rejecting the challenge out of
hand, one may hover in the abysmal depths of despair. Fleeing the challenge,
one may attempt to flee dread as well by various time-tested escape routes.
Chief among the avenues of flight is the way of *divertissements*—including
moneymaking, status seeking, philandering, overeating, and wine tippling—
cataloged by the ancient Stoics, explored perceptively by Blaise Pascal,
dramatically illustrated, in its most refined species, by the notorious fin-de-
siècle movement of decadence, and portrayed, in a more pervasive form, by
the banality of modern consumer society. A related road of escape, frequently linked to *divertissements,* but one more nefarious because it bears the signpost of vertical finality, is what Saint Augustine named concupiscence, the
concentration of infinite craving on a finite object, usually power, fame, or
sex. This is a disease of the spirit that can perniciously attack religion itself or,
deflecting its unrestricted drive, can corrupt it, whence anxious flight from reality parades, with the various biases, under the banner of the sacred. This
same disposition is what Kierkegaard called the "sickness unto death," the
self's relation to itself whereby the self defines itself in terms of some finite relationship, object, goal, destiny, or fate, pouring into this frail vessel of a definition all of its infinite concern. It is here that another deformation joins concupiscence, namely, *ressentiment;* for concupiscence, hiding, as it does, the
infinite in the finite, must protect itself from an outburst of the dreaded infinite, which threatens to break its feeble chains, and must also lash out at the

57. On "vertical finality," see *Collection,* 19–23. "Horizon and Dread," in *Notes on Existentialism,* 9–10.

boredom and anomie inevitably accompanying the loss of a true relation to the infinite by finding an appropriate scapegoat. This it can strive to accomplish through *ressentiment,* the state of mind, identified by Nietzsche and then Scheler, that belittles the value of a superior and eventually distorts the whole hierarchy of values.[58] Would not the values most immediately in the firing line of the allied forces of *ressentiment* and concupiscence be those of the sacred, truth, and philosophy?

This triad of dread of transcendence, flight into concupiscence, and collusion of *ressentiment* has its unmistakable, ominous parallel in the history of communities. Every society bears a relation to transcendence, symbolizing this orientation to the mystery of being in a civil theology, which expresses a legitimation of the society as an actor in the drama of history. Every society faces historical challenges to its horizon of cultural expressions, traditions, and social practices and may indeed experience dread at these threats from beyond and the concomitant awareness of its own finitude, if not of its possible demise. Every society may respond to the dreadful challenge by a dazed willingness to be seduced by the wily bias of common sense with its shortsighted, narrow practicality, by excursions into the sweet land of *divertissements* on a mass scale, or—in the extreme—by collapsing its symbols of ultimate concern, representing the known unknown, into decidedly finite projects, interests, and compulsions: always with a dreaded, and infinite, earnest. When concupiscence thus becomes the pied piper of a society, the blind leading the blind, it is because that society has already brought on itself an eclipse of reality, a refusal, fortified by anxiety, to be open to the horizon of being. Is it, therefore, surprising that a Western civilization marked by anomie, decadence, hedonism, stilted behavior, and dogmatic adherence to social conventions should, at the same time, suffer from periodic outbursts of nationalism breaking all bounds of rationality, as in the heady days of August 1914? Can one not perceive beneath the foreign policy preoccupations, diplomatic procedures, and international crises of European nation-states the boiling cauldron of infinite concern, the fever of the sickness unto death? Why, in truth, do we witness modern obsession with the nation, or the class, or the race? Clearly, concupiscence can deftly nurture group bias, substituting the

---

58. On the psychopathology of the Stoics, see Voegelin, *Anamnesis,* 47–103. On Pascal, see Voegelin, *From Enlightenment to Revolution,* 51–59. On the consumer society, see Voegelin, *Conversations with Eric Voegelin,* 139–40. On concupiscence, see *Collection,* 49–51. Søren Kierkegaard, *The Sickness unto Death: A Christian Psychological Exposition for Upbuilding and Awakening.* Max Scheler, *Ressentiment; Method in Theology,* 33, 273.

nation, the class, or the race for ultimate reality and value.[59] This process of deformation is only accentuated when group bias is tied to the inflammatory pronouncements of neognostic revolutionary movements that would beguile their followers into an apocalyptic dream where the imminent victory of a class or a race would herald its apotheosis and the veritable resurrection of history. Every society in the grip of concupiscence, however, would have to defend its intoxication against the call of being by belittling openness to reality; increasingly, this *ressentiment* would distort the hierarchy of values, assaulting religion, authentic selfhood, and the unrestricted desire to know. Following in the train of *ressentiment* would come a benumbed social conscience, the host of biases, and then a regressive cycle of ever more fragmented and incoherent cultural viewpoints.[60]

We have been depicting here what Lonergan has termed an "existential gap," an operatively limited horizon in which an atrophied interpretation of human reality is fundamentally at odds with what human beings can be and ought to be. The philosopher has the imperative to close such a gap, to expose by his very life of commitment and fidelity the blind spots of the dominant horizon. Specifically, the philosopher counters the antipathetic aspect of dread with the sympathetic attraction of eros; the deceitful closedness of concupiscence with the openness of the spirit of questioning; and the deep-seated weakness of *ressentiment* with the strength and integrity of living the truth. The issue at stake is not ultimately a proper set of propositions (which can be repeated without any understanding) or a defective system of philosophy in its isolated conceptual splendor; the issue is ultimately a transformation in the mode of life, in the drama of existence, in the pattern of thinking, a leap beyond the present horizon (including any defective philosophy) insofar as it is at odds with the spirit of inquiry—a conversion.[61] The philoso-

---

59. On the problem of "challenge and response," see *Third Collection,* 10, 103–6, where Lonergan mentions Toynbee's thesis. On the eclipse of reality, see Eric Voegelin, *What Is History? And Other Unpublished Writings,* chap. 3. Modern forms of social concupiscence are usually tied to the goal of a universal, or ecumenical, empire; as Voegelin argues, the idea of an ecumenical empire is the idea of a "concupiscential exodus from reality," an unlimited drive to expansion, which was proclaimed in its purest form in the "Melian Dialogue," recorded by Thucydides. Whereas the modern drive of imperial concupiscence is couched in the language of world-immanent ideologies, ancient empires, confronting their own finitude, began to associate themselves with ecumenical religions (see *Published Essays, 1953–1965,* chap. 9; *Order and History,* 4: chaps. 2–3, pp. 260–71).

60. On the cycle of cultural decline, see *Insight,* 251–57, 262.

61. On the "existential gap," see "Subject and Horizon," in *Notes on Existentialism,* 9; on exposing the existential gap, see "Horizon and Dread," in ibid., 12; on conversion, see "Subject and Horizon," in ibid., 9.

pher of any era can profit from the example of Plato in this regard. Plato in his youth had experienced the convulsions of the Peloponnesian War, a conflict diagnosed by the historian Thucydides as an infection of Hellas by the "lust for power." For Plato, in his dialogue *The Charmides,* the antidote to this existential malady was certain, the charm of fair words, the words of philosophical discourse that would cure such a "headache." Although the remedy of philosophy, of course, is not guaranteed to be successful on the stage of historical events, at least in the short run—as the fate of Socrates ironically attests—its religious therapy is nonetheless vital. The therapy of philosophy meets the inevitable resistance of the existential gap by appealing to the desperateness and hopelessness of the situation and by cutting down its pretensions through the signal importance of satire and humor. The philosopher offers not enforced dogmas or even theoretically compelling assent but an invitation to self-awareness and openness to being, an appeal to dwell in the Heraclitean *koine cosmos* permeated by the divine Logos.[62]

Philosophy and Intellectual Culture

The religious task of philosophy is also a cultural task. Philosophy must carry out a cultural mission to promote the responsible direction of history. Philosophy, in its existential sense, infuses cultural life, institutions, and politics with its spirit. Although it thus permeates culture, institutions, and politics, it has no utopian commission, for it does not create ideal institutions; it does not spawn a bureaucracy, which would equate policy with the definitiveness and universality of concepts; it does not consider politics as technique (as it does not consider academics as technique). In a word, it does not act directly on social policy. More important, though, it acts indirectly. Through its imprint on cultural ideals, through education, and through the arts of communication it reaches down to the proverbial "person on the spot," the person familiar with the classroom, the economy, or international affairs, guiding and inspiring such a person to grasp the fuller relevant insights into the concrete situation that only he or she can grasp while, at the same time, cultivating an appreciation of the long-term perspective.[63]

---

62. Thucydides, *The Peloponnesian War* 190. Plato, *Charmides* 156D–157C. On the function of satire and humor, see "Horizon and History," in *Notes on Existentialism,* 13–14; and *Insight,* 647–49. On the invitation to openness, see "Horizon and Dread," in *Notes on Existentialism,* 11–12.

63. For an attack on conceptualism, see *Insight,* 259–60; and *Third Collection,* 60–61. For praxis and its difference from technique, see *Third Collection,* 103–4, 184. For the insight of the person on the spot, see *Insight,* 259–60.

If the sway of the love of wisdom indirectly touches a large circle of people, it extends more directly to the much smaller number preoccupied with higher intellectual culture, though one still greater than those engaged in philosophy strictly in its systematic aspect. The love of wisdom is, in fact, the origin of the sciences, scholarly disciplines, and literature, even as they differentiate themselves from philosophy in its systematic sense. To separate themselves completely from philosophy would be to cut themselves off from their existential source, and this would be to court cultural disaster. Why? It is the love of wisdom that creates the nucleus, and the only nucleus, of a true academic community by creating a common field of experience, understanding, judgments, and commitments. We can breathe new meaning into the old Platonic idea of the polis by conceiving it as a cultural community informed by the love of wisdom, or, perhaps more accurately, we can impart contemporary significance to that ancient term by identifying it with, to employ Lonergan's language, borrowed from the Stoics, a cosmopolis. Those persons engaged in true *paideia* would acknowledge as their horizon the horizon of the pure question with its immanent norms: this is the substance of a real sense of community embracing all academic and scientific pursuits. Undoubtedly, this polis must first reside in the formative efforts of a creative minority. And in a time of cultural fragmentation, philosophical illiteracy, and anti-intellectual intellectuals, when it may often seem that among one's immediate contacts the only member of such a community is oneself, then the advice of the Platonic Socrates stands across the ages: incessantly build the polis in oneself.[64]

The cultural task of philosophy, however, does topple over into its objective pole. The systematic aspect of philosophy exerts a methodological influence over higher culture. Philosophy, after all, is the "basic science of human living" as it thematizes the norms of authentic human living and systematically articulates metaphysical principles. A properly validated metaphysics challenges every restricted cultural viewpoint that would eclipse reality. Avoiding reductionism as well as any monocausal interpretation, metaphysics comprehends the nuanced reality of human being as a synthesis of matter and spirit. Because of the isomorphism of knowing with the object of inquiry,

64. For Lonergan's discussion of community, see *Method in Theology,* 79, 356–57. On cosmopolis, see *Insight,* 263–67; and Chapter 6 above. On the "creative minority," see *Third Collection,* 10, 103–4; and *Topics in Education,* 51–52, 54, 60. Plato, *Republic* 591E–592B; Jaeger, *Paideia,* 2:354–57. See Voegelin, *Anamnesis,* 3–6, for his personal struggle against the "school philosophies" of his youth.

metaphysics can thereby promote the integration of the various scientific and academic fields that investigate the many-sided nature of human reality.[65] Philosophy can also unify itself, historical scholarship, and social policy on the level of methods; it can lay the foundations for intellectual collaboration by demonstrating how these fields are fundamentally related specialties in the ongoing appropriation of historical tradition by higher culture as it encounters the past, explores substantive philosophical problems, and decides on essential policy and doctrines for future development. Philosophy, above all else, can emphasize how human studies must be critical, normative, and evaluative; how the current technical, social, and cultural situation can contradict authentic human possibility and objectify the existential gap; how present turmoil and breakdown can be traced to past errors; and how, given new ideas, feelings, and decisions, historical agents can alter the historical situation.[66] Such an appreciation of the critical role of historiography can spur healthy cooperation among fields in the history of thought so that psychohistory, history of culture, history of ideas, intellectual history, and history of philosophy can be organized together to stress the increasingly explicit presence of philosophical assumptions.

The enterprise of philosophy, then, is at once diagnostic and therapeutic.[67] The philosopher can neither succumb to the zeitgeist by devaluating the intellectual currency nor speak in vague generalities that ignore concrete historical circumstances. The philosopher must address the issues of maximum import for human welfare and for human disaster in the given historical situation. Philosophy must unveil the true springs of progress. As Lonergan has so precisely stated, its basic function is to illuminate the effort of intelligent, reasonable, free, fully responsible self-constitution.[68] Philosophy, therefore, rather than fleeing historical consciousness must support it by its own species of religious experiences and its own decisive role in culture.

In the meaningful concreteness of the present historical situation, philosophy, I would urge, has two main tasks: first, to recover the fullness of the ex-

65. On human reality as synthesis of matter and spirit, see *Insight*, 494–504, 538–43; on the integration of the methods of human studies, 5, 415–16, 587–91, chaps. 7, 15.
66. On philosophical praxis: foster critical human studies, ibid., 260–61; objectify the existential gap, "Horizon and History," in *Notes on Existentialism*, 13; expose past errors, ibid., and *Insight*, 265–66, 735–39; plea for new ideas, "Horizon and History," in *Notes on Existentialism*, 13–14.
67. See Voegelin, *Order and History*, 1:xiv.
68. "Horizon and Dread," in *Notes on Existentialism*, 11–12.

istential pole—cognitive, moral, religious, and affective—along with recognition of historicity; and, second, to renew systematic philosophical thought, carrying it beyond materialism, positivism, scientism, naive or dogmatic realism, and transcendental idealism. But how do we know whether the philosopher's religious experience is not merely a subjective illusion or whether the hope for intrinsic intelligibility is not a forlorn hope? To raise these questions is to enter the terrain of epistemology and metaphysics. To wrestle with these questions is to work out the epistemological and metaphysical implications of the normative process of inquiry. Far from eschewing epistemological and metaphysical matters, our conclusion of this chapter must be that historical responsibility demands that we take up these ancient concerns in order to regenerate contemporary culture.

Part III

Authentic Existence

8

Dread and the Horizon of Existence

IN LONERGAN'S SEMINAL LECTURES on existentialism, the discussion of dread occupies a central position. Dread has what Heidegger would call an *ontological status:* it is a constituent of *human being.* In typically brief, but incisive, remarks that penetrate to the heart of the matter, Lonergan points out how one's horizon—one's "concrete synthesis of conscious living"—is "anchored by dread." For dread is the "conservative principle that offers a spontaneous, resourceful, manifold, plausible resistance" to a change in one's horizon. "Whenever one's world is menaced, one seeks spontaneously to ward off dread by appealing to what is obvious and logical" from within the perspective of the horizon under attack (*Selbstverstandlichkeiten*). As an example, imagine that one's philosophy (say, critical realism) is false. Authentic human existence, that is, the effort of intelligent, reasonable, free, fully responsible self-constitution, entails conversion, moving to a new horizon—and hence dread. Not only must one stand the dread, but one must also cope with the spontaneous resistance.[1]

Thus, Lonergan's approach here seems to highlight the *negative* dimension of dread. Dread is, for Lonergan, a constitutive element of human being because of two principles: first, the stream of consciousness has an underlying sensitive flow, which is an integration of a biological manifold of neural de-

1. "Horizon and Dread," in *Notes on Existentialism,* 10–11; Whereas dread "offers" the spontaneous resistance, dread, this statement would seem to imply, is more than simply resistance. See Heidegger, *Being and Time,* 228–35.

mands, and a stream of consciousness that runs too freely has the nemesis of an anxiety crisis, in which the stream of consciousness threatens to break down, or does break down; but, second, the stream *can* be threatened precisely by a change of horizon, by a conversion, by an expansion of the horizon.[2]

The analysis seems to parallel that of the master psychologist of dread, Kierkegaard, in his *Concept of Dread:* "If a man were a beast or an angel, he would not be able to be in dread. Since he is a synthesis [that is, finite and infinite] he can be in dread, and the greater the dread, the greater the man."[3]

Still, Kierkegaard's discussion seems, in the precision of his existential analysis, to have a more positive note, as we see in the following passages:

> He therefore who has learned rightly to be in dread has learned the most important thing. . . . Dread is the possibility of freedom. Only this dread is by the aid of faith absolutely educative, consuming as it does all finite aims and discovering their deceptions. . . . He who is educated by dread is educated by possibility, and only the man who is educated by possibility is educated in accordance with his infinity. . . . If the individual cheats the possibility by which he is to be educated, he never reaches faith. . . . But he who went through the curriculum of misfortune offered by possibility lost everything, absolutely everything, in a way that no one has lost it in reality. If in this situation he did not behave falsely toward possibility, if he did not attempt to talk around the dread which would save him, then he received everything back again, as in reality no one ever did even if he received everything tenfold, for the pupil of possibility received infinity. . . . Then when the individual is by possibility educated up to faith, dread will eradicate what it has itself produced.[4]

Dread, then, is fundamentally tied to freedom and to possibility. It indeed is itself the possibility of freedom. It educates. It "saves." It opens up to infinity. It can lead to faith, and only through it can there be genuine faith. It eradicates "what it has itself produced."

By no means are these conclusions incompatible with those of Lonergan. But they do impel us to build upon Lonergan's perceptive treatment of dread and horizon and to connect that treatment to the larger corpus of his works, including other sections of his Lectures on Existentialism.

If we focus on Lonergan's idea of the process of *self-transcendence,* I believe, we have the key to unlocking the dynamics of dread. We can then tie dread,

---

2. "Horizon and Dread," in *Notes on Existentialism,* 10.
3. Kierkegaard, *The Concept of Dread,* 139.
4. Ibid., 139–43.

in some systematic fashion, to suffering, depression, and despair; to guilt; to shame; and to *ressentiment.* I propose a brief sketch of these relations as a way of introducing the topic.

Self-Transcendence

First, we must examine self-transcendence.[5]

The self, as the existentialists have shown, ex-ists, stands outside itself; it pro-jects, hurls ahead of itself. The self is therefore a relation to itself. The relation is established by the *question;* in other words, the self is precisely the dynamic of the relation, and the relation, the link between self and self (self as choosing and self as chosen), is precisely the question: that is, the *quest.*[6]

The quest carries with it the hallmarks of drama, a tension of call and response, of fidelity and infidelity, of knowledge and ignorance, of person and community, of human and divine.

The drama, furthermore, has its own inherent hermeneutics. For the performance in the drama evokes interpretation, and the interpretation enters into future performance. Thus is established the ongoing narrative of life. But this drama, this story, is played out before a larger horizon than that of the theater of the self: the self also stands outside itself in dialogue with an audience. Its story must be told. But who—or what—is the audience? The audience, in part, is the patrimony of a community, its traditions, the experience of its historical destiny. The audience is also significant others met in intersubjective encounter. Yet, amid the very concreteness and particularity of the communication to an audience and the responsive dialogue with an audience, the *unrestricted* nature of the question opens the self to a universal audience, the horizon of being itself.[7] Herein the dialectic of relative horizons and basic horizon obtains.

The project of being a self, then, is one of self-transcendence: going beyond through the process of inquiry. The questioning regards not only the particular meanings within one's horizon but also the orientation of the horizon as a whole, its presuppositions, its assumptions.

And do we not find a tension here? We must indeed, if we are not to be inauthentic, identify ourselves with basic horizon, the horizon of the pure de-

5. On self-transcendence, see *Insight,* 494–504; and *Method in Theology,* 35, 104–5.
6. See Kierkegaard, *Either/Or,* 2:179ff; Fackenheim, *Metaphysics and Historicity,* 83–89; and Fackenheim, *The God Within,* 143–44.
7. Voegelin, *Published Essays, 1966–1985,* 112–14.

sire to know and the intention of the good. Yet, at the same time, we must each live within a particular relative horizon—a concrete synthesis of conscious living—at a particular time and particular place as a sensitive, finite creature. We face here the tension of limitation and transcendence—and the measure of psychic health is the degree to which we can effectively *live this tension*.[8]

The call to transcendence means we must come to grips with the phenomenon of *dread;* the weight of limitation means we must struggle with the primordial fact of *guilt;* the interpretive role of the audience means we are exposed to the eye of *shame;* the resistance to the call means we are susceptible to the bile of *ressentiment.* In the odyssey of existence we must endure; we must "suffer."

Dread

Let us turn, second, to dread and consider a possible interpretation of the experience.

Lonergan, as we have noted, demonstrates how the psyche offers a spontaneous resistance to self-transcendence. Still, does it not also provide resources impelling one *toward* self-transcendence? Is it not this ambivalence, or tension, within the psyche that accounts for a dual quality to dread: dread as both *repulsive* and *attractive*? Why this paradoxical, if not totally shocking, quality of ("sweet") dread? What is the nature of the experience that might "leave one now aghast, now amazed, now entranced"?[9] The sensitive psyche, as Lonergan emphasizes, is a storehouse rich in treasures of symbols, images, and affects, containing the explosive powers of awe, wonder, and eros.[10] They can carry us beyond our limited, known world into the horizon of mystery, the known unknown, pulling us to the good and the infinite. In our encounter with the known unknown through questioning, the unknown can be the sweet known unknown of mystery, beckoning us, as equally as it can be the threatening unknown, evoking "uncanny feelings of horror, loathing, dread."[11] Is not the *dizziness* of dread precisely the intensive experience of a *simultaneous* presence of, and struggle between, repulsion and attraction?

8. *Insight,* 497–503.
9. Ibid., 556.
10. Ibid., 482, 555–58, 569–72; *Method in Theology,* 64–69; "Reality, Myth, Symbol," 33–34, 37.
11. *Insight,* 556 n.

Hence, Kierkegaard calls dread "a sympathetic antipathy and an antipathetic sympathy." Plato's description of the prisoner pulled out of the cave and dazed by the luminosity of the rays of the *Agathon* is a classic metaphor of this experience of dread.[12]

Suffering

Third, dread *is* suffering. Dread is an anticipation of possibility, and, as such, it anticipates both loss and gain. If one authentically pursues the possibility—by walking through the dizzying fog of dread—one experiences dislocation and loss of self, that is, loss of self as the not-chosen or loss of self as the transcended or loss of self as the not-yet-transcended. This entails an ontological *suffering*, an enduring of discomfort, dissatisfaction, even pain. Yet, "parting is such sweet sorrow." One also experiences the gain of self as chosen, indeed—most fundamentally—the gain of self as *questing*.

Still, if the negative side of dread is too strong, dread can become *depression,* the increasing inability to experience the self in a meaningful, coherent way. And if, in turn, depression becomes too potent, it can become *despair,* the loss—with all its sensory-motor, affective power—of hope in the "existence" of self.

Guilt

Fourth, guilt is related to dread as antecedent and as consequent.

We are called to transcendence, and hence we experience dread. Yet, we experience dread as partly repulsive, and this *can* have the constricting effect of holding us back from inquiry. Here dread can be an ontological factor *preceding guilt.*

Dread, though, is also intimately and essentially related to guilt as a *response* to guilt. For guilt is a privation of being—of the self as faithful in the loving quest for the true and the good. Guilt is the gap between openness as a demand and openness as an achievement. This gap can occasion the dread that Kierkegaard names "dread of the evil": the excessive *remorse* that would linger—dazed—on past deprivations rather than utilize the energy to pro-

12. Kierkegaard, *The Concept of Dread,* 38; Plato, *Republic* 515C–516C.

ceed anew on the path toward the good.[13] But why is this "remorse" dread? Because the gap, the privation, is a revelation of moral finitude. It is a revelation of possibility. Can we "exist" in such a condition? How can we resolve this diminution of our being? How can we survive the dislocation of its recognition? Can we? Is despair avoidable?

The problem is magnified because we are guilty simply as human: Just as dread is not mere fear of this or that object within a horizon but is the generic apprehension of that which is beyond the present horizon as such, so there is an aspect of guilt that is not guilt for this or that deed or omission but is a *generic guilt* of perpetual failure to be a perfect incarnation of the good. Lonergan commends Aquinas's analysis that even if we had the superabundant energy of will to transform instantly our explicitly acknowledged inauthentic acts and to reject explicitly acknowledged temptation, we would hardly possess the energy of mind to uncover all our inauthentic *habits* and the acts that stem from them, all of which function within the realm of our freedom, though without our full deliberation.[14] The greater our noble attempts to bring to light our ignoble habits and to alter them, the more we head for breakdown.

Lonergan does indeed suggest a solution to the gap between openness as a demand and openness as an achievement: openness as a gift, where the fire of unrestricted love heals the gap of generic guilt. But the fog of dread may again envelop us. The relation to what is experienced as the "Wholly Other" forces a rupture in our horizon that may exact the price of dread.[15]

Shame

Fifth, if dread is an antecedent and consequent of guilt, it seems to be an accompaniment of shame.[16]

Guilt and shame are not identical. Let me suggest that guilt is a relation of self-to-self-to-the-good, whereas shame is a relation of self-to-other-to-the-

---

13. Kierkegaard, *The Concept of Dread*, 101–5.

14. The term *generic guilt* is that of Sebastian Moore in "Christian Self-Discovery," 197ff; Lonergan, *Grace and Freedom*, 48–52.

15. *Collection*, 186–87. Peter J. Drilling seems to be addressing this issue in his discussion of "terror" as an authentic component of religious love in "Mysterium Tremendum."

16. My reflections on shame and other matters in this chapter have been inspired and nurtured by countless discussions with two practicing psychotherapists in Seattle, Faith Smith and Rick Meyer.

good. This does not mean, of course, that guilt has no social dimension, for the interpretation of the good is mediated by tradition and concern for the other. Nor does this mean that shame is not a self-interpretation, for the response of others provokes precisely a nonthematic, affective self-interpretation.

We may say that guilt and shame are dialectically related as self and community. Just as tradition, according to Gadamer, is an ontological condition for understanding, so the sense of shame—inculcated through communal experience and wisdom, through incarnate examples, through moral tutors, and through moral codes acting as heuristic signs and guideposts—is an ontological condition for moral understanding. What must be avoided is not perhaps shame as such but an overdose of shame.[17] This would paralyze moral autonomy, which looks to guilt as the chief barometer of moral life. An overdose of shame would highlight the negative pole of dread with respect to guilt. It would be the result of inauthentic interpretive responses on the part of the audience that would place in jeopardy our sense of selfhood and possibility. It would be an affective state in which we would seek to hide.

On the other hand, does not neglect of "authentic" shame engender confusion, inattentiveness, and perhaps ultimately acute anxiety? For shame is a revelation of our performance as other than anticipated or desired in relation to the pursuit of the good. It is indeed a revelation of our *possibility* and hence is necessarily linked to dread.

Dread, however, is most pervasively associated with *generic shame*: not shame over this or that act or omission before this or that audience, real or imagined, at this or that time but the experience of finitude as such along with the concomitant dread over assuming a proper relation to the *otherness* and *transcendence* of reality. It is a startling revelation of our situatedness on the landscape of reality, and of our possibility. Generic shame is shame before the otherness of social being, the interpreted experience that we are only part of the social world; before the otherness of cosmic being, the interpreted experience that we are only part of the order of the cosmos; before the otherness of being itself, the interpreted experience that we are transcended by the order of being; and before the otherness of the Wholly Other, the interpreted experience that we are not absolute Transcendence. Yet, we have the natural

---

17. On tradition as a precondition of understanding, see Gadamer, *Truth and Method*, 225–40, 245–74. It is instructive to note Plato's position, according to Richard Patterson, that the one and only proper cause of shame for a philosopher is "to cling obstinately to his own views in the face of cogent criticism simply because they are his own views" ("Plato on Philosophical Character," 344–45).

right—and the obligation—to be! Do we, then, by our very act of existing as a self, dare disturb the universe? What can heal the native dislocation and disorientation of generic shame?

If love is the most efficacious power to call one out of hiding in the face of shame, if love's wings carry one over the abyss of dread accompanying shame, then the solution to the existential reality of generic shame is participation in unrestricted, or generic, or divine, love: the call to self-acceptance as a partner in the community of being.

Ressentiment

But, sixth, authentic selfhood must appropriate dread not only in its relation to suffering, guilt, and shame but also in its relation to the poison of *ressentiment*. For *ressentiment,* as we have seen more fully in Chapter 7, is in service with a nefarious and eternally flawed plot to eliminate dread.

If we were to refuse to navigate the waters of dread gracefully and to accept the challenge of the thrust of what Lonergan calls "vertical finality," then the most bold avenue of escape from the unrestricted openness of the process of self-transcendence—most bold because it bears the signpost of vertical finality—would be to concentrate infinite craving on a finite object or project: the self, then, would relate itself to itself in such a manner that it would define itself in terms of some finite relationship, object, goal, destiny, or fate, pouring into this frail vessel of a definition all of its infinite concern. However, this hiding of the infinite in the finite would have to protect itself from an outburst of the *dreaded* infinite, which threatens to break its feeble chains, and it would *have to* lash out at the boredom and anomie inevitably accompanying the loss of a true relation to the infinite by finding an appropriate scapegoat. This it would strive to accomplish through *ressentiment,* the state of mind, identified by Nietzsche and Scheler, that belittles the value of a superior and eventually distorts the whole hierarchy of values. This triad of dread, flight into concupiscence, and collusion of *ressentiment,* I would suggest, is an existential root of the bias of egoism, and it has its unmistakable, ominous parallel in the history of communities, where it conspires with group bias and the bias of common sense.[18] For every society faces *historical challenges* to its horizon of cultural expressions, traditions, and social practices and may indeed experience dread at these threats from beyond and the concomitant awareness of its own

---

18. *Insight,* 214–27, 242–57.

finitude, if not its possible demise. Flight from such dread could lead to collapsing its symbols of ultimate concern, representing the known unknown, into decidedly finite projects, interests, and compulsions: always with a dreaded, and infinite, earnestness. Here there would be a dazed willingness to be seduced by the wily bias of common sense. When concupiscence thus becomes the pied piper of a society, the blind leading the blind, it is because that society has already brought on itself an eclipse of reality, a refusal, fortified by the negative pole of dread, to be open to the horizon of being. Clearly, concupiscence can also deftly nurture group bias, substituting the nation, the class, or the race for ultimate reality and value. The process of deformation is only accentuated when group bias is tied to the inflammatory pronouncements of neognostic revolutionary movements that would beguile their followers into an apocalyptic dream where the imminent victory of a nation, class, or race would herald its apotheosis and the veritable resurrection of history.[19] Every society in the grip of concupiscence, however, would have to defend its intoxication against the call of being by belittling true openness to reality through *ressentiment:* in the immediate firing line would be the values of the desire to know, of truth, and of the sacred. Dread still lurks around the corner, though, and the cycle of decline feeds on itself—a regressive cycle of ever more fragmented, distorted, and incoherent viewpoints.

Conversely, we can ask whether the creative periods of a civilization—its birth in the Dark Ages, its flowering, its renaissance—are times when dread is encountered in its positive spiritual side as cultural energy bursts forth to expand horizons and spur progress.[20]

This sketch suggests only a few of the rich lines of inquiry opened up by Lonergan's penetrating remarks on dread. The following questions may focus on some of those directions:

1) Is the attractive aspect of dread an inherent feature of the experience or rather a consequence of working through the dread?

2) Why is dread such a concern of modern inquiry? What does this tell us about modern life and culture?

3) Is dread immediately linked to shame but only mediately linked to guilt either as an antecedent or as a consequent?

---

19. Voegelin, *New Science of Politics,* chap. 4; Voegelin, *Modernity without Restraint,* 175–95; Voegelin, *Order and History,* 1:452–54, 4: chaps. 2–3, pp. 260–71; Voegelin, *Published Essays, 1953–1965,* chap. 9.
20. Franz Borkenau, *End and Beginning: On the Generation of Cultures and the Origins of the West.*

4) Is the flight from dread the main cause of bias?

5) Is dread, and possibly shame, ever-present as an existential factor in intellectual dialogue?

6) Is there a distinction between "dread," with its potent, overwhelming sense of possibility, and "pathological anxiety," which freezes thinking and possibility?[21]

In considering these, and allied, questions, it is important to recall that it is the project of self-transcendence that offers the key to the complex affiliation of dread with such existential phenomena as suffering, guilt, shame, and *ressentiment.*

---

21. The original article proposed distinguishing, along similar lines, simply between "dread" and "anxiety" as a convention.

Noetic Science

Aristotle, Voegelin, and the Philosophy of Consciousness

PERHAPS MORE THAN any other philosopher in the twentieth century, Eric Voegelin has offered a philosophy of consciousness that parallels and complements that of Lonergan. Voegelin, whose life spanned much of the twentieth century, was educated in a German philosophical environment that emphasized neo-Kantian methodologies and Husserl's transcendental ego. Voegelin's own philosophical development took him beyond the perspectives of these restricted horizons, as he would come to view them, to consider the true experiential origins of order in personal life and in historical existence. Voegelin's prodigious scholarly work in numerous volumes of his history of political ideas and his history of symbols, comparable in scope to that of Toynbee's, had as its motivating center his philosophy of consciousness.[1]

The foundation of philosophy, for Voegelin, is, as we shall explore later in this chapter, neither propositions nor observations but the concrete consciousness of a concrete person. More exactly, it is the concrete consciousness

---

1. Voegelin, *History of Political Ideas;* Voegelin, *Order and History.* For references to Voegelin's intellectual development, see Voegelin, *Anamnesis,* 3–7, 14–19; Voegelin, *Autobiographical Reflections,* 86; and Voegelin, *On the Form of the American Mind,* intro., 62–63.

of a concrete person engaged in the process of inquiry that has no bounds save those of the radical scope of questioning itself, that questions up to the very ground of existence, that operates in an expanding horizon primordially open to transcendence. Breaking, as does Lonergan, from the model of subject confronting object, Voegelin stresses that concrete consciousness is participatory consciousness. Self-transcending consciousness participates in the very transcendence it seeks. This means, then, that there is no privileged position outside of the process of consciousness—and the process of history—to contemplate consciousness. The philosophy of consciousness therefore grounds, and is inextricably connected to, a philosophy of history. Voegelin pours his vast historical erudition into a kind of retrospective appropriation of the differentiating insights into the structure of participatory consciousness. This effort is itself a continuation of the event of philosophy under the concrete historical conditions of our age.

This chapter and the two concluding ones will engage in a dialogue between the positions of Lonergan and Voegelin, a dialogue that moves from the philosophy of consciousness to the philosophy of history. To initiate the dialogue we shall consider in this chapter Voegelin's own engagement with Aristotle over the prospect of a noetic science. Since, for Voegelin, noetic science must necessarily become a philosophy of consciousness, Voegelin's retrieval of Aristotle's position on noetic consciousness is part and parcel of his development of a contemporary philosophy of consciousness. Lonergan, too, develops his cognitional theory through his encounter with Aquinas and Aristotle, and does so in a way that clearly suggests a parallelism of his approach with that of Voegelin. It should come as no surprise, then, that Lonergan's cognitional theory might help make sense of some of the more difficult Aristotelian texts so as to validate Voegelin's interpretation. Thus, our discussion of Aristotle and Voegelin on noetic science will be given direction by Lonergan's cognitional theory. This introduction to Voegelin's philosophy of consciousness will also prepare us to consider what Lonergan regards as pivotal for a critical philosophy of consciousness and for a resultant philosophy of history, namely, the project of self-appropriation, the subject matter of the next chapter.

Political Science and Noetic Science

Political science is a late bloomer in the history of human consciousness, and it rarely blossoms at that. It can arise only when certain technological, economic, and civilizational conditions allow for the flourishing of a theoretical culture (as in the case of ancient Hellas), and, Voegelin notes, it need arise only when the predominant myths of the political cosmion have lost their magic and enchantment (as, for example, during the great crisis of the Peloponnesian War). However, there are also decidedly philosophical and spiritual conditions for the emergence of political science. For political science is nothing less than the articulation of the roots of the order of the polity, and these roots are precisely the dynamics for the very search for order itself. The search is a reflective, self-transcending process of openness to transcendence. Explicit identification of the source of order, moreover, takes its poignancy from an acute experience of disorder in the surrounding society, placing authentic political science in critical contention with the prevailing interpretations of social order.[2]

Such is Voegelin's understanding of political science and of what the originators of political science, Plato and Aristotle, meant by that enterprise. Political science therefore has as its foundation a reflective awareness of the normative structure of human existence. This structure is "noetic consciousness," and its reflective awareness—which gives rise to theoretical culture—is the "noetic differentiation of consciousness." Thus, for Voegelin, political science is based upon, if not virtually equivalent to, noetic science. Indeed, he suggests that we can substitute for *political science*—with its modern positivist and ideological connotations—the term *noetic interpretation*. If by "science" Voegelin means the more inclusive sense of the German *Wissenschaft*, which embraces more than modern natural science, then "noetic science" is simply the explication of the normative structure of human existence, that is, noetic science is the explication of the self-transcending process of cognitive, moral, and spiritual inquiry. Whenever the self-interpretation that is constitutive of the polity seeks to interpret its own intelligibility, norms, and ground, whenever we have such a critical interpretation of the self-interpretation of society, we have an attempt at "noetic exegesis."[3]

---

2. On political science as response to disenchantment, see Voegelin, *History of Political Ideas,* 1:228–33. On the search for order, see Voegelin, *Order and History,* 1: intro. On the response to disorder, see ibid., 1:xiv, 3:62–63, 5:13–14, 41; Voegelin, *Anamnesis,* 89; Voegelin, *Published Essays, 1966–1985,* 45–46, 265, 371–74.

3. On "noetic differentiation of consciousness," see Voegelin, *Order and History,* vols. 3–4, 5: chap. 1; Voegelin, *Published Essays, 1966–1985,* chap. 10; Voegelin, *What Is History?* chap. 5. On "noetic interpretation," see Voegelin, *Anamnesis,* 146. On Voegelin and *Wissenschaft,* see Manfred Henningsen, introduction to *Modernity without Restraint,* by Voegelin, 10. On "noetic exegesis," see Voegelin, *Anamnesis,* 148.

Voegelin and Aristotle

There is a peculiar quality to noetic science. We have used such terms as *reflection, explication,* and *exegesis* to describe the way noetic science formulates meaning. Since the subject matter of noetic science is the normative structure of human existence, the subject matter is not a distant object that can be known either by logical deduction or by simple empirical observation. One must participate in the structure of existence in order to know it. The participation has a double dimension to it, for the structure of existence is itself a participation in transcendence. And, furthermore, since the structure of existence is a dynamic, normative process of self-transcending openness to the horizon of transcendence, its reality cannot be adequately captured in a conceptual system or the type of definitions that refer to objects in the external world. So Voegelin concludes that the language of noetic science is that of "linguistic indices," which explicate the "movement of participation" in "nonobjective reality."[4]

If, however, this is what we take to be noetic science, we must consider whether this kind of science could possibly be what Aristotle means by science (*episteme*) and reason (*nous*).

Voegelin indeed claims that noetic science, as he conceives of it, is consonant with the basic direction and impetus of Aristotle's thought. Aristotle, he argues, portrays the dynamics of noetic consciousness in a complex of symbols, ranging from those expressing human self-transcending unrest ("wonder" as the source of all science, the "desire to know" as a drive all humans share by nature, and the correlative "flight from ignorance") to those identifying the divine transcendent ground of unrest (the pure act of *nous*).[5] Aristotle, according to Voegelin, highlights the participatory nature of noetic consciousness in his treatment of the activity of *nous* as the process of immortalizing ("making noetic life divine compared to human life") and in his insistence that the goals of political life are excellences that can be known only by the person who possesses them, the *spoudaios*.[6]

Nevertheless, a commonplace reading of various Aristotelian texts on *episteme* and *nous* would conclude that *episteme* is exclusively a matter of demonstrative knowledge and that *nous,* by total contrast, is an intuition of the indemonstrable principles of demonstration. In addition, many interpreters

---

4. Voegelin, *Anamnesis,* chap. 9.
5. Ibid., 91–97.
6. Voegelin, *Order and History,* 3:301.

would presuppose that indemonstrable principles are foundational propositions upon which all definitions must be grounded. The connection of *episteme* and *nous* would seem to be an elusive one. If *episteme* is exclusively an
ordered set of propositions, then how can there be a noetic science of the type
Voegelin proposes? Would not such an Aristotelian science fall into the trap
of what Voegelin would consider a propositionalist fallacy? Not only would
this putative Aristotelian science fail to do justice to the participatory nature
of noetic consciousness, but it would also make a retrieval of interiority highly problematic. Reinforcing this tendency is a traditionalist interpretation,
held by Ross among others, that would see Aristotle's account of the origin of
universals as that of a somewhat mechanical process from sense perception to
memory to repeated experiences.[7] Would not noetic science, for Aristotle, be
an oxymoron?

We are therefore faced with the question of whether Voegelin had read too
much of his own position into Aristotle. Behind this question, however, is a
much more fundamental hermeneutical issue. Can an interpreter ever "read"
Aristotle's meaning by some kind of simple perception of the text? The
Hermeneutics of the Empty Head, the interpretive model favored, for example, in positivist circles, would locate a textual meaning "out there" to be
looked at "in here."[8] In fact, if interpreters have minds, their horizons will always come into play in their interpretations, and their horizons will include,
explicitly or implicitly, philosophical assumptions—even in the case of pure
philologists. However, the richer, the more insightful, the horizon of the interpreter, the richer, the more insightful, the interpretation.

The Aristotelian corpus indeed poses special hermeneutical difficulties.
Aristotle did not write systematic treatises. He employed terms in different
senses for different occasions. Perhaps, as Werner Jaeger suggests, they were
something like school *logoi,* intended for reading out loud, for partial memo-
rization, and for discussion.[9] Whatever the nature of the texts, their philosophical content demands philosophical insight on the part of the interpreter.
The only relevant question is which philosophical perspectives will be most
successful in entering Aristotle's philosophical horizon: That of Voegelin? That
of conceptualists (for whom science equals a set of propositions)? Or that of

7. Citations in Byrne, *Analysis and Science,* 173 n. 27.
8. *Method in Theology,* 157.
9. Jaeger, *Studien zur Entstehungsgeschichte der Metaphysik des Aristoteles,* 138–48, cited
approvingly by Joseph Owens, *The Doctrine of Being in Aristotelian Metaphysics,* 75; and by
W. D. Ross, *Aristotle's Metaphysics,* 1:xiv n. 1.

empiricists? It is interesting to note that both of the latter perspectives have frequently been adopted by philologists, reflecting the contemporary climate of opinion.

It is the burden of this chapter to show how a series of plausible interpretations of *episteme* and *nous* vindicates Voegelin's assertions about Aristotelian noetic science. It will be helpful, first, to recall briefly how in the pre-Aristotelian tradition the terms *nous* and *theoros* had religious and existential resonances. Our main focus will then be on the possibilities that *episteme* is not restricted to demonstrations and that it is intimately tied to the activity, potentialities, and habits of *nous*. In so doing we can shed light on how *nous* could simultaneously be the principle of the principles of *episteme,* the dynamism of human inquiry, the norm of human existence, the participation in the divine, and the basis of authentic political life. We can also discern how, in one respect, *nous* transcends *episteme* but how, in another respect, it exhibits the rudimentary features of *episteme*.

Nous and *Theoros:* The Historical Context

Aristotle certainly coined words to fit his philosophical needs and distinctions. Yet, he did not live in a historical vacuum. The terms *nous* and *theoros*—used extensively by Aristotle—had, as we have seen, traditional meanings that conveyed a decidedly existential theme of a participatory movement of human quest and of divine presence.[10]

The original meaning of the word *nous,* associated with the revolution of the sun god, evoked a sense of returning home from darkness and death to light and consciousness. Reflecting this cycle were the names of the fabulous creatures the hero Odysseus encountered on his perilous journey home: the Cyclops, Circe, and Calypso. Odysseus, "the wanderer," who "saw the townlands and learned the minds of many distant men," in his return home to Ithaca had to contend with the forces of darkness, whether in the cave of the barbarous Cyclops, the cave of seductive Calypso, or the twilight cavernous bay of the frightful Laistrygones. Whereas Odysseus's *nous* extricated him from the entrapment by the Cyclops, Parmenides' journey with the goddess above "the beaten track of men" and the "abode of the night" granted him through the exercise of his *nous* a vision of being. The original imagery of the journey of

10. For discussion and references, see Chapter 7, 155–56, nn. 23–24, above.

nous was given its most celebrated and vivid portrayal as the upward ascent of the prisoner in Plato's allegory of the cave.

Likewise, the original Greek meaning of the word *theorist* referred to a sacred journey in search of meaning. The *theoros* was a person sent on a sacred mission to oracles or to religious festivals, such as the Olympic Games. The theorist had to venture forth, searching along the road, in order to question and transmit faithfully a divine message. Indeed, the *theoeroi* were simultaneously spectators and participants on their journey, not disengaged Cartesian observers, since *theorion* was the place where they competed in the games as official participating delegates. Thus, the theorists guarded against dogmatism as they traversed beyond the pale of the everyday to the "festive and awesome realm of the divine," but, like Plato's prisoner from the cave, they would eventually return, transformed, to the home country where their journey began. In Plato's *Laws*, the *theoroi* were precisely to embark upon a course of inquiry about the outside world, most especially to visit divinely inspired men, only to come back to the native polis to share the spectacle. Out of this religious background emerged the Greek idea of reason: for gradually *theoria* came to be connected with travel inspired by the desire to know, and eventually it referred to the knowledge acquired while traveling. Thus, philosophers were *theoroi* on the noetic road of inquiry.

We can infer that no less for Aristotle than for his predecessor Plato, the use of the terms *nous* and *theoros* expressed experience of an irruption of divine reality on the road of inquiry. And when we carefully examine strategic meanings of *episteme* and *nous* in Aristotle's writings, we find confirmation of this postulate.

Episteme and *Nous*

Aristotle is a philosopher whose overriding insights come as a result of making incisive and powerful distinctions. He handles, for example, Parmenides' problem of motion by distinguishing between potential being and actual being. He solves numerous quandaries of the pre-Socratic nature philosophers by differentiating four causes. So we must pay attention to the distinctions he brings to bear in his treatment of *episteme* and *nous*.

In particular, as Patrick Byrne notes, we must pay attention to distinctions of act, potency, and habits. This should not be surprising since *nous* is "rational soul," and, according to Aristotle, there are three kinds of things in the soul: *pathe, dunameis,* and *hexeis. Pathe,* literally "passions" and frequently translated as "emotions," are not restricted to emotions but seem to include sensations, memories, and various kinds of thoughts. The *pathe* are endurings or receivings of the potential of motion, change, or movement. If we recall Aristotle's definition of motion (*kinesis*) as the "fulfillment of potency as potency," then we can say that the *pathe* are really motions or acts.[11] *Dunameis,* on the other hand, are the potentialities of the soul relative to the acts. Finally, *hexeis,* as recurrent activities of the potentialities, are habits. Let us then elucidate Aristotle's conceptions of *episteme* and *nous* by applying these distinctions.

Cognitive Habits

The strongest argument for restricting *episteme* to demonstrations seems to be found in a passage from the *Posterior Analytics* where Aristotle claims that there can be no *episteme* of the first principles of demonstration since these principles cannot themselves be demonstrated.[12] If science cannot demonstrate the undemonstrable principles of demonstration, then it must be an intelligence other than science, namely, *nous,* that can grasp those principles. But the contrast between *episteme* and *nous* in this passage is not an absolute one. Rather, it is a contrast between *episteme* and *nous* precisely as "cognitive habits" (*hai peri ten dianoian hexeis*). The habit of *episteme* is the studied ability to work on a certain range of facts, to employ proofs about the facts, and to master sets of related proofs all pertaining to a unified field of inquiry. *Episteme,* in this sense, is the skill, familiarity, and ease of one capable of drawing together interconnected demonstrations of reasoned fact. One has at one's disposal, for example, theorems that one retains in the background of one's horizon, present habitually rather than actively. This habit of *episteme,* is not, however, an isolated one, but, on the one hand, is grounded in lower habits that it both incorporates and subsumes and, on the other hand, is, in turn, incorporated and subsumed by a still higher habit. The lower habits that ground *episteme* are memory and "experience" (*empeira*).[13] Memory is the drawing together recurrently of sense perceptions. *Empeira* is the habitual association of memories of sense perception. Far from arguing for some mechanical model

---

11. Byrne, *Analysis and Science,* chap. 7. The following analysis relies heavily on his arguments. On kinds of things in the soul, see Aristotle, *Nicomachean Ethics* 2.2.1105b20. On *pathe,* see *On Interpretation* 1.16a4–9. On *kinesis,* see *Physics* 3.1.201a28–29.

12. Aristotle, *Posterior Analytics* 2.19.100b5–17.

13. On the cognitive habits, see ibid., 2.19.100b5–6. On the lower habits, 2.19.99b38–100a9; *Metaphysics* 1.1.980b26–981a12.

of universals as derived from sensations, Aristotle is presenting the emergence of higher habits of the soul from lower habits.[14] Just as *empeira* is a higher habit than memory since the person of "experience" can grasp a single connection, a *logos*, among different memories, making such a person of "experience" one capable of good judgments, so *episteme* is a higher habit of *empeira*. For *episteme* grasps the reason why of the connection. The person of experience, for example, may use various mathematical techniques, but the person of *episteme*, the mathematician, formulates precisely the operations and rules involved in the techniques. Without *empeira* there could be no material basis for *episteme*, but *episteme* transcends that basis. So, too, *nous* as habit transcends *episteme* as habit. *Nous* as habit is the studied ability to penetrate beyond the demonstrations of *episteme* to the preconceptual, pre-propositional intelligibility of the reason why. Without the habitual familiarity with the sciences there would be no material basis for *nous* as habit, but *nous* goes beyond *episteme* by grasping the undemonstrable principles.

We notice here that Aristotle's approach is to postulate dynamically interrelated sets of habits, ranging in ascending order from memories of sense perceptions, to *empeira*, to *episteme*, to *nous*. They give us a glimpse of the structure of human existence, an existence whose locus is the physical world but whose reach goes beyond increasingly into the nonmaterial realm: from the physical connections of memory, to the intelligible connections of *empeira*, to the reason why of the intelligible connections in *episteme*, to the reason why of the reason why in *nous*. But we must consider further distinctions of *episteme* and *nous* to witness an even further opening of the structure of human existence.

Cognitive Acts

We have thus far dealt with Aristotle's treatment of *episteme* and *nous* as distinct but functionally related habits in his effort to differentiate scientific demonstrations from the undemonstrable principles of demonstrations. How, then, are we to take Aristotle's seemingly paradoxical, if not contradictory, assertions that not all *episteme* is demonstrable and that there is an epistemic grasp of immediate principles?[15]

14. Byrne, *Analysis and Science,* 171–78.
15. Aristotle, *Posterior Analytics* 1.33.72b19–24, 1.33.88b38.

The paradox, and contradiction, disappears if we interpret *episteme* in this context as act.[16] For a cognitive act to be epistemic it can meet either of two requirements: (1) it can know the cause of a fact and that it could not be otherwise; and (2) it can be the answer to the scientific question, what is it?[17] A clear example of such an epistemic act would be knowing a scientific demonstration, for a demonstration entails knowing that a fact is, knowing that it could not be otherwise, and knowing what it is. The knowing what it is *(to ti estin)* provides the middle term of a syllogism, but it is not itself ultimately the result of deduction; it is a preconceptual insight into a formal cause. Although the insight plays off images, it is not reducible to images, percepts, or sensations. Here Aristotle extends the meaning of science beyond an ordered set of propositions and rejects the reduction of scientific meaning to sense experiences, thereby avoiding both conceptualism and radical empiricism.

The meaning of science is extended still further, however, when *episteme* is applied to the type of cognitive act that grasps immediate principles. Knowing an immediate principle is to know that it is, what it is (formal cause), and that it cannot be other than it is (also formal cause). To know the principle of noncontradiction, for example, is precisely to know that it is, what it is, and that it cannot be other than it is. This kind of knowing thus meets the two criteria for an epistemic act adumbrated above. The startling conclusion, then, is that *episteme* can grasp indemonstrable principles. Is this not to say that such an act of *episteme* is also an act of *nous* and that therefore *nous*, in this sense, is science? And can we not, by extension, likewise call the epistemic act that grasps the middle term as noetic? Indeed, Aristotle is quite unmistakable in identifying *nous* as the act of cognition *(to noetikon)* that grasps *(noiei)* the forms in the images.[18] Noetic consciousness therefore is inherently scientific consciousness.

Principle of Science

Nous is also the principle of science. Here we can turn to another set of distinctions Aristotle makes about *nous*, one involving its potentialities. Aristotle differentiates two kinds of noetic potencies, namely, to use the terms of Scholastic commentators, active potency and passive potency. Active *nous* has the potential "to make all things" *(to panta poiein)*. This *nous poetikos*, as scholars have frequently called it, is a cause of the *nous* receiving intelligible forms.

16. See Byrne, *Analysis and Science*, 179–81.
17. Aristotle, *Posterior Analytics* 1.1.71b9–12, 2.1.89b23–25.
18. Aristotle, *De Anima* 3.7.431b2.

Nous poetikos makes (*poiei*) thinking as a kind of habit (*hos hexis tis*) just as light makes potential colors into actual colors. The *nous*, conversely, is able to receive the intelligible forms because it, as passive *nous*, has the potency "to become all things" (*to panta gignesthai*). The nature of active *nous*, as Aristotle muses, is a "baffling problem."[19] Is active *nous* my *nous* as well as your *nous*? Is it the divine Nous? Is it, as immaterial, immortal?

While these questions have generated controversy among Aristotelian philosophers for two millennia, we can focus on one area for a degree of clarity. When we recall that *nous* grasps the forms in the images, we may be lead to ask, what moves *nous* to grasp forms in the images? Although the answer could be the divine Nous, an equally compelling answer, if we are to follow Byrne, and one not at all incompatible with the former, is that the mover is wonderment.[20] It is wonderment—it is the process of inquiry, or, as Lear puts it, the desire to understand—that transforms and perfects images to move *nous* to receive intelligible forms. The relation of *nous* to reality, then, is not one of passive perception but rather one of active engagement. Mind is not, for Aristotle, a mirror of nature. *Nous* is able "to make and become all things" because the horizon of wonderment is an expansive, self-transcending horizon correlative to the unrestrictedness of the desire to know that is embedded in human nature.[21] *Nous* itself is also the norm of scientific inquiry and thus its inherent principle. *Nous*, as wonderment, sets the criteria for the asking of scientific questions; *nous*, as passive potential, sets the criteria for the answering of scientific questions and hence the criteria of scientific propositions and scientific demonstrations.[22] This means that the standard for what makes *episteme episteme* is the luminosity of *nous*.

Nous as Episteme

To be sure, if *episteme* were solely demonstrative, then noetic science might be an oxymoron. The gap between the undemonstrable *nous* and demonstra-

---

19. On active *nous*, see ibid., 3.5.430a14–15. On *nous poetikos*, see W. K. C. Guthrie, *A History of Greek Philosophy*, 6:315 n. 1. On active *nous* making thinking as a "kind of habit," see Aristotle, *De Anima* 3.5.430a14ff. On passive *nous*, see 3.4.429b20–31, 3.5.430a15. On acting *nous* as a "baffling problem," see Aristotle, *Generation of Animals* 2.3.736b5–8.

20. Byrne, *Analysis and Science*, 167–69; that the divine Nous is the mover of creative intelligence is the thesis of Jonathan Lear, *Aristotle: The Desire to Understand*.

21. See Aristotle, *Metaphysics* 1.1.980a22.

22. Byrne, *Analysis and Science*, 187.

ble *episteme* would be a chasm. For how could the undemonstrable shed light on the demonstrable? Conversely, how could there be a demonstration of the undemonstrable? And, furthermore, how could the demonstrable demonstrate itself? And the undemonstrable explain itself? But in the face of these apparent quandaries we have the luminosity of *nous* as the measure of science. The quandaries arise from the horizon of conceptualism, which demands that the essence of science be an ordered set of propositions. Wonder, on the contrary, is the source of science, and wonderment causes the reception of intelligible forms.

Moreover, noetic inquiry about *episteme* bears the hallmarks of *episteme* in its proper and extended meaning. For *nous* affirms that *episteme*—both as epistemic acts that grasp forms and as habits of demonstration—is a fact and that it cannot be otherwise than it is, and *nous* inquires about what it is. More remarkable and startling is the sense in which noetic inquiry about *nous* likewise bears the hallmarks of *episteme*. *Nous* is a fact; it cannot be otherwise than it is; inquiry about it asks what it is. Noetic discourse about *episteme* and *nous* surely follows the same cognitive and logical laws that govern *episteme,* for the source is the same: *nous.*

The Self-Luminosity of *Nous*

Yet, we must not lose sight of the absolutely unique status of *nous* in the structure of human existence. We can consider *nous* again in terms of Aristotle's threefold distinction of potentialities, habits, and acts. As potentiality it is dynamic; as habit it is self-transcending; as act it is divinelike perfection. All these characteristics are interconnected as part of a unity.

The active potency of wonderment is a moving principle of intelligence and discovery. It is always greater than the propositions that it generates and the habits that it nourishes. Its fluid character makes it elusive, and its creative power renders it "baffling." We can postulate that the spirit of wonder is the self-transcending transformative mover of the aforementioned series of habits: from memories of sense perception, to the *empeira* of the person of judgment and good sense, to the procedures of the practiced scientist.

We can now add specific noetic habits to the series. Indeed, a person familiar with a range of sciences can inquire about what is science itself. This kind of inquiry would go beyond raising questions about the principles of any given science to pose questions about the principles of *episteme* itself. And here we encounter an incredible eruption of cognitive energy. We certainly have a *nous* of *episteme*. Still, if *nous* grasps the undemonstrable principles and if *nous* is the principle of science, then *nous* grasps itself. *Nous* of *episteme* leads by its own dynamic necessity to *nous* of *nous*. According to Aristotle, the *nous*, as immaterial, can be the object of thought.[23] This self-luminosity of *nous* sparks a new level of habits beyond that associated with *nous* of *episteme*. This is the habit of *sophia*, which, concerned with the highest things, reflects upon both *episteme* and *nous* of *episteme* to understand *nous* as pure act. Whereas *episteme* and *nous* grasp intelligible forms in images, *sophia* reflects on the intelligible forms already grasped by *episteme* and *nous*. It seeks the highest principles, those most unchanging, intelligible, and universal, namely, the subject matter of metaphysics.

The activity of *theoria* is correlated with the habit of *sophia*, and, accordingly, Aristotle considers *theoria* the most perfect and self-sufficient human activity.[24] In *theoria* the dynamics of *nous* attain their loftiest manifestation. As all acts of *nous*, *theoria* is "pure act" (*energeia*), but *theoria* is *energeia* in its most perfect form, not tainted by potentiality.[25] This leads us to the highest thing and highest principle that *theoria* can contemplate: *nous* itself. *Theoria* grasps that the ultimate cause of cosmic order is the unmoved mover. Nature is a mirror of mind.[26] But the unmoved mover is *nous* thinking itself. *Theoria*, then, is *nous* contemplating *nous* thinking *nous*. This is indeed the summit of Aristotle's investigation, where all major paths converge, whether in his *Metaphysics*, his *Physics*, or his *Nicomachean Ethics*. In the former two works Aristotle depicts the most perfect life, the life of the divine, as *noesis* understanding *noesis*.[27] Still, every human act of *nous* shares in the divine life, albeit momentarily.[28] This is precisely why the ultimate horizon of human existence, including political existence, is defined by self-transcending openness to the divine ground.

Nous and Phronesis

Although less perfect than the theoretical life, the ethical life and the political life, too, share in the activity of *nous*. Practical intelligence (*phronesis*) is

23. Aristotle, *De Anima* 3.4.430a2–5.
24. Aristotle, *Nicomachean Ethics* 10.7.1177a18–1178a4.
25. Elizabeth Murray Morelli, "Aristotle's Theory Transposed," 7.
26. Lear, *Aristotle*, 306–7.
27. Aristotle, *Metaphysics* 12.7.1072a19–b30, 12.9.1074b15–1075a11.
28. Ibid., 12.7.1072b26; Aristotle, *Nicomachean Ethics* 10.7.1177b30–1178a8.

an act of *nous*. It is less perfect than *theoria* because its objects—whether the individual choices of goods that would foster the well-being (*eudaimonia*) of the individual or the legislative arrangements that would promote human flourishing (*areté*) within the polis—are less unchanging, intelligible, and universal.[29] We need not dwell on the obvious: how contingency, flux, and particularity pervade the human world. So political science will be science to a much lesser degree than such a discipline as geometry. To a large extent the analytical side of political science, amid a plethora of contingent circumstances, adjusts means to ends. The ends are the excellences of human nature. The meaning of excellence (*areté*) is to "function well," and to "function well" as a human being is to realize the potentialities of human nature. But what is human nature? Human nature, like every nature, is an "internal principle of change and rest."[30] What is this specifically human principle? The answer is the process of cognitive, moral, and spiritual inquiry, with its own built-in norms, a process of incarnate beings who can nonetheless participate—precariously—in the life of the divine Nous.[31] The principle, in short, is noetic consciousness. Noetic science, therefore, by explicating the structure of human existence, provides political science with the goals of political endeavor. The "single science" of government, which aims to determine which government is best, must determine what is the best human life.[32] The best human life, of course, is the life of *nous,* and the perfection of *nous* is *theoria*. But *theoria* needs *phronesis* since practical wisdom, including political wisdom (which frames legislation), is the precondition for engaging in *theoria*.[33]

Noetic science in asking the question what is *nous* is asking about the dynamic principle of human nature. *Nous,* with its acts, potentialities, and habits, is the self-transcending normative principle of change and rest in human life. Whereas the contemplative life seeks knowledge for its own sake, employs scientific demonstrations, and focuses on the universal and the necessary, and though the practical life seeks action, employs the "practical syllogism," and focuses on the particular and the contingent, these differences should not obscure the fact that they both share what is highest in human life. They both participate in the self-transcending normative process of question-

---

29. Aristotle, *Nicomachean Ethics* 6.8.1141b23–24.
30. On *areté,* see ibid., 1.7.1097b23–1098a19; on "nature," see Aristotle, *Physics* 2.1.195b21–22.
31. *Third Collection,* 172.
32. Aristotle, *Politics* 4.1.1288b22–23, 6.1.1323b15–16.
33. Aristotle, *Nicomachean Ethics* 6.13.1144b17–1145a6.

ing, which ranges from involvement with the images of physical things to the self-luminosity of the pure act of *nous*. They both share in noetic consciousness. All the virtues, both theoretical and practical, are inherently interrelated.[34] This means that in authentic political life—a kind of *phronesis* that Aristotle calls the virtue of political wisdom—that which is best and divine in us is actualized.[35] The subject matter of political science therefore concerns the participation of human *nous* in the activity of the divine Nous.

Limits of Aristotle's Analysis

If we can extrapolate this core of noetic science from the writings of Aristotle with some plausibility, we nevertheless should not be surprised that it has been muddled, overlooked, or even denied by commentators and philosophers. Aristotle, however, has himself contributed to the confusion.

Aristotle first develops terminology applicable to the most generic discipline possible: that which deals with being as being. From the *Metaphysics* he then can gather terms for his investigation of being as changing, his *Physics*. From both the *Metaphysics* and the *Physics* he can employ terms in his study of being as self-changing, his *De Anima*. This hierarchy of disciplines causes problems when he reaches the specifics of the human situation. When he examines, for example, *nous,* he is examining a principle of rational self-change, but the categories of metaphysics, physics, and psychology cannot do strict justice to the nuances of noetic consciousness. The faculty psychology Aristotle relies upon differentiates souls by potencies, potencies by acts, acts by objects, and objects by either efficient or final cause. This approach will strain any attempt to explore such "elusive" aspects of noetic consciousness as self-transcendence, interiority, and spiritual presence.[36] And the language of faculty psychology might not be very suggestive of an "exegesis" of "nonobjective reality." It can easily tempt one to look at *nous* as part of a system or as a theoretical object "out there." This temptation will become more acute if one interprets *episteme* as an ordered set of propositions. Voegelin notes how Aristotle's use of such categories from his metaphysics and physics as matter and

---

34. Ibid., 6.13.1144b32–1145a6.

35. Hans Georg Gadamer, *The Idea of the Good in Platonic-Aristotelian Philosophy,* 174–76.

36. *Verbum,* 2–5. On Aristotle's differentiation of the soul, see Aristotle, *De Anima* 2.4.415a14–20.

form hampers his investigation of political topics (for example, constitutional order) and contributes to a "derailment" of his political philosophy.[37]

Another barrier Aristotle erects to an ample treatment of noetic consciousness is his identification of being with substance.[38] This may be rooted, as
Voegelin argues, in Aristotle's "immanentizing" tendency, the propensity to di-
vinize the eternal recurrence of cosmic order, the positing of a transcendent,
completely immaterial unmoved mover notwithstanding.[39] In any event, the
distinction of essence and existence, such as Aquinas, for example, makes,
would seem to provide metaphysical categories better suited to addressing the
participatory nature of noetic consciousness. Aquinas equates being with to-
be *(esse)*. Only divine transcendence is pure to-be; all other beings exist by
participation in pure to-be. Aquinas's metaphysics, of course, was still attached to an Aristotelian faculty psychology, so that his philosophy could not
fully exploit his metaphysical distinction of essence and existence to explore
human interiority.[40]

Whatever the limits of Aristotle's analysis of noetic consciousness, noetic
science does pervade the Aristotelian corpus, and to recognize it is not to read
into Aristotle's text some idiosyncratic philosophical position. The contemporary task is rather to appropriate the insights of Aristotle about noetic consciousness and in appropriating the insights to develop his ideas so as to transcend his limitations.

Since the time of Aristotle, Christian pneumatic consciousness has radically emphasized both divine transcendence of the cosmos and human participation in divine presence; the recent study of comparative religion has
indicated parallels in other religious traditions; Aquinas, Schelling, and Kierkegaard have differentiated essence and existence; the scientific revolution has
discovered a universe that is no longer a cosmos of eternal recurrence; phenomenology has replaced faculty psychology; and historical consciousness
has expanded the theological and political horizons. In light of these developments the task today is to transpose Aristotle's noetic science into a philosophy of consciousness. And this, of course, is what Voegelin has attempted to do, moved by the spirit of wonderment in the face of the disorder of his
time.

37. Voegelin, *Order and History,* 3:333–35.
38. Gilson, *Being and Some Philosophers,* chap. 2.
39. Voegelin, *Order and History,* 3:307–10, 362–66.
40. On Aquinas's focus on *esse,* see David B. Burrell, *Knowing the Unknowable God: Ibn-
Sina, Maimonides, Aquinas;* on Aquinas's faculty psychology, see *Verbum,* intro.

Noetic Science as Philosophy of Consciousness

The foundation of political science, for Voegelin, is neither a set of propositions nor a set of observations about objects in the external world. It is the concrete consciousness of a concrete person. Or, rather, it is the concrete consciousness of a concrete person under certain concrete, existential conditions.[41] For human consciousness ordinarily exhibits intentionality —which Voegelin defines as awareness of objects in the spatial field, as befitting the embodied nature of human consciousness. Human consciousness, however, can also exhibit luminosity when the concrete consciousness is of a concrete person engaging in the concrete process of questioning.[42] The more radical and open the questioning—the more it questions about the meaning of human life, the more it searches for the ground of human existence—the more self-reflective can the luminosity be. Luminosity is therefore an inherently participatory act. It is, moreover, a participatory act that is experienced as a theophanic event at the intersection of time and the timeless.[43] The horizon of luminosity is the horizon of an incarnate inquirer in search of the transcendent ground of existence. This horizon, according to Voegelin, using the materials of the phenomenology of comparative religion, is that of the Greek mystic philosophers, including Aristotle, but it equally embraces the spiritual quests expressed, in more differentiated fashion, in the writings of the Israelite prophets, the Gospels, and the Pauline Epistles and, in less differentiated fashion, in the *Upanishads,* the teachings of the Buddha, the Amon hymns, and Babylonian incantations.[44] Voegelin's philosophy of consciousness explores noetic consciousness directly without the cage of a faculty psychology or the intrusion of metaphysical categories. Informed by phenomenology and modern existentialist concerns, it is also quite consonant with Aquinas's focus on being as the act of existing.

The philosophy of consciousness is the foundation of political science because the participatory consciousness of questioning is the source of order in both personal existence and the life of the polity. To ignore the normative status of noetic consciousness, including its spiritual dimensions, is to ignore the most substantial element of political existence. Indeed, when political science,

41. Voegelin, *Anamnesis,* chap. 11.
42. On "intentionality" and "luminosity," see Voegelin, *Order and History,* 5:14–16.
43. Voegelin, *Anamnesis,* chap. 7; Voegelin, *Published Essays, 1966–1985,* chaps. 3, 7.
44. On the horizon of the search, see Glenn Hughes, *Mystery and Myth in the Philosophy of Eric Voegelin,* chap. 2; Voegelin, *Order and History,* 1:85–87, chap. 13; 4: chap. 5, pp. 316–30; Voegelin, *Published Essays, 1966–1985,* chap. 7, p. 294.

and intellectual culture as a whole, ignores, distorts, or denies noetic consciousness, then it is an active accomplice to the cumulative cycle of decline.
Since, in Voegelin's view, this is, in fact, what modern political science and
modern intellectual culture have done, it is incumbent upon him, as a genuine political scientist, above all else, to restore noetic science under the un-
propitious historical conditions of the modern situation.

This supreme task of restoration should not, however, lead us to conclude
that Voegelin does not appreciate the more "earthly" features of political existence. He commends the *proemium* of the *Institutes of Justinian* for dividing authority into three facets: power, reason, and spirit.[45] Power concerns internal
order and defense against external enemies. If a polity has the authority rooted in power, it has articulated itself as an agent that can act in history, and it,
accordingly, has "existential representation," an institutional embodiment of
its capacity for action.[46] Articulation and representation have technological,
economic, social, and cultural preconditions. Here it is quite appropriate to
examine the polity in terms of efficient cause. It is precisely this manner that
Aristotle conducts empirical investigations to shed light on how to avoid "revolutions" and how to promote the stability of a regime by considering such
factors as the form of government and the degree of participation of citizens.
Voegelin, too, is acutely aware of the authority of power. Indeed, he praises
the insight of such "realist" thinkers as Machiavelli and Hobbes into the exigencies of power and admires their avoidance of moralizing clichés.[47] Not surprisingly, Voegelin is totally conversant in his writings with the major political trends throughout history from the Mesopotamian city-states to the cold
war. He traces in great detail, for example, the articulation of the English polity in the late Middle Ages, arguing that its parliamentary style of representation was based upon historical accidents. He shows in a book-length study
that, by contrast, his own Austria after World War I had no adequate politi-

45. Voegelin, *The Nature of Law and Related Legal Writings,* 70–71; Voegelin, *Hitler and the Germans,* 79–80; Thomas J. McPartland, "Authenticity and Transcendence: Lonergan and Voegelin on Political Authority," 50–75.

46. Voegelin, *New Science of Politics,* chap. 1; Voegelin, *History of Political Ideas,* vol. 3, *The Late Middle Ages,* ed. David Walsh, vol. 21 of *Collected Works of Voegelin,* 145–54.

47. Voegelin, *History of Political Ideas,* vol. 4, *Renaissance and Reformation,* ed. David L. Morse and William M. Thompson, vol. 22 of *Collected Works of Voegelin,* chap. 1; Voegelin, *History of Political Ideas,* vol. 5, *Religion and the Rise of Modernity,* ed. James L. Wiser, vol. 23 of *Collected Works of Voegelin,* 248; Voegelin, *History of Political Ideas,* vol. 7, *The New Order and Last Orientation,* ed. Jürgen Gebhardt and Thomas A. Hollweck, vol. 25 of *Collected Works of Voegelin,* chap. 1; Voegelin, *History of Political Ideas,* 1:228; Voegelin, *New Science of Politics,* 179; Voegelin, *Modernity without Restraint,* 234.

cal articulation.[48] As a result, Voegelin insists, its appropriate constitution is an authoritarian one. To impose democratic self-rule would be to foster the collapse of the incipient political society and would succumb to utopian formalism, if not utopian fancy.

Voegelin's own focus on the authorities of reason and of spirit also avoids such a utopian deformation of reality. The norms of noetic consciousness are not abstractions that dwell in some noetic heaven. They are concretely operative in the process of history—or if concretely inoperative, there are dire historical consequences. Voegelin, inspired by Max Weber's lecture "Science as a Vocation," pours vast erudition into his study of reason and spirit, an endeavor in which he attempts to incorporate the most recent historical scholarship.[49] His monumental *History of Political Ideas* is not a conventional history of political ideas because it is a genuine history. It does not treat political ideas as freely floating abstractions or as reified doctrines. As mentioned above, political ideas, for Voegelin, are critical responses to historical crises in which the evocations of society have lost their luster. He locates intellectual and religious developments in their political contexts, and he displays remarkable insight and sensitivity in relating the political contexts to technological, demographic, economic, and social factors. Unlike most orthodox histories of medieval political ideas, for example, which skip from Augustine to Aquinas, Voegelin devotes considerable attention to the German migrations. He relates the rise of millenarian sentiments to the expansion of urban population in the High Middle Ages. He views the popularity of Luther's ideas as, in part, a function of the printing press. He pinpoints the traumatic influence of Tamerlaine's conquests on the political sensitivity of Renaissance political theorists. He sees the Enlightenment project of establishing a new meaning of Western civiliza-

---

48. On the articulation of English political society, see Voegelin, *History of Political Ideas,* 3: chap. 19; Voegelin, *New Science of Politics,* 38–45; Voegelin, *Modernity without Restraint,* 117–23. For contrast, see Voegelin, *The Authoritarian State: An Essay on the Problem of the Austrian State,* trans. Ruth Hein, vol. 4 of *Collected Works of Voegelin,* ed. Gilbert Weiss, commentary by Erika Weinzierl.

49. The abundant bibliographical materials in Voegelin's *History of Political Ideas* and *Order and History* amply demonstrate this. But, to cite anecdotal evidence, when Voegelin visited the University of Washington to deliver a series of lectures, I, then a graduate student, was asked to direct him to Prof. Carol Thomas, an expert in Mycenaean and Dark Age Greek history, since Voegelin wanted to keep up on the latest developments in this field. Thomas's work has recently been published (Carol G. Thomas and Craig Conant, *Citadel to City-State: The Transformation of Greece, 1200–700* B.C.E.).

tion as a response to a complex of such historical factors as global exploration, commercial expansion, religious fragmentation, and nation-state building.[50]

Voegelin's enterprise does justice to the full range of noetic consciousness, which can well up from the unconscious, gain insight into images, and ultimately reflect on its own luminosity. His approach is consonant with Aristotle's idea of human reality as a "synthetic nature," stretching from the apeironic depths, through inorganic nature, vegetable nature, animal nature, the passionate psyche, the noetic psyche, to the divine Nous. All in all, he clearly follows the empirical bent of Aristotle (not to be confused with modern empiricism). This is illustrated not only by Voegelin's interest in and grasp of detail but also in his quite Aristotelian procedure of relating means to ends in light of the details. Again, as a case in point, Voegelin's comprehensive rationale for an authoritarian Austrian constitution is based on his assessment of what in the concrete circumstances of post–World War I Austria would best nurture democratic habits by a kind of political education. Voegelin, however, in one important respect expands the empirical range beyond that of Aristotle by addressing in a more explicit and thematic way the historical dimension of human existence.[51]

Nonetheless, as dedicated as Voegelin is to empirical sobriety he never loses sight of the core philosophical issue in political science: authority is not exhausted by power but also must be rooted in reason and in spirit. In addition to the polity's representation as a power on the field of history, there is the polity's representation of transcendent truth through the evocations of reason and spirit.[52] And when the entire texture of modern civilization has been to downgrade reason into merely instrumental reason and either to deny spirit or to fuse it diabolically into totalitarian revolutionary movements, then, as Voegelin's entire corpus attests, noetic science must proclaim the proper roles of reason and spirit in political existence. From the beginning of Voegelin's career we witness this calling. In opposition to his teacher, Hans Kelsen, whose positivistic formal theory of law investigated law in terms of the horizon in

---

50. On the German migrations, see Voegelin, *History of Political Ideas,* vol. 2, *The Middle Ages to Aquinas,* chap. 12. On the urban context of medieval millennialism, see *History of Political Ideas,* 4:150–51. On Tamerlaine and the Renaissance, 218–20. On Luther and the printing press, 43–55. On the historical context of the Enlightenment, see Voegelin, *History of Political Ideas,* vol. 6, *Revolution and the New Science,* ed. Barry Cooper, vol. 24 of *Collected Works of Voegelin,* 31–34.

51. Voegelin, *Anamnesis,* 92; Voegelin, *Published Essays, 1966–1985,* 268.

52. Voegelin, *New Science of Politics,* chap. 2; Voegelin, *Modernity without Restraint,* 129–48.

which it operated, Voegelin in the 1930s searched for the "existential experiences" that gave rise to the horizon. He urged a "transformation of the dogmatic system of natural right into an analysis of existential experiences that made regulation of certain institutions . . . the inevitable component of any legal order."[53] Voegelin's search for "existential experiences" led to his restoration of noetic science in the form of his philosophy of consciousness. And thus the prime task of Voegelin's philosophy of consciousness is the restoration of noetic consciousness as the central concern of political science in response to the disorder of the age.

---

53. Voegelin, *Race and State*, 4.

10

Self-Appropriation in Lonergan and Voegelin

WHAT DOES IT MEAN to appropriate the self? Is the self somehow a "something" that can be "appropriated"? Is this mysterious appropriation something added on to the mysterious self coming from outside the self? Or is it an enrichment of the already present self? Or is it a fundamental constituent of the very being of the self? Indeed, if Kierkegaard is correct and the self is a relation that relates itself to itself, then perhaps self-appropriation concerns the very being of the self.[1] Lonergan and Voegelin would, in fact, agree with Kierkegaard's assessment, each from his own distinct, but substantially equivalent, perspective, Lonergan highlighting more the role of mediation (and intentionality) in the enterprise, Voegelin more the role of meditation. But, given their respective emphases on mediation and meditation, how can we speak of their equivalent positions? For the former conveys the image of scientific discourse, whereas the latter suggests the practice, if not the silence, of the mystic.

1. Kierkegaard, *Sickness unto Death*, 13.

Lonergan's Reflective Subjectivity

Since *self-appropriation* is Lonergan's technical term, we can start first with his analysis.[2]

What, then, is the self? Interestingly enough, the self, for Lonergan, is a thing. But it is not a thing like an instance of the Cartesian *res extensa* or like a Kantian phenomenal object, both of which are "bodies" in the "already-out-there-now-real." No, the self is a thing simply because it is a unity, identity whole grasped in data as individual.[3] Its unity, however, is a unity that marks it off from the unity of other kinds of things: it is a unity that is simultaneously intelligible and intelligent. To use Hegel's language, as does Lonergan, it is subject and not just substance. Thus, metaphysical categories, equally applicable to plants, animals, and humans, are not adequate to explore the being of the self.[4] To say that the self is intelligent is to say that the self is the subject of conscious and intentional operations that spontaneously constitute a dynamic structure: the successive levels of experiencing, understanding, judging, and deciding. Thus, we can equate self and subject and consciousness. It is furthermore an incarnate consciousness since it is a higher integration of otherwise coincidental manifolds of subatomic, chemical, organic, and psychic manifolds. It is thus conditioned by the lower, material manifolds but not determined by them. It is not only not determined by them but also oriented to something wholly beyond them. For, as Lonergan makes clear, the subject's performance of conscious and intentional operations is underpinned by the pure unrestricted desire to know and the all-encompassing unrestricted intention of the good neither of which will find rest save in the unrestricted being of the transcendent beyond. Although conditioned by the empirical residue, the self is not intrinsically conditioned. Thus, the self, so defined, is the central form of a concrete human being.[5]

---

2. *Insight,* 13–17; *Method in Theology,* 95, 262; *Understanding and Being,* 3–23, 261–66, 270–74, 297–99, 381–83.

3. On definition of a "thing," see *Insight,* 271; contrast to Cartesian or Kantian object-as-extroverted, 275–79.

4. On self as intelligible and intelligent, see ibid., 538–43. On self as subject not substance, see *Method in Theology,* 96; *Understanding and Being,* 11–12, 297–98; "Philosophy of History," 71; *Topics in Education,* 80–81; *Verbum,* 3–11; and *Collection,* 222–24. On inadequacy of metaphysical categories applied to the self, see *Method in Theology,* 95–96; *Verbum,* 4–6; *Topics in Education,* 209–10; and *Second Collection,* 72–73.

5. On self as conditioned by lower manifolds, see *Insight,* 494ff; on basic intentionali-

Still, as we have seen above, the metaphysical category of central form is not sufficient to explore the dynamics—nay, even the seeming paradox—of the self. We can capture this dynamic by stating quite simply that the self is a process of self-transcendence. We can be selves as we can be subjects, by degrees, minimally when we are in deep sleep and maximally when we are deliberating and deciding. The entire movement and flow and direction of conscious and intentional operations are the tendency of questioning, and the entire process of inquiry is under the guidance of the existential level of consciousness, where we decide not just about X, Y, or Z but equiprimordially about who we are to be as we decide about X, Y, or Z.[6] In deliberating about any course of action, we are also, at least implicitly in subsidiary awareness, asking about what we are, what we can be, and what we ought to be. And the context of the questions—where our selves are at issue—changes the "what" to "who." The self, then, is the tension of self as questioner and self as questioned, self as choosing and self as chosen.[7] The self is the relation that relates itself to itself. The self is not therefore some pure "given," an "already-in-here-now-real."

Here we first witness self-appropriation and mediation. For to choose the self is to appropriate the self. And to appropriate the self requires the mediation of an interpretation of what the self has been, what it can be, and what it ought to be. This mediation is obviously conducted for the most part in what Polanyi calls subsidiary awareness rather than in what he terms focal awareness, and it is usually expressed in a combination of nonthematic, or elemental, meanings and commonsense language. It takes place on the level of the cultural infrastructure, where meaning is spontaneously apprehended and communicated. Since moral deliberation typically involves commonsense insight in the self-correcting process of moral learning, this kind of self-appropriation and this kind of mediation may seem adequate to the task of selfhood.[8]

---

ty of self, 539; on self as not conditioned intrinsically by empirical residue, 541; on self as central form, 460–63, 542–43.

6. On degrees of selfhood, see *Collection*, 222; and *Second Collection*, 80. On self-constitution, see *Method in Theology*, 121–22; *Collection*, 223–24, 229–30; and *Second Collection*, 79–80, 83.

7. See Chapter 1, n. 20, above.

8. Polanyi, *Personal Knowledge*, vii, 55–56. On the cultural infrastructure, see *Insight*, 594–95; *Method in Theology*, 86–90, 97–99, 272–73; *Collection*, 236; and *Second Collection*, 91, 102. On commonsense inquiry, see *Insight*, 196–204, 311–12, 314–16.

Nonetheless, this is not what Lonergan means by self-appropriation. There remains the Delphic imperative, "Know thyself." What ought the self to choose? Clearly, the true self, the authentic self. And what is the authentic self? The self-transcending self faithful to the transcendental precepts of being attentive, intelligent, reasonable, and responsible. Indeed, on the level of the cultural infrastructure there can be an "implicit intellectual conversion" that in a somewhat spontaneous and perhaps inchoate manner through commonsense understanding identifies true responsibility with the openness of questioning. Still, this identification can be a tricky business, especially since most people are not too attentive to the apparently fuzzy structure and dynamics of interiority and since common sense, not being reflective, can easily merge with common nonsense. Hence, in the hermeneutics of performance and interpretation, where past performance becomes data for present interpretation as the self relates itself to itself, it is easy for there to be an operative existential gap between the reality of authentic selfhood and the interpretations.[9] Unfortunately, the misinterpretations can mediate future performance in a cycle of decline, whereas what is needed is increased lucidity about the authentic self that can foster progress.

Here we turn, then, to the meaning of self-appropriation and mediation in *Insight*. Lonergan's cognitional theory aims at adequate self-knowledge on the critical and reflective level of the cultural superstructure. It promotes an explicit intellectual conversion that defines cognitive and moral truth in terms of the norms ingredient in the process of inquiry. As Lonergan makes clear at the beginning of *Insight*, such self-appropriation places a premium on intelligence as the spring of progress and, in closing the existential gap, combats bias as the primal source of decline.[10]

We must emphasize that mediation in this project is not the mediation of some reified speculation. Mediation has two precise loci. On the one hand, mediation must always necessarily be carried out by the concrete person. Self-appropriation, Lonergan proclaims, issues in a decisive, personal act.[11] It is not knowledge of an abstract self that is at stake; it is the experiment of one's self-consciousness taking possession of itself.

---

9. On the transcendental precepts, see *Method in Theology,* 20, 53, 104, 302; and *Collection,* 227ff. On common nonsense, see *Insight,* 4; on the "existential gap," see "Horizon and History," in *Notes on Existentialism,* 13.

10. On intellectual conversion, see *Method in Theology,* 238–40; on self-appropriation and progress, see *Insight,* 8.

11. *Insight,* 13.

On the other hand, the self-appropriation of a sufficient number of persons can form the nucleus of a community in dialogue, a critical culture, a dimension of consciousness. What Lonergan calls "cosmopolis" can act through (nonpolitical) indirection, through example, through satire and humor, through critical historical scholarship, through plainspokenness about the truth, through addressing issues of maximum consequence for human welfare or human disaster—it can act through all these means precisely as a mediating force in society.[12] It can mediate in an ongoing fashion in the hermeneutic of performance and interpretation through the functional cooperation of specialties in the cultural superstructure. It can criticize contemporary deculturation in light of the dialectic of progress and decline, guiding culture toward the openness of the basic horizon of inquiry. Lonergan is well aware of the ordinary mediating functions of tradition and belief through acculturation, socialization, and education in what he characterizes as the "movement from above downwards." To this he would add cosmopolis. Like Plato's true polis, cosmopolis first and foremost resides in the souls of authentic inquirers, whether a sole representative figure, a small remnant, or, in more golden moments of history, a larger segment of the cultural superstructure.[13] Cosmopolis, says Lonergan, can formulate statements about cognitive, moral, and spiritual reality—statements he would term "doctrines." Lonergan emphasizes, however, that these "doctrines," which can play a positive role of mediating self-appropriation, must themselves be mediated by self-appropriation in the foundational enterprise of appealing to the data of consciousness and the engendering experience of self-transcending inquiry.[14]

Although in Insight Lonergan focuses on mediation, his post-Insight work offers the prospect of forging links between meditation and self-appropriation.

Consider again the self. The authentic self performs within a self-assembling structure of cognitive and moral operations underpinned by the basic intentionality of unrestricted questioning. The self is located between lower, material manifolds and the beyond correlative to the unrestricted sweep of questioning. This creates a tripolar tension—tension below and tension above. The hallmark of this location, then, is the tension of limitation and transcendence.

12. Ibid., 263–67, 647–49; see Chapter 6 above.

13. On tradition as mediating from above, see Third Collection, 181. Lonergan invokes Toynbee's ideal-type of the "creative minority" (16, 103–4, 214).

14. On doctrines, see Method in Theology, chap. 12; on foundations, chap. 11. The issue of authenticity regards both the authenticity of the tradition and the authenticity of the person within the tradition (78–80; Collection, 227–28). The criterion of authenticity is self-transcendence. See n. 9 above.

Another word for this tension is _anxiety_. To carry out self-appropriation requires that we come to grips with this permanent existential mood. If we become, in Kierkegaard's language, pupils of possibility in the curriculum of anxiety, then we must engage in something like existential meditation.[15]

There is also the task of negotiating with the psychic depths in the twofold manner described by Ricoeur, namely, the archaeological retrieval of repressed unwanted materials, largely vital urges of image and affect, and the teleological conscription of psychic energy supporting the process of inquiry. Lonergan speaks of a self-appropriation of the sensitive psyche involving "genuineness," which brings to light unconscious components of development that need integration with the life of intelligence. Genuineness might then bring about a kind of psychic conversion. Particularly in the case of the teleology of the psyche, this would seem to entail a type of psychic meditation on the symbolic and affectively charged anticipations and virtualities of higher living.[16]

Finally, and perhaps most important, the self has a relation—perhaps an intrinsic relation—to divine presence. Lonergan in his later writings, we must underscore, focuses on three dimensions of interiority: not only on the structure of cognition and on the basic intentionality driving it but also, third, on the existential state of being-in-love that engulfs the directional tendency and the structured operations. As the desire to know and the intention of the good are unrestricted, so the existential state that engulfs them is unrestricted. The unrestricted state of being-in-love is the experience of divine presence, the consciousness of divine presence as object (the object of the unrestricted desire to know and the unrestricted intention of the good) and of divine presence as subject (the experience of participation in divine reality analogous to vital intersubjective union).[17] The experience of divine presence is the existential condition for sustained moral commitment and for the effort of cognitive self-appropriation.[18] Meditative practices of the most traditional sort not

---

15. On the tripolar tension, see *Insight*, 749; on the tension of limitation and transcendence, 497–99. On anxiety, see Chapter 8 above; and Kierkegaard, *The Concept of Dread*, 139–43.

16. On Ricoeur, see Chapter 1, n. 27, above. On genuineness, see *Insight*, 499–504. The term *psychic conversion* is that of Robert Doran (see *Psychic Conversion and Theological Foundations: Toward a Reorientation of the Human Sciences* and *Theology and Dialectic of History*, 8–9, chap. 2). For Lonergan's positive reference to Doran's idea, see "Reality, Myth, Symbol," 36–37. On psychic process as anticipation of higher living, see *Insight*, 482.

17. On being-in-love, see *Method in Theology*, 104–7; and *Third Collection*, 171–75. On religious experience as an analogue of intersubjective union, see *Method in Theology*, 101–3, 105–7.

18. *Method in Theology*, 237–43.

only can be woven into the fabric of the originating experiences but presumably can also assist materially in the task of self appropriation of spiritual consciousness. In other words, meditation on religious experience can assist the project of *fides quaerens intellectum,* which, among other things, would mediate, or objectify, spiritual interiority.

Voegelin's Existential Exegesis

It is obvious that in his later writings Lonergan has entered the territory of Voegelin. We see Lonergan articulating the reality of tension as the equivalent of Voegelin's in-between participatory reality; suggesting the negotiation of the psychic depths, reminiscent of Voegelin's portrait of consciousness opening to the unfathomable psychic reaches below, as depicted in Plato's *Timaeus;* and showing the centrality of the divine human encounter.[19] Voegelin, however, has a somewhat precise and perhaps novel idea of meditation as it is related to his version of self-appropriation. Voegelin, of course, has explored his own territory in a more concerted and detailed manner by a style evocative of the very existential consciousness being investigated.

Voegelin does not mention the "self" often, and when he does, he usually refers to the creation of imaginary selves as "second realities," as substitute, false selves, exemplifying what Lonergan calls the existential gap. The idea of a false self, however, points, by contrast, to a true self. And Voegelin indeed speaks of a "true self": the self that experiences the divine pull and responds with the loving search for being; the self whose reaction to the anxiety of existence is not flight but instead the search for the ground; the self who exists in the tension, the in-between, of time and the timeless, the human and the divine; the self who is aware of participating in the order of being.[20]

Rare is the thinker—philosopher, prophet, or saint—who can successfully elucidate the true self and the participatory, in-between structure of the human experience with its worldly and transcendent poles. When such elucidation occurs, it is because the thinker has had differentiating insights into transcendence as the ground of being and into the soul as the sensorium of transcendence. This identification, for Voegelin, is the key moment in his ver-

19. See Chapter 11, nn. 5, 92, 94, below.
20. On self as "second reality," see Voegelin, *Published Essays, 1966–1985,* 16, 33–34, 242–54, chap. 2; Voegelin, *What Is History?* 111–21, 136–39. On true self as tension to transcendence, see Voegelin, *What Is History?* 137–39.

sion of self-appropriation, which is nothing less than the "truth of existence." The latter term Voegelin defines as "the awareness of the fundamental structure of existence together with the willingness to accept it as the *conditia humana*."[21] The thinkers of first rank with differentiated consciousness (Plato, for example), or their followers, articulate their experiences in the language of symbols or of reflective distance, which are eventually written down.[22] Such texts become normative for a genuine tradition of higher culture. They are truly mediators. But the texts themselves can be misinterpreted. The tradition can become inauthentic and adhere to dogmas, in the negative sense, that are cut off from the engendering experiences. There is always the temptation to interpret the texts about the in-between of participatory existence (which is concomitant with the luminosity of consciousness) as though they refer to bodies in the external world, which are the content of the intentionality of consciousness (modeled on perception). This temptation follows almost inevitably from the fact that since human consciousness is incarnate, human language tends to mirror the externality of bodily relations in space and time.[23]

Every person, according to Voegelin, experiences the anxiety of existence, including the mystery of death, and every political society needs to address it by creating symbols of participation in the wider network of reality (in the community of being shared by person, society, nature, and the divine). When these symbols break down and are no longer effective, then the society faces a severe crisis of anxiety, usually leading, at least since Hellenic times, to philosophies of hedonism (in order to avoid pain), to contract theories of government based on a psychology of the passions, and, more nefariously and more typical of recent times, to activist ideologies and movements that would mold idols of transcendence in speculative gnostic systems or in radical revolutionary regimes.[24]

21. Voegelin, *Published Essays, 1966–1985,* 49.

22. Voegelin, *New Science of Politics,* 60, 63–64, 70, 75, 77–80; Voegelin, *Modernity without Restraint,* 135–36, 138–39, 143, 147–48, 151–52; Voegelin, *Order and History,* 1:370, 3:10–14; Voegelin, *Published Essays, 1966–1985,* 111, 180, 192–93, 201; Voegelin, *What Is History?* 47, 49.

23. On dogmatism, see Voegelin, *Order and History,* 4:36–57; Voegelin, *Anamnesis,* chaps. 8–10; Voegelin, *Published Essays, 1966–1985,* 52–57, 119–22, 173–76; and Voegelin, *What Is History?* 181–87. On the "intentionalist" fallacy, see Voegelin, *Order and History,* 5:14–18; Voegelin, *Anamnesis,* 168, 178–81; and Voegelin, *Published Essays, 1966–1985,* chap. 3.

24. On the anxiety of existence and political symbols, see Voegelin, *Order and History,* 1:1–2, 3:62; Voegelin, *Anamnesis,* 95–96; Voegelin, *Published Essays, 1966–1985,* 176, 268–70; Voegelin, *What Is History?* chap. 2; and Voegelin, *History of Political Ideas,* 1:225–

It is at this juncture that the philosopher is motivated to respond to the disorder of the age by meditative exegesis, namely, the effort, in the meaningful concreteness of the present, to recover the original noetic experiences behind the language of higher intellectual culture and the original pneumatic experiences behind the language of higher religions and to expose the distortion of meaning, the closed existence, and the contracting of reality of the contemporary climate of opinion.[25]

Comparative Assessment

Self-appropriation, then, for Lonergan and for Voegelin regards the same reality: the self as inquirer. Lonergan objectifies inquiry as structure, as intentionality, and as existential state. Voegelin objectifies inquiry as process. What are the specific advantages of the respective focus of each thinker?

Voegelin's existential exegesis draws the reader into the historical drama surrounding the origin of a text and brings home in a compelling fashion the struggle against the forces of disorder that would block access to formative texts of differentiated consciousness. Whether engaged in a historical narrative or a reflective essay, the reader is invited to enter into the very process of inquiry being discussed. And since Voegelin conceives of the process of inquiry as a theophanic event, he presents entry into the process of inquiry as also entry into the dynamics of divine movement and human countermovement. Voegelin's style is uniquely crafted through meditative reflections to honor the participatory nature of human consciousness in the experiences of wonder, questioning unrest, search for the ground, and the pull of transcendence. Voegelin never lets the reader lose sight of the fact that the reality in which we participate is mystery. Conversely, Voegelin's skills as a critic are fine-tuned to expose in historical case studies the flight from anxiety and from an encounter with transcendence and to analyze the various deft maneuvers of concupiscence to deflect the drive to the beyond onto some finite domain of

---

33. On ideological response to political crisis, see Voegelin, *New Science of Politics,* chap. 4; Voegelin, *Modernity without Restraint,* 175–95; Voegelin, *Order and History,* 1:452–58; Voegelin, *Anamnesis,* 97–103; Voegelin, *Published Essays, 1966–1985,* 273–79; Voegelin, *Science, Politics, and Gnosticism,* 83–114; Voegelin, *Modernity without Restraint,* 295–313; Voegelin, *History of Political Ideas,* 1:79–84; and Voegelin, *From Enlightenment to Revolution,* chap. 2.

25. Voegelin, *Order and History,* 1:xiv, 3:62–63, 5:13–14, 41; Voegelin, *Anamnesis,* 89; Voegelin, *Published Essays, 1966–1985,* 45–46, 265, 371–74.

being as an imaginary substitute, thereby seeking to hide the flight from anxiety.[26]

If both Lonergan and Voegelin hold what Lonergan would call "positions" on the self, the advantage of Voegelin's perspective is that his invitation to self-appropriation highlights living the truth as an inquirer who participates in mysterious divine reality on the road of inquiry itself. Voegelin's writings would challenge interpreters of Lonergan, as it apparently did Lonergan himself, to consider more carefully and thoroughly inquiry as process and as existential state.[27]

The advantage of Lonergan's perspective, on the other hand, is that he has perhaps the most comprehensive and detailed explanatory account in the philosophical literature about inquiry as structure. With his cognitional theory as a base, he can develop an epistemology and metaphysics consonant with the openness, dynamism, and directional tendency of inquiry. His invitation for self-appropriation is supported by a vast amount of material all geared toward promoting intellectual conversion. But what are the real benefits of intellectual conversion? Lonergan's cognitive self-appropriation offers two distinct positive challenges to interpreters sympathetic to Voegelin's enterprise.

One is captured in the injunction "develop positions."[28] When examining a text—whether a text of Voegelin or a text Voegelin investigates—one can employ Lonergan's cognitional theory as a powerful tool to distinguish the insights from an inadequate epistemological framework. The purpose of such a "hermeneutic of the philosophical position" would be to tap more deeply into the solid core of a thinker by eliminating obstructions. Lonergan's cognitional theory, for example, would critique Voegelin's concept of intentionality as too narrow and rigid because it is rooted in the model of perception.[29] A reformulated concept of intentionality might allow for a more nuanced treatment of such issues as the origin of symbols, the criteria of genuine myths, and the authentic role of doctrines in mediating differentiated insights. It

---

26. On inquiry as theophanic event, see Voegelin, *Order and History*, 4:241–44; Voegelin, *Anamnesis*, chap. 6; and Voegelin, *Published Essays, 1966–1985*, chaps. 7, 10. On the participatory nature of consciousness, see Voegelin, *Order and History*, 1:1–2, 4:330, 5:14–16; and G. Hughes, *Mystery and Myth*. On the flight from anxiety, see Voegelin, *Order and History*, 5:198–201, 260–66; Voegelin, *Anamnesis*, 97–103; Voegelin, *Published Essays, 1953–1965*, chap. 9; Voegelin, *Published Essays, 1966–1985*, 33–34, 242–54, 273–79; Voegelin, *What Is History?* chap. 3; and Voegelin, *From Enlightenment to Revolution*, chap. 2.
27. "Philosophy of History," 65–66; *Third Collection*, chaps. 12–13.
28. *Insight*, 413.
29. *Third Collection*, 201 n. 46.

would also show the close link between the cognitive structure discerned by Lonergan and the existential state explored by Voegelin.

Second, evaluative historical studies that seek to identify intellectual decline, including the history of political ideas and the history of symbols, will have their critical powers enormously expanded in the measure that they can recognize epistemological assumptions as decisive influences on thinkers and as contributors to precipitous cultural deformation. In evaluating Hobbes, for example, one can neither ignore the fact that he eliminates the orientation to transcendence as a constitutive factor behind political order nor ignore the fact that the first part of the *Leviathan* is about an empiricist epistemology as the foundation of the rest of the text.[30] To understand adequately the unfolding of the dialectic of dogmatism and skepticism in modernity one needs both Voegelin's existential analysis of how ideas are tied to dispositions, sentiments, and spiritual aspirations and Lonergan's cognitional analysis of how ideas are tied to epistemological counterpositions. In general, intellectual decline is a complicated cycle with roots in both existential deformation and epistemological confusion. The existential gap is a gap between interpretations and the reality of the self as both cognitive subject and existential subject.

Thus, for both Lonergan and Voegelin, self-appropriation, which recognizes inquiry as the in-between state of human existence, is in accord with the norms of human nature, is concerned with human nature, and is an enrichment of human nature—that is to say, self-appropriation is in accord with authentic selfhood, is concerned about the being of the self, and is an enrichment of the self. But self-appropriation does not transcend human nature since human nature, at its very core, is self-transcending.

Hence, Voegelin stresses how the truly great thinker's inquiry about inquiry is always framed by a "balance of consciousness," presuming both epochal differentiating insight into the process of inquiry and awareness of the participatory nature of the process of existence, including that of the philosopher's understanding.[31] The task of philosophy, whether in fifth-century Athens, thirteenth-century Europe, or the twenty-first century, like the discovery of historical existence in Israel and Hellas, has its concrete origins, in part, as a response to existential disorder. Whereas in the case of Israel the disorder is the threat of a universal empire to extinguish by brute force a spiritually advanced and creative society, in the case of philosophy the disorder also stems

---

30. Hobbes, *Leviathan,* pt. 1, chaps. 1–16.
31. Voegelin, *Order and History,* 4:227–37. See G. Hughes, "Balanced and Imbalanced Consciousness."

from intellectual culture itself, either from the sophistic intellectuals who deny the in-between status of self-transcending human being or from the court theologians who neglect the nature of the self.[32] The philosopher can see the act of self-appropriation as marking a "before" and an "after" in personal, civilizational, and world history but not as thereby standing above history.[33]

According to Lonergan, self-appropriation plays a role in self-constitution, but this role operates in the dialectic of performance and interpretation in the process of self-transcendence and does not differ in kind from any other genuine role in that dialectic. Self-appropriation indeed arises from the exigency of questioning and is an expression of the selfhood of the philosopher. Still, far from creating moral and religious conversion, it ordinarily stems from the latter. Philosophy itself, as the unrestricted love of wisdom, bears the hallmarks of a variety of religious experience, and it is this unrestricted eros of the mind that inspires and sustains the effort of self-appropriation.[34] Moreover, it is on the level of existential consciousness, where we act as moral agents and undergo religious experiences, that we are most fully subjects. And though self-appropriation points to openness as a demand, it is openness as a gift that heals the gap between openness as a demand and openness as an achievement.[35]

We can conclude that Lonergan's cognitional theory is no more a reification of subjectivity than Voegelin's meditative exegesis is an exercise in mystical obscurantism. Both approaches invite us to engage in self-appropriation, both approaches deal with the same self, the same unity, identity whole, to be appropriated, both approaches keep self-appropriation within the process of self-transcendence—and both approaches provide us with searching texts to help mediate that self-appropriation.

32. Voegelin, *Anamnesis*, 122–23. See n. 24 above.
33. Voegelin, *Order and History*, 4:2–20; Voegelin, *Published Essays, 1966–1985*, 195–96.
34. See Chapter 7 above, 150–54.
35. *Collection*, chap. 12.

11

Equivalence of Meaning
Lonergan's Cognitional Theory and Voegelin's History of Symbols

AS WE ASSESS THE STATUS of philosophy at the beginning of the twenty-first century, the temptation may arise to compare it to the situation of philosophy at the turn of the twentieth century. The latter period, Voegelin reminds us, was a "difficult time for men of a philosophical bent, so bad a time indeed that a Wilhelm Dilthey refrained from publishing because he deemed the effort useless."[1] In the era of the Weimar Republic dominating the public scene were, as Voegelin characterizes them, "restricted school philosophies and methodologies." Writing in the 1960s, Voegelin saw a repetition in the United States of these same "German ideologies, methodologies, value theories, Marxisms, Freudianisms, psychologies, phenomenologies, hermeneutical profundities"—with an actual lessening of the intellectual quality of the debate.[2] By no means have these currents of thought died out in our own time. Instead, they have been joined by deconstructionism, which in the United States has mingled with streams of pragmatism, positivism, and analytic philosophy.[3] This latest wave has seemingly ushered in the victory of sophistry over its old opponent, philosophy.

1. Voegelin, *Published Essays, 1966–1985*, 57.
2. Voegelin, *Anamnesis*, 7.
3. See, for example, Richard Rorty, *Contingency, Irony, and Solidarity*.

This, of course, is not the whole story. Philosophy, we can argue, made a vigorous comeback during the twentieth century, in some cases precisely in response to the movements mentioned above. That philosophy at the turn of the twenty-first century had had such a healthy turnaround is in no small measure because philosophy has recovered the experience of its origins—origins both historical and, in the broad philosophical sense, psychic. And that philosophy has recovered the experience of its origins is in no small measure because of the pioneering efforts of Voegelin's history of symbols and Lonergan's cognitional theory. Although Voegelin and Lonergan have considered both the historical and the psychic origins of philosophy, Voegelin has focused more on the former, Lonergan on the latter.

On perhaps a superficial level, sociological evidence would suggest a substantial convergence of the two philosophers. Lonergan and Voegelin in their later years participated on many panels together, often with Gadamer. Voegelin himself attended Lonergan conferences as a main speaker. Both Lonergan conferences and Voegelin conferences in recent years have regularly incorporated discussions about the other thinker.[4]

Still, on the surface, as the terms *history of symbols* and *cognitional theory* might imply, no two philosophers might seem more different in philosophical temperament, method, and claims about reason. Are their respective approaches more complementary or more contradictory?

The term *history of symbols* is an abbreviated way of capturing in language Voegelin's project of a meditative exegesis of the great historical symbols that articulate the experience of authentic existence. The experience is nothing less than the process of reality becoming luminous to itself, and the symbols, themselves tied to the engendering experience, therefore are integral to the process. For Voegelin, the order of history truly emerges from the history of order, but there are nevertheless lines of meaning that are not temporal. Hence, Voegelin focuses primarily on history as the in-between, the intersection of the timeless and time, which is the "locus" of the divine movement and the human countermovement. The history of symbols explores this nonobjective (nonthinglike) reality as the luminous process that not only enfolds within a reality—the Mystery—it can never fully comprehend but also, with-

---

4. Most notable are the Lonergan workshops held each June at Boston College and at sessions sponsored by the Eric Voegelin Society. See Fred Lawrence, ed., *The Beginning and the Beyond: Papers from the Gadamer and Voegelin Conferences*. See also the proceedings of a Thomas More Institute symposium involving Lonergan and Voegelin: Elaine Cahn and Cathleen Going, eds., *The Question as Commitment: A Symposium*.

in the Mystery, achieves differentiated leaps in being through the pneumatic revelatory consciousness of Israel and Christianity and the noetic conscious-ness of the mystic philosophers of Hellas.[5] Whereas the history of symbols seeks to appropriate the engendering experience, various derailments of phi-losophy, not heeding the vital distinction between luminosity and intention-ality (the latter modeled on perception of external things), would separate ex-perience and symbols and "hypostatize" reality, including historical being, as the object of a putative intentional act, thereby treating the divine, the human inquirer, and reality as a whole as "things."[6] Most metaphysical speculation and philosophical system-building either ignore or cannot do adequate jus-tice to the reality of subjectivity, the mystery of human existence, and the spir-itual and self-transcending nature of human being. Voegelin would thus seem to rule out of court both Lonergan's metaphysics and perhaps even his cogni-tional theory, which has as one of its major concentrations the focus on in-tentional acts.

Lonergan, by contrast, seeks the meaning of the terms *knowledge, truth,* and *reality* in the transcultural and transcendental structure of knowing.[7] Hence, his foundational philosophical discipline is cognitional theory, which, in ex-plicating the recurrent and normative structure of conscious and intentional operations, establishes the basis for epistemology, metaphysics, ethics, and the philosophy of history. Highlighting the significance of intentionality in his method, Lonergan's philosophy of history pinpoints the great differentiations of history as the great objectifications of the transcendental structure of the horizon of inquiry.[8] Lonergan's notion of intellectual conversion, grounded in his cognitional theory, would criticize such a philosopher as Jaspers—and by implication Voegelin—who would conduct existential analysis but not arrive at objective knowledge. And, in fact, Lonergan has explicitly contrasted his own critical realism with Voegelin's "immanentism."[9]

---

5. On symbols and the luminosity of the process of reality, see Voegelin, *Order and His-tory,* 4:227–38; Voegelin, *What Is History?* 178; and Voegelin, *Anamnesis,* 175–82. On temporal and atemporal lines of meaning, see Voegelin, *Order and History,* 1:ix, 4:2; and Voegelin, *Anamnesis,* 91–97, 103–5. On history as the in-between, see Voegelin, *Published Essays, 1966–1985,* 175–76, 267–73, 279–81; Voegelin, *What Is History?* 178; and Voegelin, *Order and History,* 4:172. On leaps in being, see Voegelin, *Order and History,* 1: pref., vol. 4.

6. On hypostatizing, see Voegelin, *What Is History?* 52–53, 65–66, 179.

7. *Insight,* 352–53, 413, 572–75; *Verbum,* 20; *Method in Theology,* chap. 1; *Collection,* chap. 14.

8. *Method in Theology,* 81–99, 172–73, 257–62, 284–87, 302–12, 314–18.

9. On Jaspers, see *Caring about Meaning,* 117–18; and *Method in Theology,* 262–65. A

It is the thesis of this chapter, however, that Lonergan's cognitional theory and Voegelin's history of symbols articulate equivalent answers to a similar, or complementary, range of questions stemming from the same crisis of culture and civilization. Linking the similar questions and the equivalent answers is the exploration, from sometimes sharply different angles, of the experience of the same, to use Voegelin's language, "moving presence of process," or, in Lonergan's language, "process of self-transcendence."[10]

Response to the Crisis

Both Lonergan and Voegelin, though from widely divergent backgrounds, have recognized the same crisis and have responded in a foundational, and equivalent, manner.

Voegelin's intellectual development took place in an Austrian environment still dominated by the influence of Kant, most particularly in the form of the "restrictive" neo-Kantian methodologies referred to above, and by various ideological theories of consciousness, including Marxist and Freudian versions. Voegelin's achievement of a "larger horizon" was stimulated by his own experience of himself as a concrete consciousness engaged in the process of inquiry; by his encounter with pre-Kantian thinkers, a preoccupation that would earn him the dubious label of "historian"; and by his trip to the United States, where he found a living tradition of common sense and what he characterized at the time as the "doctrine of the open self."[11] His own training and interest in political philosophy was matched by firsthand experience of totalitarian politics in the 1930s. He was warned by friendly Marxist students that as much as they personally admired him, they would have to kill him when they seized power.[12] When it was the National Socialists who actually gained control of Austria in the *Anschluss,* Voegelin had to flee for his life as the author of books highly critical of the National Socialist theory of race. Voegelin's mature work was always animated by his concrete experience with totalitarian disorder. He once remarked in a symposium that whenever he appeared before an academic audience, he always asked himself how many

---

point stressed by Eugene Webb, *Philosophers of Consciousness: Polanyi, Lonergan, Voegelin, Ricoeur, Girard, Kierkegaard,* 95, 97. On Voegelin, see *Third Collection,* 218.

10. Voegelin, *Published Essays, 1966–1985,* 131–32; *Method in Theology,* 241.

11. Voegelin, *On the Form of the American Mind,* 62–63; *Anamnesis,* 3–6.

12. Voegelin, *Autobiographical Reflections,* 86.

of those in the audience would succumb to the pressures of a totalitarian regime and consent to his murder.[13] The dramatic, serious, and uncompromising tone of much of his writing, which is evocative of the very subject matter investigated, is testimony, on the one hand, to his own highly personalized and nondogmatic search for "larger horizons" and, on the other hand, to his personal familiarity with the pernicious evil and horror of ideology.

Lonergan's intellectual development took place in Canada, England, and Rome within the atmosphere, perhaps equally open and restrictive, of scholastic theology. In this climate of development, Lonergan's open horizon of inquiry would not have to grapple with the formidable presence of a Kant so much as the domineering figure of the Aquinas of the neo-Thomists. Lonergan himself took a unique path. Witnessing the contentions of the various schools of theology, many of them, in fact, opposing strands of Thomism, he realized that the battle of theological dogmas was really, at the root, a battle of conflicting philosophical dogmas. What could cut through the discord of the contending philosophical schools? His own aspiration to be a theologian who could meet the challenges of the twentieth century demanded that he discover, if possible, the foundational principles of a philosophy of philosophies. Struggling with his earlier nominalism, he encountered the texts of Aquinas. Raising his mind up to that of Aquinas simultaneously changed him profoundly and changed radically his interpretation of Aquinas. Lonergan argued that the epistemology of Aquinas, in fact, was not that of a Thomist and that it was quite consonant with the spirit of inquiry in modern physical science and the *Geisteswissenschaften*.[14] Whereas Voegelin was working his way out of a Kantian horizon that proscribed metaphysics, Lonergan was working his way out of a Thomist horizon that started out with a metaphysics. Not surprisingly, Lonergan's style is more technical, precise, and systematic than that of Voegelin. Perhaps Lonergan's most creative intellectual response to the disorder of his age was in his *Essay on Circulation Analysis,* occasioned by the economic breakdown of the Great Depression. Yet, as we shall see, his larger project of understanding understanding he viewed as quite germane to offsetting the long-term decline that has ravished Western civilization through its apparent climax in the deformation of totalitarianism itself.

13. See Cahn and Going, *Question as Commitment,* 113. According to Voegelin, "the answer always is: the majority."
14. On raising his mind up to that of Aquinas, see *Insight,* 769. On the isomorphism of Aquinas's epistemology and modern scientific method, see *Verbum; Collection,* chap. 9, 193–203; and *Insight,* 432–33.

We can trace back to the late Middle Ages the intellectual component of the crisis to which both Voegelin and Lonergan responded out of their distinctly different backgrounds in their characteristically different manners. For in the late Middle Ages philosophical discourse operated under the ground rules of the confrontation theory of truth, which posits, simply, that knowing has to be at least analogous to perception. If we follow Lonergan—and to some extent Voegelin—who argues that there is no such philosophically relevant perception, then we see that the advocate of the confrontation theory of truth has ultimately two logical alternatives: either suppose some kind of dogmatic perception of concepts, grounding an objectivist metaphysical system, or accept as the only perception perception itself, embracing a skepticism about the claims of philosophy with respect to truth and reality.[15] In the late medieval period, intellectual culture seemed ruled by these alternatives, held, respectively, by the conceptualist metaphysics of Scotus and by the nominalism of the followers of Ockham. We witness here a dialectic of dogmatism and skepticism that at the dawn of modern philosophy was only repeated with the movements of rationalism and empiricism carrying on, respectively, the earlier horizons of conceptualism and nominalism.[16]

The Enlightenment, the first grand attempt at a comprehensive modern cultural synthesis, inherited the dialectic of dogmatism and skepticism as it constructed its new worldview. It sought to apply the method of science, which had been used so successfully by Isaac Newton to uncover for the first time the laws of nature, to uncover also for the first time the laws of history, social dynamics, and human nature, thereby liberating the world. But the Enlightenment tended to oscillate between the extremes of dogmatic materialism, in the systems, for example, of D'Holbach and LaMettrie (the latter, in particular, influenced by rationalist, Cartesian assumptions about reality as the *res extensa*), and the mitigated skepticism of Hume, who essentially reduced science to habit and custom. The ambivalence was essentially continued in the various waves of positivism—Comte's social positivism, Spencer's evolutionary positivism, Mach's critical positivism, and the Vienna Circle's logical positivism—with an increasing tendency, however, toward skepticism

---

15. Voegelin, it should be noted, models intentionality, which is directed to things in the external world, on perception.

16. The epistemological component of this dialectic of dogmatism and skepticism might further elucidate this phenomenon, which Voegelin sees as a leitmotiv in modern culture. See Voegelin, *Anamnesis,* chap. 10; and Voegelin, *Published Essays, 1966–1985,* 54–55, 64–75.

about the power of the human mind to understand the true structure of nature let alone establish any moral, metaphysical, or spiritual truth. Positivism, by the turn of the twentieth century, was joined by various forms of pragmatism, vitalism, and voluntarism.[17] The other major current of thought from the nineteenth century until the present, the dialectical twin of positivism, namely, romanticism, shared the Enlightenment tradition's severe restriction of the scope of reason and opted instead for nonrational, usually irrational, avenues to reality. If we compare, on the one hand, the romanticism of Wordsworth with his sense of "something far more deeply interfused" or of Emerson with his participation in the Over-Soul ("I" eye "I") and, on the other hand, the neoromanticism of fin-de-siècle decadence and the neo-neoromanticism of the 1960s counterculture, we observe an increasing retreat into the self. Thus, by the end of the twentieth century the main currents of intellectual culture exhibited ever narrower, fragmented viewpoints, all hallmarks, according to Lonergan, of precipitous cultural decline.[18]

In essence, the intellectual crisis, experienced in his youth by Voegelin and diagnosed with his sensitivity to epistemological issues by Lonergan, has been an assault on the integrity and worth of intellectual culture itself, of the ability of the human mind to grasp truth about natural, moral, and spiritual matters—and hence an assault, by this curious phenomenon of anti-intellectual intellectuals, on philosophy in any traditional sense. In Lonergan's view, the pragmatic solution to the problems of this effete intellectual culture with its eclipse of reason has been "totalitarian practicality," which substitutes itself for reason. In fact, Lonergan turns his epistemological analysis in *Insight* to address the practical implications of the long-term decline of Western civilization. Carefully differentiating between the sources of progress and of decline, he identifies the simultaneous restriction of the scope of reason and the eclipse of mystery as the radical precipitants that have brought us "to the profound disillusionment of modern man and to the focal point of his horror." In language reminiscent of that of Voegelin, if not literally inspired by *The New Science of Politics,* Lonergan's critical brand of history would expose the "nonsense that the rising star of another nation or class is going to put another human nature in the saddle."[19] Indeed, the careful reader of *Insight* will notice that in

---

17. H. S. Hughes, *Consciousness and Society.*

18. *Insight,* 254, 262; *Method in Theology,* 54–55.

19. On "totalitarian practicality," see *Insight,* 256–57; on the longer cycle of decline, 250–57; on the eclipse of reason and of mystery, 8, 259–60, 572; for the fallacy of positing a change in human nature, 265.

the chapters on common sense, in contrast to the style of much of the book, Lonergan's passion and urgency, even eloquence, leap out from the pages.[20] The response to the cultural crisis and to the crisis of civilization, then, goes to the heart of *Insight*.

Thus, we see that the intellectual crisis interpenetrates with the crisis of civilization. As Voegelin points out, Nietzsche was a prophet in this respect, predicting "wars of the spirit" and calamity. If Lonergan stresses the epistemological origins of the crisis, Voegelin emphasizes the origins in the sentiments, images, and feelings of the cultural infrastructure that often works beneath the surface of explicitly formulated ideas. As Voegelin shows, the Enlightenment in seeking to make sense of, and to validate, the defining experiences of the modern world eschewed any appeal to the symbols of Christendom, which seemed irrelevant, dogmatic, and, in truth, discredited. In the wake of the old symbols, the Enlightenment embraced neognostic sentiments of transforming human nature and eliminating the major source of evil in society through esoteric wisdom about the meaning of history. Hence was born Enlightenment progressivism, displaying a family resemblance to ancestral millenarian and Joachite aspirations. However, the logic of these sentiments of modernity was in the direction of immediate action, not gradualism, violence, not talk—in short, revolution, not progressivist reform.[21] Totalitarianism, then, was the logical outcome of the deepest yearnings of modernity.

Clearly, Lonergan's critique of the confrontation theory of truth and Voegelin's critique of neognosticism complement each other. The epistemological crisis whittled down adherence to the standards of rational civilized life, opening the door for the flood of neognostic sentiments, whereas the neognostic dream, as Freidrich Heer suggests, was always pressuring the higher culture of reason from below.[22] Both Lonergan and Voegelin, though analyzing the crisis from different backgrounds, experiences, and intellectual perspectives,

---

20. For the centrality of Lonergan's concern with economic, political, and social questions in his early writings and for the possibility that he wrote the chapters on common sense out of sequence, see "Editors' Preface," in ibid., xxii.

21. Voegelin, *Published Essays, 1940–1952,* chap. 5. Voegelin, *From Enlightenment to Revolution,* chap. 1. On millennialism, see Cohn, *Pursuit of the Millennium;* on the connection between millenarianism and progressivism, see Voegelin, *New Science of Politics,* chap. 4; Voegelin, *Modernity without Restraint,* 175–95; and Tuvenson, *Millennium and Utopia;* on modern neognostic movements and their locations in traditional hotbeds of heresy, see Heer, *Intellectual History of Europe,* 2. On the revolutionary tenor of modernity, see Voegelin, *New Science of Politics,* 121–32; and Voegelin, *Modernity without Restraint,* 187–95.

22. Heer, *Intellectual History of Europe,* 1–2.

are describing the same crisis. What their respective approaches reveal is that the crisis has these interpenetrating layers of superstructure and infrastructure. Indeed, any contemporary thinker who attempts to understand the one crisis in its historical complexity is obligated to employ the categories of both Lonergan and Voegelin.[23]

The response of each to the crisis, however, has some significant areas of solidarity, not just complementarity. Voegelin, too, addresses key features of the confrontation theory of truth as he seeks a fundamentally alternative framework to the paradigm of a subject "in here" confronting an object of cognition "out there" in his treatment of consciousness, divine presence, human existence, and the history of symbols. Voegelin in the 1920s made a decisive break with Husserl's phenomenology of a self-contained transcendental ego constituting intentional objects, where intentionality, so interpreted, was modeled primarily on auditory perception. Voegelin conceived of consciousness as the consciousness of a concrete person with a life embedded in the body, society, and history. In a similar vein, he considered the neo-Kantian categories of cultural forms, which were constituted as objects "out there" by a methodologically postulated ego, to be artificial and restrictive devices. Instead, he proceeded to study cultural horizons as they developed in concrete history.[24]

If the subject does not confront culture as an object, neither is the subject, or, more properly, human existence, an object to be confronted. It is here that Voegelin differentiates between the intentionality of consciousness (modeled, as we have seen, on perception of external things) and the luminosity of consciousness.[25] Consciousness, to be sure, is incarnate consciousness; indeed, bodily movements and rhythms give to consciousness its sense of time.[26] But this also implies that consciousness is not just in time. Concrete consciousness extends to the network of social institutions, beyond that to the histori-

---

23. In assessing Voltaire, for example, one cannot ignore either the epistemological situation that made Voltaire suspicious of metaphysics and attracted to Lockeanism or the deeper longing and sentiments that made Voltaire substitute the story of the birth, decline, and rebirth of civilization for the birth, death, and resurrection of Christ as the *eidos* of history. See Voegelin, *From Enlightenment to Revolution,* chap. 1; Voegelin, *New Science of Politics,* 119–21; and Voegelin, *Modernity without Restraint,* 185–86.

24. On the break with Husserl, see Voegelin, *Anamnesis,* 14–19. Voegelin seems to commend Santayana's "critical realism" as an advance over phenomenology (*Form of the American Mind,* 74). On concrete consciousness, see Voegelin, *Anamnesis,* chap. 11. On cultural horizons as historically concrete, see Voegelin, *Form of the American Mind,* intro.

25. Voegelin, *Order and History,* 5:14–16.

26. Voegelin, *Anamnesis,* 15–18.

cal traditions embedded in society, and beyond that to the grand movement of human history itself. Consciousness, in fact, is a process. It is a process with its own dynamics, including the search for order and the ground of being, a reflexivity concomitant with the search, and a dramatic urgency about the right direction. Human existence, then, is the luminous process with its directional tendency. Human beings are actors in the drama of existence without knowing fully what is the role. Consciousness cannot step outside the drama and take a look at it.[27] The relation of consciousness to body, to society, and to history is not the relation of one external thing to other external things. Thus, the confrontation theory of truth with its subject-object bifurcation fails to do justice to the reality of human existence as a process with an ever widening field. The category of luminosity captures the absolute distinctness of this "nonobjective" reality of human existence.[28]

However, there is yet a further dimension to the dynamics of the process of existence that marks it as unique from any "external thing," namely, that the search is experienced precisely as a response to divine presence. This human-divine encounter is not something added on to human nature as a cosmic afterthought or a helping hand from above. It is of the very essence of human being. Voegelin therefore speaks, in Platonic language, of human reality as "in-between": in-between the divine (as transcendent) and the human (as purely world-immanent); in-between the timeless (the atemporal presence of consciousness, its openness, and its participation in the Beyond) and time (the flow of things in the world); in-between knowledge (the luminosity of consciousness and its directional tendency) and ignorance (about the Mystery of reality and the meaning of the drama of existence). Neither the divine nor the in-between status of human existence is an object to be perceived as part of a speculative system. The luminosity of consciousness is an event *within reality;* it is reality becoming luminous for its structure in the process of history. Reality cannot be confronted outside the participatory process.

Does this mean, then, that, for Voegelin, there are no norms or standards by which to evaluate human history, human society, or individual human behavior? After all, since there is no standpoint outside the process, would not any attempt to evaluate within the process be forced to succumb to relativism? This disjunction, of course, is set up by the confrontation theory of truth. It argues that either there is a standard external to the process or there are no

27. Voegelin, *Order and History,* 1:1–2.
28. Voegelin, *Anamnesis,* 29, 147, 153, 175, 178–79; Voegelin, *What Is History?* 106. Voegelin also formulates it as "nonexistent" reality (*Published Essays, 1966–1985,* 52, 54).

standards. But Voegelin finds a constant in the process: the Question. Norms are immanent in the process of the Question, which, with its property of openness, is oriented to the "common world" (the *koine cosmos* of Heraclitus).[29]

The great symbols of the historical tradition arise out of this normative process of inquiry, which is their engendering experience, and cannot be severed from the process or their meaning is lost. To understand the meaning is to enter the process. Hence, the historian of symbols does not confront them as objects. The history of symbols is not an object of doxiographical research.[30] Nor is the writing of the history of symbols a dry report; rather, at least as practiced by Voegelin, it is an evocative entry into the horizon of openness with its engendering experience, which can, in turn, spur creative effort, possibly leading to the expression of new symbols.[31]

Voegelin, then, is quite serious about intellectual culture escaping the spell of the confrontation theory of truth, and he is able to do so the extent to which he articulates the norms of authentic existence in relation to the open horizon of the Question. Herein we see substantive agreement with Lonergan: for Lonergan radically locates the meaning of objectivity, truth, and reality with the self-transcending process of questioning. Objectivity, according to Lonergan, is the fruit of authentic subjectivity, that is, fidelity to the imperatives of being attentive, intelligent, reasonable, and responsible—in a word, openness.[32]

Yet, we must still ask just how equivalent is Lonergan's cognitional theory to Voegelin's history of symbols. How can Lonergan address, as does Voegelin, the "within" of existence, the luminosity of consciousness, which is distinct from intentionality, and the in-between of human being—in particular, what Voegelin calls the "nonobjective reality" of the luminous human-divine encounter at the very core of open existence? Indeed, are Lonergan's cognitional theory and Voegelin's history of symbols equivalent in such a foundational

---

29. On the question, see *Order and History*, 4:316–35; on the *koine cosmos*, 2:232ff; Voegelin, *New Science of Politics*, 28; and Voegelin, *Modernity without Restraint*, 109.

30. Voegelin, *What Is History?* 1–13. The historian of symbols may find "traces" of symbols as "givens" in the external world (like Kantian phenomena), but to understand the symbols the historian must "encounter" them. Voegelin, *Published Essays, 1966–1985*, 120–21, 289; and Voegelin, *Anamnesis*, 113.

31. Voegelin, for example, notes that the symbol *history* is not in either the Platonic corpus or the Aristotelian corpus, but by wrestling with the Platonic and Aristotelian texts, he also finds that the symbols fit the Platonic and the Aristotelian analyses of human existence (*Published Essays, 1966–1985*, 268; *Anamnesis*, 92).

32. *Method in Theology*, 20, 265, 292, 302; *Collection*, 186.

way as to oblige the contemporary philosopher to encounter in a serious fashion the horizon of both thinkers?

Lonergan's Cognitional Theory

Insight is surely Lonergan's magnum opus, and interpreters naturally focus on this difficult and challenging book. At least by contrast to his thorough, even seemingly systematic, treatment of issues in *Insight*, Lonergan's investigations in his post-*Insight* work, including *Method in Theology*, appear more suggestive, more scattered, more in need of development. Students of Lonergan's post-*Insight* material, accordingly, offer different interpretations of the implications of his ideas.[33]

We must be clear that in *Insight* Lonergan neither presents dogmas nor proposes that there be "Lonerganians" to interpret them.[34] He gives an invitation for a personal, decisive act of self-appropriation and urges collaboration in the enterprise of gaining an insight into insight.[35] *Insight* itself is written from a "moving viewpoint," where earlier statements must be qualified and revised by later statements in an ever expanding horizon of inquiry, and it is written about a moving viewpoint, the process of inquiry. We must, however, consider the "moving viewpoint" from a larger context than that simply of *Insight* itself. Lonergan tells us that he "rounded off" *Insight* for publication in light of impending teaching duties. He wrote *Insight* from a moving viewpoint that continued to unfold beyond that monumental achievement. Lonergan, for example, eliminated his reliance on a faculty psychology in his analysis of moral and spiritual consciousness by his introduction of the seminal notion of the "intention of the good."[36] To use Lonergan's language, he was developing his own "position" with respect to such items as the good, myth, and divine presence. If, consequently, we interpret a post-*Insight* idea, however briefly ex-

33. Much of the discussion, for example, in a recent volume of *Method: Journal of Lonergan Studies* 13 (fall 1995) was devoted to the question of the number of levels of consciousness.

34. "The word Lonerganian has come up in recent days. In a sense there's no such thing. Because what I am asking is people to discover themselves and be themselves" (*Second Collection*, 213).

35. *Insight*, 6–7, 12–14.

36. On a "moving viewpoint," ibid., 17–21; and *Second Collection*, 222–23, 275. On rounding off *Insight*, see *Second Collection*, 213, 275; and *Caring about Meaning*, 70. On the intention of the good, see *Second Collection*, 79–84, 223; and *Method in Theology*, 268, 340, 343.

pressed, even mentioned as *dicta,* to be, in fact, a substantive enrichment of his basic position and a perceptive response to further, relevant questions arising from his very method of inquiry, then we must consider that idea to be a significant part of Lonergan's developing position. Although in his post-*Insight* work Lonergan had penetrating remarks and a characteristic grasp of nuance as he dealt with such topics as the good, myth, and the divine, he did not treat those topics with the same thoroughness and detail as he had given to the process and structure of cognition in *Insight.* His most comprehensive post-*Insight* book, *Method in Theology,* had as its theme the functional cooperation of distinct specialties. To be sure, it relied on *Insight* to provide a broad framework for a developed position on the good, myth, and the divine and had chapters on the good and on religion, but the framework was more like the rudiments for an *Insight 2* than a work equal in depth of articulation to *Insight.* Whether Lonergan ever envisioned something like the more detailed *Insight 2,* which by virtue of its emphasis on existential orientation and existential state may have challenged his style of presentation, or to what extent factors of health and age hampered his efforts, or to what degree he was increasingly preoccupied with such other areas as economic analysis are matters more suitable for an intellectual biography. What concerns us here—and this is a major premise of this chapter—is that we cannot discuss Lonergan's ideas on the good, myth, and the divine solely from the perspective of *Insight* any more than we can discuss those ideas without recourse to *Insight.*

With these preliminary issues of method kept in mind, we can now address the extent to which Lonergan's philosophy of history is the equivalent of Voegelin's.

Cognitional theory, for Lonergan, is at the core of philosophical reflection. At the beginning of *Insight,* Lonergan sets out his philosophical program: all metaphysical, ethical, and epistemological statements can be reduced to statements of cognitional theory, and statements of cognitional theory can be tested by cognitional fact.[37] Lonergan's cognitional theory is an objectification of inquiry as structure, or, more precisely, an objectification of conscious and intentional operations as structure. We must be careful, then, at the outset of not misconstruing such key terms as *objectification, structure, conscious,* and *intentional.* We must at least try to take seriously Lonergan's claims that he is engaging in a radical foundational enterprise, one that requires an "intellectual conversion."[38] Thus, Lonergan's use of language may seem idiosyncratic from the viewpoint of the climate of opinion.

---

37. *Insight,* 5.
38. *Method in Theology,* 238.

To objectify the structure of cognition is, of course, to make it into an object. But what does Lonergan mean by an "object"? An object is simply what is intended in a question. Since we have yet to define how Lonergan would conceive of "intend," the meaning of "object" may still seem a bit obscure. Suffice it to say that "object" is not a Cartesian "thing," either a pure thinking substance divorced from the world or an instance of the *res extensa*, the latter being what Lonergan refers to as "body," having the attributes of "already out there now real." Nor is "object" a Kantian "thing" determined by an appropriate filling in of the categories of the mind to give us the world of appearances described in Newtonian physics. Nor is the object necessarily a thing in Lonergan's sense, namely, a "unity, identity, whole grasped in data as individual," the intelligibility of which Lonergan calls a central form.[39] Only if what we inquire about has the properties of a Cartesian *cogito,* Cartesian *res extensa,* or Kantian phenomenal substance would the object of inquiry be a *cogito,* instance of *res extensa,* or phenomenal substance. Since Lonergan emphatically denies the existence of a pure *cogito,* or *res extensa,* or phenomenal substance, none of these "things" can be objects outside the framework of a Cartesian or Kantian philosophy.[40] To Lonergan's way of thinking, if we can inquire about the self, the self can be an object. If we can inquire about God, God can be an object. If we can inquire about justice, justice can be an object. If we can inquire about inquiry, inquiry can be an object. So if we can inquire about the structure of cognition, then it, too, can be an object. To say of something that it is an object is not to determine the status of our answers, for our answers can be complete, or partial, or analogous, or, in principle, radically incomplete, depending upon what we inquire about. If what we inquire about is mystery, then the object is mystery because the object is nothing less than what we inquire about. Finally, to say of something that it is an object does not, as we have seen, mean that it must be any kind of thing, in Lonergan's proper sense.

The structure of cognition is not a thing. Lonergan cannot be accused of reifying the structure of cognition out of the process of subjectivity and thereby making it some kind of autonomous thing like "bodies" in the external world. Cognitional structure, for Lonergan, is like any structure, a whole defined in terms of dynamically and functionally related parts.[41] In this case, the

---

39. On "object," see ibid., 341; and *Second Collection,* 121, 123–24. On "body," see *Insight,* 276–77; on "thing," 271, 460–63.

40. *Insight,* 362–66, 430–31, 433–36; *Collection,* 193–94, 203; *Second Collection,* 75–79, 122; Giovanni Sala, *Lonergan and Kant: Five Essays on Human Knowledge.*

41. *Collection,* 205–6.

functionally related parts are the operations of experiencing, understanding, and judging; the dynamism is the process of inquiry linking the operations; and the whole is the totality of distinct operations that alone constitute human cognition. The functional connections of the structure of cognition form, literally, an intelligible set of relations, what Lonergan appropriately calls a "conjugate form," which is to be differentiated from Lonergan's "thing," or "central form." Conjugate form, for Lonergan, bears a resemblance to Aristotle's "accidental form," and, as is the case with Aristotle, the conjugate form exists not by itself but only in a concrete being.[42] To put it in Voegelin's language, the structure of cognition exists in the concrete consciousness of a concrete person.

We turn, then, to consciousness. Recall that cognitional operations are conscious. Here perhaps more than anywhere else Lonergan departs from the conventional philosophical usage. For consciousness, as Lonergan speaks of it, is not an inner look; it is, rather, with respect to cognition, the awareness concomitant with cognitional operations. It is a self-presence.[43] I can look at a painting. I am present to the painting as seen but also present to myself as looking. I can seek, perhaps somewhat spontaneously, to understand what the painting means. I am present to the content of my thinking but also present to myself as thinking. I can judge, again perhaps somewhat spontaneously, the adequacy of my interpretation of the meaning of the painting. I am present to the content of my judgment but also present to myself as judging. Consciousness, in Lonergan's deliberately narrow and technical use of the term, is the self-presence of the knower prior to any objectification. It is not the awareness of the content of cognitional operations, whether the contents be sensible, intelligible, or rational. But consciousness itself can be an object of inquiry, in Lonergan's aforementioned sense of object. This does not mean, therefore, that one must approach consciousness through a radical Cartesian self-doubt, or a Kantian transcendental deduction, or a Husserlian transcendental reduction.[44] One objectifies consciousness, according to Lonergan, by appealing to inner experience—not the content of conscious operations but the self-presence of the operator—and one does that by a heightening of self-presence as one performs the cognitional operations. Then one can inquire about what one does. By emphasizing inner experience, the data of con-

---

42. *Insight*, 460–63.
43. On consciousness as awareness, see ibid., 344–46, 636–38; as self-presence, see *Method in Theology*, 7.
44. *Insight*, 440; and n. 40 above.

sciousness prior to any interpretation, Lonergan argues that we can posit the unity of consciousness—and hence a conscious self—because the unity is an experiential given.[45] This may seem at odds with Voegelin, who opposes the idea of the unity of consciousness. But Voegelin's opposition is framed within his critique of Husserl's transcendental ego, which is a pure self-contained *cogito* that constitutes unity by constituting the *noema* of cognition by acts of *noesis*. Lonergan, by contrast, would transpose Descartes's *cogito* to concrete living. He would furthermore deny there is a transcendental ego. Husserl's pure ego is, for Lonergan, the concrete knowing subject attenuated to intentional acts under the shadow of the influence of extroversion.[46]

Underpinning the operations of cognition and its structure is the factor of intentionality. This, too, is a troublesome word. Voegelin struggled with the phenomenologists' idea of intentionality. Early in his writings Voegelin criticized intentionality as too narrowly associated with auditory perception.[47] Later, as we have seen above, he felt the need to differentiate luminosity as a dimension of consciousness from intentionality, which was modeled on perception of external things. Although Lonergan does not deny that there are intentional operations "heading" for contents of perception, he does not restrict intentionality to perception. Instead, when dealing with cognition he would model intentionality more on the immediate relation to an object through a question.[48] The intentionality of knowing obviously involves perception, but "what is obvious in knowing is not what knowing obviously is."[49] Knowing also involves two qualitatively distinct questions and hence two distinct intentions: the question what is it?—the intention of the intelligible; and the question is it so?—the intention of the real. Here cognitive intention and cognitive object can be defined only mutually since one cannot make sense of one without reference to the other.[50]

Not only does cognitional process exhibit intentional operations other than those of perception or analogous to perception, but also the process of cog-

---

45. On heightening of consciousness, see *Insight*, 345; on unity of consciousness, 349–52.

46. Voegelin, *Anamnesis*, 19; on transposition of the *cogito* to concrete living, see "Horizon and the Problem of Philosophy," in *Notes on Existentialism*, 15; on critique of Husserl's pure ego, see *Insight*, 440.

47. Voegelin, *Anamnesis*, 19; Voegelin, *Form of the American Mind*, 66–72.

48. *Collection*, 211–14.

49. *Insight*, 441.

50. On the distinct questions of cognition, see ibid., 297–99; on implicit definition, the hallmark of explanation, 37.

nition exhibits a number of salient features that approximate Voegelin's luminosity (and not his intentionality).

Recall that, for Lonergan, the structure of cognition is a whole. But it is a whole because there is a dynamism running through the process and its structured operations. The dynamism is a basic intentionality, the intention of being.[51] All cognitive operations of sensing, perceiving, imagining, all questions for intelligence and operations of understanding, and all questions for reflection and operations of reflective understanding, weighing and marshaling evidence, and judging are underpinned by the intention of being. Interpreters of *Insight* have tended to focus on Lonergan's model of levels of consciousness. If, though, the levels of consciousness are not always intimately and essentially tied to the underlying dynamic intentionality, then indeed the structure of cognition will seem to be a reified external thing. This basic intentionality, always that of the concrete consciousness of a concrete person, constitutes the unity of cognition.

The intention of being is an unrestricted intention. It is the unrestricted desire to know. Given Lonergan's internal definition embracing the terms *cognitive intention* and *cognitive object,* it follows that the unrestricted desire to know intends an unrestricted object, that is, one not known by a restrictive horizon of inquiry, namely, being.[52]

The intention of being in its unrestricted sweep is also normative. The norms of what is real are not, as the confrontation theory of truth would have it, bound up with a putative look at objects "out there" but are ingredient in the process of inquiry itself, just as the norms of objectivity reside not in some antiseptic distance from objects but in fidelity to the project of questioning. Therefore to speak of the object correlative to the unrestrictive nature of questioning as real is not to indulge in wishful thinking. Indeed, the intention of being is the core of meaning.[53]

Since the normative dimension of the intention of being, the directional tendency of questioning, if you will, is conscious, the intention of being is heuristic. Every question is situated midway between knowledge and ignorance: without the latter, there would be no need to ask; without the former, as Plato explored in the *Meno,* there would be no basis for asking.[54] The un-

51. Ibid., 379; *Collection,* 205–8, 211–14.
52. *Insight,* 372–76, 667–68.
53. On immanent norms of the real and of objectivity, see ibid., 404–5, 413; and *Verbum,* 20. On transcendent object not wishful thinking, see *Second Collection,* 40–42. On core of meaning, *Insight,* 381–83.
54. Lonergan's probable reference to the *Meno* in *Insight,* 16.

restricted question, the pure question, is situated between heuristic anticipations of the reality sought and mystery. Lonergan, at one point, defines being as the totality of correct answers to the totality of authentic questions. This is a heuristic definition and, most important, one rooted in the intention of being latent and operative and conscious prior to any thematization. Hence, he speaks not of the concept of being but the notion of being. In his favorable commentary on Voegelin's "Gospel and Culture," Lonergan calls this conscious heuristic anticipation the "inner light."[55]

The intention of being, as unrestricted, normative, and heuristic, is likewise transcendent. The raising of a question is the source of transcendence.[56] Every question takes us beyond. Thus, the unrestricted question takes us radically beyond. Here we must not misconstrue Lonergan's definition of being, for if the definition of being as the totality of correct answers to the totality of correct questions is heuristic, it is also analogous. The unrestricted sweep of our questioning places both the questioner and the world in question—and thereby already has gone beyond the universe of finite being. No finite mind could grasp the insights to be able to answer the "totality of questions" contained virtually in the energy, dynamism, and directional tendency of the pure unrestricted desire to know. Every concrete horizon has its "known unknown," its realm of mystery where there are questions (the known) but no answers (the unknown).[57] The field of mystery can be contracted by expanded knowledge but never eliminated. The implications of Lonergan's ideas, then, are clear: mystery, in principle, is permanent for humans. Only an unrestricted act of understanding could understand being, and that unrestricted act of understanding would have to be being itself.[58] If our heuristic anticipation of being is our conscious notion of being, that is, our self-presence as the question of being, then true knowledge of being would be the self-presence in which there would be a radical identity of knower and known. Still, as inquirers we have a fundamental orientation to Transcendent Mystery. And indeed it is this orientation that underpins all activities of knowing, even of things in the world.

Finally, the orientation to transcendent Mystery is the search for the divine ground. Unrestricted questioning asks about the purpose of life, the meaning of death, the fact of evil; about the ultimate nature of the unrestricted intelli-

55. On notion of being as heuristic definition, see *Insight,* 374–76, 383–384; as "inner light," see *Third Collection,* 190, 219.
56. *Insight,* 658.
57. *Method in Theology,* 77.
58. *Insight,* 669–71.

gibility, reality, and goodness we seek in our questions; and about the ground for a world whose intelligibility, reality, and goodness do not match what the norms of the process of inquiry point to as the proper object of its unfettered open quest. Simply put, the unrestricted desire to know is the question of God.[59]

If focus on Lonergan's levels of consciousness in *Insight* runs the risk of missing the significance of intentionality, so focus on Lonergan's strategically chosen instances of intentionality in the fields of mathematics and science (chosen for their precision and methodical dynamism) runs the danger of restricting intentionality to the intellectual pattern of experience alone. Lonergan's idea of "patterns of experience" is a crucial one. Our predominant interests, concerns, questions constitute the way we organize our experience. Correlative to certain types of questions are corresponding kinds of methods, modes of expression, and realms of meaning (similar to Alfred Schütz's "finite provinces of meaning").[60] To cite an example, three persons look at a river. One is a plumber concerned about the hydraulics of water control, another is a scientist interested in the biochemical makeup of the stream, and the third is a painter moved by the beauty of it all. The plumber operates in the practical pattern of experience with commonsense procedures, the scientist operates in the intellectual pattern of experience with explanatory categories, and the painter operates in the aesthetic pattern of experience with artistic criteria in which meaning and judgments are collapsed onto a purely experiential level. Although insight obviously occurs in the intellectual pattern and all its numerous subdivisions of science and scholarship, it is present also in the common sense of the practical pattern and in the artistic vision of the aesthetic pattern. Moreover, and this is crucial for the theme of this paper, if we examine carefully the phenomenon of myth, we can discern in mythopoesis all the hallmarks of a distinct pattern of experience. We can imagine a fourth person present beside our proverbial river, one who views the river as symbolic of the mysterious depths out of which human life has emerged. We must be careful, as Lonergan later warned in an interview, not to identify his later understanding of "myth" with the purely pejorative way that he used the term in

---

59. *Method in Theology,* 101–3.

60. On patterns of experience, see *Insight,* 204ff: on the intellectual pattern, 209–10; on the practical pattern, 232–34; on the aesthetic pattern, 207–9; *Method in Theology,* 61–64; and *Topics in Education,* chap. 9. On realms of meaning, see *Method in Theology,* 272, 286–87; Alfred Schütz, "On Multiple Realities," in *Collected Papers,* 1:207–59; Schütz, *On Phenomenological and Social Relations,* 252–62.

Insight. Instead, we should look in *Insight* at his analysis of "mystery" and "symbols" for his idea of "myth."[61] To be a genuine pattern of experience, mythopoesis would have to have its own distinct questions ("why" questions that explore rather than explain), its own mode of inquiry (regarding heuristic anticipations, where it would overlap with the aesthetic pattern and what Lonergan calls the "dramatic pattern"), its own form of expression (symbols and narratives), and its own world of meaning (the mystery of the known unknown). Although in *Insight* Lonergan does not, then, develop an explicit and lucid theory of mythic consciousness, he does provide the critical tools for such a theory and prepares the way for a more sophisticated and serious treatment of myth in the enriched and expanded cognitional theory of his later writings.

Before we discuss that enriched context, let us assess what we have covered in this section. If an object, in Lonergan's sense, is not an external thing, Cartesian or Kantian, if consciousness is not constituted by a transcendental ego, if intentionality is not modeled on perception, and if myth is a possible genuine mode of inquiry, then the apparent distance separating Lonergan's cognitional theory and Voegelin's history of symbols has been narrowed considerably. Instead, basic lines of affinity have become prominent with the two thinkers' emphasis on the dynamic process of inquiry with its directional tendency oriented to transcendence.

Lonergan's Expanded Cognitional Theory

In *Insight,* Lonergan employs his method artfully to detail the structured conscious and intentional operations of cognitional process. When he deals with moral consciousness, however, he resorts to an antiquated faculty psychology rooted in metaphysical categories as suitable for plants as for humans.[62]

In his post-*Insight* writings, however, Lonergan extends the base of his intentionality analysis from conscious and intentional cognitive operations to include conscious and intentional volitional operations on the existential level of consciousness, broadens the field of intentionality to embrace the inten-

61. *Insight,* 556–57, 569–72, 585; *Second Collection,* 275.
62. *Insight,* 72–73, 79, 170, 223, 277; *Method in Theology,* 268, 343; *Verbum,* 4–5.

tion of the good, and links intentionality itself to existential moods and spiritual presence.

When we examine existential consciousness, which involves operations of apprehending values, evaluating, and deciding, we witness how, contrary to any charge of excessive rationalism, for Lonergan, human reality is a concrete unity of affectivity, intelligence, and volition. Apprehension of values is a spontaneous affective response to what is worthwhile, evaluation is the fruit of a deliberative process in which, most ordinarily, commonsense-type insights coalesce in the self-correcting process of moral inquiry (Aristotle's *phronesis*), and deciding is an irreducible exercise of responsible freedom.[63] The criterion of moral objectivity is self-transcendence, going beyond what is merely satisfying to what is truly worthwhile. This criterion is at once cognitive and affective since in deliberation consciousness becomes conscience, where the "nagging conscience is the recurrence of the original question that has not been met." Moral self-transcendence is fuller participation in being than cognitive self-transcendence. Here the issue is living the truth. If the commitment to living the truth of existence in fidelity to the intention of the good is firm enough, then it is accompanied by the vertical exercise of freedom Lonergan terms "moral conversion." To function well in the entire process of conscious and intentional operations is to be Lonergan's equivalent of the Aristotelian *spoudaios*. As Aristotle's ethics is the study of the *ethos* (character) of the *spoudaios* (mature person), who is the norm and measure of good acts, so, for Lonergan, philosophy is the study of the self-transcending subject.[64] The operations of moral consciousness retain but go beyond those of cognition. Moral deliberation must take into account knowledge of human reality, but, at the same time, moral operations guide the process of cognition. The desire to know is, in fact, a spontaneous apprehension of value. To respond to it, however, requires judgment of its worth and decisions to pursue it through the process of cognition, perhaps in the face of anxiety and biases.

As the process of cognition is underpinned by the intention of being with its unrestrictive, normative, heuristic, and transcendent dimensions, so, too, the process of moral inquiry is underpinned by the unrestrictive, normative, heuristic, and transcendent intention of the good. Similarly, as the operations

63. *Method in Theology,* 31–32, 36–39; *Insight,* 197–98, 311–12, 314–16, 631–42.
64. On moral objectivity, see *Method in Theology,* 35, 37–38; on conscience, 35, 40, 121, 268–69; and *Third Collection,* 174. On cognitive and moral self-transcendence, see *Method in Theology,* 37–38; on moral conversion, 40, 240–42. On Aristotle, see ibid., 41; and *Second Collection,* 82.

of moral consciousness retain but go beyond cognitive operations, so the intention of the good is the fuller unfolding of the intention of being.[65] It is that fuller unfolding because it seeks fuller participation in being. The intention of the good is oriented to being as to what is worthwhile: this invites participation, that is, real self-transcendence. It also simultaneously turns on the subject. For the question regarding this or that object of deliberation and decision is also the question regarding who is the moral agent.[66] The question of who one is is the question of being.[67] It is a question that relates the self as questioner to the self as questioned. Fidelity to the intention of the good is to live the tension between self as questioning and self as questioned. This is a prime existential manifestation, to employ Lonergan's language, of the "tension of limitation and transcendence." Since the intention of the good is an unrestricted question, it is a question of my self-transcendence in relation to transcendent mystery, where my self-transcendence itself, as we have just seen, is the tension of question and questioned. Thus, it is entirely appropriate, following Lonergan's explication of the dynamics of questioning on the existential level of consciousness, to say that I am in my being the question of being (who I am to be in relation to being). I am a known unknown. Who I am is a mystery.

Lonergan's depiction of the self as mystery is only more pronounced when his moving viewpoint goes beyond intentionality to the existential moods that expand and enrich the commitment to value. Perhaps a better metaphor than "going beyond" would be "engulf." What engulfs intentionality is the state of being in love, embracing love of family, friends, country. Love creates its own discernment of values through "faith," which Lonergan defines as "knowledge born of love."[68]

Furthermore, if the intention of the good is unrestricted, then the love that nourishes it must be an unrestricted love. Lonergan maintains that such an unrestricted love is a datum of consciousness. Since Lonergan is not too clear on terminology here, let us provisionally call the entire complex of experiences of being in a state of unrestricted love "spiritual consciousness." It is important to keep in mind that spiritual consciousness is not the awareness of any new intentional operation added onto those of cognition and volition.

---

65. *Method in Theology*, 34–35; *Second Collection*, 82.
66. *Method in Theology*, 121, 240.
67. *Collection*, 229.
68. *Method in Theology*, 289; *Third Collection*, 175; on "faith," see *Method in Theology*, 115.

Thus, Lonergan terms it a "state," and we have described it as an "existential mood" that "engulfs." If spiritual consciousness is present sufficiently, it has momentous consequences for changing the existential disposition. It brings with it a new discernment of what is worthwhile, a new commitment to living in the universe of being—a spiritual faith, whose "reasons of the heart," to quote Pascal, as Lonergan does, are born of the experience of unrestricted love. This leads to a vertical exercise of liberty that transforms the horizon in which conscious and intentional operations occur. Such a transformation Lonergan calls "religious conversion." Indeed, ordinarily, religious conversion is the existential condition for moral conversion, as religious conversion and moral conversion are the existential conditions for intellectual conversion.[69]

Lonergan tends to emphasize two components or dimensions of spiritual consciousness. We may say that the state of being in unrestricted love is both an unrestricted love of an unrestricted object and an unrestricted love with an unrestricted subject. To put it another way, in the traditional language of Western theology, unrestricted love is the love of God, where "of" means both love "for" God (Augustine's infinite yearning for God) and love "by" and "with" God (God's infinite love for us). Or we can speak, in the same vein, of divine presence as object and divine presence as subject.

Recalling Lonergan's unique definition of "object" as what is intended in questioning, we can unpack the meaning of the previous statement about divine presence as object. For an object can be what is intended in unrestricted questioning, the content of which can be heuristically anticipated in the transcendental notions of the intelligible, the real, and the good. Divine presence as object would be the immediate relation of the inquirer to what is questioned in the unrestricted drive to understand, the unrestricted openness to being, and the unrestricted attraction to the good. Lonergan, however, goes on to describe unrestricted being-in-love as the experienced fulfillment of the thrust for self-transcendence. Clearly, Lonergan does not mean that unrestricted being-in-love constitutes some kind of revelation or vision or look at the entire content of the intelligible, the real, and the good that we seek as questioners. That might be what an advocate of the confrontation theory of truth would be anticipating, including a speculative gnostic. Rather, Lonergan points out that the transcendental notions "constitute our capacity for self-transcendence" and that unrestrictedly being-in-love actualizes that ca-

---

69. *Method in Theology*, 243; on unrestricted love, 106, 116, 242, 289; on Pascal, 115; on religious conversion, 240ff.

pacity.[70] What, then, does fulfillment of our capacity for self-transcendence mean? We can follow here James Price's suggestion about one possible interpretation of "fulfillment" and call "religious consciousness" the component of spiritual consciousness that is the drive to self-transcendence working at full operational capacity. "Religious consciousness," so defined, would seem to approximate Voegelin's *zetesis,* the loving search for being, portrayed by Plato in his myth of the puppet player in the *Laws* as a response to the pull of the golden cord and in his allegory of the cave as the result of being drawn.[71] To actuate fully the dynamic process of self-transcendence would be to be faithful to the norms of intentionality without reservation or qualification within a perspective of love and faith. For Lonergan, too, as for Voegelin, this is a response to a pull. What Price has labeled religious consciousness is one dimension of spiritual consciousness; it cannot be separated from the other dimension: the divine as subject.

Fulfillment of the capacity for self-transcendence also takes place in what can be described, by analogy with a human intersubjective relation, only as divine-human intersubjective consciousness or, by metaphor, as participatory consciousness. Here intentionality is not immediately at issue even though it is at work in meditative disciplines that would effect a "mediated return to immediacy" and is operating unrestrictedly as a response to divine presence as subject. Thus, ordinarily, divine presence as subject is not objectified; rather, Lonergan variously describes it as an "undertow of consciousness," a "fateful call to dreaded holiness," a "consolation without a cause," a "cloud of unknowing." Again following Price, we can term this spiritual experience "mystical consciousness." The longing of the human spirit for ultimate intelligibility, being, and goodness is a love of the divine that can be satiated only in a union with the divine. Mystical consciousness is the experience of the fulfillment of that longing in an actual encounter with divine reality, and it carries with it a "clouded revelation" of the ultimate intelligibility, being, and goodness sought.[72] This "clouded revelation"—not to be confused with some inner look proposed by the confrontation theory of truth, or, more crudely,

70. On heuristic anticipations, see ibid., 11–12; on fulfillment of the thrust of self-transcendence, 109; on actualizing the capacity for self-transcendence, 105.

71. James Robertson Price III, "Lonergan and the Foundations of a Contemporary Mystical Theology," 182; Voegelin, *Published Essays, 1966–1985,* 183–87, 269–70, 281.

72. On "mediated return to immediacy," see *Method in Theology,* 77; on unobjectified spiritual presence, 106, 113, 266, 342; on mystical experience, see Price, "Lonergan and the Foundations," 184–90; on "clouded revelation," see *Method in Theology,* 116.

with some external look at bits of information—is, properly interpreted, with respect to its source, the fruit of intersubjective consciousness and, with respect to its content, heuristic insights that guide the *zetesis* with its inner light.

We must not destroy the intricacy of the complex of experiences that make up spiritual consciousness by creating a narrow temporal cause-and-effect relation. We cannot say, for example, that the path of spiritual development is simply that the orientation of our intentionality as search leads to meditative practices, which eventually achieve the goal of mystical experience. Lonergan makes clear that the latter experience is not principally our doing. Rather, it is more likely that the intense longing of our conscious intentionality is a countermovement to the moving experience, however inchoate, of divine presence as subject. Lonergan quotes Pascal: "Take Comfort, you would not be seeking me if you had not already found me." Because mystical consciousness is the experience of the very reality sought in the intentional orientation to transcendent mystery and because mystical consciousness is the experience of the divine as subject, Lonergan concludes that "on the primary and fundamental meaning of the name, God, God is not an object."[73] It is in this very precise but significant sense that Lonergan could agree with Voegelin's description of God as "nonobjective" reality.

Still, it is the very experience of the nonobjective reality of the divine subject that impels us to seek the divine as object and to know and love all that participates in being. We desire to know without restriction the unrestricted love that we have encountered.[74] The basic awareness of God is the experience of openness as a gift. This is the openness that calls us to inquiry, sustains us in our inquiry, and heals us of the wounds from counterpulls that would force us in the direction of living in untruth off the path of inquiry.[75]

We are now in a position to see the centrality of divine presence in Lonergan's philosophy. To elucidate this, we can now legitimately translate Lonergan's analysis into Voegelin's terminology. What we have called divine presence as subject and Lonergan has characterized as the "transcendent mystery of awe and love" is surely what Voegelin symbolizes by the "Beyond," referring to the movement of the divine in the soul. We can also associate Lonergan's "openness as a gift" with Voegelin's divine draw, taken from Plato's allegory of the cave, where the prisoner is drawn (*helkein*) to turn around to make the rough ascent, and from the Gospels, where the divine son draws (*helkein*)

73. *Method in Theology,* 340–42. For divine as object, see *Second Collection,* 130–31.
74. *Method in Theology,* 116, 278, 283, 340–41.
75. Ibid., 105–6, 109; *Collection,* chap. 12; *Third Collection,* 106; *Insight,* chap. 20; *Grace and Freedom.*

men to himself by the prior draw of the Father.[76] Openness as a gift, as we
have seen, is the call to inquiry as well as that which can sustain and heal on
the road of inquiry. The cooperating unrestrictive love that animates the cognitive and moral operations of intentionality, it would seem, both longs for
the divine Beyond that called it and searches for the divine Beginning that is
the ground of the intelligibility of worldly being and existence.

The centrality of divine presence for human existence, Lonergan makes
clear in his post-*Insight* writings, is such that it must be considered at the core
of human nature. Following Voegelin's lead, Lonergan would have us conceive
of nature not abstractly in terms of a conceptualist or essentialist approach but
as operating concretely along the lines of Aristotle's interpretation. Citing Aristotle's definition of nature as an "immanent principle of movement and rest,"
Lonergan views the process of raising a question and getting an answer as fit-
ting the definition.[77] But there are questions for intelligence, for reflection,
and for deliberation. Thus, Lonergan asks, are there three principles of human nature? There is, in fact, he answers, a deeper and more comprehensive
principle, itself a nature, of which the transcendental intentions are but aspects: "a tidal movement that begins before consciousness, unfolds through
sensitivity, intelligence, rational reflection, responsible deliberation, only to
find its rest beyond all of these." The point beyond is precisely unrestricted
being-in-love, "a principle of movement at once purgative and illuminative,
and a principle of rest in which union is fulfilled."[78] If this point, which has
all the attributes of divine presence as subject and divine presence as object,
is, as Lonergan argues, a nature, then it would appear that Lonergan's moving
viewpoint has led him to break with faculty psychology not only with respect
to its distinction of intellect and will but also—and this would mirror
Voegelin's frequent contention—with respect to its distinction of natural and
supernatural.[79] Although the exact implications of Lonergan's position here
are perhaps a bit murky, he seems to be as much Augustinian as Thomist. This

---

76. On the "beyond," see *Method in Theology,* 106, 113–14; and Voegelin, *What Is History?* 173–74. On the *helkein,* see *Third Collection,* 188–92; Voegelin, *Published Essays,
1966–1985,* 182, 184, 202; Plato, *Republic* 515E; John 6:45, 12:32.

77. *Third Collection,* 172, with reference to Voegelin n. 5; Aristotle, *Physics* 2.1.195b21–
22.

78. *Third Collection,* 174–75.

79. Lonergan refers to Voegelin's contention at ibid., 219. Lonergan charts the origin of
the medieval theological distinction of natural and supernatural in *Grace and Freedom.* In
Method in Theology, 310–11, he expresses his "reservation" that the treatment of issues employed the framework of Aristotle, which has now been superseded and its defects brought
to light.

much is evident: we cannot, for Lonergan, talk of human nature concretely unless we also talk of the divine-human encounter at its core.

There is one final area of convergence between Lonergan and Voegelin worth noting, and that is the spiritual dimension of philosophy, which Voegelin stresses in his study of classical philosophy, an approach praised by Lonergan.[80] What concerns us here are the implications of Lonergan's developing position for the religious and mystical nature of philosophy. If philosophy is truly the love of wisdom and if the love of wisdom is unrestricted, then is not philosophy itself a state of unrestricted being-in-love? Would there not be born from this love a philosophical faith with its heuristic insights guiding the direction of the quest for truth with luminosity? Would not the most appropriate expression of this faith be in symbols, saving tales, and biographical anamnetic reflections (as carried out, for example, by Voegelin and proposed by William Matthews, who has been influenced by Lonergan's focus on interiority)?[81] Would not the philosopher experience the *zetesis* as a response to openness as a gift? And, finally, would not the absolutely distinct quality of philosophy as a variety of spiritual consciousness be the experience of the divine as intrinsically—unrestrictedly—intelligible?[82]

If, to summarize our argument thus far, *Insight* showed significant lines of affinity between Lonergan and Voegelin, then the expansion of cognitional theory brings Lonergan's intentionality analysis and its larger framework of existential analysis to the point of equivalence of meaning with Voegelin's history of symbols. A friendly interpreter of Voegelin perhaps might suggest that if the most interesting developments in Lonergan take him beyond cognitional theory, then it might be well and good simply to drop, or at least to downplay, the cognitional theory along with the expanded intentionality analysis. However, this would be for Lonergan to become Voegelin. What makes the equivalence of Voegelin and Lonergan so important and exciting is that the equivalence comes out of different frameworks, where Lonergan is not Voegelin and Voegelin is not Lonergan, thus offering the prospects for fruitful dialogue and creative exchange. Lonergan's perceptive and tantalizing explication of intentionality beyond cognition and of existential mood beyond intentionality is still rooted in his cognitional theory: it is defined in relation to, by the effect upon, and in terms of the goal of cognitional structure; it is interpreted in light

---

80. *Third Collection*, 190–91, 219.

81. Voegelin, *Anamnesis*, chap. 3; Matthews, "On Journalling Self-Appropriation" and "Personal Histories."

82. For working out these implications, see Chapter 7 above, 150–54.

of the epistemological and metaphysical position derived from cognitional theory. The base remains cognitional theory even as it is the base for higher viewpoints.

Historical Existence

Since Voegelin wrote as a philosopher of history and historian of symbols, it is vital to the topic of this chapter to provide a synthetic view of how Lonergan's position, adumbrated above, takes into account historical existence. Such a synthetic view will reveal striking parallels—in spite of the sharp differences of emphasis—with Voegelin's crucial ideas on the self-interpretation, or hermeneutical, nature of society, the "integral nature" of human being as participating in complex reality, the in-between status of history, the identity of the Question in the drama of history, and the historical movements of differentiation.

In Voegelin's first book, *On the Form of the American Mind,* he sought to interpret his subject matter free of the a priori forms of culture posited by neo-Kantian methodologies. To do so he had to consider American cultural activities in terms of the concrete form of the American mind, or what Lonergan would call the concrete horizon of American culture, the set of meanings and values that inform American life.[83] The concrete horizon is embodied in a concrete society with a concrete history. Similarly, for Lonergan, culture is situated in a network of political institutions, economic patterns, and technological achievements all part of a historical tradition of beliefs.[84] Voegelin later articulated the "within" character of the horizon: "Human society is not merely a fact, or an event, in the external world to be studied by an observer like a natural phenomenon. Though it has externality as one of its important components, it is as a whole a little world, a cosmion, illuminated with meaning within by the human beings who continuously bear and create it as the mode and condition of their self-realization." In fact, the "meaning within" is the "self-illumination" of society, that is, its understanding of itself as a participant in the whole that transcends it.[85] Although Voegelin eschews the "hermeneutical profundities" stemming from the German philosophical scene in the

83. Voegelin, *Form of the American Mind,* 5; *Method in Theology,* xi.
84. Voegelin, *Form of the American Mind,* 6; *Insight,* 232–34, 725–39.
85. Voegelin, *New Science of Politics,* 27–28; *Modernity without Restraint,* 109–10.

Weimar Republic, he has his own distinct hermeneutic.[86] A cardinal principle of his historical inquiry, then, is that it must take as a fundamental datum
the self-interpretation of society.

Lonergan echoes this approach in his analysis of horizons, both individual
and collective. Each horizon is formed, with varying degrees of fidelity, by inquiry into being and inquiry into the good. Inquiry is a project springing from
the very imperatives of human nature, the concrete principles of movement
and rest. The concrete principles are embedded in the concrete historical circumstances that give rise to the concrete challenges that spark the concrete
responses of concrete inquiry. Thus, Lonergan is attracted to Toynbee's conception of the dynamics of history as the dynamics of challenge and response.[87] Through the intention of being we inquire about the reality in which
we participate and about our being. Through the intention of the good we
inquire about the right path to participation in our unique historical circumstances. Every question about every particular good is also a question
about who concretely we are to be, individually or collectively. Every performance—whether in thought or action, word or deed—becomes, according to Lonergan's cognitional theory, data for interpretation (understanding
and judging), and interpretation can inform performance, which provides, in
turn, evidence for further interpretation in an ongoing dialectic of performance and interpretation. Now interpretation is a "within" in a double sense:
it arises from "within" as an exigency of questioning unrest, and it is the self-
interpretation of a person or a society. Performance, too, has its "within" since
its source—inquiry—is the same as that of interpretation, which, in turn, reflects on it. Still, performance and interpretation both can be externalized, and
must be externalized, given the conditions of embodied human existence, in
technological products, social institutions, and cultural sedimentations. These
externalizations express self-interpretation and enter into the dialectic of performance and interpretation. Lonergan's cognitional theory, then, identifies in
a sophisticated manner the dynamics, normative principles, and structured
operations of the "self-illumination" of historical horizons, all the while explicitly free from the incubus of treating them primarily as objects in the external world.

A second area of emphasis for Voegelin is that a proper study of human affairs must avoid any monocausal interpretation of history. Voegelin hails Aristotle's study *peri ta anthropina* as a tour de force that grasps the complex "integral" reality of human being, involving personal ("rational animal"), social

86. Voegelin, *Anamnesis*, 7.
87. *Insight*, 234; *Third Collection*, 10, 103–4, 214.

("political animal"), and, by implication, historical dimensions that all partic-ipate in a "synthetic nature," stretching along the chain of being from the apeironic depths, through inorganic nature, vegetable nature, animal nature, the passionate psyche, the noetic psyche, to the divine Nous.[88]

Lonergan's philosophy of history, profoundly influenced by the Aristotelian tradition, not surprisingly offers a direct parallel. Lonergan would neither re-duce the horizon of the person as inquirer to a function of technological, so-cial, or cultural forces impinging from the external world, thereby overlook-ing the self-transcending nature of humans as inquirers (as rational animals), nor reduce the horizon of society, in a nominalist fashion, to the individuals who are parts of society, thereby overlooking the inherently communal di-mension of human living and the perduring of social patterns and cultural forms through historical traditions (as political animals). Lonergan recog-nizes, in his theory of "perspectivism," the finitude of human knowledge and the historical conditionedness of the ongoing dialectic of performance and in-terpretation illuminating human society from within.[89]

Lonergan, though, has worked out an impressive and comprehensive "worldview of emergent probability" to rival, and, in Lonergan's view, super-sede Aristotle's earlier theory of "synthetic nature" formulated within the framework of a now antiquated cosmology. Lonergan's key category is "levels of integration." By this he means that there are lower and higher levels in an ascending order, in which the lower levels exert what Voegelin calls "condi-tioning causality" on the higher levels and the higher integrations unify schemes of recurrence that are merely coincidental on the lower manifolds. The ascending order goes from prime potency, which Lonergan links to basic energy, to subatomic elements, to chemical compounds, to biological organ-isms, to organisms with animal sensitivity, to animals with human cognition and moral operations, to the experience of divine presence. Lonergan does not postulate, as does Samuel Alexander, that divinity is emergent as the lat-est stage of evolution, but Lonergan does see the divine-human encounter as a higher integration from the Beyond that, in contrast to any gnostic dreams of salvation from the cosmos, honors, that is, is conditioned by, the probabil-ity schedules of emergent world process.[90]

---

88. Voegelin, *Published Essays, 1966–1985,* 267–68, 289–90.
89. *Method in Theology,* 214–20.
90. On emergent probability and Aristotle, see *Insight,* 138–52. On levels of integra-tion, 476–84; on "conditioning causality," see Voegelin, *Published Essays, 1966–1985,* 290. On spiritual life as a higher integration, see *Insight,* 270–71; on Alexander, see R. G. Collingwood, *The Idea of Nature,* 155–65.

Unlike the static Aristotelian universe of eternal recurrence, Lonergan's universe of emergent probability has, as its hallmark, the tension of development. A higher integration is indeed a precarious achievement, a balancing act, a tension, between the lower manifold whose laws of operation must be respected and the higher level, which, to emerge, must necessarily go beyond. It is not surprising that such a universe is a universe of trial and error, success and failure, breakthrough and dead end. It is not an aseptic world of "chrome and plastic." It is a universe, quite succinctly, that exhibits throughout the whole field of development the tension of limitation and transcendence. This tension is only heightened in human development, for human development is not bipolar but tripolar.[91]

On the one hand, intelligence is a higher integration that transcends the rhythms of the sensitive psyche but must not destroy the psychic base and its neural demand functions. Lonergan defines "genuineness" as precisely bringing "unconscious" and conscious components of development into harmony. This can mean a Freudian-type archaeology of the psyche to recover repressed contents of neural demands seemingly at odds with the higher levels, and, equally, it can mean, in Paul Ricoeur's words, a teleology of the psyche to conscript the psychic energy with its "anticipations and virtualities" of higher activities. This teleology of the psyche appears to be what Voegelin is depicting in his commentary on Plato's *Timaeus,* where Voegelin speaks of mythic content arising from the psychic depths with "assuaging expression."[92]

On the other hand, human intelligence—both theoretical and practical, in all of its operations of understanding, judging, and deliberating—is a limit to be surpassed in the mysterious divine-human encounter and, at the same time, an achievement to be preserved in the enriching and transformative context of religious conversion. The experience of the divine is simultaneously both the experience of what is utterly beyond human intelligence as the fullness of being and goodness and the experience of what is intrinsically related to human intelligence both as the "object" of the desire to know and the intention of the good and as that which calls, sustains, and heals human inquiry. Openness as a gift comes from what is beyond the merely human exercise of

---

91. On world process as trial and error, see *Insight,* 474; on the tension of limitation and transcendence, 476–79, 497; on human development as tripolar, 749.

92. On genuineness, see ibid., 499–503; *Method in Theology,* 33–34. On the teleology of the psyche, see *Insight,* 482; and Ricoeur, *Freud and Philosophy.* For Lonergan's references to Ricoeur, see *Method in Theology,* 68; and *Third Collection,* 65, 72, 157. Voegelin, *Order and History,* 3:186.

intelligence, reason, and responsibility, yet the state of being unrestrictedly in love is, as we have seen, at the core of human nature, as the veritable principle of movement and rest sweeping through all the conscious and intentional operations of human questioning. There can be a real history of religion because the integration of spirituality occurs in a world of emergent probability at the intersection of time and eternity. But this is not the same as an "evolution of religion" conceived according to some speculative progressivist spiritual categories. Lonergan does not, for example, postulate an early stage where human intelligence performs without any experience of divine presence or a later stage where spiritual integration eliminates the need for genuineness to negotiate the psychic depths. On the stage of human history, the tripolar tension is a permanent feature.

This tripolar tension of existence points to a third feature of the philosophy of history: its status as an in-between. Indeed, Voegelin's word for what Lonergan calls the "tension of limitation and transcendence" is our now familiar term, the *in-between*. Thus, for Voegelin, echoing Plato's description of Eros in the *Symposium*, human existence is between the human and the divine, time and eternity, ignorance and knowledge.[93] The in-between cannot be known save from participating in it. It is not an external object to be known in the mode of intentionality, as Voegelin conceives of intentionality. Rather, it is to be known in the mode of participating luminosity and, in light of that, through the reflective distance of the philosopher's inquiry.[94] The equivalent of luminosity, for Lonergan, is the complex of consciousness and intentional operations, cognitive and moral; of the underpinning directional tendency of these operations ("intentionality" in Lonergan's sense); of the engulfing unrestricted state of being-in-love; and of the concomitant interpretations of the operations, orientation, and experience of divine presence in an emerging historical process with its differentiating insights.[95] The advantage of Voegelin's approach is that he can emphasize in his term *luminosity* the participatory nature of the whole process. The advantage of Lonergan's approach is that he can encompass the whole range of elements and relations that constitutes the same participatory process without succumbing to the confrontation theory of truth that would make the process a reified something to look at. Lonergan's expanded cognitional theory and linked existential analysis can, in its

93. See n. 5 above.
94. Voegelin, *Order and History*, 5:40–47.
95. See also Frederick Lawrence, "On 'The Meditative Origin of the Philosophical Knowledge of Order,'" 61–65.

detailed explication, bring home with clarity and precision that in-between reality is not some strange, rarely traversed region of the globe but rather the reality of faithfully pursuing the familiar process of inquiry with its inherent norms. At least one aspect of the participatory nature of the process can be formulated quite simply in Lonergan's cognitional theory in terms of the dialectic of performance and interpretation. One's conscious performance is data for understanding and judging the process. Unless one performs, there are no data. If there are no data, there can be no meaningful interpretation. If there are data, there is ordinarily some kind of interpretation whose expression of meaning can range from compactness to differentiation.

Because, in Lonergan's philosophy, unrestricted love is at the core of human nature, human history is between divine transcendence and merely world-immanent process. Because human inquiry with its locus at particular times and places is oriented to what is not only beyond particular times and places but also beyond time and place as such and is a human response to divine, otherworldly presence, it is between the timeless and time. And because human inquiry is the constant in history and inquiry by its very nature is a tension of anticipation and not knowing, human history is between knowledge and ignorance. The ever expanding horizon of inquiry and achievement of knowledge is situated between heuristic insights that give inquiry its direction and the mystery that is sought by the directional tendency of inquiry.

Although both Voegelin and Lonergan focus on the process of inquiry, they escape the dangers of historical relativism by the same focus, and here is a fourth area of equivalence in their respective philosophies of history. Voegelin sees the constant among the myriad expressions of meaning as the Question.[96] This is the structure of openness, which is in search of the Heraclitean "common world."[97] Exclusive concentration on answers will miss the unity of historical expressions of meaning and hence nourish relativism. It can also support dogmatism in its pejorative sense. The meaning of an answer is the meaning of the question from which it arose. Without a question there is no genuine meaning to the answer. For answers are to questions. Moreover, the question is itself a reality in the participatory process of being. Awareness of the question as the fundamental structure of existence is the truth of existence.[98] The structure of existence, which is the structure of the question, is

96. Voegelin, *Order and History,* 4:326.
97. See n. 29 above.
98. On dogmatism, see Voegelin, *Published Essays, 1966–1985,* 175; on the question as participatory in being, ibid.; on the truth of existence, 49.

the state of questioning unrest in response to the divine mover. Herein, then, reside norms.

For Lonergan, too, the process of inquiry is a normative structure. By Lonergan's extensive treatment of epistemology, he can give a detailed explication of cognitive, moral, and spiritual norms. These are the norms of open existence associated with fidelity to the process of inquiry, captured in Lonergan's "transcendental precepts": be attentive, intelligent, reasonable, responsible, and loving. The precepts are transcendental because they are ingredient in the transcultural structure of the basic horizon of inquiry. They are manifest in all concrete relative horizons of inquiry—in all fields of inquiry, in all patterns of experience, at all times and places—insofar as these relative horizons are not blinded by bias and inauthenticity. There is, however, a necessary tension between basic horizon and relative horizons, exhibiting the in-between status of human existence. Basic horizon cannot exist apart from relative horizons. For Lonergan, there is no more a pure transcendental horizon than there is a pure transcendental ego. Relative horizons, on the other hand, cannot exist without at least a modicum of participation in basic horizon. A relative horizon, whether individual or social, not so participating, that is, a completely private world cut off completely from the *koine cosmos,* would soon collapse, if it could ever be born, through self-destruction. Basic horizon, the source of unity amid different historical horizons, is also the source of diversity, for the pure desire to know, the intention of the good, and unrestricted love impel every concrete historical horizon to go beyond itself. Lonergan defines a horizon in terms of the range of meaningful, significant, and relevant questions. The unrestricted normative scope of the basic horizon of inquiry always raises further questions that would necessarily challenge any concrete horizon to expand with wonder, anxiety, and awe. Insofar as there is a common origin and goal of the search for meaning, there is a "universal viewpoint" of hermeneutics that can link divergent historical contexts, assess major horizon shifts in human history, and criticize concrete horizons in light of the norms of basic horizon.[99]

We turn here to a fifth topic in the philosophy of history: the movement from compactness to differentiation. We surely cannot overlook the fact that Voegelin addresses this theme almost as a leitmotiv in his history of symbols, whereas

---

99. On the transcendental precepts, see *Method in Theology,* 20; and *Third Collection,* 10. On the concept of horizon, see *Method in Theology,* 235–36; and "Subject and Horizon," in *Notes on Existentialism,* 7. On the "universal viewpoint," see *Insight,* 587–91; and *Method in Theology,* 53 n. 1, chap. 10.

Lonergan discusses the idea in a much more brief and abstract manner. Never-theless, we must observe that there are profound parallels in the way the two thinkers approach the basic principles, identify the differentiation of philoso-phy and revelation, and consider the permanence and integrity of myth.

Voegelin holds that the basic experience of living in truth remains constant, but the symbols engendered by the experience can range from compactness to differentiation. The more differentiated symbols arise later in the history of or-der, specifically, the symbols of Hellenic philosophy, which articulate the noet-ic consciousness of the search for the divine ground of being in response to the divine pull, and the symbols of Israel and Christianity, which express the pneu-matic consciousness of a moving divine presence from beyond the cosmos. The symbols of philosophy and revelation do not replace the structure of ques-tioning but elucidate it. The elucidation creates a tension with myth. It replaces not myth as such but earlier "cosmological" myths, which portray human be-ings, society, nature, and the divine as participants within the overriding cos-mic order. By contrast to the cosmological myth, the noetic consciousness of philosophy and the pneumatic consciousness of revelation differentiate the realm of transcendence: either the Beginning (the philosopher's ground of be-ing, the Book of Genesis's creator) or the Beyond (the philosopher's *helkein*, the biblical inner word of the spirit). Still, to differentiate the realm of transcen-dence is not to abolish the in-between of the human condition. It is, rather, to heighten the sense of transcendent mystery. Thus, Voegelin breaks from any tendency to view either philosophy or revelation as superseding myth let alone any tendency to view science as superseding the differentiating movements of philosophy and revelation. Bluntly stated:

> Myth is not a primitive symbolic form, peculiar to early societies and pro-gressively to be overcome by positive science, but the language in which the experience of human-divine participation in the In-Between becomes artic-ulate. The symbolization of participating existence, it is true, evolves his-torically from the more compact form of the cosmological myth to the more differentiated form of philosophy, prophecy, and the gospel, but the differ-entiating insight, far from abolishing the *metaxy* of existence, brings it to ful-ly articulate knowledge.[100]

100. On the movement from compactness to differentiation, see Voegelin, *Order and History*, 1:5, 60. On differentiations of consciousness, vols. 2, 4. On cosmological myth, 1: intro., pt. 1. On the realm of transcendence, 5: chap. 1; and Voegelin, *What Is History?* chap. 5. On the enduring relevance of myth, see Voegelin, *Published Essays, 1966–1985*, 188.

Lonergan also posits a constant experience, the experience of basic horizon as it concretely exhibits its basic existential state of unrestricted love, its basic existential disposition of the intention of being and the intention of the good, and its basic operations that are the unfolding of the basic intentions. Basic horizon, however, as experience, is always an interpreted experience in the aforementioned dialectic of performance and interpretation. The interpretations can range from elemental meanings, which require participatory experiences to be understood (examples of which include intersubjective meaning, symbolic meaning [in Lonergan's narrow sense of "images tinged with affects"], artistic meaning, and incarnate meaning [great words and deeds that embody what they mean]); to commonsense, ordinary language, expressions; to theoretical formulations. The history of expression of meaning is the history of a developmental tendency from the generic to the differentiated.[101]

The early, compact stages of the history of consciousness would be characterized by lack of differentiation in three areas: patterns of experience, expressions of meaning, and realms of meaning. The cosmological societies, for example, that Voegelin discusses would, for Lonergan, have not achieved differentiation of the intellectual pattern of experience, that is, explicit recognition of the exigencies and norms of theoretical inquiry and the institutional matrix to sustain it; they would communicate ideas in a combination of elemental meanings and commonsense expressions; and they would articulate clearly neither the realm of being defined by explanatory relations nor the realm of transcendence.[102] What Lonergan calls differentiations of consciousness are epochal horizon shifts associated with strategic differentiations of patterns of experience, which, in turn, affect the expression of meaning, the orientation to what is to be known, and, perhaps most important, the interpretation of basic horizon itself. Lonergan, in fact, sees two such epochal shifts, or, to adopt Jaspers's term, "axial periods," in the history of consciousness. In the first such horizon shift, a distinct "cultural superstructure" emerges to reflect upon and criticize through the intellectual pattern of experience the spontaneous apprehension and communication of meaning. The dynamic model of this intellectual culture is the Socratic enterprise of "con-

101. On elemental meaning, see *Method in Theology*, 57–69, 73. On commonsense meaning, see ibid., 71–72; and *Insight*, 196–204. On theoretic meaning, see *Insight*, 209–10; and *Method in Theology*, 72, 81–83. From generic to differentiated meaning, see *Insight*, 589–90.

102. *Method in Theology*, 86–90; see McPartland, "Meaning, Mystery, and History," 215–25.

trolling meaning" by asking the Athenians to define their moral terms. The cultural superstructure can approach reality through metaphysical and scientific accounts. The second epochal transformation, which has occurred recently, involves a shift to interiority and historicity. Here the radical focus of intellectual culture, at least for the creative minority operating within the new horizon, is not on theories, whether metaphysical or scientific, as its foundation but on the concrete consciousness that creates the theories.[103] If the first differentiation of consciousness could speak, with Socrates, of "knowing thyself," where the self, particularly in the Aristotelian tradition, would be subsumed under the category of a metaphysical object, the second differentiation of consciousness talks, as does Lonergan, of "self-appropriation," where each self, with his or her concrete existential project under concrete historical circumstances, is his or her own "unique edition."[104]

Now Lonergan's schema would seem to be vastly different from Voegelin's idea of noetic and pneumatic differentiations. Voegelin, like Lonergan, has two differentiations. Nonetheless, for the former, they are more or less synchronic since they are basically within the same time frame; for the latter, they are diachronic, with a gap of more than a millennium. Voegelin's noetic differentiation is a spiritual quest rather than just an effort at theoretical control of meaning. Nor is Voegelin's pneumatic differentiation the same as Lonergan's shift to interiority. Lonergan mentions the spiritual traditions of Israel and Christianity in the context of differentiation of consciousness principally when he discusses how theologians have utilized theory for reflection on the content of those traditions.[105] Moreover, Lonergan's emphasis on the project of theoretical control of meaning might suggest he is at odds with Voegelin's insistence on the permanence of myth.

---

103. On the emergence of the cultural superstructure, see *Method in Theology*, 90–93, 302–12; *Second Collection*, 91–92; and McPartland, "Meaning, Mystery, and History," 226–37. On Socratic control of meaning, see *Collection*, 235–38. On the shift to interiority, see *Method in Theology*, 83–85, 93–99, 314–18; *Collection*, 238–45; *Second Collection*, 1–9; *Third Collection*, 63–65, 137–40, 170–71; and McPartland, "Meaning, Mystery, and History," 237–47. In *Collection*, 237–38, Lonergan refers to Jaspers's idea of an "axial period" of history, covering the time of the great philosophers and prophets of Hellas, Israel, Iran, India, and China in antiquity. Lonergan applies the idea of an axial period to the shift to interiority (*Second Collection*, 226–27). Voegelin, on the other hand, expresses reservations about the category of axis-time and speaks of the danger of treating the epoch as an object in the external world (*Order and History*, 2:19–23, 3:312).

104. *Second Collection*, 69–86.

105. See, for example, *Way to Nicea*.

Still, as argued above, the differences are ones of emphasis, not of principle, an emphasis caused, in part, by Voegelin actually writing a history of symbols and Lonergan writing on methodology. We must also recall that Lonergan gives a much more restricted and technical meaning to *consciousness* than does Voegelin. Hence, we must look to a larger context of discussion in Lonergan's work if we wish to find an equivalent to Voegelin's differentiations of consciousness. Here, once again, we must consider Lonergan's moving viewpoint, one at certain junctures materially influenced by Voegelin himself. What is common to both Voegelin's noetic differentiation and his pneumatic differentiation is the articulate awareness of transcendence. This awareness impels the philosopher's *zetesis,* or quest, and locates the *pneuma* as the prophet's or saint's center of order and sensorium of divinity. Lonergan, too, recognizes the historical import of the differentiation of transcendence. The intellectual pattern of experience is driven by the desire to know, which can rest only in a complete intelligibility beyond the world. Any genuine metaphysics must affirm transcendence.[106] As we have seen above, Lonergan's expanded cognitional theory and existential analysis can fully regard philosophy as a variety of spiritual experience, and indeed Lonergan has explicitly agreed with Voegelin's depiction of philosophy as a theophanic event. Furthermore, Lonergan recognizes Israelite and Christian revelatory experiences precisely as differentiations of transcendence and commends Voegelin's analysis of pneumatic consciousness, which Lonergan explicates, in the Christian case, with his own categories of "inner word" and "outer word."[107] As far as Lonergan's shift to interiority is concerned, Voegelin has not labeled any such historical phenomenon a differentiation of consciousness, nor should he if by "differentiation" he means primarily differentiation of transcendence. Nevertheless, Voegelin has been quite clear that the classical analysis of human existence must be supplemented by the category of historical existence.[108] In addition, Voegelin obviously does not base his philosophy upon an appeal to metaphysical principles or philosophical dogma; rather, he places a premium on the self's experience of living the truth of existence as a foundation of his theory of consciousness. Voegelin's and Lonergan's philosophies, then, are complementary philosophies of interiority, Voegelin's focusing more, with his reflective distance, on inquiry as process, Lonergan focusing more, with his

106. *Insight,* chap. 19.
107. On philosophy as a theophanic event, see *Third Collection,* 188–92, 220–21; on "inner word" and "outer word," 195.
108. Voegelin, *Published Essays, 1966–1985,* 268, 289–290.

expanded cognitional theory, on inquiry as a complex of state, orientation, and structure. Voegelin performatively recognizes the differentiation of interiority.

Finally, there is the issue of myth. Lonergan stresses that mystery cannot be eliminated from the horizon of inquiry, both as "object" of questioning and as divine presence calling to inquiry. Mythopoesis, as intimated above, would seem to be a genuine pattern of experience. It represents the field of mystery to human sensitivity for effective living and expresses an inchoate understanding of mystery that is part and parcel of human existence as in-between, for mystery itself, as defined by Lonergan, is the paradoxical in-between of the known unknown. Myth would be a story told and a drama enacted exploring the mystery of the known unknown through symbols and analogies. Myth would express the clues, hints, heuristic insights that ground inquiry itself. As such, myth is the ground of philosophical inquiry, providing heuristic images to guide the project of inquiry. Lonergan, echoing Voegelin, agrees with Aristotle that the lover of myth and the lover of wisdom are equivalent.[109] Myth in this sense cannot be merely a matter of communication (for that would reduce myth to allegory) but must also be a foundational concern.[110] When Lonergan discusses his functional specialty of foundations, he operationally defines it in terms of three conversions: intellectual, moral, and religious. In a manner that is reminiscent of Plato's treatment of characters and regimes in books 8 and 9 of the *Republic,* Lonergan sees the foundation of philosophy and intellectual culture in the kind of person one is. The conversions are manifestations of the openness of existence, the foundational criterion. In his later writings, Lonergan reacts positively to Robert Doran's suggestion to add a fourth conversion, psychic conversion, which would negotiate the psychic depths to get in touch with the teleological thrust of psychic energy, or what Bergson called the *élan vital,* or what Lonergan himself in *Insight* called the psychic "virtualities and anticipations" of higher living.[111] In a similar vein, one interpreter of Lonergan, William Matthews, has urged the project of "journaling" one's life history in a narrative sensitive to the development of

---

109. On the permanence of mystery, see *Insight,* 569–72; *Method in Theology,* 116, 278, 283, 340–41; and *Collection,* chap. 12. On the known-unknown, see *Insight,* 569–70. On myth as heuristic insight, see "Reality, Myth, Symbol," 33–34. On myth as the ground of philosophy, see *Collection,* 241–42; *Insight,* 43, 556–57; and Chapter 7 above, 169–70. On Aristotle and myth, see "Reality, Myth, Symbol," 33; Voegelin, *Published Essays, 1966–1985,* 269; and Aristotle, *Metaphysics* 282b18ff.

110. See Chapter 7 above, 168–73.

111. "Reality, Myth, Symbol," 34, 37; *Insight,* 482.

one's imagination and affectivity, a project resembling Voegelin's own effort of anamnetic reflections on childhood images.[112] Such foundational explorations of the psyche can provide a basis for critique of myths, discriminating between genuine myths that express openness to mystery and deformed myths that reveal closed existence and psychic aberration.[113] Myths also reflect historicity. There is the inner word of mythopoesis and the outer word of historical tradition (that presents the store of mythic material) and historical situation. Lonergan's own theory of differentiation of consciousness would seem, in principle, to distinguish among myths prior to the differentiation of theory, myths after the differentiation of theory but prior to the differentiation of interiority, and myths after the differentiation of interiority. In any case, myth, for Lonergan, is a permanent feature of authentic existence.

We are not claiming here that Lonergan has developed a systematic treatment of myth or given a rich historical portrait of myth. What we are claiming here is that Lonergan has statements about myth that have a striking parallel with Voegelin's ideas and are fully in accord with, and a true development of, Lonergan's position. And this has been the thesis of this chapter all along.

Lonergan-Voegelin Dialogue

Philosophy is an ongoing venture of *anamnesis* lit by the radiance of the spirit.[114] It is ongoing, both Lonergan and Voegelin would agree, because it is the process of inquiring about the process of inquiry, a process that manifests the dialectic of basic horizon and relative horizons. It is an anamnetic venture because, again as both Lonergan and Voegelin recognize, the event of philosophy first emerged in Hellas within, to use Voegelin's language, the in-between reality of human-divine participation at the border of time and the timeless. Lonergan's position would be that the development of philosophy is both from above downward, the assimilation of a living historical tradition, and from below upward, the personal insight of the philosopher—in other words, a creative tension of the outer word of philosophical tradition and the inner word of the philosopher's spirit of inquiry.[115] Voegelin would formulate the same creative tension of philosophical inquiry as recapturing the engendering ex-

112. See n. 81 above.
113. "Reality, Myth, Symbol," 33; *Insight*, 499–503, 557.
114. See Chapter 7 above, 159–62.
115. *Method in Theology*, 112, 119; *Third Collection*, 196–97.

periences of historically effective symbols in the meaningful concreteness of the present circumstances by the concrete consciousness of a concrete inquirer. So Voegelin himself recovered the engendering experiences of philosophy in the Platonic symbols, refuting the interpretation of Plato as an "idealist." So Lonergan saw Aquinas as precisely appropriating the genuine movement of Greek theory for the medieval Scholastic period, and Lonergan, in turn, recovered the genuine cognitional performance of Aquinas, refuting the interpretation of Aquinas as a "naive realist."[116]

And so now, as we seek from the meaningful concreteness of the turn of the twenty-first century to appropriate the event of philosophy as it erupted in Hellas and in medieval Scholasticism, we ourselves have the mediating efforts of Voegelin and Lonergan. For the works of Voegelin and Lonergan challenge us to enter into their engendering horizon of inquiry, spark us to engage in a similar fashion with the great texts of the philosophical tradition, and invite us to a personal act of self-appropriation.

In this chapter we have argued that Lonergan's cognitional theory and Voegelin's history of symbols exhibit an equivalence of meaning. But such equivalence is not identity. Therefore, the mediating efforts of Lonergan and Voegelin also challenge us to relate the two philosophies to each other in a critical dialogue, the value of which will be a rich clarification of issues both theoretical and historical.

In such a Lonergan-Voegelin encounter, Lonergan's stress on intellectual conversion (which bases the meaning of truth, objectivity, and reality on the directional tendency of questioning) would encourage a complete break from a Kantian framework, particularly with respect to Voegelin's restriction of "intentionality" to picture thinking, with a corresponding change in the conception of "object" and "objective reality."[117] Related to Lonergan's conception of intellectual conversion is his idea of a "cosmopolis," a dimension of consciousness that would foster a critical intellectual culture whose foundation of critique would be the norms ingredient in the process of inquiry.[118] Lonergan's explicit technical language regarding the state, orientation, and structure of inquiry provides a sophisticated basis for discriminating between progress and decline in history, between position and counterposition in philosophy—and, perhaps most important in a Lonergan-Voegelin dialogue—

116. Voegelin, *Order and History,* 3:82f, 274–76, 281–82; *Verbum,* esp. chap. 3.
117. See n. 40 above. For possible Kantian assumptions in Voegelin's thought, see G. Hughes, *Mystery and Myth,* 130–31.
118. Chapter 6 above; *Insight,* 263–67; *Collection,* 39, for an earlier formulation as the "great republic of culture."

between genuine myths and deformed myths. Voegelin, of course, distinguishes between expression of open existence, where "the movements of the unconscious are allowed to express themselves in myth in free recognition of their nature," and expressions of closed existence; he also distinguishes between "primary symbols" of open existence and "secondary symbols" (or dogmas or doctrines) that get cut off from their engendering experience.[119] Yet, through Lonergan's detailed explication of the state, orientation, and structure of open existence—quite consonant, as we have seen, with Voegelin's concept of the in-between—Lonergan can add precision to the evaluation of myths that might help avoid any charges of "circularity" or "romanticism" in the selection of certain myths as normative.[120] Moreover, Lonergan's unique approach to intentionality and its dynamic relation both to the state of unrestricted love and to the structure of cognition offers the prospect of a critical differentiation between genuine philosophical myths, representing the known unknown, and philosophical objectifications (in Lonergan's sense of "object") of the process of inquiry. Voegelin's philosophical symbols may, then, embrace both philosophical myths and philosophical objectifications in Lonergan's precise meaning of the term. Such clarification might also overcome the mistaken impression that talk of the philosopher's "luminosity" or "vision," particularly as it is associated with language of the "spontaneous generation of symbols out of experience," is just another example of the confrontation theory of truth.[121] Voegelin, for example, speaks of insights into participatory existence as expressed in "images," which, if adequate, must properly be considered "linguistic indices" rather than propositions since the mind is not a "mere automatism that infallibly produces pictures of reality." By contrast, according to Voegelin, concepts may indeed be based upon exegesis of noetic consciousness, but they inevitably refer to phenomena beyond that area, namely, to things in the spatio-temporal world. All discourse about "objects" necessarily reflects the condition of the human inquirer as an embodied knower. Hence arises the danger of dogmatism, where exegesis of participation in being is replaced by propositions about things.[122] Although Voegelin

---

119. Voegelin, *Order and History,* 3:187; *Published Essays, 1966–1985,* 16, 21, 36–37. Eugene Webb, in *Eric Voegelin: Philosopher of History,* 181, 183–84, 193–94, 259, 288, uses the terms *primary symbols* and *secondary symbols.*

120. For such analysis of Voegelin's hermeneutics of myth, see Webb, *Philosophers of Consciousness,* 120–29.

121. Ibid., 122–23.

122. On images as linguistic indices, see Voegelin, *Anamnesis,* 168–69, 176; on concepts and embodied knowing, 179; on dogmatism, 163.

obviously rejects the idea that there is a look at "nonobjective" reality, his language might suggest that the ground rules of the confrontation theory of truth could still be operative. Lonergan raises the challenge whether there can be propositional truth in philosophy about interiority that is qualitatively distinct from propositional truth about things in the external world. Lonergan, of course, would, in principle, exclude from the latter philosophical statements about "bodies" in the "already out there now real." The issue here is that Lonergan would not reject out of hand every version of the correspondence theory of truth but rather "woodenheaded" versions based on the confrontation theory of truth.[123]

Voegelin's resolute focus, on the other hand, on historical existence as participatory existence in divine reality, as mystery, and as process would spur the moving viewpoint Lonergan espoused to develop on a more comprehensive and detailed scale his position on moral and spiritual consciousness, fostering something like an *Insight 2*. Furthermore, Voegelin's uncompromising differentiation of interiority would insist that such a moving viewpoint make unmistakably clear the qualitative distinction between statements about interiority, if they are to be allowed legitimately in the framework of the Lonergan position, and statements about things.

Perhaps the project of dialogue discussed thus far has more of the earmarks of Lonergan's approach. Even to suggest that dialogue would lead to identification of differences, to criticisms, and to revisions or refinements on both sides with respect to theoretical formulations is to talk more in the mediating technical language of Lonergan's cognitional theory than in the language of meditative exegesis of Voegelin's history of symbols. On the other hand, we cannot ignore that the burden of this chapter has been, in fact, to show the correspondence of Lonergan's position with Voegelin's exegesis, thereby assuming from the outset, at least implicitly, the compelling nature of Voegelin's explication of existence! Nevertheless, we cannot overlook how dialogue would also promote in a substantive way the project of the history of symbols.

Lonergan's own work in the history of ideas, although impressive—his recovery of Aquinas's epistemology, in particular, is a stunning achievement of philosophical scholarship—is hardly comparable in scope to Voegelin's prodigious effort, greatly admired by Lonergan.[124] What Lonergan offers most to

123. *Second Collection,* 15–16.
124. Lonergan's historical works are *Way to Nicea, Gratia Operans,* and *Verbum.* He comments on Voegelin's enterprise of *Order and History* in *Third Collection,* 200–201 n. 45; "Philosophy of History," 65–66.

the enterprise is what he calls the "upper blade" of hermeneutics, that is, heuristic concepts that allow for interpretation of the history of consciousness.[125] These heuristic concepts are derived from his expanded cognitional theory, as outlined above: the structured operations of human cognition and volition; the basic intentionality underpinning those operations in the direction of open existence; the divine presence and human response at the core of the process of inquiry; the dynamic play of communal tradition and individual creativity; the norms of inquiry and their violation in closed existence; the unfolding of the process of inquiry in the various patterns of experience, their corresponding expressions of understanding, and corresponding realms of meaning; and the differentiations of these patterns of experience.

This "upper blade" of interpretation must cooperate with a "lower blade" of interpretation immersed in the details of historiography to provide a scissorslike action to cut through the data.[126] Voegelin, to be sure, has his own "upper blade," his theory of consciousness and of history. However, he articulates his theory most often in response to actual historical material. Lonergan holds that the relation between "upper blade" and "lower blade" is an ongoing and creative one. Categories of the "upper blade" can stimulate historical questions, insights into developments, and new and richer interpretations, while the historiography of the "lower blade" can revise and lend precision to the categories of the "upper blade." It is precisely this latter possibility that Voegelin's unprecedented work offers. Voegelin's penetrating account of noetic and pneumatic differentiations of consciousness can inspire and even demand, as we have suggested above, the further development of Lonergan's moving viewpoint on myth and divine presence.

At the same time, Lonergan's methodical hermeneutics articulates a "universal viewpoint," a basic horizon, that aims at ongoing collaboration among researchers, philologists, historians, and philosophers. This is the task formulated in *Insight* and elaborated in terms of the cooperation of functional specialties in *Method in Theology*.[127] It would urge the collaboration of many thinkers to continue the kind of historical investigation carried on heretofore by one man, Voegelin. Investigating the major horizon shifts in human history, it would emphasize the transition from cosmological myth to philosophy and noetic symbols, the differentiation of transcendence, and the recognition

---

125. *Insight,* 600–601; *Method in Theology,* 285–88; McPartland, "Meaning, Mystery, and History," 211–15.
126. *Insight,* 600.
127. Ibid., 724; *Method in Theology,* chap. 5.

of interiority and historicity. This is not to propose, of course, "upper blade" categories as dogmas. Lonergan's vision of functional cooperation includes the exigency to identify philosophical differences, to address them with foundational questions, and to address the foundational questions by appealing to foundational reality: the concrete consciousness of a concrete person concretely animated by the norms of inquiry. What counts for Lonergan, as for Voegelin, is the personal self-appropriation of the engendering experience of open existence.

Lonergan expresses this openness performatively by his ceaseless questioning, beyond any obscurantism, as he seeks insight into the foundations of epistemology, metaphysics, and indeed all philosophical, theological, and intellectual discourse and as he establishes a critique of historical reason adequate to the task of distinguishing between progress and decline. Voegelin expresses this openness performatively by his dramatic historical inquiry—evocative of the truth of existence, of moral and spiritual conversion, and of the passion of philosophical inquiry—as he encounters both noetic and pneumatic leaps in being and the derailment of noetic and pneumatic symbols both by dogmatic believers and by skeptical unbelievers who are lovers of closed existence.

The fundamental thesis, then, of this chapter has been that, obvious differences in background, temperament, style, emphasis, and philosophical vocabulary notwithstanding, Lonergan and Voegelin on the most substantive issues converge to the point of equivalence. They consider the same materials of authentic existence. Although operating from their different perspectives, Lonergan working out of a Thomist framework, Voegelin out of a Kantian framework, they issue the same injunction: (borrowing from Rilke) "to live the question."[128] The affinity of these two thinkers of rank overrides their differences. Prior to the task of identifying, exploring, and criticizing the differences is the task of recognizing the equivalence. To bring home that prior task has been the concern of this chapter. For, as Eliot puts it (in a passage quoted by Voegelin),

> . . . there is no competition—
> There is only the fight to recover what has been lost
> And found and lost again; and now, under conditions
> That seem unpropitious.[129]

---

128. Rainer Maria Rilke, *Rilke on Love and Other Difficulties: Translations and Considerations of Ranier Maria Rilke*, 25.

129. Voegelin, *Published Essays, 1966–1985*, 80, with quotation from T. S. Eliot, "East Coker," *Four Quartets*.

If, to turn again to our opening theme of the crisis at the turn of the twenty-first century, the conditions are now more propitious, it is, in part, because of the anamnetic ventures of Lonergan and Voegelin. And if this is the case, then it is the obligation of the philosopher of the twenty-first century to build upon their mediating efforts.

Bibliography

Works by Bernard J. F. Lonergan

"Analytic Concept of History." *Method: Journal of Lonergan Studies* 11 (1993): 5–35.

"Bernard Lonergan Responds." In *Foundations of Theology: Papers from the International Lonergan Conference, 1970,* ed. Philip McShane, 223–34. Notre Dame: University of Notre Dame Press, 1972.

Caring about Meaning: Patterns in the Life of Bernard Lonergan. Ed. Pierrot Lambert, Charlotte Tansey, and Cathleen Going. Thomas More Institute Papers 82. Montreal: Thomas More Institute, 1982.

Collection. Vol. 4 of *Collected Works of Bernard Lonergan,* ed. Frederick E. Crowe. Toronto: University of Toronto Press, 1988.

Grace and Freedom: Operative Grace in the Thought of St. Thomas Aquinas. Ed. J. Patout Burns. New York: Herder and Herder, 1971.

Insight: A Study of Human Understanding. Vol. 3 of *Collected Works of Bernard Lonergan,* ed. Frederick E. Crowe and Robert M. Doran. 5th ed. Toronto: University of Toronto Press, 1992.

Method in Theology. New York: Herder and Herder, 1972.

Notes on Existentialism. Author's notes for lectures given at Boston College, summer 1957. Reprinted by Thomas More Institute, Montreal.

"Philosophy and the Religious Phenomenon." *Method: Journal of Lonergan Studies* 12:2 (1994): 121–46.

"Philosophy of History." In *Philosophical and Theological Papers, 1958–1964.* Vol. 6 of *Collected Works of Bernard Lonergan,* ed. Robert C. Croken, Frederick E. Crowe, and Robert M. Doran, chap. 3. Toronto: University of Toronto Press, 1996.

"Questionnaire on Philosophy." *Method: Journal of Lonergan Studies* 2 (1984): 8.

"Reality, Myth, Symbol." In *Myth, Symbol, and Reality,* ed. Alan M. Olson, 31–37. Notre Dame: University of Notre Dame Press, 1980.

A Second Collection. Ed. William F. J. Ryan and Bernard J. Tyrell. Philadelphia: Westminster Press, 1974.

A Third Collection: Papers by Bernard J. F. Lonergan. Ed. Frederick E. Crowe. New York: Paulist Press, 1985.

Topics in Education: The Cincinnati Lectures of 1959 on the Philosophy of Education. Vol. 10 of *Collected Works of Bernard Lonergan,* ed. Robert M. Doran and Frederick E. Crowe. Toronto: University of Toronto Press, 1993.

Understanding and Being: The Halifax Lectures on Insight. Vol. 5 of *Collected Works of Bernard Lonergan,* ed. Elizabeth A. Morelli, Mark D. Morelli, Frederick E. Crowe, and Robert M. Doran. 2nd ed. Toronto: University of Toronto Press, 1990.

Verbum: Word and Idea in Aquinas. Vol. 2 of *Collected Works of Bernard Lonergan,* ed. Frederick E. Crowe and Robert M. Doran. Toronto: University of Toronto Press, 1997.

The Way to Nicea: The Dialectical Development of Trinitarian Theology. Trans. Conn O'Donovan. Philadelphia: Westminster Press, 1976.

Other Sources

Antoni, Carlo. *From History to Sociology: The Transition in German Historical Thinking.* Trans. Hayden V. White. Detroit: Wayne State University Press, 1959.

———. *L'Historisme.* Trans. Alain Dufour. Geneva: Droz, 1963.

Appleby, Joyce, Lynn Hunt, and Margaret Jacob. *Telling the Truth about History.* New York: W. W. Norton, 1994.

Arendt, Hannah. *The Human Condition.* Garden City, N.Y.: Doubleday, Anchor Books, 1959.

Aristotle. *The Basic Works of Aristotle.* Ed. Richard McKeon. New York: Random House, 1941.

Aron, Raymond. "Relativism." In *The Philosophy of History in Our Time,* ed. Hans Meyerhoff, 153–61. Garden City, N.Y.: Doubleday, Anchor Books, 1959.

Augustine, Saint. *City of God.* Trans. Marcus Dods. New York: Modern Library, 1950.

Barth, Karl. *Protestant Thought: From Rousseau to Ritschl.* Trans. Brian Cozens. Rev. ed. New York: Simon and Schuster, 1959.

Baumer, Franklin L. *Modern European Thought: Continuity and Change in Ideas, 1600–1950.* New York: Macmillan, 1977.

Bellah, Robert, et al. *Habits of the Heart: Individualism and Commitment in American Life.* Berkeley and Los Angeles: University of California Press, 1958.

Bendix, Reinhard. *Max Weber: An Intellectual Portrait.* Garden City, N.Y.: Doubleday, Anchor Books, 1962.

Berger, Peter, and Thomas Luckmann. *The Social Construction of Reality: A Treatise in the Sociology of Knowledge.* Garden City, N.Y.: Doubleday, Anchor Books, 1967.

Bergson, Henri. *Time and Free Will: An Essay on the Immediate Data of Consciousness.* Trans. F. L. Pogson. New York: Harper and Row, 1960.

Berlin, Isaiah. *Vico and Herder: Two Studies in the History of Ideas.* New York: Viking Press, 1976.

Binswanger, Ludwig. *Being-in-the-World: Selected Papers of Ludwig Binswanger.* Ed. Jacob Needleman. New York: Harper and Row, 1968.

Boehner, Philotheus. *Collected Articles on Ockham.* Ed. Eligius M. Buytaert. St. Bonaventure, N.Y.: Franciscan Institute, 1958.

Booth, Wayne C. *Modern Dogma and the Rhetoric of Assent.* Notre Dame: University of Notre Press, 1974.

Borkenau, Franz. *End and Beginning: On the Generation of Cultures and the Origins of the West.* Ed. Richard Lowenthal. New York: Columbia University Press, 1981.

Bracher, Karl Dietrich. *The Age of Ideologies: A History of Political Thought in the Twentieth Century.* Trans. Ewald Osers. New York: St. Martin's Press, 1984.

Brumfitt, J. H. *Voltaire, Historian.* Oxford: Oxford University Press, 1958.

Burrell, David. *Analogy and Philosophical Language.* New Haven: Yale University Press, 1973.

———. *Knowing the Unknowable God: Ibn-Sina, Maimonides, Aquinas.* Notre Dame: University of Notre Dame Press, 1986.

Burtt, E. A. *The Metaphysical Foundations of Modern Science.* Garden City, N.Y.: Doubleday, Anchor Books, 1954.

Byrne, Patrick H. *Analysis and Science in Aristotle.* Albany: State University of New York Press, 1997.

Cahn, Elaine, and Cathleen Going, eds. *The Question as Commitment: A Symposium.* Thomas More Institute Papers 77. Montreal: Perry Printing, 1979.

Cassirer, Ernst. *The Philosophy of the Enlightenment.* Trans. Fritz C. A. Koelln and James P. Pettegrove. Boston: Beacon Press, 1955.

Clark, Norris. "On Facing the Truth about Human Truth." *American Catholic Philosophical Association Proceedings* 43 (1969): 4–13.

Clark, R. T. Rundle. *Myth and Symbol in Ancient Egypt.* London: Thames and Hudson, 1959.

Cohn, Norman. *The Pursuit of the Millennium.* Rev. ed. Oxford: Oxford University Press, 1970.

Collingwood, R. G. *The Idea of History.* New York: Oxford University Press, 1956.

———. *The Idea of Nature.* Oxford: Oxford University Press, 1945.

Collins, James. *Interpreting Modern Philosophy.* Princeton: Princeton University Press, 1972.

Conn, Walter. *Conscience: Development and Self-Transcendence.* Birmingham: Religious Education Press, 1981.

Copleston, Frederick. *A History of Philosophy.* 9 vols. Garden City, N.Y.: Doubleday, Image Books, 1984.

Cornford, F. M. *From Religion to Philosophy: A Study in the Origins of Western Speculation.* New York: Harper and Row, 1957.

D'Alembert, Jean le Rond. "Preliminary Discourse." In *Denis Diderot's The Encyclopedia,* trans. Stephen J. Gendzier, 1–43. New York: Harper and Row, Torchbooks, 1967.

Descartes, René. *Discourse on Method.* Trans. Laurence J. Lafleur. New York: Macmillan, 1956.

Dilthey, Wilhelm. *Gessamelte Schriften.* 12 vols. Stuttgart: B. G. Teubner Verlag, 1959–1962.

———. *Pattern and Meaning in History.* Ed. H. P. Rickman. New York: Harper and Row, 1962.

Doran, Robert. "Duality and Dialectic." In *Lonergan Workshop,* ed. Fred Lawrence, 7:59–84. Atlanta: Scholars Press, 1988.

———. *Psychic Conversion and Theological Foundations: Toward a Reorientation of the Human Sciences.* Atlanta: Scholars Press, 1981.

———. "Subject, Psyche, and Theology's Foundations." *Journal of Religion* 57 (July 1977): 279–80.

———. *Subject and Psyche: Ricoeur, Jung, and the Search for Foundations.* Washington, D.C.: University Press of America, 1979.

———. "The Theologian's Psyche: Notes toward a Reconstruction of Depth Psychology." In *Lonergan Workshop,* ed. Fred Lawrence, 1:93–137. Missoula, Mont.: Scholars Press, 1978.

———. *Theology and the Dialectic of History.* Toronto: University of Toronto Press, 1990.

Drilling, Peter J. "Mysterium Tremendum." *Method: Journal of Lonergan Studies* 5 (1987): 58–72.

Dudley, Guilford. *Religion on Trial: Mircea Eliade and His Critics.* Philadelphia: Temple University Press, 1977.

Dunne, Tad. *Lonergan and Spirituality: Towards a Spiritual Integration.* Chicago: Loyola University Press, 1985.

Edelstein, Ludwig. *The Idea of Progress in Classical Antiquity.* Baltimore: Johns Hopkins University Press, 1967.

Eliade, Mircea. *Cosmos and History.* Trans. Willard R. Trask. New York: Harper and Row, 1959.

———. *Images and Symbols.* Trans. Philip Mairet. New York: Sheed and Ward, 1969.

———. *Patterns in Comparative Religion.* Trans. Rosemary Sheed. New York: Meridian Books, 1963.

———. *The Sacred and the Profane.* Trans. Willard R. Trask. New York: Harcourt, Brace, and World, 1959.

———. *Shamanism: Archaic Techniques of Ecstasy.* Trans. Willard R. Trask. Bollington Series 76. New York: Pantheon Books, 1964.

Fackenheim, Emil L. *The God Within: Kant, Schelling, and Historicity.* Ed. John Burbrage. Toronto: University of Toronto Press, 1996.

———. *Metaphysics and Historicity.* Aquinas Lecture, 1961. Milwaukee: Marquette University Press, 1961.

Fallon, Timothy P., and Philip Boo Riley, eds. *Religion and Culture: Essays in Honor of Bernard Lonergan.* Albany: State University of New York Press, 1987.

Fitzpatrick, Joseph. "Lonergan and Poetry." *New Blackfriars* 59 (1978): 441–50, 517–26.

Foucault, Michel. *The Archeology of Knowledge.* Trans. Rupert Sawyer. New York: Harper and Row, 1976.

Frame, Donald M., ed. *Montaigne: Selections from the Essays.* Arlington Heights, Ill.: Harlan Davidson, 1973.

Frame, Douglass. *The Myth of Return in Early Greek Epic.* New Haven: Yale University Press, 1978.

Frankfort, Henri. *Kingship and the Gods: A Study of Ancient Near Eastern Religion as the Integration of Society and Nature.* Chicago: University of Chicago Press, 1948.

Frankfort, Henri, et al. *The Intellectual Adventure of Ancient Man: An Essay in Speculative Thought in the Ancient Near East.* Chicago: University of Chicago Press, 1949.

Freeman, Kathleen. *Ancilla to the Pre-Socratic Philosophers.* Cambridge: Harvard University Press, 1957.

Gadamer, Hans Georg. *Dialogue and Dialectic: Eight Hermeneutical Studies on Plato.* Trans. P. Christopher Smith. New Haven: Yale University Press, 1980.

————. *The Idea of the Good in Platonic-Aristotelian Philosophy.* Trans. P. Christopher Smith. New Haven: Yale University Press, 1986.

————. *Philosophical Hermeneutics.* Trans. David E. Linge. Berkeley and Los Angeles: University of California Press, 1976.

————. *Truth and Method.* New York: Seabury Press, 1975.

Gay, Peter. *The Enlightenment: An Interpretation.* 2 vols. New York: Alfred A. Knopf, 1969.

Gershoy, Leo. *The Era of the French Revolution, 1789–1799: Ten Years That Shook the World.* New York: D. Van Norstrand, 1957.

Gilson, Etienne. *Being and Some Philosophers.* 2nd ed. Toronto: Pontifical Institute of Mediaeval Studies, 1952.

Gunnell, John G. *Political Philosophy and Time.* Middletown, Conn.: Wesleyan University Press, 1968.

Guthrie, W. K. C. *A History of Greek Philosophy.* 6 vols. Cambridge: Cambridge University Press, 1981.

Habermas, Jürgen. *Knowledge and Human Interests.* Trans. Jeremy Shapiro. Boston: Beacon Press, 1971.

————. "Summation and Response." *Continuum* 8 (1970): 123–33.

————. *Theory and Practice.* Trans. John Viertel. Boston: Beacon Press, 1973.

————. *Toward a Rational Society: Student Protests, Science, and Politics.* Trans. Jeremy J. Shapiro. Boston: Beacon Press, 1970.

Hadot, Pierre. *Philosophy as a Way of Life.* Ed. Arnold I. Davidson. Oxford: Blackwell Publishers, 1995.

Havelock, Eric. *Preface to Plato.* Cambridge: Harvard University Press, 1963.

Heer, Friedrich. *The Intellectual History of Europe.* Trans. Jonathan Steinberg. Cleveland: World Publishing, 1966.

Hegel, Georg Wilhelm Freidrich. *Lectures on the Philosophy of Religion.* Trans. E. B. Speers and J. Burdon Sanders. London: Kegan Paul Trench, Truebner, 1895.

————. *The Phenomenology of Mind.* Trans. J. W. Baillie. New York: Harper and Row, Torchbooks, 1967.

————. *Reason in History: A General Introduction to the Philosophy of History.* Trans. Robert S. Hartman. Indianapolis: Bobbs-Merrill, Library of Liberal Arts, 1953.

Heidegger, Martin. *Being and Time.* Trans. John Macquarrie and Edward Robinson. New York: Harper and Row, 1962.

————. "Letter on Humanism." In *The Existentialist Tradition,* ed. Nino Languilli, 204–45. Garden City, N.Y.: Doubleday, Anchor Books, 1971.

————. *The Question Concerning Technology and Other Essays.* Trans. William Lovitt. New York: Harper and Row, Colophon Books, 1977.

Heiler, Friedrich. "The History of Religion as a Preparation for the Cooperation of Religions." In *The History of Religion: Essays in Methodology,* ed. M. Eliade and J. Kitakawa, 142–53. Chicago: University of Chicago Press, 1959.

Heisenberg, Werner. *Physics and Philosophy: The Revolution in Modern Science.* New York: Harper and Row, 1962.

Helminiak, David A. *Spiritual Development: An Interdisciplinary Study.* Chicago: Loyola University Press, 1987.

Hobbes, Thomas. *Leviathan.* Everyman's Library. London: J. M. Dent and Sons, 1914.

Hodges, H. A. *The Philosophy of Wilhelm Dilthey.* London: Routledge and Kegan Paul, 1952.

Homer. *The Odyssey of Homer.* Trans. Richmond Lattimore. New York: Harper and Row, 1961.

———. *The Odyssey of Homer.* Trans. Robert Fitzgerald. Garden City, N.Y.: Doubleday, 1961.

Hughes, Glenn. "Balanced and Imbalanced Consciousness." In *The Politics of the Soul: Eric Voegelin on Religious Experience,* ed. Glenn Hughes, chap. 7. New York: Rowan and Littlefield, 1999.

———. "A Critique of 'Lonergan's Notion of Dialectic,' by Ronald McKinney, S.J.," and "A Reply to Ronald McKinney, S.J." *Method: Journal of Lonergan Studies* 1:1 (1983): 60–67, 70–73.

———. *Mystery and Myth in the Philosophy of Eric Voegelin.* Columbia: University of Missouri Press, 1993.

Hughes, H. Stuart. *Consciousness and Society: The Reorientation of European Social Thought, 1890–1930.* New York: Random House, Vintage, 1958.

Hume, David. *Treatise of Human Nature.* Ed. L. A. Selby-Biggs. Oxford: Oxford University Press, 1955.

Husserl, Edmund. *Ideas: General Introduction to Pure Phenomenology.* Trans. W. R. Boyce Gibson. New York: Collier Books, 1962.

Iggers, George. *The German Conception of History.* Middletown, Conn.: Wesleyan University Press, 1968.

Jacobsen, Thorkild. *The Treasures of Darkness: A History of Mesopotamian Religion.* New Haven: Yale University Press, 1976.

Jaeger, Werner. *Paideia: The Ideals of Greek Culture.* Trans. Gilbert Highet. 3 vols. New Haven: Yale University Press, 1943.

———. *Studien zur Entstehungsgeschichte der Metaphysik des Aristoteles.* Berlin: Weidmann, 1912.

———. *The Theology of the Early Greek Philosophers.* The Gifford Lectures, 1936. Oxford: Oxford University Press, 1947.

Jager, Bernd. "Theorizing, Journeying, Dwelling." In *Duquesne Studies in Phenomenological Psychology,* ed. Amedo Giorgi, Constance Fisher, and Edward L. Murray, 2:235–60. Pittsburgh: Duquesne University Press, 1975.

Jaspers, Karl. *Man in the Modern Age.* Trans. Eden Paul and Cedar Paul. Garden City, N.Y.: Doubleday, 1957.

Jay, Martin. *The Dialectical Imagination: A History of the Frankfurt School and the Institute of Social Research, 1923–1950.* Boston: Little, Brown, 1973.

Jonas, Hans. *The Gnostic Religion.* Boston: Beacon Press, 1963.

Kant, Immanuel. *Critique of Pure Reason.* Trans. Norman Kemp Smith. New York: St. Martin's Press, 1965.

Kelly, George Armstrong. *Idealism, Politics, and History: Sources of Hegelian Thought.* Cambridge: Cambridge University Press, 1969.

Kierkegaard, Søren. *The Concept of Dread.* Trans. Walter Lowrie. 2nd ed. Princeton: Princeton University Press, 1957.

———. *Concluding Unscientific Postscript.* Trans. David F. Swenson and Walter Lowrie. Princeton: Princeton University Press, 1941.

———. *Either/Or.* Trans. Walter Lowrie. 2 vols. Princeton: Princeton University Press, 1944.

———. *The Sickness unto Death: A Christian Psychological Exposition for Upbuilding and Awakening.* Trans. Howard V. Hong and Edna H. Hong. Princeton: Princeton University Press, 1980.

Kilcup, Rodney. "Burke's Historicism." *Journal of Modern History* 49 (1977): 394–410.

———. Introduction to *The History of England,* by David Hume. Classics of British Historical Literature. Chicago: University of Chicago Press, 1975.

Kirk, G. S., and J. E. Raven, trans. *The Presocratic Philosophers: A Critical History with a Selection of Texts.* Cambridge: Cambridge University Press, 1971.

Kisiel, Theodore. "Ideology Critique and Phenomenology: The Current Debate in German Philosophy." *Philosophy Today* 14 (1970): 151–60.

Koller, H. "Theoros und Theoria." *Glotta, Zeitschrift fur Griechische und Lateinische Sprache* 36 (1958).

Krutch, Joseph Wood. *The Modern Temper: A Study and a Confession.* Rev. ed. New York: Harcourt, Brace, and World, 1956.

Kuhn, Thomas S. *The Structure of Scientific Revolutions.* 2nd ed. Chicago: University of Chicago Press, 1970.

Lakatos, Imre, and Alan Musgrave, eds. *Criticism and the Growth of Knowledge.* Cambridge: Cambridge University Press, 1970.

Langer, Suzanne K. *Feeling and Form: A Theory of Art.* New York: Scribner, 1953.

Lauer, Quentin. Introduction to *Phenomenology and the Crisis of Philosophy,* by Edmund Husserl. New York: Harper and Row, 1955.

Lawrence, Fred. "On 'The Meditative Origin of the Philosophical Knowledge of Order.'" In *The Beginning and the Beyond: Papers from the Gadamer and Voegelin Conferences.* Supplementary issue of *Lonergan Workshop,* ed. Fred Lawrence, 4:43–51. Chico, Calif.: Scholars Press, 1984.

Lear, Jonathan. *Aristotle: The Desire to Understand.* Cambridge: Cambridge University Press, 1988.

Leff, Gordon. *The Dissolution of the Medieval Outlook: An Essay on the Intellectual and Spiritual Change in the Fourteenth Century.* New York: Harper and Row, 1976.

Leibniz, Baron Gottfried Wilhelm von. *Basic Writings.* Trans. George R. Montgomery. LaSalle, Ill.: Open Court Publishing, 1968.

Lewis, Charlton T., and Charles Short. *A Latin Dictionary.* Oxford: Oxford University Press, 1969.

Liddel, Henry George, and Robert Scott. *A Greek-English Lexicon.* 9th ed. New York: Oxford University Press, 1996.

Linge, D. E. "Historicity and Hermeneutic: A Study of Contemporary Hermeneutical Theory." Ph.D. diss., Vanderbilt University, 1969.

Locke, John. *Essay Concerning Human Understanding.* Ed. Alexander G. Fraser. 2 vols. New York: Dover Publications, 1959.

Löwith, Karl. *From Hegel to Nietzsche.* Trans. David E. Green. Garden City, N.Y.: Doubleday, Anchor Books, 1967.

———. *Martin Heidegger and European Nihilism.* Trans. Gary Steiner. European Perspectives. New York: Columbia University Press, 1995.

———. *Meaning in History.* Chicago: University of Chicago Press, 1949.

———. *Nature, History, and Existentialism and Other Essays in the Philosophy of History.* Northwestern University Studies in Phenomenology and Existentialist Philosophy. Evanston: Northwestern University Press, 1966.

Luijpen, William. *Existential Phenomenology.* Duquesne Studies, Philosophy Series 12. Pittsburgh: Duquesne University Press, 1969.

MacIntyre, Alasdair. *After Virtue: A Study in Moral Theory.* Notre Dame: University of Notre Dame Press, 1981.

Makkreel, Rudolf A. *Dilthey: Philosopher of the Human Studies.* Princeton: Princeton University Press, 1975.

Mandelbaum, Maurice. "Historicism." In *The Encyclopedia of Philosophy,* ed. Paul Edwards, 4:22–25. New York: Macmillan, 1967.

———. *History, Man, and Reason: A Study in Nineteenth-Century Thought.* Baltimore: Johns Hopkins University Press, 1971.

Marcel, Gabriel. *Man against Mass Society.* Trans. G. S. Fraser. Chicago: Henry Regnery Press, Gateway Edition, 1962.

Marx, Karl. *Early Writings.* Trans. and ed. T. B. Bottomore. New York: Mc-Graw-Hill, 1964.

Masur, Gerhard. *Prophets of Yesterday: Studies in European Culture, 1890–1914.* New York: Macmillan, 1966.

Matthews, William. "Journalling Self-Appropriation." *Milltown Studies* 7 (1981): 96–184.

———. "Personal Histories and Theories of Knowledge." *Milltown Studies* 8 (1981): 58–73.

Matson, Floyd W. *The Broken Image: Man, Science, and Society.* Garden City, N.Y.: Doubleday, Anchor Books, 1966.

May, Rollo. *Love and Will.* New York: W. W. Norton, 1969.

McCarthy, Michael H. *The Crisis of Philosophy.* Albany: State University of New York Press, 1990.

McCarthy, Thomas. *The Critical Theory of Jürgen Habermas.* Cambridge: MIT Press, 1979.

McCoy, Charles N. R. *The Structure of Political Thought: A Study in the History of Ideas.* New York: McGraw-Hill, 1963.

McDonald, Forrest. *Novus Ordo Seclorium: The Intellectual Origins of the Constitution.* Lawrence: University Press of Kansas, 1985.

McPartland, Thomas J. "Authenticity and Transcendence: Lonergan and Voegelin on Political Authority." Paper presented at Lonergan Philosophical Society, Santa Clara University, October 29, 1999.

———. "Meaning, Mystery, and the History of Consciousness." In *Lonergan Workshop,* ed. Fred Lawrence, 8:203–67. Atlanta: Scholars Press, 1988.

Meinecke, Friedrich. *Historism.* Trans. J. E. Anderson. London: Routledge and Kegan Paul, 1972.

Meynell, Hugo. *The Nature of Aesthetic Value.* Albany: State University of New York Press, 1986.

Moody, Ernest A. *The Logic of William of Ockham.* London: Sheed and Ward, 1935.

Moore, G. E. *Principia Ethica.* Cambridge: Cambridge University Press, 1903.

Moore, Sebastian. "Christian Self-Discovery." In *Lonergan Workshop,* ed. Fred Lawrence, 1:187–221. Missoula, Mont.: Scholars Press, 1978.

Morelli, Elizabeth Murray. "Aristotle's Theory Transposed." Paper presented at the Lonergan Philosophical Society, Santa Clara University, November 1997.

———. "The Feeling of Freedom." In *Religion and Culture: Essays in Honor of*

Bernard Lonergan, S.J., ed. Timothy P. Fallon and Philip Boo Riley, 95–106. Albany: State University of New York Press, 1987.

Morgan, Edmund S. *Inventing the People: The Rise of Popular Sovereignty in England and America.* New York: W. W. Norton, 1988.

Navone, John. *The Jesus Story: Our Life as Story in Christ.* Collegeville, Minn.: Liturgical Press, 1979.

Newman, John Henry. *An Essay in Aid of a Grammar of Assent.* Garden City, N.Y.: Doubleday, 1955.

Nietzsche, Friedrich. *The Use and Abuse of History.* Trans. Adrian Collins. Indianapolis: Bobbs-Merrill, Library of Liberal Arts, 1957.

Nisbet, Robert. *History of the Idea of Progress.* New York: Basic Books, 1980.

Ockham, William of. *Philosophical Writings.* Trans. Philotheus Boehner. Indianapolis: Bobbs-Merrill, Library of Liberal Arts, 1964.

Owens, Joseph. *The Doctrine of Being in Aristotelian Metaphysics.* 2nd ed. Toronto: Pontifical Institute of Mediaeval Studies, 1963.

Palmer, R. E. *Hermeneutics: Interpretation Theory in Schliermacher, Dilthey, Heidegger, and Gadamer.* Northwestern University Studies in Phenomenology and Existentialist Philosophy. Evanston: Northwestern University Press, 1969.

Pangle, Thomas L. *Montesquieu's Philosophy of Liberalism.* Chicago: University of Chicago Press, 1973.

Pascal, Blaise. *Pensées.* Trans. A. J. Krailsheimer. New York: Penguin Books, 1966.

Patterson, Richard. "Plato on Philosophical Character." *Journal of the History of Philosophy* 25 (1987): 325–50.

Peccorini, Francisco L. "Knowledge of the Singular: Aquinas, Suarez, and Recent Interpreters." *Thomist* 38 (July 1974): 606–55.

Piscitelli, Emil J. "Paul Ricoeur's Philosophy of Religious Symbol: A Critique and Dialectical Transposition." *Ultimate Reality and Meaning* 3 (1980): 275–313.

Plato. *Collected Dialogues of Plato Including the Letters.* Ed. Edith Hamilton and Huntington Cairns. Bollingen Series 71. Princeton: Princeton University Press, 1963.

Polanyi, Michael. *Personal Knowledge: Towards a Post-Critical Philosophy.* New York: Harper and Row, 1958.

Polybius. "Histories." In *The Portable Greek Historians,* ed. M. I. Finley, 441–501. New York: Penguin Books, 1959.

Popkin, Richard. *The History of Scepticism from Erasmus to Descartes.* New York: Harper and Row, 1968.

Popper, Karl R. *Conjectures and Refutations: The Growth of Scientific Knowledge.* New York: Harper and Row, 1968.

————. *The Logic of Scientific Discovery.* New York: Harper and Row, 1965.

————. *The Poverty of Historicism.* New York: Harper and Row, 1964.

Praz, Mario. *The Romantic Agony.* Trans. Angus Davidson. 2nd ed. London and New York: Oxford University Press, 1970.

Price, James Robertson, III. "Lonergan and the Foundations of a Contemporary Mystical Theology." In *Lonergan Workshop,* ed. Fred Lawrence, 2:163–95. Chico, Calif.: Scholars Press, 1985.

Pritchard, James B., ed. *Ancient Near Eastern Texts, Relating to the Old Testament.* 3rd ed. Princeton: Princeton University Press, 1969.

Progoff, Ira. *At a Journal Workshop: The Basic Text and Guide for Using the Intensive Journal Process.* New York: Dialogue House Library, 1975.

————. *The Practice of Process Mediation.* New York: Dialogue House Library, 1980.

————. *The Symbolic and the Real: A New Psychological Approach to the Fuller Experience of Human Existence.* New York: McGraw-Hill, 1973.

Prufer, Thomas. "A Protreptic: What Is Philosophy?" In *Studies in Philosophy and the History of Philosophy,* 2:1–10. Washington, D.C.: Catholic University of America Press, 1963.

Radnitzky, Gerhard. *Contemporary Schools of Metascience.* Chicago: Henry Regnery, 1973.

Randall, John Herman, Jr. *The Career of Philosophy.* 3 vols. New York: Columbia University Press, 1962–1977.

Reill, Peter Hans. *The German Enlightenment and the Rise of Historicism.* Berkeley and Los Angeles: University of California Press, 1975.

Rescher, Nicholas. *The Philosophy of Leibniz.* Englewood Cliffs, N.J.: Prentice-Hall, 1967.

Ricoeur, Paul. *The Conflict of Interpretations: Essays in Hermeneutics.* Northwestern University Studies in Phenomenology and Existentialist Philosophy. Evanston: Northwestern University Press, 1974.

————. "Ethics and Culture: Habermas and Gadamer in Dialogue." Trans. David Pellauer. *Philosophy Today* 17 (1973): 153–55.

————. *Freud and Philosophy: An Essay on Interpretation.* Trans. Denis Savage. Terry Lectures. New Haven: Yale University Press, 1970.

————. *Time and Narrative.* Trans. Kathleen McLaughlin and David Pellauer. Vol. 1. Chicago: University of Chicago Press, 1984.

Rilke, Rainer Maria. *Rilke on Love and Other Difficulties: Translations and Considerations of Rainer Maria Rilke.* Trans. and ed. John J. L. Mood. New York: W. W. Norton, 1975.

Rorty, Richard. *Contingency, Irony, and Solidarity.* Cambridge: Cambridge University Press, 1989.

Ross, W. D. *Aristotle's Metaphysics.* 2 vols. Oxford: Oxford University Press, 1924.

Roth, Gunther. "History and Sociology in the Work of Max Weber." *British Journal of Sociology* 27 (1976): 308–18.

Ryan, John K., and Bernardine M. Bonansea, eds. *John Duns Scotus, 1265–1965.* Vol. 3 of *Studies in Philosophy and the History of Philosophy.* Washington, D.C.: Catholic University of America Press, 1965.

Sala, Giovanni. *Lonergan and Kant: Five Essays on Human Knowledge.* Trans. Joseph Spoerl. Ed. Robert Doran. Toronto: University of Toronto Press, 1994.

Sallis, John. *Being and Logos: The Way of Platonic Dialogue.* Duquesne Studies, Philosophical Series 33. Pittsburgh: Duquesne University Press, 1975.

Scheler, Max. *Ressentiment.* Trans. Lewis A. Coser. New York: Schocken Books, 1972.

Schütz, Alfred. *Collected Papers.* Ed. Maurice Natanson. 3 vols. The Hague: Martinus Nijhoff, 1962.

———. *The Phenomenology of the Social World.* Northwestern University Studies in Phenomenology and Existentialist Philosophy. Evanston: Northwestern University Press, 1967.

Scotus, John Duns. *Philosophical Writings.* Trans. Allan Wolter. Indianapolis: Bobbs-Merrill, Library of Liberal Arts, 1962.

Shackleton, Robert. *Montesquieu: A Critical Biography.* Oxford: Oxford University Press, 1961.

Shrag, Calvin O. *Experience and Being: Prolegomena to a Future Ontology.* Northwestern University Studies in Phenomenology and Existentialist Philosophy. Evanston: Northwestern University Press, 1969.

Sorokin, Piritim. *Social and Cultural Dynamics.* 4 vols. New York: American Book, 1934–1941.

Spengler, Oswald. *The Decline of the West.* Trans. Charles Francis Atkinson. 2 vols. New York: Alfred A. Knopf, 1929.

Stromberg, Roland N. *After Everything: Western Intellectual History since 1945.* New York: St. Martin's Press, 1975.

Thomas, Carol G., and Craig Conant. *Citadel to City-State: The Transformation of Greece, 1200–700* B.C.E. Bloomington: Indiana University Press, 1999.

Thompson, J. M. *Robespierre and the French Revolution.* New York: Macmillan, Collier Books, 1962.

Thucydides. *The Peloponnesian War.* Trans. Richard Crawley. New York: Random House, Modern Library College Editions, 1951.

Toulmin, Stephen. *Cosmopolis: The Hidden Agenda of Modernity.* Chicago: University of Chicago Press, 1990.

Troeltsch, Ernst. "Die Krise des Historismus." Part 1. *Die Neue Rundschau* 33 (1922): 573.

Tuveson, Ernest Lee. *Millennium and Utopia: A Study in the Background of the Idea of Progress.* New York: Harper and Row, 1964.

Van der Leeuw, Gerhardus. *Religion in Essence and Manifestation: A Study in Phenomenolgy.* Trans. T. E. Turner. New York: Harper and Row, 1962.

Van Groningen, B. A. *In the Grip of the Past: Essay on an Aspect of Greek Thought.* Leiden: E. J. Brill, 1953.

Vasari, Giorgio. *Lives of the Artists.* Trans. George Bull. New York: Penguin Books, 1981.

Vico, Giambattista. *The New Science of Giambattista Vico.* Trans. Thomas Goddard Bergin and Max Harold Fisch. Ithaca: Cornell University Press, 1970.

Voegelin, Eric. *Anamnesis.* Trans. Gerhart Niemeyer. Notre Dame: Notre Dame University Press, 1978.

———. *Autobiographical Reflections.* Ed. Ellis Sandoz. Baton Rouge: Louisiana State University Press, 1989.

———. *Conversations with Eric Voegelin.* Ed. R. Eric O'Connor. Montreal: Thomas More Institute Papers, 1980.

———. *From Enlightenment to Revolution.* Ed. John Hallowell. Durham: Duke University Press, 1975.

———. *History of Political Ideas.* Vols. 19–26 of *The Collected Works of Eric Voegelin,* ed. Ellis Sandoz. Columbia: University of Missouri Press, 1997.

———. *Hitler and the Germans.* Vol. 31 of *The Collected Works of Eric Voegelin,* trans. Detley Clemens and Brendan Purcell. Columbia: University of Missouri Press, 1999.

———. *Modernity without Restraint: "The Political Religions," "The New Science of Politics," and "Science, Politics, and Gnosticism."* Vol. 5 of *The Collected Works of Eric Voegelin,* ed. Manfred Henningsen. Columbia: University of Missouri Press, 2000.

———. *The Nature of Law and Related Legal Writings.* Vol. 27 of *The Collected Works of Eric Voegelin,* ed. Robert Anthony Pascal, James Lee Babin, and John William Corrington. Baton Rouge: Louisiana State University Press, 1991.

———. *The New Science of Politics.* Chicago: University of Chicago Press, 1952.

———. *On the Form of the American Mind.* Vol. 1 of *The Collected Works of Eric Voegelin,* trans. Ruth Hein, ed. Jurgen Gebhardt and Barry Cooper. Baton Rouge: Louisiana State University Press, 1996.

———. *Order and History.* 5 vols. Baton Rouge: Louisiana State University Press, 1956–1987.

————. *Published Essays, 1940–1952.* Vol. 10 of *The Collected Works of Eric Voegelin,* ed. Ellis Sandoz. Columbia: University of Missouri Press, 2000.

————. *Published Essays, 1953–1965.* Vol. 11 of *The Collected Works of Eric Voegelin,* ed. Ellis Sandoz. Columbia: University of Missouri Press, 2000.

————. *Published Essays, 1966–1985.* Vol. 12 of *The Collected Works of Eric Voegelin,* ed. Ellis Sandoz. Baton Rouge: Louisiana State University Press, 1990.

————. *Race and State.* Vol. 2 of *The Collected Works of Eric Voegelin,* trans. Ruth Hein, ed. Klaus Vondung. Baton Rouge: Louisiana State University Press, 1996.

————. *Science, Politics, and Gnosticism.* Chicago: Henry Regnery Press, 1968.

————. *What Is History? And Other Unpublished Writings.* Vol. 28 of *The Collected Works of Eric Voegelin,* ed. Thomas A. Hollweck and Paul Caringella. Baton Rouge: Louisiana State University Press, 1990.

Wagar, W. Warren. *World Views: A Study in Comparative History.* Hinsdale, Ill.: Dryden Press, 1977.

Webb, Eugene. *Eric Voegelin: Philosopher of History.* Seattle: University of Washington Press, 1981.

————. *Philosophers of Consciousness: Polanyi, Lonergan, Voegelin, Ricoeur, Girard, Kierkegaard.* Seattle: University of Washington Press, 1988.

Weber, Max. "Politics as a Vocation." In *From Max Weber: Essays in Sociology,* ed. H. H. Gerth and C. Wright Mills, pt. 1. New York: Oxford University Press, 1958.

————. "Science as a Vocation." In *From Max Weber: Essays in Sociology,* ed. H. H. Gerth and C. Wright Mills, pt. 1. New York: Oxford University Press, 1958.

Weber-Schaefer, Peter. *Oikumeme und Imperium: Studien zur Ziviltheologie des chineischen Kaiserreichts.* Munich: n.p., 1968.

Weinberg, Julius R. *A Short History of Medieval Philosophy.* Princeton: Princeton University Press, 1964.

Wellmer, Albrecht. *Critical Theory of Society.* Trans. John Cumming. New York: Seabury Press, 1974.

Whitehead, Alfred North. *Science and the Modern World.* New York: Mentor Books, 1948.

Willey, Basil. *The Seventeenth-Century Background: Studies in the Thought of the Age in Relation to Poetry and Religion.* Garden City, N.Y.: Doubleday, Anchor Books, 1953.

Winter, Gibson. *Elements for a Social Ethic: Scientific Perspectives on Social Process.* New York: Macmillan, 1966.

Wolter, Allan. *The Transcendentals and Their Function in the Metaphysics of Duns Scotus.* St. Bonaventure, N.Y.: Franciscan Institute, 1946.

Index

Academic praxis, 122. *See also* Functional specialties

Acculturation, 45, 120. *See also* Development

Act, 29, 32–40 passim; Aristotle's idea of, 29, 32, 41; as metaphysical equivalent of judging, 32

Adamites, 48

Agathon, 168, 187

Albert, the Great, 153

Alembert, Jean le Rond d', 56, 89

Alexander, Samuel, 255

Amon hymns, 209

Anabaptists, 48

Anamnesis, 160, 172, 265–66

Anaxagoras, 154

Anaximander, 111, 157–58

Antoni, Carlo, 79–80, 83n13

Anselm, Saint, 153

Anxiety. *See* Dread

Apostolic Brethren, 48

A priori construction of meaning of history, 108, 114

A prioris of human condition: bodily, 67, 131–32; communal (social), 67, 131–32; horizon of openness, 67; temporal, 67, 131–32

Aquinas, Thomas, 21, 39, 153, 160, 161, 188, 208, 209, 211, 230, 266, 268

Architecture, 138

Areté, 30, 127n5, 154, 206

Aristotle, 21, 26, 39, 31n15, 58, 65n16, 101, 102n46, 153, 161, 194, 195, 196–98, 199–208, 212, 251n79; and act, 29, 32, 41, 199, 202; and *areté,* 30, 206; and being as substance, 208; and change (*kinesis*), 28, 200; and development, 25, 27–31; and dialectical analysis of predecessors, 56, 63; and empirical investigations, 210; and experience (*empeira*) and faculty psychology, 207; and final cause, 29, 51; and form, 29, 32, 240; and habits (*hexeis*), 199–201, 204; and hierarchy of intellectual disciplines, 207; and history as not scientific, 111; and human existence as synthetic nature, 201, 206–7, 212, 254–55; and human form as "rational animal," 29–30; and idea of nature, 28–29, 41, 111, 127, 129–30, 205, 206, 251; and judgment as synthesis of concepts, 40; and limits of historical responsibility, 111–12; and lover of myth as philosopher, 264; and memory, 200–201, 204; and myth, 171n54; and *pathe* as acts, 199–200; and political science, 206, 207; and potency, 28, 29, 32, 41, 199, 200, 202–3; and practical wisdom, 30; and problem of interpreting his texts, 197–98; and questioning, 30, 196, 206; and science as true, certain knowledge of causal necessity, 35, 127n5; and *spoudaios,* 29, 196, 246; and static universe, 33, 256; and unmoved mover, 205

—and *episteme,* 199–207; as cognitive habit, 200–201; and demonstrative knowledge, 196–97, 200; as preconceptual act, 202; and relation to *nous,* 196–97, 198, 201, 202, 203–4, 205

—and *nous,* 198, 199–207; as active potency (*nous poetikos*), 202–3, 204; as cognitive habit, 201, 204–5; as divine in us, 155, 196, 198, 204, 205, 206; as divine transcendent ground, 196, 205; as epistemic act, 202, 203–4; and images, 202, 203; as indemonstrable principle, 196–97, 200; as passive potency, 202–3; as *phronesis,* 205–7, 246; as principle of human nature, 206; as

Aristotle (*cont.*)
  principle of science (*episteme*), 198,
    202–3; self-luminosity of, 204–5; as
    sophia, 205; as *theoria,* 205, 206; as
    wonderment, 203, 204
Art, 137, 138. *See also* Poetry
Augustine, Saint, 38, 113, 128, 153, 174,
  211, 248; and theology of history, 113,
  128
Authenticity, 4–5; as criterion of human
  development, 45; in negotiating tension
  of limitation and transcendence, 4; and
  self-transcendence, 5; as *Sorge* (Heidegger), 98; as withdrawal from inauthenticity, 135
Authorities, 139
Authority. *See* Voegelin, Eric: and authority
Awareness: focal, 23, 216; subsidiary, 23,
  216

Babylonian incantations, 209
Bach, 3*n*5
Basic horizon. *See* Horizon(s): basic
Baumer, Franklin, 76, 107
Behaviorists, 11
Being: affirmation of transcendent being,
  50, 263; and core of meaning, 242; as
  esse in Aquinas, 208, 209; heuristic notion of, 243; inquiry about, as constitutive of self, 43, 247; relation to through
  inquiry, 148, 171; as self-presence of
  unrestricted understanding, 243; as
  substance in Aristotle, 208. *See also* Intention: of being
Being-in-love: engulf's intentionality, 2,
  219, 247–48; as essence of religious
  experience, 152n16; existential state of,
  16, 19–20, 149, 259; as nature, 251; as
  solution to generic shame, 190; participation in, 139, 174; philosopher's participation in, 152–53, 158–59, 167,
  252; unrestrictedly, 152. *See also* Spiritual
Belief: and genesis of knowledge, 135–36,
  218; and reason, 120. *See also* Tradition
Bergson, Henri, 18, 44, 120, 138, 157,
  169, 264. *See also* *Élan vital*
Bias, 68, 70, 117, 173, 176, 217; of common sense, 68, 117, 136, 164, 173,
  175–76, 190–91; existential roots of,

173–76; group, 68, 117, 164, 173,
  175–76, 190–91; individual, 68, 117,
  190, 164, 173; psychoneurotic, 68,
  117, 164, 173
Bios, 152
Body, 215, 268
Boethius, 38
Boltzmann, Ludwig, 38
Bonaventura, Saint, 153
Buddhist: *nirvana,* 158; teachings, 209
Burke, Edmund, 80, 81*n*8
Burtt, E. A., 88
Byrne, Patrick H., 199, 203

Calypso: and *nous,* 155, 198
Cartesian: alienation of subject and world,
  95, 98; doubt, 240; idea of scientific
  method, 104n52; idea of tradition as
  object to be confronted, 99; observer,
  156; *res extensa,* 215, 231, 239
Cause, final, 29, 51, 51n63
Change, 28, 29, 45; Aristotle's definition
  of, 28
China, 48, 110, 154, 157, 158n25
Christian: beatific vision, 158; idea of history, 112–13; spiritual tradition, 262
Circe: and *nous,* 155, 198
Civil theology, 175
City of God, 128
Classic (great book), 139, 160
Classical laws (in science), 33
Classicism, 4, 109–16, 121, 129, 132,
  136; explicit in Greco-Roman, medieval, and Renaissance cultures, 109;
  and fragmentary view of human reality,
  116; and historicism, 109–16; ideas of
  found in preclassical societies, 109;
  places premium on concepts, 115;
  places reason above history, 109–12
Classicist culture, 27, 51, 93, 112, 142,
  146; as ideal-type, 112; as worldview,
  51. *See also* Classicism
Cognitional theory, 120, 123, 138, 143–
  44, 147, 148, 162, 194, 217, 223, 225,
  237–53, 254; as methodology, 149,
  238; as reflection on basic method, 149
Collins, James, 165n39
Common sense: bias of, 68, 117, 136,
  164, 173, 175–76, 190–91; language,
  216; self-interpretation, 22, 119
Community: as constituted by common

experience, understanding, judgments, and decisions, 47, 178; historicity of, 46–47; and triad of dread, concupiscence, and *ressentiment,* 175–76

Comte, Auguste, 80, 92

Conceptualism, 144, 197, 202, 204, 231, 251

Concupiscence: and collapse of mystery, 175, 222–23; and community, 175–76; defined, 174; and ecumenical empire, 176n59; nurtures group bias, 175–76, 191; in relation to dread and *ressentiment,* 174–76, 256–57

Condorcet, Marie Jean Antoine Nicolas Caritat, Marquis de, 73

Confrontation theory of truth, 11, 85–94, 99–100, 142–43, 148, 150, 234–36, 248, 257; and biological extroversion, 150, 164; and body as already-out-there-now-real, 215; break from, 94, 96, 98, 99–100, 105, 194; defined, 85; as dominant assumption of modern culture, 90–91, 142–43, 231–33; and the Enlightenment, 87; and historical understanding, 85–87, 143; and historicism, 85–94; joined with neo-gnostic sentiments, 233–34; and object, 239, 245; and ocular model, 31, 92–94, 143, 144, 240, 242; posits objectivity versus subjectivity, 11, 85, 153, 194; and romanticism, 87; and tradition, 99–100

Confucian philosopher, 154

Conn, Walter, 41

Conscience, 246

Consciousness, 3–4, 5; age of, 10–12; as data, 4, 14, 18–21; heightening of, 24; historical, 77–78, 83, 85; Hobbes on, 9; ideological theories of, 229; as incarnate, 18, 21, 131, 215; integration of with psyche, 44; levels of, 15, 31, 75, 117, 121–22, 130, 215, 242; Locke on, 9, 11; as luminosity, 13, 21, 242–45, 257; normative flow of, 16, 17, 64–65, 75; philosophy of, 193–203; as self-presence, 14, 21; stream of, 15, 183–84; structure of, 2–3, 239–40; of subject-with-subject, 19, 249; symbolic, 20; unity of, 16, 240–41, 242. *See also* Deciding; Differentiations of consciousness; Experience: as level of con-

sciousness; History: of consciousness; Mystical consciousness; Religious consciousness; Spiritual consciousness; Understanding: as level of consciousness; Voegelin, Eric: and consciousness
—is not: an operation, 13; nonthematic interpretation, 23; self-knowledge, 14; subsidiary awareness, 23

Constitution: Austrian, 210–11, 212; of the United States, 59, 63

Conversion, 20, 134, 140, 167, 183; intellectual, 131, 144–45, 146, 154, 167, 217, 223, 228, 264; moral, 131, 144–45, 146, 167, 246, 264; psychic, 219, 219n16, 264; religious, 131, 144–45, 146, 167, 256, 264

Correspondence theory of truth, 268

Cosmopolis, 5, 125–40, 218, 266; and City of God, 128; as coined by Diogenes, 126; embraces art, media, and historiography, 132–33; and historicity, 125, 129–35; and humor and satire, 137; as normative community, 131, 178; rests on norms inherent in human existence, 131; Stoic ideal of, 126; as tribunal of history, 125

Cosmos, 126–29; as cosmic-divine order of archaic civilizations, 126; as created by God, 128; as emergent world process, 129, 162; as hierarchical, 162; as machine in modern thought, 128–29; as rational order of Greeks, 127–28, 127n4; and teleology, 127

Counterpositions: defined, 68–69, 164; epistemological, 224; invite reversal, 69, 73, 164; of philosophy, 12, 164, 166

Creative minority, 54, 159, 185, 234, 347

Critical realism, 31, 37, 75, 228, 234n24

Croce, Beneditto, 80

Cultural superstructure, 74, 218; historicity of, 122, 136–37

Cultus and culture, 146

Cyclops and *nous,* 155, 198

Decadence, 174, 175, 232

Deciding: as level of consciousness, 117, 130, 215, 216, 246

Decline, 3, 61, 64, 70, 72, 103, 106, 116, 119, 124, 129, 133, 136, 217, 270; cumulative process of, 47, 73, 111, 121,

Decline (*cont.*)
134, 209–10; epistemological assumptions and, 224, 231–32; Marx's explanation of, 61–62; offset by philosophy, 174, 176–77; reversal of, 118, 121, 134, 174, 176–77; symbolized in archaic societies, 110; therapy of society in, 134. *See also* Social surd

Deconstructionism, 12, 108, 115, 115*n*11, 124, 132, 226

Deliberation. *See* Conscience; Evaluation

Descartes, René, 3, 10, 12, 13, 23, 89–91 passim, 128, 141, 143, 161; and extended substance, 24, 87; and modern idea of objectivity, 87. *See also* Cartesian

Desire to know, 16, 102–4 passim, 117–18, 118*n*15, 120, 121, 122, 130, 139, 144, 147–48, 149, 152, 156, 164, 166, 167, 174, 185–86, 191, 196, 203, 215, 219, 242, 246, 259; as question of God, 244, 250. *See also* Intentionality: basic

Destiny, 145, 159, 169; of philosophical tradition, 169

Development: Aristotle's notion of, 25, 27–31; authenticity as criterion of human, 40–45; defined, 39; goal of individual development as fulfillment of operational capacity, 45, 49; historical, 45–51; Leibniz's theory of, 43; liberal view of, 25; Marxist view of, 25; no God's-eye view of, 51; of individual through socialization, education, and acculturation, 45, 120, 130, 218; Plato's notion of, 25; of positions, 68–69, 73, 164; romanticist view of, 25; self-transcendence as goal of, 45; tension of limitation and self-transcendence, 4, 45, 67, 121, 132, 218, 256, 257; tripolar tension of, 218–19, 256, 257

Dialectic, 4; and analysis of historiography, 72–73; of contradictories, 65, 68; of contraries, 65–68; defined, 64; distorted, 65*n*16; Hegel's, 60–61; of human and divine, 66; of individual and community, 45–46, 66, 119–20, 130, 159–60, 255; of intersubjective community and practical intelligence, 66; of performance and interpretation, 21–22, 44, 67, 70, 119, 121, 130–31, 133–34, 138, 145, 150, 157, 167, 168, 217,

218, 255, 258, 261; of philosophers and tradition, 159–62, 265; of positions and counterpositions, 68–69; of progress and decline, 64, 121–22, 133–34, 218

Differentiations of consciousness, 46, 73–74, 75, 123, 138, 228, 259–64; as axial periods of history, 261, 262*n*103; defined, 261; as grand-scale ideal-types, 74; and myth, 265; and shift to interiority and historicity, 261–62, 263–64; and Socratic enterprise of controlling meaning, 261–62; and transcendence, 263; and undifferentiated cosmological societies, 261. *See also* History: of consciousness; Voegelin, Eric: and differentiations of consciousness

Dilthey, Wilhelm, 11, 12, 59–60, 75, 77, 80, 81*n*8, 82–84, 83–84*n*13, 85, 86–87, 93, 99, 108, 115, 143; and crisis of historicism, 83; dream of, 2, 5, 83; and philosophy of worldviews, 59–60, 83, 141; and positivist strains in his thought, 86–87; and war against dogmatism, 60, 83

Diogenes, 126

Divertissement, 10, 174, 175

Divine: logos, 154, 177; *nous,* 154, 157, 167, 203, 203*n*20, 206, 207, 212; religious experience, 50. *See also* Human-divine encounter

Divine presence: as central to human existence, 250–52; at core of human nature, 351–52, 256, 258; as object, 219, 248, 256, 264; as subject, 219, 248, 249–50, 264. *See also* Mystical consciousness

Doctrines, 218, 223

Dogmatism, 78, 83, 136, 221, 231, 258, 267, 270; Dilthey's war against, 60; and positivism, 91–92; versus openness of religious experience, 50, 118. *See also* Skepticism: as dogma

Doran, Robert, 18–19, 19*n*24, 65, 65*n*16, 219*n*16, 264

Drama, 138; of history, 70, 72*n*34, 101–2, 121*n*22, 136, 146, 150, 153–54, 175; of philosophy, 164, 166, 168–69, 170; of self, 185

Dread, 5, 68, 183–84, 186–87, 218–19; as antecedent to guilt, 187; as attractive

and repulsive, 186–87; and community, 175; and cultural creativity, 191; flight from, 68, 173–76, 220, 221; and mystery, 186, 222–23; and philosopher, 167–68; as possibility of freedom, 184; in relation to concupiscence and *ressentiment,* 173–76, 190–91; as response to guilt, 187–88; and shame, 189; and suffering, 187
Drilling, Peter, 188n15
Dunne, Tad, 20
Durée pure, 138, 157

Education, 45, 120, 138–39; liberal, 139. *See also* Development
Élan vital, 18, 44, 169, 172, 264
Eliade, Mircea, 94, 97, 97n39
Eliot, T. S., 173, 270
Emergence: as development of form, for Aristotle, 29; insight as prototype of, 33; of new forms, 33, 34–35, 38
Emergent probability, 4, 33–39, 55, 117n14, 255; argument for, 35–38, 36n31, 37n34; defined, 34; and ideal frequencies, 34; and nonsystematic processes, 34, 38; opposed to gnosticism, 51; opposed to reductionism, 38–39, 39–40, 50, 51; opposed to static essentialism, 39; posits no final cause, 51; reason as executor of, 117; in relation to dialectic of contraries, 67; and schemes of recurrence, 34; trials and successes in, 47–48, 256; as uniquely probable as worldview, 35–38
Emergent world process: as cosmos, 129, 162; heuristic anticipations of, 50–51; human reason as contributing to, 117
Emerson, Ralph Waldo, 232
Empedocles, 154
Empirical residue, 215
Empiricism, 117, 143, 202
Encylopedia, 128
Engels, Friedrich, 25
Enlightenment, 77, 79, 82, 97, 113–14, 211–12, 231, 233; and attack on myth and mystery, 50, 75, 232–33; and confrontation theory of truth, 87; and disassociation of progress from the sacred, 118, 139; and empiricist idea of reason, 117; and idea of progress, 25, 128–29,

233; and idea of tradition as object to be confronted, 99, 100, 135; and materialism (D'Holbach and LaMettrie), 231; and relation to romanticism, 82, 86–87, 232; and scientism, 87, 88; and social engineering, 128
Episteme, 111. *See also* Aristotle: and *episteme*
Epistemology, 162, 180, 223, 228, 230, 259
Epistles, Pauline, 209
Eros, 44; and psyche, 44, 186; of the mind, 225
Eschaton, immanentization of, 113
Esse, 208
Eternity, 120, 157
Evaluation, 246
Existential: gap, 22, 69, 70, 133–34, 176, 179, 217, 220, 224; history, 71, 120, 122, 133; moods of wonder, doubt, and dread, 16; roots of bias, 173–76; roots of human living and knowing, 98. *See also* Deciding
Existentialism and Existentialists, 117, 141, 209
Experience: and art, 137; as level of consciousness, 15, 31, 32, 117, 121, 130, 144, 148, 165, 215. *See also* Patterns of experience; Religious experience
Externalization, 254

Faith: as born of love, 20, 152, 247, 248; and philosophy, 167; and reason, 153–54, 158–59
Fides quaerens intellectum, 220
Flagellants, 48
Form, 31–40 passim; Aristotle's idea of, 29, 33; central, 215, 239; as classical laws, 33, 37–38; conjugate, 33, 240; as goal of development, 29; as metaphysical equivalent of understanding, 32
Foucault, Michel, 108, 115
Foundational: concerns, 136–37; enterprise, 12–14, 218, 238; myths, 173; philosophy, 3, 13, 108, 116, 123, 136, 143, 171, 228; reality, 13, 270
Frame, Douglass, 155
Freedom: operational range of, 118
Functional specialties, 122, 136–37, 138, 165–68, 218, 269

Gadamer, Hans Georg, 58, 77, 94, 99–100, 104n52, 142, 189, 227; and dialogue with tradition, 99–100, 135; and fusion of horizons, 58, 100, 103–4; and hermeneutical circle, 166
Galileo Galilei, 89
Genetic fallacy, 89–90
Genius and tradition, 161–62
Genuineness, 219, 256
German idealism, 88, 92–93; and speculative gnosis, 92–93
Geschichlichkeit, 77n2. *See also* Historicity
Gilson, Etienne, 90n27
Gnosticism (neognosticism), 132, 164, 248, 255; in German idealism, 92–93; in Hegel's theory of history, 61, 114n8, 141; and meaning of history, 3, 118, 123, 141, 233; opposed by worldview of emergent probability, 51; and revolution, 73, 176, 191, 233
God: not object, 250
Goethe, Johann Wolfgang von, 80n6
Gospels, 209, 250
Greek (Hellenic) intellectual culture, 101, 107, 126–28, 154–58
Guilt: defined, 188; and dread, 187–88; generic, 188; and weight of limitation, 186

Habermas, Jürgen, 77, 83–84n13, 94, 100–101, 104n52, 106n54, 142; and critical human science, 100; and depth hermeneutics, 133; and dialectical relation with tradition, 100; and emancipatory interest, 101, 135
Heer, Friedrich, 233
Hegel, Georg Wilhelm Friedrich, 10, 12, 60–61, 73, 75, 77, 80, 81n8, 108, 114, 114n8, 141; and dialectic, 60–61; and intersection of time and eternity, 61; and objective spirit, 162n33; and the subject, 13, 143, 215
Heidegger, Martin, 77, 77n2, 94, 96, 97–99, 104n52, 142, 162, 183; and attack on Cartesian alienation of subject and world, 98; and basic norm of inquiry, 98; and question of Being, 98; and *Sorge* as authenticity, 98
Heisenberg, Werner, 38, 94–95
Helkein, 250–51
Helminiak, Daniel, 41

Heraclitus, 102n46, 127n6, 153; and *koine cosmos,* 154, 177, 236, 258
Herder, von Johann Gottfried, 58, 80, 89
Hermeneutics: circle of, 166; depth, 18, 133; dialectical, 55–56; of Empty Head, 197; and historicity, 135–36; and project of history, 70, 121, 130; questioning as standard of, 99–100; romanticist, 57–58, 59, 60, 75, 114; and two blades of interpretation, 37, 269–70; universal viewpoint of, 72, 122, 259, 269. *See also* Dialectic: of performance and interpretation; Historical: evaluation
Herodotus, 110, 111, 157–58; and Anaximander, 111, 157–58
Higher integrations, 18, 19, 33, 34–35, 39–40, 44, 50, 67, 215, 255; of human nature and transcendent spiritual reality, 50; insight as prototype of, 33; of psyche with organism and consciousness, 44
Historical: consciousness, 76–79, 83, 85, 109, 113, 129, 141–42, 144, 162, 208; description, 72, 136; development, 45–51; development of philosophy, 162–64; evaluation, 62–63, 71–72, 75, 84, 85–86, 100, 121–22, 134, 136–37; existence, 79, 117, 121n22, 130; explanation, 72, 136; human existence as, 79, 98, 121n22; knowledge, 111, 117; limits of in Plato and Aristotle, 112; narration, 72, 121n22; revolution, 107; understanding and confrontation theory of truth, 85–86. *See also* Historicism; Objectivity: and history
Historical-mindedness, 4, 26–27; and collective responsibility, 46, 71, 101, 117, 122, 129, 134–35, 145, 173; and natural right, 116
Historicism, 4, 12, 71, 75, 79–94, 109–16, 121, 141, 144, 258; Antoni's theory of, 79–80; and classicism, 109–16; and concept of human nature, 81, 114, 141–42; and confrontation theory of truth, 85–94, 115, 143; crisis of, 76–79, 83, 85, 93; and disappearance of human nature and history, 115; epistemological assumptions of, 82–94, 143; and fragmentary view of human reality, 116; and genetic fallacy, 89–90; Man-

delbaum's theory of, 81; Meinecke's theory of, 80; method of, 80–81; places premium on concrete process, 115; places reason under historical process, 109, 115; Popper's theory of, 80; and religion, 97; and scientific truth, 95; versus historicity, 4, 104, 106

Historicity, 4, 47, 49, 70–71, 94–106, 120, 129; between classicism and historicism, 109, 114–15; of community, 46–47; as constituted by intersection of time and eternity, 49–50, 121, 156–57; as core of human existence, 79, 98; and cosmopolis, 129–35; of cultural superstructure, 122, 136; and hermeneutics, 135–37, 149–50; and human-divine encounter, 146, 156–57; as in-between, 106; of myth, 172; of philosophy, 168; of reason, 122; and religion, 97, 146–47; as tension of basic and relative horizons, 132, 149–50; as translation of *Geschichlichkeit,* 77n2; of science, 95; of tradition, 99; versus historicism, 4, 104, 106, 116. *See also* Perspectivism

Historiography, 71–73; and conflict with universal empire, 157; critical and dialectical, 71–72, 122, 134; dialectical analysis of, 72–73. *See also* Historical; Objectivity: and history

Historismus, 77n2. *See also* Historicism

History, 69–74; a priori constructions of, 108, 114; challenge and response as complex of factors, 70; of consciousness, 74, 123, 134, 261–64, 268–70; and dialectic, 70–71; and dialectic of performance and interpretation, 70, 121, 130–31; as drama, 69–70, 72n34, 101–2, 121n22, 146, 175; as dynamism of, 254; goal of as transcendental ideal of historical action, 70, 105, 212, 145–46; as hermeneutical project, 69–70, 75, 105, 121, 121n22, 130–31; identity and difference in, 67, 103, 105, 121, 146; at intersection of time and eternity, 49, 121, 156; mystery as plot of, 49, 105; philosophy of, 69–74; of philosophy, 138, 170, 179; placed above reason by historicism, 109, 115; placed below reason by classicism, 109–12; of religion, 49–50; sacred, 128; of thought, 138, 179. *See also* A

prioris of human condition; Existential history; Philosophy: of history
—ideas of: archaic mentality, 109–10; Augustine's, 113, 128; biblical, 56–57; Christian, 113; cyclical, 58–59, 108; Dilthey's, 59–60; Enlightenment, 56; Hegel's, 60–61, 108, 114; Indian (Hindu) as escape from, 110; Israelite, 112–13; Marxist, 47, 61–62, 108, 114, 118; Mesopotamian, 109–10; Muslim, 112; Polybius's, 58–59; progressivist, 57, 114, 118; romanticist, 57–58; Sorokin's, 59; Spengler's, 58–59; three stage theory, 56–57; Vico's, 58

Hobbes, Thomas, 88, 129, 210; on consciousness, 9

Hope, 20

Horizon(s): basic, 67, 75, 102–4, 121, 122, 131–32, 135, 149–50, 163, 261; as concrete synthesis of conscious living, 21, 186; defined, 96, 259; defined by questions, 119; dialectical relation with (Habermas), 100; dialogue with, 99–100; fusion of, 58, 99–100, 103–4, 116; as historically situated, 253; historicity as tension of basic and relative horizon, 132, 259; as interrelated sets of profiles, 16–17; objective pole of, 96; of openness, 67; relative, 58, 63, 75, 104, 121, 131–32, 135, 149; religious, 97; subjective pole of, 96; as way of being, 149. *See also* Philosophy: horizon(s) of

Hughes, H. Stuart, 83, 84n14

Human: living, basic science of, 144, 178; science, critical and normative, 100–101, 106, 136–37, 179. *See also* Development
—existence: as historical, 79, 98, 121n22; mystery of, 123; normative structure of, 195; as odyssey, 145; ontological philosophy of history, 69–71; as project, 134–35. *See also* Aristotle: and human existence as synthetic nature; Historical: existence; In-between
—nature: historical development as second nature, 49; historicist concept of, 81; as inquiry, 41; transformation of, 48

Human-divine encounter, 156–57, 220, 251–52; at core of historicity, 146; at core of philosophy, 150–54

Hume, David, 89, 231
Humor and satire, 137, 177, 218
Husserl, Edmund, 94, 96–98, 97n39, 104n52; and horizon, 96; and intentionality, 96; and transcendental ego, 88, 234, 241, 245; and transcendental reduction, 241

Ideal frequencies, 34
Ideal-types, 69, 74, 75, 112, 115
Ideology, 164; defined, 164n37
Iggers, George, 83n13
In-between, 3, 67, 101, 102n46, 106, 121, 132, 243–44, 257–58, 259; and historicity, 106; and Plato, 102n45, 132, 257; as status of human being, 67, 101–2, 224. *See also* Voegelin, Eric: on "in-between"
Indian (Hindu) culture, 110, 154; and *moksha,* 158
Individual development. *See* Development
Inner light. *See* Consciousness: as luminosity
Inquiry: about being constitutes the self, 43, 130, 224; basic intentionality of, 2, 98, 102–4, 118n15, 149, 218, 222, 263–64, 266; and emancipatory interest (Habermas), 101; existential state of, 222, 223, 263–64, 266; as expansion of selfhood, 16; as immanent source of transcendence, 48–49; into self, 14; as natural principle, 41, 129–30, 251, 254; norms of, 1–4, 15–16, 41, 64–65, 72, 102, 118, 121, 131, 139, 140, 144, 146, 149, 164, 217, 224, 242, 257–58, 259, 270; notion of *Sorge* as basic norm of, 98; as orientation to the real, 31–32; process of, 1, 31, 42, 49, 117–18, 146, 148, 222, 223, 240; spiritual, 149; and standard of hermeneutics, 99–100; structure of, 2, 15, 31, 117, 118n15, 121–22, 131, 136, 138, 144, 148, 149, 165, 215, 218, 222, 223, 239, 264, 266. *See also* Horizon(s): basic
Insight: as prototype of emergence, 33; as prototype of higher integrations, 33
Insight: status of in Lonergan's corpus, 237–38
Intellectual: conversion, 131, 144–45, 146, 217, 264; crisis, 10; patterns of experience, 42, 149, 244

Intelligibility, complete: as divine, 153, 252; search for, 148, 152, 170, 180
Intention: of being, 242, 247, 254; of the good, 16, 102–4 passim, 121, 122, 130, 131, 144, 149, 174, 185–86, 215, 219, 237, 247, 254, 259. *See also* Intentionality: basic
Intentionality, 2, 16, 96, 102–4, 119, 121, 241–42; basic, 2, 98, 102–4, 118n15, 121, 149, 218, 242; broader than perception, 223, 241; as engulfed by state of being-in-love, 2, 219; and method, 149; modeled on questioning, 241; and reason, 119. *See also* Inquiry; Voegelin, Eric: and consciousness, as intentionality
Interiority, 10; turn toward, 10. *See also* Subjectivity
Interpretation. *See* Hermeneutics; Self-interpretation
Intersection of time and eternity: as constitutive of historicity, 49; Hegel's view of, 61
Intersubjective meaning. *See* Meaning: intersubjective
Ionians, 154
Isomorphism: of dynamism of knowing and dynamism of the known, 35; of genetic-classical-statistical methods and potency-form-act, 37–39; of structure of knowing and structure of the known, 32, 178–79
Israelite: spiritual tradition, 262, 263; view of history, 112–13, 157, 158n25, 224

Jacobins, 48
Jaeger, Werner, 170, 197
Jager, Bernd, 156n23
Jaspers, Karl, 162, 261
Judgment: as level of consciousness, 15, 31, 117, 121–22, 130, 144, 148, 165, 215; as synthesis of concepts, for Aristotle, 40; as virtually unconditioned, 136
Justinian, 210

Kant, Immanuel, 12, 13, 63, 88, 89, 90n27, 91n29, 141, 143, 150, 161, 229; and critique of intellectual intuition, 91; and phenomena, 24, 215; and transcendental deduction, 240

Kelsen Hans, 212

Kierkegaard, Søren, 94, 142, 154, 208; and dread, 168, 174, 184, 187; and indirect communication, 170; and self, 214; and subject, 13, 143

Kimmerians and *nous,* 155

Kinesis, 28, 110, 200

Knowledge: and belief, 135–36; of consciousness, 12; historical, 111, 117

Known unknown. *See* Mystery

Kuhn, Thomas S., 95–96n36

Laistrygones and *nous,* 155, 198

Langer, Suzanne K., 138

Laws: classical, 37; statistical, 34

Lear, Jonathan, 203, 203n20

Learning: self-correcting process of, 136; moral, 149, 216, 246

Legal pragmatism, 63

Leibniz, Gottfried Wilhelm, 43, 51, 60, 80n6, 91; and development of monads, 43, 51

Levels of integration. *See* Higher integrations

Liberty, 118. *See also* Conversion

Limitation and transcendence, 49–50; as hallmark of human development, 4, 45; tension of, 48–49, 74

Linge, D. E., 84n13

Linguistic philosophers, 11

Locke, John, 89; on consciousness, 9, 11

Logos, 127n6, 154, 201

Love. *See* Being-in-love; Eros

Love(r) of wisdom, 123, 127, 127n6, 147–48, 151, 154, 159, 162, 164, 168–69, 171, 173, 225, 252; as nucleus of academic community, 177; as origin of science, scholarship, and literature, 177

Luther, 211

McCarthy, Michael, 23

Machiavelli, Niccolò, 210

MacIntyre, Alasdair, 135

Makkreel, Rudolf A., 84n13

Malebranche, Nicolas, 91

Mandelbaum, Maurice, 81

Marcel, Gabriel, 162

Marcoux, Paul, 3n5

Marx, Karl, 61–62, 73, 75, 77, 80, 81n8, 128; and explanation of decline, 61; and group bias, 61; and idea of humanity as species-being, 62; and theory of history, 61–62, 108, 114

Marxism, 25, 47, 48, 114, 118; and restriction of questions to worldly matters, 50

Matthews, William, 172, 252, 264–65

Meaning: aesthetic, 137, 261; core of, 242; elemental, 22–23, 119, 160, 261; incarnate, 23, 160, 170, 261; intersubjective, 23, 119, 261; symbolic, 22–23, 119, 261

Mediation, 216–18, 220–21

Meditation, 218–20, 222, 249

Meinecke, Friedrich, 80

Mesopotamian idea of history, 109–10

Metaphysics, 147, 180, 230, 231; challenges eclipse of reality, 178; grounded in cognitional theory, 148, 162, 223, 228, 238, 252–53; inadequate to explain human development and the self, 41, 215; potency, form, and act, terms of, 32; promotes integration of methods, 178–79

Method(s): basic, 149–50; classical, 55, 117n14; collaboration of, 137–38, 178–79; contrasted to technique, 149; defined, 149; dialectical and hermeneutical, 55–56; genetic, 37, 38, 55, 117n14; of historicism, 80–81; as *methodos,* 149; of neo-Kantians, 149, 226, 229, 253; of positivist, 63, 149; statistical, 38, 55, 117n14

Methodology. *See* Cognitional theory

Millenarianism, 48, 118–19, 211, 233

Moksha, 110, 154

Montaigne, Michel Eyquem de, Seigneur, 1

Montesquieu, Charles de Secondat, Baron, 89

Moore, G. E., 89

Moral. *See* Conversion: moral; Learning: moral; Objectivity: moral; Self-transcendence: moral

Music, 138

Muslim view of history, 112

Mysterium iniquitatis, 49

Mystery (known unknown), 20, 49, 105; collapse of by concupiscence, 175, 222–23; defined, 264; and drama of philosophy, 170, 171; and dread, 186; of human existence, 123, 126; of hu-

Mystery (*cont.*)
   man freedom, 73; as plot of history, 49,
   105; as permanent, 171, 243; of self,
   247; transcendent, 243–44, 250, 256
Mystical consciousness, 19, 21; and
   clouded revelation, 249; as experience
   of divine presence as subject, 249–50,
   250; not objectified, 349–50
Myth, 74, 97, 110; and archetypes and
   anagogic symbols, 169–70; critique of
   distorted myth, 265, 267; defined, 264;
   and differentiation of consciousness,
   265; as foundational concern, 264; as
   genuine form of understanding, 97,
   171, 245; as heuristic insight, 169–70,
   245, 264; historicity of, 172, 265; as
   neither allegory nor mere pedagogy,
   170; as permanent, 265; and philosophy, 168–73, 171n54, 264. *See also*
   Psyche

National Socialism, 48, 229
Natural: right and historical-mindedness,
   116; and supernatural, 251
Naturalistic fallacy, 89, 114
Nature: Aristotle's definition of, 28, 127;
   inquiry as nature principle, 41
Neural demands, 65
Newman, John Henry, 142
Newton, Isaac, 89, 113, 231
Niebuhr, Barthold, 77
Nietzsche, Friedrich, 78, 81n8, 94; and
   ressentiment, 175, 190
Nirvana, 158
Nisbet, Robert, 139
Nominalism, 91, 137, 143, 231, 255
Norms. *See* Consciousness: normative
   flow of; Inquiry: norms of; Self-
   transcendence: norms ingredient in
Nous: and cave imagery, 155, 198–99;
   and cycle of sun, 155, 198. *See also*
   Aristotle: and *nous*

Object: Cartesian, 24, 239, 245; Kantian,
   24, 239, 245. *See also* Metaphysics
Objective pole of horizon. *See* Horizon(s):
   objective pole; Philosophy: horizon(s)
   of
Objectivism, 144, 147
Objectivity, 148; Descartes and modern
   idea of, 87; of facts, 71, 122; as fidelity

to inquiry, 24, 36, 143–44; as fruit of
   authentic subjectivity, 16, 94, 102–3,
   104–5, 122, 131, 236; historical, 62–
   63, 71–72, 75; and history, 12, 85–86,
   86n19, 100–101, 121–22; moral, 71–
   72, 103, 122, 246; and science, 36; versus subjectivity, 11, 82. *See also* Knowledge
Ockham, William of, 91, 231
Odysseus: and journey of *nous,* 155, 198
Openness: as achievement, 44, 187, 225;
   as demand, 44, 187, 225; as gift, 118,
   131, 151–52, 188, 225, 250–51, 252,
   256–57; and religious experience, 50,
   139; to transcendence, 131, 139
Orphic tale, 154

Painting, 138
Paleolithic societies, 110
Parmenides, 153, 154, 198, 199
Participation: of human and divine, 50
Pascal, Blaise, 1, 174, 248, 250. *See also*
   Divertissement
Patterns of experience, 3, 42, 75, 122,
   138, 149; aesthetic, 42, 149, 244, 245;
   defined, 244; dramatic, 245; intellectu-
   al, 42, 149, 244; mythic, 244–45, 264;
   practical, 42, 149, 244
Patterson, Richard, 189n17
Peloponnesian War, 177, 194–95
People: as modern symbol of legitimacy,
   113
Persian Empire, 157
Perspectivism, 132, 255
Phenomenologists and phenomenology,
   10, 16, 96–100, 208, 209, 241
Philosopher(s), 147–48, 150–54; and
   autobiographical narrative, 172; biography of, 170; combats dread, concupiscence, and *ressentiment,* 176–77; dialectic of and tradition, 159–62, 265;
   as incarnate meaning, 160, 170–71;
   mystic, 153, 154, 209, 227; related to
   being through inquiry, 148; religious
   experience of, 151–53; and saints, 153;
   and self-appropriation, 150, 160, 161,
   166–67, 168, 172. *See also* Love(r) of
   wisdom
Philosophy: acts indirectly on social policy, 177; addresses issue of maximum
   import, 179, 218; and *anamnesis,* 160,

265–66; and call to being, 151–52; classics of, 160; combats existential roots of bias, 173, 176–77; as conditioned by historical situation, 162; and counterpositions, 12, 164, 166; and destiny, 169; event of, 168, 265; existential, 133; existential conditions of, 146–47; and experience of human-divine encounter, 151–52, 169; and experience of intrinsic intelligibility of being, 152, 169–70; and functional specialties, 165–68; and genius, 160–62; historical development of, 162–64; as historical drama, 164, 166, 168–69, 170; historicity of, 168; history of, 138, 170; as horizon bound, 163; and intellectual culture, 177–80; and intellectual, moral, and religious conversions, 167; as interpretation of basic horizon, 150, 153; as invitation to self-transcendence, 179; and myth, 168–73; and openness as a gift, 151–52; as oriented to mystery, 169, 171; as participation in unrestricted love, 152–53, 158, 159, 167; of philosophies, 12–13, 230; and positions, 12, 163, 164, 166; and praxis, 173; and progress, 163; and psyche, 169, 171–72; and relativism, 162–64; and religious traditions, 158–59; as search for complete intelligibility, 148, 152, 169–70, 171; as self-interpretation, 150; story of, 170; as systematic, 147; therapy of versus existential gap, 176–77; and triad of faith, hope, and love, 153, 167, 170, 252; as variety of religious experience, 4, 147, 150–54, 155–59, 169, 173, 180, 225, 252; as way of being, 150, 172
—of history: epistemological, 69, 71–73; of German idealism, 92–93; ontological, 69–71; of positivism, 92; speculative, 69, 73–74. *See also* History
—horizon(s) of, 147–50; and basic horizon, 163; genetic sequences of, 163; objective (systematic) pole of, 147–48, 178–79, 180; subjective (existential) pole of, 147–48, 159, 179–80. *See also* Cognitional theory; Metaphysics
Phronesis, 205–7, 246
Physis, 28, 154
Pindar, 156

Plato, 19, 26, 27, 31*n*15, 40, 101, 127*n*6, 153, 155, 159–62 passim, 177, 189*n*17, 195, 199, 218, 242, 256, 266; and *agathon,* 168; and decline, 111; on development, 25; and dialectic of individual and society, 46, 264; and dramatic artistry, 30, 168, 170, 171*n*54; and *helkein,* 250; and history as not object of science, 111; and "in-between," 102*n*46, 132, 257; and limits of historical responsibility, 111; and normative analysis of horizons, 30–31, 127; and science as true, certain knowledge of causal necessity, 35; and sense of historical epoch, 157; and universe as *kosmos,* 127*n*4; and *zetesis,* 249
Plotinus, 153
Plutarch, 111
Poetry: epic, 138; lyric, 138; metaphysical, 173
Polanyi, Michael, 2, 23, 94–95, 101, 142, 216
Polis: as intelligible cosmion, 127
Political science, 194–95, 205–7, 209–10, 212
Polybius, 58–59, 111–12
Pope, Alexander, 113
Popper, Karl, 36, 80
Positions, 68–69, 73, 237; defined, 68–69; and development, 69, 73, 164, 223; and philosophy, 12, 163, 164, 166
Positivism, 63, 71, 75, 91–92, 93, 100, 141, 143, 180, 195, 197, 226; and dogmatism, 91–92; as legacy of Enlightenment, 87; and method, 63, 149; and trend toward skepticism, 231–32; types of, 231
Potency, 32–41 passim, 45, 67; Aristotle's idea of, 28, 29, 32, 41; as empirical residue, 32; genetic method grounded in, 37; as metaphysical equivalent of experience, 32; as objective ground of dynamism of reality, 32–33; as principle of limitation, 32–33; as tension of opposites, 33
Practical: intelligence, 138; patterns of experience, 42, 149, 244; wisdom, for Aristotle, 30. *See also Phronesis*
Pragmatism, 117, 226, 232
Praxis, 173
Price, James Robertson, III, 249

Propositional truth, 267–68
Progoff, Ira, 172
Progress, 3–4, 57, 64, 72, 75, 106, 116, 119, 124, 133, 136, 163, 217, 270; basic horizon source of, 103; cumulative process of, 47, 121; Enlightenment view of, 25, 128; and norms of self-transcendence, 70; pure line of, 47, 49; symbolized in archaic societies, 110; as tied to the sacred, 50, 118, 139
Psyche, 65; archeology of, 18–19, 18n23, 219, 256; and conversion, 219; and eros, 44; integration of with organism and consciousness, 44, 65; and negotiation by mind, 44, 65, 219, 256; and self-appropriation, 171; as source of transcendence, 44, 132; and symbols, 219; teleology of, 18, 18n23, 219, 256, 264; therapy of, 133–34; and wonder, 44, 132
Psychology, faculty, 207, 208, 209, 237, 245, 251
Pythagoreans, 154; and universe as *kosmos*, 127n4

Questioning. *See* Inquiry

Ranke, Leopold von, 49, 77, 86–87
Raphael: *School of Athens,* 2, 5, 83
Rationalism, 117, 143
Real: as "already out there now real," 32n16; as object of questioning, 32, 143–44; and principle of isomorphism, 32; and world as dynamic relation of potency, form, and act, 32
Reality, eclipse of, 173, 175, 178, 191
Reason, 10–11, 101; and belief, 119–20; classical experience of, 101; conceptualist idea of by rationalists, 117; eclipse of, 10–11; empirical concept of, 117; as executor of emergent probability, 117; and faith, 153–54, 158; historicity of, 121–22; and history, 120–24; as inquiry, 118n15; and intentionality, 119; placed above history by classicism, 109–12; placed under history by historicism, 109, 115; as tied to religious experience, 139; voluntarist concept of, 117. *See also* Inquiry: process of; Inquiry: structure of; *Nous*
Red Turbans, 48

Reformation, 77, 113
Relativism, 71, 75, 78–79, 81, 83, 85, 86, 86n19, 89–90, 95–96n36, 101–2, 104, 132; and philosophy, 162–64; and scientific truth, 95. *See also* Historicism
Religious experience, 50. *See also* Divine presence; Philosophy: as variety of religious experience
Religious consciousness: as experience of divine presence as object, 249; as fulfillment of capacity for self-transcendence, 249; and transcendental notions, 248
Religious conversion, 131, 145, 146, 264; as condition for intellectual and moral conversions, 219, 225, 248
Religious horizon, 97
Religious symbols, 97
Renaissance, 109, 113, 211
Ressentiment, 68, 173–76; and community, 175–76; defined, 174–75; in relation to dread and concupiscence, 173–76, 186, 190–91
Revolution, 48, 212; French, 77, 80; and group bias, 176, 191
Ricoeur, Paul, 18n23, 135, 167, 219, 256
Rilke, Ranier Maria, 173, 270356
Robespierre, Maximilian, 128
Romanticism, 45, 77, 82, 93, 144; and confrontation theory of truth, 86–87; and hermeneutics, 57–58, 59, 60, 75, 114; and idea of development, 25–26; and relation to Enlightenment, 82, 86–87, 232; and retreat into the self, 232; and voluntarist idea of reason, 117
Ross, W. D., 197
Rousseau, Jean Jacques: and idea of general will, 62

Sacred presence. *See* Religious experience
Scheler, Max, 175, 190
Schelling, Friedrich Wilhelm Joseph von, 208
Schemes of recurrence, 34. *See also* Emergent probability
Schlegel, August Wilhelm von, 160
Schütz, Alfred, 244
Science: conceptualist view of, 197; as giving probable truth, 36; and historicity, 95; Newtonian, 24; and norms of inquiry, 94–95; as not applicable to history (Plato and Aristotle), 111; as not

true, certain knowledge of causal necessity, 35; as opposed to historicism, 95; and process of inquiry, 94–95; and self-transcendence, 95

Scientific revolution, 77, 113, 208

Scientism, 87, 88

Scotosis, 135, 136

Scotus, John Duns, 90, 90n27, 91, 231

Self, 17–24; authentic, 17, 43–44, 174, 217; drama of, 185; ex-ists and projects, 185; expansion of, 16, 216; as function of dialectic of performance and interpretation, 21–22, 185, 217, 254; historicity of, 42–44; inauthentic, 44; inquiry about being constitutes, 43, 130; as metaphysical object, 262; nature of, 17–18, 215–16; personal edition of, 45; as project of historical existence, 130; as question of being, 247; and relation to audience, 185; and tension of basic horizon and relative horizons, 185; as tension of questioner and object of question, 17, 130, 174, 185, 216, 247. *See also* Self-transcendence; Subject

Self-appropriation, 1, 13, 139, 143–44, 194, 214–24, 237, 262, 270; cognitional, 1, 146–47, 167; and philosophy, 149–50, 160, 161, 166–67, 168, 172, 225; and psyche, 171; and religious experience, 219. *See also* Intellectual: conversion

Self-interpretation, 131; commonsensical, 22, 119; as constitutive of polity, 195; critical interpretation of, 195; and existential history, 122; nonthematic, 22–23, 44, 119; of philosopher, 150; and process of history, 145; of society, 254; theoretic, 22, 119

Self-knowledge. *See* Self-appropriation

Self-transcendence, 69–70, 74, 132, 185–86; authenticity and, 4–5, 174; and community, 175–76; at full operative capacity, 249; as goal of human development, 45; moral, 246; and negotiation of tension of limitation and transcendence, 67, 186, 247; norms ingredient in, 64–65, 69–70, 136; and progress, 70; and religious experience, 139; of scientific inquiry, 95; and triad of dread, concupiscence, and *ressenti-*

ment, 173–76, 190–91. *See also* Religious consciousness; Voegelin, Eric: and transcendence

Shaman, 110

Shame, 186; defined, 188–89; generic, 189–90; as ontological condition of moral understanding, 189; related to guilt as community is to self, 189

Shelly, Percy Bysshe, 112

Sickness unto death, 68, 174

Skepticism, 60, 90, 91, 93, 132, 137, 231–32, 270; as dogma, 60, 78

Social Darwinism, 58

Socialization, 45, 120. *See also* Development

Social surd, 118, 123, 133, 134, 136, 137. *See also* Decline

Socrates, 140, 155, 160, 170, 177, 262

Socratic enterprise of controlling meaning, 127, 261–62

Solon, 154, 156

Sorge, 98

Sorokin, Pitirim, 59

Specialization, 137

Spencer, Herbert, 25

Spengler, Oswald, 58–59, 80

Spinoza, Baruch, 1, 91

Spiritual consciousness: as entire complex of being-in-love, 247; as religious and mystical, 247–48

Spiritual inquiry, 149

Spiritual virtues, 20

Spoudaios, 29, 30, 127n5, 196, 246

Stoics, 174

Suarez, Francis, 90n27

Subject: existential, 42–44; not mere substance, 130, 215; as subject, 13, 23, 24, 143. *See also* Cognitional theory

Subjective pole. *See* Horizon(s): subjective pole; Philosophy: horizon(s) of

Subjectivism, 124, 143, 144, 147; not identical to subjectivity, 95

Subjectivity, 11, 16, 82, 94, 95, 96, 102–3, 105–6; authentic, 16, 103, 105; as core of objectivity, 94; intelligent, 102; not identical to subjectivism, 95; versus objectivity, 11, 82

Substance: not identical with subject, 130

Sumerian king list, 110

Symbolic: "symbolic animal" replaces "rational animal" as definition of human

Symbolic (*cont.*)
being, 42; symbolic consciousness, 20; symbolic meaning, 22–23, 119, 261; symbolic operator, 19. *See also* Voegelin, Eric: and history of symbols

Taborites, 48
Tai Ping, 48
Tamerlaine, 211
Taoist sage, 154
Tension of limitation and transcendence. *See* Development; Limitation and transcendence
Theodicy, 50*n*61
Theoria and *Theoros:* 156, 167, 169, 173, 198, 199, 205, 206; etymology of, 156*n*23
Therapy: of psyche, 133–34; of society in decline, 134
Thing, 215, 239; defined, 215*n*3, 239
Thomas, Carol, 211*n*49
Thomism, 230
Thucydides, 110, 177
Tien Ming, 110
Tien Xia, 110
Time: elementary, 120, 156–57; psychological, 120, 157
Totalitarian practicality, 129, 232
Toulmin, Stephen, 128
Toynbee, Arnold, 22*n*31, 75, 254
Tradition, 99–100, 119–20, 135–36, 139, 145, 218, 253, 265; and authenticity, 218*n*14; critique of, 139; dialectical relation with (Habermas), 100; dialogue with, 99–100; Enlightenment idea of as object to be confronted, 99, 100, 135–36; and genius, 161–62; historicity of, 99; as ontological condition of understanding, 189; philosophical, 159–62; and reason, 119–20. *See also* Belief
Transcendence: inquiry as immanent source of, 48–49; meaning of as raising further question, 21; psyche as source of, 44; relation of society to, 175–76. *See also* Mystery: transcendent; Voegelin, Eric: and transcendence
Transcendental precepts, 119, 217; defined, 259
Trinity, 159
Troeltsch, Ernst, 76

Truth. *See* Confrontation theory of truth; Correspondence theory of truth; Propositional truth
Twentieth century, cultural crisis of, 10–12, 107, 116, 141–42, 226, 232–33; in both infrastructure and superstructure, 233–34

Unconscious: cosmic, 18–19, 169; energy, 18, 19, 169, 171–72; generic, 19
Understanding: historical, 85–86; as level of consciousness, 15, 31, 117, 212–22, 130, 144, 147–48, 165, 215; mythic, 97, 171
Universal viewpoint. *See* Hermeneutics: universal viewpoint of

Values: apprehension of, 246; hierarchy of, 175, 176
Value-free. *See* Historical: evaluation
Vasari, Giorgio, 56
Vertical finality, 174, 190
Vico, Giovanni Battista, 58
Voegelin Eric, 3–5, 94, 101–2, 133, 142, 154, 170, 176*n*59, 194–98, 207, 209–13, 220–22, 226–71 passim; and Austrian constitution, 210–11, 212; on "burden of polis," 158; on community of being, 221; on "conditioning causality," 255; on divine-human encounter, 220, 222, 223, 227, 235, 236; on drama of existence, 235; on generic unconscious, 19, 220, 256, 267; *History of Political Ideas,* 211–12; and horizon of American culture, 253; on "in-between," 3, 101, 132, 209, 220, 227, 235, 236, 257, 260; and Kantian assumptions about intentionality and object, 266–68; on nonobjective reality, 196, 227, 235, 236; on noetic science, 194–96; on normative structure of human existence, 195; on permanence of myth, 260, 262; on Plato's *helkein,* 250–51, 260; on Plato's *zetesis,* 249, 263; on political science, 194–95, 209–10, 212–13; on "realist" political thinkers, 210; on reason and religious experience, 139, 209; on Santayana's "critical realism," 234*n*24; on symbol of historical existence, 236*n*31, 263; on truth of existence, 220–21,

258, 263; and "within" of society, 253–54
—and Aristotle's idea of: noetic science, 196–98, 207–8; synthetic nature of human reality, 212, 254–55
—and authority: of power through existential representation and articulation, 210; of reason and of spirit, 210, 211–12, 212–13
—and consciousness, 209–13; balance of, 224; biography of, 172, 252, 264–65; of concrete person, 193–94, 209, 234, 240; as intentionality, 209, 221, 223, 228, 231n15, 234, 236, 241, 257; as luminosity, 209, 221, 228, 235, 236, 241, 257; participatory nature of, 3, 194, 196, 209, 220, 221, 222, 235, 268; as process with directional tendency, 234–35, 245; reification of (propositionalist fallacy), 196, 197, 221, 228, 267
—and critique of: confrontation theory, 194, 234–36; false self as "second reality," 220; flight from anxiety of existence, 220, 221, 222–23; gnosticism, 221, 233; political ideas as reified, 211; sentiments and symbols of cultural infrastructure, 233; totalitarian revolution, 212, 221, 229–30
—and differentiations of consciousness, 220–21, 260; noetic, 195, 222, 224–25, 227–28, 260, 262, 263, 269–70; pneumatic, 222, 227–28, 260, 262, 263, 269–70
—and history of symbols (meditative exe-

gesis), 221–22, 227–28, 234–36, 260; defined, 227; not confronted as objects, 236; primary symbols versus secondary symbols, 267
—and the Question: as open to the *koine cosmos* of Heraclitus, 236, 258; norms immanent in, 236, 258
—and transcendence: as the Beginning, 251, 260; as the Beyond, 250, 251, 260; political representation of, 212; self-transcending openness to, 194, 195, 245

Voltaire, de François Marie Arouet, 56, 89, 234n23

Weber, Max, 11, 62, 82, 84n16, 84–85, 93, 115, 211; and value free historical scholarship, 62, 84–85
Weimar Republic, 226, 253–54
Whitehead, Alfred North, 18, 88
Wittgenstein, Ludwig, 23
Wonder, 44; and psyche, 44
Word, inner, 263, 265
Wordsworth, William, 232
World: as objective pole of horizon, 96; *See also* Cosmos; Emergent world process

Xenophanes, 154

Yellow Turbans, 48

Zeitgeist, 161, 166
Zetesis, 249, 263

Permissions

Not advocating extension of Therapeutic Model -
its presupposition - it has its place but not
a Totalization of issues.

- Rather a questioning - a conversion.

170 - The Love of wisdom generates the understanding
of faith and the affect-laden urge of hope